AF247484

Modernist Studies

Rima Drell Reck, Editor

Neo-Impressionism
and the Search
for Solid Ground

Neo-Impressionism and the Search for Solid Ground

Art, Science, and Anarchism in Fin-de-Siècle France

John G. Hutton

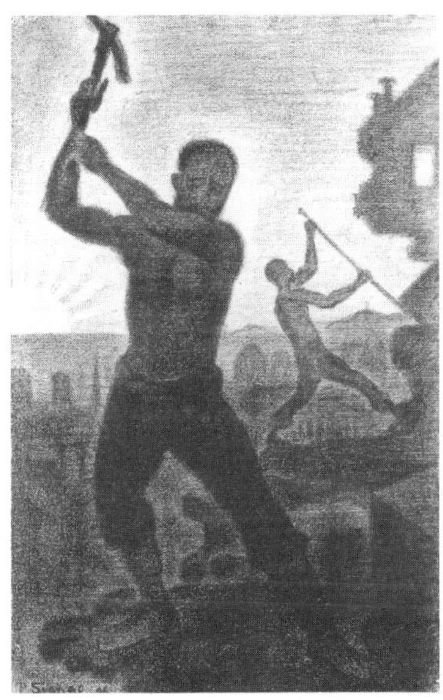

Louisiana State University Press
Baton Rouge and London

Copyright © 1994 by Louisiana State University Press
All rights reserved
Manufactured in the United States of America
First printing
03 02 01 00 99 98 97 96 95 94   5 4 3 2 1

Designer: *Glynnis Phoebe*
Typeface: *Bembo*
Typesetter: *G&S Typesetters, Inc.*
Printer and binder: *Thomson-Shore, Inc.*

LIBRARY OF CONGRESS CATALOGING-IN-PUBLICATION DATA

Hutton, John Gary, date.
   Neo-impressionism and the search for solid ground : art, science,
and anarchism in fin-de-siècle France / John G. Hutton.
      p.   cm. — (Modernist studies)
   Includes bibliographical references and index.
   ISBN 0-8071-1823-0 (cloth)
   1. Neo-impressionism (Art)—France.   2. Art, French.   3. Art—
Political aspects—France.   4. Art and society—France—
History—19th century.   I. Title   II. Series.
N6847.5.N37H88   1994
759.4′09′034—dc20   93-26334
                                                         CIP

The illustration on the title page is Paul Signac's *Les Démolisseurs* (Paul Signac, French, 1863–1935, The Wreckers [Les Démolisseurs] lithograph, 1896, 47 × 30.5 cm, Gift of Martin A. Ryerson, 1928.643, photograph © 1994, The Art Institute of Chicago, All Rights Reserved).

Contents

Illustrations

Acknowledgments

It is difficult to acknowledge major influences on one's work without sounding a bit like the character in Frederick C. Crews's *The Pooh Perplex* who cites everyone from Karl Marx to Nietzsche, Sacco and Vanzetti, Jung, and Saint John of the Cross. Nonetheless, it is important to note that any study is inevitably grounded in the work and insights of others. Hollis Clayson requires special recognition for helping me convert a random pile of note cards and partial drafts into a completed document. It was through her help and example as well that I first came into contact with a range of social historians of art whose work exemplified what I hoped to do. In my case, the investigations of Tim Clark, Tom Crow, Carol Duncan, Robert Herbert, and Griselda Pollock have been a continuing inspiration.

My initial research took place at the Northwestern University Library and at the Ryerson Art Library of the Art Institute of Chicago. More recently, the collections of the Trinity University Library and the libraries of the University of Texas at Austin have proved of worth. I acknowledge gratefully the individual assistance extended by Russell Maylone and the entire staff of the Special Collections Department of the Northwestern University Library, as well as by the staff of the interlibrary-loan offices at Northwestern and Trinity.

It would be impossible to list fully the other collections and institutions I drew on in my research. Recognition must go to the Institut Français d'Histoire Sociale and the Centre de Recherche des Mouvements Sociaux, both in Paris; the Ashmolean Museum, in Oxford; and the International Institute of Social History, in Amsterdam. The International Institute's materials were of particular importance, and its personnel were unfailingly courteous. Other research collections of major use to me were those of the British Museum Reading Room and the British Newspaper Library; the Library of Political and Economic Science of the London School of Economics; the Rylands University Library, of the University of Manchester; and the Bibliothèque Nationale, the Bibliothèque de l'Arsenal, the Bibliothèque des Arts Décoratifs, and the Archives Nationales, all in Paris.

A number of museums, galleries, and private collectors have shown particular consideration in aiding me to acquire the necessary images. I am notably indebted to Walter and Janet Brown and to the Jean Claude Bellier Galleries for their gracious assistance.

Many people have been both professionally and personally helpful to me, offering encouragement and suggestions. I would like to thank especially Christopher Lloyd, Sally Medlyn, Richard and Belinda Thomson, and Anne Thorold, in Great Britain, and Sura Levine, Robyn Roslak, Nancy Troy, David Van Zanten, Martha Ward, and Carol Zemel, in the United States. Several people assisted with translating materials from French into English, including Alan Astro, Nanette LeCoat, and especially Vanita Blessing.

Research is not free, of course. My studies would not have been possible without generous grants from the Samuel H. Kress Foundation and from Northwestern University. Trinity University has conferred considerable assistance, including three successive Maria and Arthur Berger Faculty Fellowships and a special grant from Dean William Walker to assist in translations. I must also note the strong supportive atmosphere provided by my colleagues in the Department of Art History at Trinity, including Lisa Reitzes, Charles Talbot, and Carolyn Valone.

This book would have been impossible without the assistance and encouragement of LSU Press. Barry L. Blose, the editor for the volume, has demonstrated both patience and tact. In addition, Rima Reck, the editor of the series Modernist Studies, has shown continuing confidence and support.

Above all, I would like to express my gratitude to my wife, Paula, who provided material, moral, and emotional support with unflagging consistency despite the pressing needs of her own research and career. I can only offer my deepest thanks and love and the promise to return the kindness and support in her life and work.

Finally, I would like to dedicate this study to my parents, John Lewis Hutton and Margaret MacDonald Hutton, and my daughter, Amy. I regret that my parents did not live to see the completion of my studies and the proof that—as they always insisted—I *could* finish something I started. I hope that Amy will come to maturity in a world where hopes for equality and social justice will once again find space to grow and thrive.

Chronology

	Social and Political	Cultural and Artistic	Neo-Impressionist
1870	French declaration of war, in July, opens Franco-Prussian War. Empire is defeated; emperor is overthrown.		
1871	Royalists win overwhelming majority in elections centering on issue of peace versus continued war. Right-wing government moves from Paris to Versailles. Paris Commune is proclaimed in March. Commune is defeated in *semaine sanglante*, week of bloody street fighting and massacres by Versailles troops in May. An estimated twenty-five to thirty thousand are killed; tens of thousands are arrested.	During Commune, Gustave Courbet inaugurates revolutionary Fédération des Artistes at a mass rally and proclaims abolition of Salon, *Ecole des Beaux-Arts*, prizes, and medals.	
1872		In first annual Salon after war and Commune, restrictions are placed on subject matter. Courbet is banned from Salon for life.	
1873	Attempted monarchist takeover collapses because of intransigence of Comte de Chambord, Legitimist pretender to throne.		

	Social and Political	Cultural and Artistic	Neo-Impressionist
1874		First Impressionist Exhibition is held at studio of photographer Nadar (Félix Tournachon). Among thirty exhibitors are Paul Cézanne, Edgar Degas, Armand Guillaumin, Claude Monet, Berthe Morisot, Camille Pissarro, Alfred Sisley, and Auguste Renoir.	
1876	Republicans win solid majority in Chamber of Deputies.	At Second Impressionist Exhibition, Gustave Caillebotte joins exhibitors.	
1877	Battle between Chamber of Deputies and monarchist president, Marshal MacMahon, results in new elections, with a continued republican majority.	Third Impressionist Exhibition is held.	
1878	Republicans win majority in Senate. MacMahon resigns and is replaced by republican Jules Grévy.		
1879	Limited amnesty is granted Communard prisoners. Peter Kropotkin and Elisée Reclus begin publishing *Le Révolté* in Geneva.	At Fourth Impressionist Exhibition, Marie Bracquemond, Mary Cassatt, and Jean Louis Forain exhibit with group. Internal dissensions lead Cézanne, Renoir, and Sisley to withdraw.	Georges Seurat and friends reportedly visit Fourth Impressionist Exhibition. Albert Dubois-Pillet joins Masonic cell inside army.
1880	Communard prisoners and exiles gain full amnesty.	At Fifth Impressionist Exhibition, Monet is also absent, but Jean Raffaëlli joins exhibitors. With disestablishment, Salon is to be run by semiprivate Société des Artistes Français (SAF).	

1881	Anarchist conference in London adopts a proposal for "direct action."	At Sixth Impressionist Exhibition, Paul Gauguin joins exhibitors. When Caillebotte's attempt to bring back "true Impressionists"—Monet, Renoir, and Sisley—fails, he withdraws as well. Revised, somewhat liberalized Salon jury awards Edouard Manet his first medal. Translation of Ogden Rood's *Modern Chromatics* is published in France. Socialist Edmond Picard founds *L'Art moderne* in Brussels.	Seurat begins to study Ogden Rood's *Théorie scientifique des couleurs*. Henri Edmond Cross exhibits in Salon for first time. Louis Hayet begins study of color theories of Ernest Chevreul.
1882	Union Générale, largest Catholic-owned bank in France, collapses. Industrial slump begins. Riots and first bombings lead to arrests of leading anarchists.	Caillebotte, Monet, Renoir, and Sisley return to Seventh Impressionist Exhibition. Cassatt, Degas, Forain, and Raffaëlli decline to exhibit.	
1883	Jules Guesde forms Parti Ouvrier, first Marxist party in France. In Geneva, Jean Grave takes over as editor of Kropotkin's *Le Révolté*.	Les XX is founded in Brussels by twenty Belgian artists.	Seurat begins work on *Bathers at Asnières*.
1884	Trade unions are legalized.	First issue of *Revue Indépendante,* edited by Félix Fénéon, appears. First Salon des Indépendants, a democratic rival to official Salon, takes place. Subsequent Salons des Indépendants are to be operated by new Société des Artistes Indépendants (SAI), chaired by Albert Dubois-Pillet (who will continue chairing it until his death). First exhibition of Les XX opens in Brussels.	Cross, Dubois-Pillet, and Seurat, along with Charles Angrand and Paul Signac, are among exhibitors at Salon des Indépendants. Seurat has first showing of *Bathers at Asnières,* and Dubois-Pillet exhibits notorious *Dead Child*. Seurat, Dubois-Pillet, and Signac meet. Seurat begins work on *Sunday Afternoon on the Isle of Grande Jatte*.

	1885	1886	1887
Neo-Impressionist	Seurat completes *Grande Jatte*. Signac meets Camille Pissarro, and Pissarro is introduced to Seurat. Lucien Pissarro meets Hayet, who is drawn into Neo circle. Maximilien Luce quits studio of Carolus Duran and discovers work of Seurat.	Neo-Impressionist works are on display in a separate room at Eighth Impressionist Exhibition. Seurat shows *Grande Jatte*, and Camille Pissarro, Lucien Pissarro, and Signac exhibit works. At second Salon des Indépendants, Angrand, Cross, Dubois-Pillet, Seurat, Signac, and Lucien Pissarro all have works hanging. Term *Neo-Impressionist* is first employed, in an article by Félix Fénéon. Dubois-Pillet holds meetings in his home with Fénéon, Seurat, Signac, and the Pissarros present. Hippolyte Petitjean affiliates with Neos. Signac begins his *Breakfast*, a parody of Gustave Caillebotte's *Luncheon*.	Seurat and Camille Pissarro are included in exhibition of Les XX in Brussels. Seurat begins *The Models*. Angrand, Cross, Dubois-Pillet, Luce, Seurat, Signac, and Lucien Pissarro are included in fourth Salon des Indépendants. Angrand completes *An Accident*; Seurat responds with *The Sideshow*. Luce's
Cultural and Artistic	Charles Henry publishes his *Introduction à une esthétique scientifique*.	Eighth Impressionist Exhibition is last one. Among exhibitors are Marie Bracquemond, Cassatt, Degas, Forain, Guillaumin, Morisot, and nascent Neo-Impressionists Camille Pissarro, Lucien Pissarro, Georges Seurat, and Paul Signac. Jean Moréas issues "Symbolist Manifesto." Jean Grave's *Le Révolté*, in attempt to make use of visual art, negotiates to purchase topical prints from news journal *L'Illustration*. Fénéon's *Les Impressionnistes en 1886* is published.	Grave begins issuing a literary supplement that relates cultural and aesthetic issues to anarchist principles. Jules Antoine establishes Théâtre Libre.
Social and Political	Former anarchist Benoît Malon organizes Société pour l'Economie Sociale to promote "integral socialism," modeled on British Fabianism. *Le Révolté* moves from Geneva to Paris. Kropotkin publishes his *Paroles d'un révolté*.	Local strikes in Belgium coalesce into a spontaneous uprising. French socialists set up a national union, Fédération Nationale des Syndicats (FNS). General Georges Boulanger begins to assemble a coalition of disaffected rightists and former radicals as a power base. Paris stock exchange is bombed.	Boulanger, dismissed as defense minister for his intrigues, embarks on a strategy to seize power. President Grévy is forced to resign in influence-peddling scandal. Sadi Carnot—called Sadi-Crétin by anarchist press—replaces Grévy. *Le Révolté* is banned; it is re-established in September as *La Révolte*.

			paintings, using divided color, attract attention of Camille Pissarro, who draws him into Neo circle. Attempt to retire Dubois-Pillet involuntarily from army fails. Article by Arsène Alexandre leads to squabble among Neo-Impressionists over "paternity" of Neo-Impressionist theory and technique. Hayet experiments with chromatic disk. Luce experiments with Neo-Impressionist portraiture. Signac, signing himself "Néo," reviews Les XX exhibition and fourth Salon des Indépendants in radical journal *Le Cri du peuple*.
1888	Parliament votes new loans for Ferdinand de Lesseps' Panama Canal Company. Company goes bankrupt, and dozens of deputies are implicated in acceptance of bribes.	Work begins on Eiffel Tower. Charles Henry's *Cercle chromatique* appears in print. Gauguin and Emile Bernard begin work in Pont Aven, in Brittany. Nabi Brotherhood is formed in Pont Aven by Pierre Bonnard, Maurice Denis, Paul Ranson, and Paul Sérusier.	
1889	Universal Exposition is held in Paris to observe centennial of French Revolution. Mass demonstrations mounted in support of General Boulanger lead to fear of a coup d'etat. Boulanger's advisers are arrested. Boulanger flees the country, and his movement collapses.	First issues of literary journal *La Plume* and insurrectionary anarchist journal *Le Père Peinard* are published. Salon splits as a minority withdraw to form Société Nationale des Beaux-Arts. First exhibition is held of Groupe Impressionniste et Synthétiste, Neos' rivals as heirs to Impressionists. Louis Anquetin, Bernard, and Gauguin exhibit with Neos' rivals. Artists and intellectuals—mostly anarchists and followers of Benoît Malon—form Club de l'Art Social.	Cross, Dubois-Pillet, Hayet, Luce, Seurat, Signac, and Lucien Pissarro all show at fifth Salon des Indépendants. Dubois-Pillet is promoted to major. Camille Pissarro produces his *Turpitudes sociales,* an album of satirical pen-and-ink drawings, together with quotations from the anarchist press. Seurat begins *The Chahut*.

	Neo-Impressionist	*Cultural and Artistic*	*Social and Political*
1890	Angrand, Cross, Dubois-Pillet, Luce, Seurat, and Signac, as well as Anna Boch and Lucien Pissarro, are all in sixth Salon des Indépendants. Dubois-Pillet dies of smallpox. Exchange of letters takes place between Seurat and Fénéon on Neo-Impressionist theory. Seurat completes *The Chahut* and begins *The Circus*. Hayet breaks his affiliation with Neos.	Vincent van Gogh commits suicide. Maurice Denis publishes his "Définition du néo-traditionnisme."	
1891	Angrand, Boch, Cross, Luce, Seurat, Signac, van Rysselberghe, and Lucien Pissarro are in seventh Salon des Indépendants. Dubois-Pillet is included posthumously. Cross joins with Neos. Seurat dies. Lucien Pissarro moves to England. Signac publishes his "Impressionnistes et Révolutionnaires" in Grave's *La Révolte*.	Jacques Huret's *Enquête sur l'évolution littéraire*, containing interviews with leading artists and writers, is released. First issues appear of Thadée Natanson's *Revue blanche* and of anarchist-oriented *L'Art social*, edited by poet Gabriel de La Salle. Gauguin moves to Tahiti.	Fourmies Massacre occurs. Protests by anarchists and socialists against shooting of unarmed civilian protesters lead to arrest of radical leaders.
1892	Les XX pays tribute to Seurat. Group exhibition of Neo-Impressionist painters is held in Paris.	Anarchist Théâtre d'Art Social is established. Peter Kropotkin's *The Conquest of Bread* is published in French. Socialist *maison du peuple* in Brussels institutes a *section d'art* with aim of enabling artists and intellectuals to educate workers about art and culture.	Anarchist Ravachol (François Koenigstein) is tried for murder, condemned, and executed. Syndicalists (worker anarchists) form Fédération des Bourses du Travail (FBT) as rival to socialist FNS.
1893	Galerie des Néo-Impressionnistes opens at 20 rue Laffitte as an anarchist cooperative. Signac begins work on *In Times of Harmony*.	Poll of artists, writers, composers, and critics by review *L'Ermitage* reveals more than half to be sympathetic to anarchist ideas.	Auguste Vaillant hurls a bomb into Chamber of Deputies to protest execution of Ravachol. French parliament votes first *lois scé-*

lérates against anarchist "associations of evildoers." Attempt by government to close down syndicalist _bourse du travil_ in Paris leads to four days of fierce riots. Government bans production of Gerhart Hauptmann's _The Weavers,_ and of _L'Automne,_ by anarchist writers Paul Adam and Gabriel Mourey. Trial of directors of bankrupt Panama Canal Company and of ten deputies implicated in bribetaking ends in a whitewash and cover-up.		

1894	Vaillant is executed. Emile Henry bombs Terminus Café in retaliation. Execution of Henry sparks assassination of President Sadi Carnot. Banning of anarchist journals and mass arrests follow. Procès des Trente, intended as first in a series of mass trials of anarchists, ends with most of the thirty acquitted. Félix Dubois' _Le Péril anarchiste_ warns that an anarchist conspiracy continues to threaten France. Captain Alfred Dreyfus is charged with providing secret papers to Germans.	Mass arrests surround Procès des Trente. Artists, writers, and critics, among them Fénéon and Maximilien Luce, are apprehended. Others, including Paul Adam, Octave Mirbeau, Camille Pissarro, and Théophile Steinlen, flee country. When Impressionist painter and collector Caillebotte dies, his bequest of a number of Impressionist paintings to Louvre ignites heated debate over appropriateness of gift.	First exhibition at Galerie des Néo-Impressionnistes includes works by Angrand, Cross, Luce, Petitjean, Signac, and van Rysselberghe, along with Antoine de La Rochefoucauld and three Pissarro siblings—Lucien, Georges, and Felix. Camille Pissarro declines to participate. Cross and Petitjean have a joint show. Luce is arrested in wake of assassination of Sadi Carnot. Camille Pissarro flees country. Luce produces _Mazas,_ an album of lithographs on prison life.
1895	Augustin Hamon's _Psychologie de l'anarchiste socialiste_ rebuts Dubois' book with a portrait of anarchists as intelligent and compassionate. Novelist Victor Barrucand launches _pain gratuit_ movement demanding free bread for poor as a basic right. Dreyfus is convicted.	_Les Temps nouveaux_ supersedes _La Révolte._ First issue of Sebastien Faure's journal _Le Libertaire_ appears. Grave's _La Société future_ is published.	Signac completes _In Times of Harmony_ (which in 1938 will be donated to _mairie_ of Montreuil). Luce tours working-class regions of Belgium.

	Social and Political	Cultural and Artistic	Neo-Impressionist
1896		*L'Art social* is reestablished as voice of anarchist Groupe de l'Art Social. *Les Temps nouveaux* commissions lithographs from sympathetic artists as a fund-raising tool. *L'Enclos,* an anarchist-oriented literary review, begins a poll of artists, writers, and intellectuals on how individuality and free expression can be tied to cause of social justice. Paterne Berrichon uses column in *Le Libertaire* to evaluate Symbolism and Neo-Impressionism from anarchist viewpoint.	Angrand, after death of his father, moves to village of Saint-Laurent, in Normandy. Luce publishes his *Les Gueules noires,* an album of scenes of working-class life in manner of Constantin Meunier. Camille Pissarro writes to Henry van de Velde to deny that his affiliation with Neo-Impressionism continues.
1897		Grave publishes his *L'Individu et la Société.*	
1898	Emile Zola publishes public letter ("J'accuse") on the Dreyfus case, charging that government and military deliberately convicted and imprisoned an innocent man. Zola is convicted of libel and flees country for England.	Reclus publishes his *L'Evolution, la Révolution et l'Idéal anarchique.*	
1899	New trial finds Dreyfus guilty, but with extenuating circumstances. Dreyfus is pardoned by French president. Anti-Semitic riots follow.	Kropotkin's *Fields, Factories, and Workshops* is published.	Signac's *D'Eugène Delacroix au néo-impressionnisme* is published in book form.

1900	FNS and FBT join in a single union federation, Confédération Générale du Travail (CGT), initially under syndicalist leadership.	
1903		Camille Pissarro dies.
1904	Quarreling socialist parties achieve unity as Parti Socialiste, Section Française de l'Internationale Ouvrière (SFIO).	
1905		Charles Albert takes twenty-first Salon des Indépendants as occasion to evaluate Neo-Impressionism critically for *Les Temps nouveaux*.

Neo-Impressionism
and the Search
for Solid Ground

Introduction

Neo-Impressionism was born just over a century ago, in May, 1886, at the Eighth (and final) Impressionist Exhibition, in a separate room built around Georges Seurat's colossal *Sunday Afternoon on the Isle of Grande Jatte*. The four artists in the subexhibition—Seurat himself (1859–1891), the veteran Impressionist Camille Pissarro (1830–1903), his son Lucien (1863–1944), and Paul Signac (1863–1935)—were convinced that they were making history. In place of what Seurat and his group saw as an antiquated "Romantic Impressionism," grounded in intuition and spontaneity, they promised to employ optical and psychobiological theories in pursuit of a grand synthesis of the ideal and the real, the fugitive and the essential, science and temperament.

Less than five years later, Seurat was dead, of a sudden attack of diphtheria. Accounts of Neo-Impressionism, centering for the most part on the views and contributions of Seurat himself, tend overwhelmingly to focus on the brief time before his death. Yet Neo-Impressionism did not die in 1891; it continued to develop over the next decade. After Seurat's death and that of his friend and colleague Albert Dubois-Pillet, who had been struck down by smallpox in the previous year, the movement began to take on a more distinct profile, with political and social strands of Neo-Impressionist theory in increasing prominence. The Neos began to forge explicit, instead of tacit, links to the anarchocommunist movement around Peter Kropotkin, Jean Grave, and Elisée Reclus. Around the surviving core—the Pissarros, Signac, Charles Angrand (1854–1926), Louis Hayet (1864–1940), Hippolyte Petitjean (1854–1929), and Maximilien Luce (1858–1941)—young artists gathered, attracted by the movement's blend of social and artistic theory, including Henri Edmond Cross (1856–1910) and the Belgian Théo van Rysselberghe (1862–1926).[1]

---

1. By the late 1890s, a second cluster was added, including a number of women; among them were students of Signac, including Lucie Coustourier, Jeanne Droz, and Jeanne Selmersheim-Desgrange, as well as the Belgian painter Anna Boch, of Les XX. The study

For someone unaware of the gradual transformation of Neo-Impressionism, much of the critique it received at the time remains at best just out of focus. In December, 1894, the critic Adolphe Tabarant took notice in his front-page column in the independent socialist daily *La Petite République* of the new Neo-Impressionist cooperative gallery in the Rue Laffitte. Focusing on the works of the "two young masters" Luce and Signac, Tabarant wrote, "The art has, perhaps, a tendency toward an ill-tempered synthesis, toward a scientific observation that is too dry. But how it vibrates, and how it rings with truth! What an expenditure of coloring, what a profusion of agitated notations, in which one senses the noble and sincere passions of those young men who, after the lamented Seurat, strive to capture all the secrets of light from the sun!"[2] There seems little in this at odds with modern accounts of Neo-Impressionism. Nine decades of criticism and analysis have thoroughly accustomed us, perhaps numbed us, to Tabarant's observations—with their reference to the young disciples of Seurat, to science, and to the drive to capture the secrets of sunlight, and with the use of such catchphrases of the late-nineteenth-century art world as *truth, synthesis,* and *vibrancy.* So commonplace have the terms and phrases become that we skim over the most important questions Tabarant's account should raise. What did such language mean to Tabarant and the readers of a socialist daily newspaper? What would it have meant to the readers that "the Neo-Impressionists affirm in an incessant manner their desire for research and synthesis"?[3] Precisely what sort of *vérité* was the science of Neo-Impressionism intended to unveil? And for whom?

Less expected perhaps by a modern reader of Tabarant's commentary is the situation he presents as that of the artistic project of Neo-Impressionism. The section quoted occurs in the course of a discussion of Luce's arrest in connection with the Procès des trente, a mass show trial of anarchists intended as the first act in repressing the anarchist movement. Sarcastically labeling the arrested artist "decidedly a dangerous anarchist," Tabarant goes on to link Luce's political beliefs and activities to his and the other Neo-Impressionists' art.

of this group—especially the women who affiliated with the Neos—is in approximately the state of research on Pre-Raphaelite women before the work of Jan Marsh. References are spotty for all but Boch, and research is all but nonexistent.

2. Adolphe Tabarant, "Impressions quotidiennes," *La Petite République,* December 16, 1894, p. 1.

3. *Ibid.*

It is scarcely surprising that Tabarant, a veteran socialist, found the politics of the Neos consequential. Yet, nearly a century later—and nearly three decades after the ground-breaking work by Robert L. Herbert and Eugenia W. Herbert on anarchism and the artistic avant-garde of the era—the precise political affiliations and political content of Neo-Impressionism remain in large part unmapped.[4] The scholarship of art history has all too frequently distorted or even ignored such matters. Even when it has addressed the topics, it has tended to deal with the anarchism of the Neo-Impressionists rather elliptically. For many historians of art and culture, the political beliefs and affiliations of the Neos are at most peripheral, if not merely a curiosity. The Neo-Impressionists, we often hear, kept up a correspondence with Grave and other anarchist militants, contributed a few francs to anarchist fund drives, and produced a handful of lithographs or drawings for the cause that were, on the whole, of only minor artistic interest when they were openly political and of only tangential political impact when they were of artistic merit.[5] A second body of modern studies enfolds the Neo-Impressionists in an amorphous, catchall "anarchism" it attributes to the intelligentsia at large—moreover, an anarchism it leaves suspended in midair and discusses in ways that rip it from the time, the place, the milieu, that is, the very conditions, within which it was generated and produced.[6] Despite

4. See Robert L. Herbert and Eugenia W. Herbert, "Artists and Anarchism: Unpublished Letters of Pissarro, Signac, and Others," *Burlington Magazine,* CII (1960), 473–82, 517–22; Robert L. Herbert, "Les Artistes et l'Anarchisme," *Le Mouvement social,* XXXVI (July–September, 1961), 2–19; Eugenia W. Herbert, *The Artist and Social Reform: France and Belgium, 1885–1898* (New Haven, 1961); Robert L. Herbert, *Neo-Impressionism* (New York, 1968); and Robert L. Herbert, "*Parade de cirque* de Seurat et l'Esthétique scientifique de Charles Henry," *Revue de l'art,* L (1980), 9–23. The Herberts' work has inspired a number of similar efforts, including those of Annemarie Springer, in "Terrorism and Anarchy: Late Nineteenth-Century Images of a Political Phenomenon in France," *Art Journal,* XXXVIII (1979), 261–66; and those of John A. Walker, in "Art and Anarchism," *Art and Artists,* XIII (May, 1978), 16–19.

5. This reaction is found, though in different forms, in most general historical studies of anarchism as well. See James Joll, *The Anarchists* (2nd ed.; Cambridge, Mass., 1980), 151. See also Raymond Cogniat, *Camille Pissarro* (New York, 1978), 72; Benedict Nicolson, "The Anarchism of Camille Pissarro," *The Arts,* II (1947), 43–51; and Françoise Cachin, "The Neo-Impressionist Avant-Garde," *Art News Annual,* XXXIV (1968), 54–65. Common to most of the reactions is an equation of politically engaged art with direct political propaganda.

6. This view finds supreme expression in Donald Drew Egbert's *Social Radicalism and the Arts—Western Europe: A Cultural History from the French Revolution to 1968* (New York, 1970), in which almost any image of someone wielding a farm implement becomes a radical statement. See especially the discussion of the Nabis and Synthetists (pp. 258–62). See also

the apparent contrast, the two approaches join in stripping Neo-Impressionism of its specificity and in slighting concerns that the artists themselves identified as primary. Neither sort of study seriously addresses what it might have meant to proclaim oneself an anarchist artist, in an era when the "propaganda of the deed" had for governments around the world made anarchism synonymous with a form of social pathology.

Both sorts of study derive ultimately from the idea that blossomed later of a Post-Impressionism capable of including everyone from Paul Gauguin to Luce, from Signac to Maurice Denis. Inherent in that idea is a teleological view of art in which each movement is of interest primarily as the antecedent of what comes next, of trends to be adopted, extended, or reversed by the following generation. Neo-Impressionism, Synthetism, Symbolism, and all their competitors gain their significance, in a critique of this sort, above all by contributing to the progressive decoupling of modern art from external subject matters, and by implication from any social preoccupations. Harold Rosenberg once wrote scathingly of a conception of the history of art according to which it consists of tombstones for dead movements. It might be more accurate to say that in much of the literature on modern art, movements and individuals are reduced to mileposts on the highway to abstraction.

I seek to approach Neo-Impressionism from a different angle. John Berger wrote of the "moment" of Cubism—of a complex interrelated, interacting network of aesthetic, social, political, cultural, and economic factors that fed into Cubism and bound it to a distinct historical period, milieu, and social fabric. Neo-Impressionism was perhaps even more distinctly a creature of its time and milieu than Cubism: it was a determined but fragile attempt to derive a "harmonious" synthetic vision from contemporary science, anarchist theory, and late-nineteenth-century aesthetic debates. Though it is impossible to recover all that collectively overdetermined Neo-Impressionism, we can at least expose and assess the key features of the world in which its artists lived, the character of the audience they addressed (and what they hoped—or claimed—to say to it), and the broad forces behind the intellectual and social climate from which their entire project emerged.

Theda Shapiro, *Painters and Politics: The European Avant-Garde and Society, 1900–1925* (New York, 1976), 15–17; John Rewald, *Post-Impressionism from Van Gogh to Gauguin* (3rd ed.; New York, 1978), 133–65; and Ralph E. Shikes, *The Indignant Eye: The Artist as Social Critic in Prints and Drawings from the Fifteenth Century to Picasso* (Boston, 1969), 200–253.

Such an exercise requires attention to issues of artistic theory, but as an integral part of a broader analysis referring to the political, economic, class, and other socially determined variables that inevitably influenced the manner in which the Neos lived, the hopes they nursed, and the theories they defended. The study must not force later notions upon the Neos—including those of the twentieth-century avant-garde—but must examine the factors that shaped their artistic production as a whole. The goal must be neither to reduce Neo-Impressionism to a mere prelude to later, supposedly more advanced, art nor to accept the claims of its proponents or its critics at face value. Instead, it must be to grasp to the fullest how a movement such as Neo-Impressionism arises and how—and why—it dies.

Even a partial dissection of Neo-Impressionism will involve an examination not only of French cultural life in the 1880s and 1890s but of the social dynamics of the time and place. Above all, the goal cannot be to establish a "context" for Neo-Impressionism. The seemingly harmless phrase "to put art into its context" falsely implies a separation between the two; all too often the "context" is reduced to the level of the program notes the operagoer skims before the lights dim. The result for Neo-Impressionism is often a discussion of formal technique in gratuitous exile from the social concerns the technique was intended in part to address. More often yet, the result is along the lines of a Romantic myth: a lone genius invents (creates, discovers) a brilliant but controversial new technique, experiments with it while rallying a company of devoted, if less talented, admirers, then tragically dies. His followers attempt to continue the movement, but they seem unable to get it right, and the whole endeavor collapses.[7] Sometimes, the entire account of Neo-Impressionism from the death of Georges Seurat to its end as a movement takes barely a paragraph or two.[8]

There are fundamental problems with this Romantic narrative. First, it seriously distorts the history of Neo-Impressionism, making it the creation, and property, of a single, gifted individual rather than the domain of a circle of artists who have come together for disparate reasons with their own concerns and contributions. Hayet's color-wheel experiments, Signac's early fascina-

7. This latter account occurs most frequently in studies of Neo-Impressionism and scientific theory. See, for example, John Adkins Richardson, *Modern Art and Scientific Thought* (Urbana, Ill., 1971), 74; and William Innes Homer, *Seurat and the Science of Painting* (Cambridge, Mass., 1964), 1–3.

8. See Rewald, *Post-Impressionism,* 398–402.

tion with the writings of Charles Henry, and other individual distinctions are minimized or lost altogether in buttressing the concept of a master genius. As a result, there is no room for exploring the *evolving* nature of Neo-Impressionism, for exploring Neo-Impressionism as a project. Changes in focus, form, technique, or subject matter register simply as failures by members of the circle to grasp adequately what Seurat intended. Perhaps more important, such an account is false as well to the manner in which any artistic movement functions in modern societies. It misstates the reality to note in passing the conditions under which the Neos produced and sold their art—the collapse of the Salon, the rise of the Indépendants, the growing dominance of the private dealer system, the general social climate of pessimism and periodic depressions that flowed from the collapse of the Union générale bank in 1882 and of the Panama Canal Company in 1888—as if they were merely hurdles the artists had to vault. Rather, Neo-Impressionism was the creature—one of many competing creatures, to be sure—of that climate and those social factors. Had any of the factors been significantly different, Neo-Impressionism would never have come into being.

Social conditions do not produce art; people do. But artists make their art for something or someone, and they produce it as part of an overdetermining web of social and cultural conditions. The nature of the art market, the profile of its patrons (and the conditions of their patronage), the dominant values of the time (which influence what art is seen to be for as well as the ways in which its subjects are most likely to be seen) all impose, if nothing else, certain unavoidable choices that the artist is compelled to make.[9]

Among popular concerns, an interest in social class emerged with special vigor in the latter half of the nineteenth century. Indeed, the relative openness with which people discussed class seems striking in comparison with the present. In recent decades, those on the political right have chosen most often to remain quiet about the class nature of artistic production. Their political forebears were far less reticent: they loudly and frequently proclaimed that artistic excellence was inseparable from a wealthy elite. The Parnassian review *La Jeune Belgique* asserted flatly that "every pro-

---

9. On overdetermination, see Louis Althusser, "Contradiction and Overdetermination," in *For Marx,* trans. Ben Brewster (New York, 1969), 89–128. For a discussion more heavily flavored by Freud than Marx, cf. Peter Gay, "On Overdetermination," in *Art and Act: On Causes in History* (New York, 1976), 1–14.

duction addressing itself to the public must be banal in basis as well as in form" and attacked democracy as the intrinsic enemy of art. Léon Daudet, looking back at what he termed the "stupid nineteenth century," asserted that "in a democracy, where everything totters, collapses, liquefies, and decomposes through political and social spasms, an Academy, which is by definition an elite and privileged body living in accordance with tradition, finds itself orphaned and abandoned." [10] The monarchist poseur Joséphin ("Sâr") Péladan saw realism in art, Protestantism and free thought in religion, and intellectual and social equality as the bitter enemies of the "true," hierarchical, and religious France he advocated. [11] On the other hand, anarchist and socialist writers and artists sought to chart a path from a class society that vulgarized and destroyed art toward a classless, harmonious world in which art would be available to all and, in the words of Camille Pissarro, "everyone will be an artist." Otherwise, "soon there will be nothing left except the lying dreams of history, the miserable wreckage of our museums and picture-galleries, and the carefully-guarded interior of our aesthetic drawing-rooms, unreal and foolish, fitting witnesses of the life of corruption that goes on there, so pinched and meagre and cowardly," William Morris told a presumably skeptical audience of English art lovers. [12]

It is vital here to avoid the image of class cleavage as involving two or more distinct, static masses of people hacking and bashing at one another. Classes, as E. P. Thompson has understood, are not "things," or even "structures," but historically evolving relationships. One class cannot exist without another; there can be, he reminds us, no "love without lovers, or deference without squires and labourers"—nor, we might add, in a market economy, artists without buyers. In evolving social relationships, centered ultimately upon the forces of production and distribution, common experiences lead to a sense of common identity and purpose, both by inclusion (common activities, status, legal restrictions, or duties) and by exclusion. The class into which one is born—or forced—provides a consciousness that finds expression in a variety

10. Albert Giraud, "Etudes esthétiques: L'Art social," *Le Jeune Belgique,* II (1882–83), 369–79; Léon Daudet, *Le Stupide XIXe Siècle* (Paris, 1922), 199.

11. Joséphin Péladan, *L'Art idéaliste et mystique: Doctrine de l'ordre* (10th ed.; Paris, 1894), 23–25.

12. William Morris, "The Aims of Art," in *Signs of Change: Seven Lectures* (London, 1888), 132. R. Vertpré quotes Pissarro in "De l'évolution de l'art," *Le Libertaire,* 3rd ser., VII (February 9–16, 1901), 3.

of customs, traditions, ideas, arts, and institutional forms. The clothes we wear, the books or journals we read (and whether we read at all), the clubs and associations we join, the recreations that divert us, the parties we vote for or against are all shaped by a variety of class pressures, expectations, and traditions.[13]

The insight that class formations are always in flux, that class identity is never altogether stable but formed in the interactions and antagonisms of social strata that are both affected by and in turn influence the interactions, also reminds us that any class itself is an aggregate or conglomerate of differing strata, of layers on the rise or in decline—layers that often have quite distinct trajectories. The "middle class" in particular is often a temporary sojourn for distinct groupings; the industrializing France at the end of the nineteenth century typically saw both a rising middle stratum of white-collar civil servants, clerks, and managers, and a declining middle stratum comprising petty merchants and skilled artisans. Both were petit bourgeois in some sense, yet their hopes, and fears, were distinct.

Much of the debate on the arts that took place in late-nineteenth-century France is incomprehensible if the process of class formation and transformation remains in the shadows. Discussions within the arts and among their audience tended to orbit, at a very small remove, ongoing debates in the country as a whole over class power and class allegiances. In the debates, it is possible to trace the shifting social and economic power relations that were belatedly recognized and codified by the revolutions and uprisings France experienced throughout the century. Under the Bourbon restoration (1815–1830), the moderate liberal Benjamin Constant was already saluting the inroads the middle classes had made into administrative circles in the wake of the Great Revolution.[14] By the 1870s, the republican leader Léon Gambetta took the power of the bourgeoisie for granted; he greeted the emergence of a "new social layer" that was asserting its rights in the new republic, and in 1875 he called for a republicanism based on an "alliance of the bourgeoisie and the proletariat," an alliance of the producing classes against the remnants of the aristos.[15]

13. E. P. Thompson, *The Making of the English Working Class* (New York, 1966), 9–11; T. J. Clark, *The Painting of Modern Life: Paris in the Art of Manet and His Followers* (New York, 1984), 7–8.

14. Jacques Droz, *Europe Between Revolutions, 1815–1848* (London, 1967), 48.

15. On the "couche sociale nouvelle," see Léon Gambetta, *Discours et Plaidoyers poli-*

A parallel, and derivative, discussion occurred in the arts. In the first half of the century, reformers called for strong ties between artists and the commercial bourgeoisie, deeming such relationships a precondition for a modernized France. Henri de Saint-Simon and Léon Halévy, in their *L'Artiste, le Savant et l'Industriel,* of 1825, grouped the three agents of their title together as the nucleus of a modern social order. In their projection, the industrialists were to impose their ideas—along with the duties the ideas entailed—on society, scientists were to demonstrate the practical utility of knowledge, and artists were to act as an ideological vanguard, giving visual and literary form to the ideals of the industrialists and scientists.[16] That became a commonplace in republican thought. For Alexandre Decamps, art and industry—and therefore artists and industrialists—were necessary allies for a democratization of society: under a tyranny both were repressed, whereas under a democracy both flourished.[17] Charles Baudelaire, in the obsequious "Aux bourgeois" that he wrote as the preface to his review of the Salon of 1846, hailed the bourgeoisie as the "majority—in number and intelligence," called for a union of proprietors and scientists to form an invincible bloc, and addressed those uniting: "You have joined forces, you have formed companies and indebted yourselves in order to attain the idea of the future in all its diverse forms, from the political to the industrial and the political . . . you are the natural friends of the arts, some because you are the rich, others because you are the learned."[18]

Coziness between the industrialist or financier and the arts did not seem auspicious to others. Edmond de Goncourt and Jules de Goncourt, in *La Révolution dans les moeurs,* described industry and art as irreconcilable. They found universal suffrage itself fatal to art, for it undermined the elite with the taste, money, and leisure

tiques, ed. Joseph Reinach (11 vols.; Paris, 1880–85), III, 101. On the call for an alliance between workers and the bourgeoisie, see IV, 294.

16. Claude Henri de Saint-Simon, *Oeuvres* (6 vols.; Paris, 1964), V, 201–57. An excerpted translation appears in *Henri de Saint-Simon, 1760–1825: Selected Writings on Science, Industry, and Social Organisation,* ed. and trans. Keith Taylor (London, 1975), 279–88.

17. Alexandre Decamps, "Les Arts et l'Industrie au dix-neuvième siècle," *Revue républicaine,* III (1834), 27–52, IV (1835), 175–94. Decamps concluded, "That is why we call our vows a social reform, which puts the people and the exercise of their rights, the influence of their will, and the authority of their beliefs back into the picture; it is in their breasts that the artists will ascertain the true and noble inspirations for their works; their needs will dictate industry's search for its true progress and its new discoveries" (p. 194).

18. Charles Baudelaire, "Aux bourgeois," in *Salon de 1846,* reprinted in *Oeuvres complètes* (2 vols.; Paris, 1976), II, 415–17.

to comprehend the artist's work.[19] Jules Fleuricamp, writing in the wake of the Commune (1871), similarly deplored the artistic climate when "the kings of the era are the bankers and the entrepreneurs, the prime ministers, engineers and architects, secretaries of state, master masons and contractors." The new "kings" inevitably demand an art "in harmony with their art: that of building trains, train stations, ballast beds, railways, steam engines, and kilometers of telegraphic poles and wire." Fleuricamp did not charge that the new cultural rulers wanted paintings only on themes of that sort; rather, he affirmed that a utilitarian mentality was inherently hostile to genuine art. Intelligence was applied to material things rather than matters of the spirit. The result was an increasingly vulgar society, dominated by the art of a Courbet or a Teniers.[20]

By the time of Fleuricamp's jeremiad, another sort of dissent was being heard as well. In 1876, the poet Stéphane Mallarmé, echoing Gambetta, extolled the development of a radical, democratic art corresponding to the emergence of a "hitherto ignored people in the political life of France."[21] Mallarmé linked that art to the Impressionists—whose project Claude Monet had described in terms of the "associationism" of lower-middle-class republicanism.[22] In anarchist writings from Pierre Joseph Proudhon's posthumous *Du principe de l'art et sa destination sociale,* of 1865, to Kropotkin's *Paroles d'un révolté,* of 1886, artists were exhorted to speak out in behalf of an artisanal working class.

19. Edmond de Goncourt and Jules de Goncourt, *La Révolution dans les moeurs* (Paris, 1854). An excerpt from their discussion on art appears in English translation in *Realism and Tradition in Art, 1848–1900: Sources and Documents,* ed. Linda Nochlin (Englewood Cliffs, N.J., 1966), 17–18. For an earlier critique of the same sort, see the anonymous "Salon de 1839," *Revue des deux-mondes,* 4th ser., I (1839), 83–103.

20. Jules Fleuricamp, "Causerie sur le Salon," *L'Artiste,* II (1871), 271–74.

21. Stéphane Mallarmé, "The Impressionists and Edouard Manet," *Art Monthly Review,* September 30, 1876, reprinted in *The New Painting: Impressionism, 1874–1886* (San Francisco, 1986), 28–34.

22. On May 5, 1873, Paul Alexis in *L'Avenir national* called for artists to commit themselves to "this powerful idea, the idea of association, [which is] not only growing in the passionate and lively world of artists [but] beginning to suffuse new blood into the anemic old world." On May 12, Claude Monet responded, "A group of painters . . . have read with pleasure the article you have published. . . . We are happy to see you defend ideas that are ours, too, and we hope that . . . *L'Avenir national* will kindly give us assistance" (Paul Hayes Tucker, "The First Impressionist Exhibition in Context," in *The New Painting,* 94–96, 101–106). On the significance of the term *association,* see William H. Sewell, Jr., *Work and Revolution in France* (New York, 1980), 201–18.

More or less taken for granted by everyone engaging in the debate was that the class paying for and commissioning art—and for whom it was intended—fundamentally determined its content and significance. Saint-Simon called for artists to give form to the ideas of the industrialists; Decamps thought they would do so naturally; Baudelaire urged the bourgeoisie to involve itself in the arts; the Goncourts and Fleuricamp complained that it had already done so. The relationship between audience or patron and message was spelled out bluntly in a speech by the anarchosyndicalist Fernand Pelloutier when he charged that capitalism did not maintain itself through the state apparatus, army, police, and courts alone but imposed its ideas on the population monopolistically when it employed art and literature as instruments of social control. Pelloutier viewed the arts as not unlike the legal system in the way they were being used to trap the population in a matrix of concepts and beliefs that left it passive and inert. At birth, a human being was a "clean slate." Each person had to be taught what was right, what was proper, what was allowed and what was not. Art—particularly with the reemergence of mysticism and the underlying idea of an "aristocracy of art"—had become "the servant, the accomplice of bourgeois society."[23]

Pelloutier's call to turn art into a force for popular emancipation fed the fervor of the French far right's complaint that art was failing in its essential task of upholding privilege and hierarchy. For Daudet, art had become reduced to the plaything of a vulgar mob; Péladan could think of no higher task for his Salons de la Rose + Croix than to uphold the faith and beauty of traditions in the brief time remaining until the barbarians came and pounded everything into rubble.

But is the existence, so widely supposed, of a socially generated and controlled art evident from the side of the art objects themselves? Nicos Hadjinicolaou has advanced the idea of a visual, imaged ideology, the expression of a class—or a significant fraction of a class—in visual art.[24] His idea has useful ramifications, most notably in inviting the examination of how certain forms are seen to codify the world views of their makers and patrons, but it is also

23. Fernand Pelloutier, *L'Art et la Révolte* (Paris, 1896), 16–17.

24. Nicos Hadjinicolaou, *Art History and Class Struggle,* trans. Louise Asmal (London, 1978), 95–102, 107–23. For criticism of the concept of *idéologie imagée,* see Alan Wallach, "In Search of a Marxist Theory of Art History," *Block,* IV (1981), 15–17; and Michel Lequenne, *Marxisme et Esthétique* (Paris, 1984), 27–38.

simplistic in its assumption that a social class has or can have a uniform way of looking at the world. It is vital to distinguish between signifier and signified, between intent and effect, between production and reception. In practice, there are always incoherences and disjunctures in a representational system. The novels of Balzac, Flaubert, the Goncourts, Hugo, and Zola all have, at some level, to do with the ways in which a dominant bourgeoisie saw the world in the nineteenth century, but their differences do not stem solely from their separate moments of production. Rather, the variations help us to perceive the boundaries of French bourgeois thought, its contradictions as well as its uniformities, its assertions and its blind spots. From them, we gain insight into debates that were occurring in French society over class, over representative institutions, and over the ways in which women and men were supposed to live. We can also get an impression of what issues were not to be raised, of which ones were at the margins of or altogether outside a dominant and privileged discourse.

Class and gender provide the clearest examples. By the end of the century, allegiance to the concept of an immutable and eternal class structure was confined to a sullen but usually powerless monarchist right. But the period in France that saw the fall of the doctrine of "natural" classes also saw the resurgence of a ritualized discourse on women that presupposed the "natural" patriarchal structure of society—this at precisely the moment that socialists and feminists were raising the issue of equality for women and the demands of a burgeoning capitalist economy were pressing millions of women into the work force. Literary and artistic images of women were generated within the compass of the debate on the status of women and the social dislocations caused by industrialization. The images often sought to impose an artificial—usually a reactionary—stability over the gap between the dominant assertions of the time and the experiences of living men and women.[25]

Griselda Pollock speaks in this connection of the "ideological baggage" viewers of nineteenth-century art brought with them to a museum or gallery—a mental jumble of novels, essays, manuals, and periodicals, all of which attempted to establish basic definitions of, for example, masculinity and femininity, through which the art viewed was to be interpreted. Although the influences in

25. Griselda Pollock, *Vision and Difference: Femininity, Feminism, and the Histories of Art* (London, 1988), 9. Pollock also notes that "reading" an art work is no simple matter, that the identity of the producer and the viewer must be factored into the equation.

such a situation are inevitably a miscellany, Pollock remarks that "in the interconnections, repetitions and resemblances a prevailing regime of truth is generated, providing a large framework of intelligibility within which certain kinds of understanding are preferred, and others rendered unthinkable."[26] In a society marked by sharply uneven access to power, the dominant discourse is stamped with the views of those at the top. In effect, not only literature, the arts, the journalistic media, and political campaigns but all the pursuits of everyday life are saturated with a certain set of views and values around which thinking is expected to revolve. This congeries of privileged values and ideas—the permeation by which Antonio Gramsci styled hegemony—embodies not so much a rigorous development of consciously worked out principles as a limiting framework within which social discussion takes place, within which certain views are routinely excluded from the outset as outmoded or alien. Raymond Williams emphasizes that the concept of hegemony "sees the relations of domination and subordination, in their forms as practical consciousness, as in effect a saturation of the whole process of living—not only of political and economic activity, nor only of manifest social activity, but the whole substance of lived identities and relationships." The result of hegemony is to make an existing system appear not a created artifact but the product of "simple experience and common sense."[27]

Hegemonic relations, like those of class, amount by their very nature less to a discrete thing than to an ongoing process, in which dominant ideas are continually challenged, revised, defended, or discarded. The metaphor is possible of a loosely woven mesh through which some ideas or projects slip easily while others are blocked and a few get through only by smashing their way. The mesh is constantly being torn and rewoven.

Tradition produces some of the sturdiest strands in the mesh, and much that tries to penetrate the barrier dresses itself to fit tradition. In nineteenth-century France, the Great Revolution of the previous century was constantly being refought. The slogans of the eighteenth-century Enlightenment were deployed by the regime, which saw itself as answering to the dreams of the *philo-*

26. *Ibid.*
27. Raymond Williams, *Marxism and Literature,* (Oxford, 1977), 108–14, 116–17. John Berger has noted in G (London, 1972) that "every ruling minority needs to numb and, if possible, to kill the time-sense of those whom it exploits by proposing a continuous present" (p. 72).

sophes, but also by at least part of a radical opposition, which put the slogans to a completely different use.[28]

It is customary to think of the battles of nineteenth-century France as war in the streets, from the *trois glorieuses* of 1830 to the *semaine sanglante* of 1871 to the brawls and riots that punctuated the last two decades of the century. But upheavals in the street were only the most visible eruptions, and the battles also involved a continuing attempt to define and delimit—in a word, to represent—social realities, as a way either of controlling them or of contesting their control. Representation in the broadest sense—not only the visual or literary depiction of the world but the entire process of conceptualizing it—was a part of the battle precisely because all the contestants were convinced that making others see the world in a certain way was a precondition of victory. Many of the same dates, traditions, flags, and icons were contested, appropriated, and reappropriated by different positions and factions attempting to prove themselves the logical end product of historical evolution.

A study of the interweavings of French art and social relations can particularly help us to grasp the fragmentation and schism that marked the art world of the 1880s and 1890s. Artists of the period—a Théophile Steinlen and a Maurice Denis, for example—might have access to some of the same sources, even drink at the same taverns, yet not produce their art for the same people, for the same reasons, or in the same way. When Steinlen opened a shop for his prints in a working-class arrondissement of Paris, advertising his work among the artisans and workers of the city, his act signaled more than a simple appeal to a broader audience. It was part of a fundamental break with dominant notions of Art as they had existed even within nineteenth-century radical circles, and an effort to restore to those the socialist leader Jean Jaurès termed the disinherited some access to education, beauty, knowledge, and hope.

The 1880s and 1890s were a period of flux, in which French society was splintering to an extent hitherto experienced only in

28. Raymond Williams has advanced the term *selective tradition* for the effort by the dominant culture to pass off its selected reading of the past as "the tradition," "*the* significant past." He adds, "But always the selectivity is the point; the way in which from a whole possible area of past and present, certain meanings and practices are chosen for emphasis, certain other meanings and practices are neglected and excluded." See his "Base and Superstructure in Marxist Cultural Theory," in *Schooling and Capitalism,* ed. Roger Dale *et al.* (London, 1975), 202–205.

periods of insurrection or civil war. Artists had to choose sides in the conflicts of the day, either by allying themselves openly with some faction or by retreating to their own homes and imaginations. It is impossible under the circumstances to speak blithely of an art, a literature, even an avant-garde. There were arts, literatures, competing visions of, and projects for, an avant-garde, blurred sometimes at the edges but differentiated by intent and audience. Certain trends in the arts following the breakup of Impressionism, for example, brought Gauguin and Pissarro together for a time; the events and struggles of the 1880s and 1890s—not only artistic but social and political, or all three at once—pulled them apart. When Pissarro complained that Gauguin was "always on the side of the bastards," or Gauguin attacked the Neo-Impressionists as chemists, more than merely aesthetic responses were at work.

Neo-Impressionism attempted alternately to address and evade the social ruptures of its time. The Neos have affinities with almost every movement spawned by the breakup of Impressionism and the collapse of the Salon, their political alliances and affiliations often pressing them in a direction contrary to that of their artistic aspirations. Theirs was a movement racked by almost unbearable tensions and contradictions from the start, engaged in a perilous balancing act. It is not surprising that when the group finally split apart, its adherents landed on different, even opposing, sides. Neo-Impressionism thus constitutes a promising field in which to conduct an examination, necessarily partial, of the response of a circle of artists bound by certain characteristics and experiences to an especially turbulent period, in which a certain form of market relations seemed to pose a special threat to the survival of art in the forms it had until then taken. Neo-Impressionism was one of the competing politicoartistic projects by which artists attempted to respond to that period and to adapt to a rapidly changing society while upholding certain values—in their paintings and their daily lives—that they regarded as crucial. Their reactions assist us to understand both how art can function as one thread in a larger social fabric and how artists can use their art to change the social fabric itself.

In a letter Pissarro wrote to his son Lucien in 1884, he provided the setting for what he saw as a compelling question of the day. In a discussion of the art of Honoré Daumier, Pissarro wrote, "In going over this book [by Champfleury], we see easily that Daumier was indeed a man of his designs, a believer, a true republican—and we sense in the rest of his drawings the breath of a great artist who marched toward a goal but never ceased to be profoundly artistic, so that even in the absence of text or explanations his drawings remain beautiful."[29] How to bridge that gap—to be at once a "true republican" and a "profound artist"? How to shape an art in which the art itself—"sans légende, sans explication"—can carry the entire burden of communicating a social message in a manner conformable to an inherited notion of the *beau?* On the effort to enlist preexisting political and artistic categories to shape a new social vision hung the entire Neo-Impressionist project, one that linked its participants to other radical artists who shared their politics but not their means of expressing it, and to other avant-garde artists who shared many of their aesthetic concerns but found their politics repugnant. The artistic and political terrain of the period was there for all: the bridge the Neo-Impressionists sought to build over it was their own. The chapters that follow will map out the terrain, examine the plans for the bridge, observe the attempts to construct it, and suggest some of the reasons why it fell.

29. Camille Pissarro to Lucien Pissarro, February 17, 1884, in Camille Pissarro's *Correspondance,* ed. Janine Bailly-Herzberg (Paris, 1980–), I, 287.

1
A New Impressionism?

Constant revolutionizing of production, uninterrupted
disturbance of all social relations, everlasting uncertainty
and agitation, distinguish the bourgeois epoch from earlier times. All fixed, fast-frozen relationships, with their
train of venerable ideas and opinions, are swept away, all
new-formed ones become obsolete before they can ossify.
All that is solid melts into air, all that is holy is profaned,
and men at last are forced to face with sober senses the
real conditions of their lives and their relations with their
fellow men.

—Karl Marx (1848)

There rolls the deep where grew the tree.
O earth, what changes hast thou seen!
There where the long street roars hath been
The stillness of the central sea.

The hills are shadows, and they flow
From form to form, and nothing stands;
They melt like mist, the solid lands,
Like clouds they shape themselves and go.

—Alfred, Lord Tennyson (1849)

The first use of the term *Neo-Impressionism*—at least in print—
came in an essay by the critic and anarchist militant Félix Fénéon in
September, 1886. Fénéon, who was to gain renown for his fondness both for high living and for anarchist bombs, wrote in passing of the manner in which "the Neo-Impressionist method demands an exceptional delicacy of the eye." In an article in April,
1887, he referred to Georges Seurat, Paul Signac, Lucien Pissarro,
and Albert Dubois-Pillet collectively as the "young clan of Neo-
Impressionists."[1] Seurat himself favored the term *chromo-luminarist,*

---

1. Félix Fénéon, "L'Impressionnisme scientifique," in *Au-delà de l'impressionnisme,* ed.
Françoise Cachin (Paris, 1966), 80; Félix Fénéon, "L'Impressionnisme, 1887," *L'Emancipa-
tion sociale,* April 3, 1887, reprinted in *Au-delà de l'impressionnisme,* ed. Cachin, 81. See Joan
Ungersma Halperin, *Félix Fénéon: Aesthete and Anarchist in Fin-de-Siècle Paris* (New Haven,

but it won little currency. A more common term initially was *impressionnisme scientifique,* meant to distinguish the new movement from the "impressionnisme romantique" of the past.[2]

The competing terminology reflected the different conceptions of what the movement was and of how it converged with and differed from the Impressionism of a Claude Monet or a Berthe Morisot. Camille Pissarro sometimes envisaged the new art as a modification or refinement of Impressionism rather than as a totally new approach. The Impressionist emphasis on motion, on spontaneous sensation and direct observation remained a continuing strain in his work—and one that in the end led him to break from the Neos.[3]

For Signac, the breach between the old and the new was far more profound. His manifesto *D'Eugène Delacroix au néo-impressionnisme,* of 1899, asserted that the use of the term *Impressionist* by both movements was merely the recognition of a common emphasis on light and color. He added, "It is in this sense that the word *Neo-Impressionist* must be understood, because the technique these painters employ has nothing impressionist about it: where the technique of their predecessors was one of instinct and spontaneity, theirs is of reflection and permanence." The contrast between the "instinct and spontaneity" of Impressionism and the "reflection and permanence" of Neo-Impressionism ran through Signac's account. He criticized Impressionism for its lack of rigor, its ad hoc character, its aversion to theory. For Signac, Neo-Impressionism had regularized, codified, rendered precise and scientific what for the Impressionists had been mere instinct and intuition.[4]

Neo-Impressionism was born in a period in which the term *scientific* carried a rather different charge from what it does today. For one faction in French society, to be scientific meant to be modern and rational, a freethinker, a believer in the essential goodness of humanity and the possibility of a golden age on earth. For that faction's opponents, though, it meant to be godless and subver-

---

1988), 266–78. Signac in his journal reported a conversation on December 26, 1894, in which Fénéon asserted that "the anarchist *attentats* have done more for anarchist propaganda than twenty years of brochures by Reclus or Kropotkin" (John Rewald, ed., "Extraits du journal inédit de Paul Signac," *Gazette des beaux-arts,* 6th ser., XXXVI [1949], 113).

2. See Camille Pissarro to Lucien Pissarro, May 8, 1886, in Camille Pissarro's *Correspondance,* ed. Janine Bailly-Herzberg (Paris, 1980–), I, 44–45.

3. Camille Pissarro to Lucien Pissarro, September 6, 1888, in Camille Pissarro's *Correspondance,* II, 251.

4. Paul Signac, *D'Eugène Delacroix au néo-impressionnisme* (1899; Paris, 1978), 100, 102.

sive, a ruthless destroyer of French traditions of faith, order, and hierarchy. Those on the side of science believed—or hoped—that education and progress would soon destroy the age-old tyranny of superstition and folly; those on the side of faith (to its defenders there could be only one faith in France) looked toward France's casting out the unbelievers and kneeling again to church and, perhaps, king. The conflicting aspirations are on display in two fin-de-siècle novels: Emile Zola's *Vérité,* of 1901, and Jean Nesmy's *Les Egarés,* of 1906. Both tales are set in rural villages; both pit a local schoolmaster, symbol of the "new" France, against the local priest and gentry. Both portray the battle between the two in apocalyptic terms. In *Vérité,* the schoolmaster, persecuted in a case loosely modeled on the Dreyfus affair, is finally triumphant, the clerical reactionaries are routed, and the secular educational system delivers a death blow to religion and capitalism. *In Les Egarés,* the outraged villagers expel the atheistic teacher, "cowardly, insurgent, depraved, enemy of order and of discipline," and work to bring back the royalist past, the "old heroic France . . . battling for the flag, in the name of the glorious traditions of history."[5]

To call art scientific was thus not merely to offer a description but to propose a sort of minimum program. Zola's novels claimed to be scientific studies of French life; René Ghil was busy constructing a "scientific poetry," although few seem to have had a burning desire to read it. In Jacques Huret's *Enquête sur l'évolution littéraire,* a series of interviews with leading literary figures of the day, professions of the new passion for the mystical and the occult are no more frequent than emphatic assertions that science is the sole basis for society and the arts. The writer Joseph Caraguel declared, "We the artists are smitten with the modern world, infused with the scientific spirit, followers of the positivist philosophy, in direct and frequent communion with the soul of the prodigious, the incomparable century in which we live." The Neo-Realist novelist J. H. Rosny agreed that "social evolution and material progress have created other visions, have stirred new emotions in beings: the emotions of some are not the emotions of others, and in order to be able to comprehend them all, translate them all, today's writers must have an understanding . . . that is historic, industrial, congruent to the era in which we live."[6]

---

5. Henry Surchamp [Jean Nesmy], *Les Egarés: Roman* (3rd ed.; Paris, 1906), 303.

6. Jacques Huret, *Enquête sur l'évolution littéraire* (Paris, 1891), 223, 232–33. See also the interview with Octave Mirbeau, pp. 207–18.

A scientific Impressionism fit neatly enough with the dichotomy between the mystical and the modernly rational. "Science" provided an interpretive framework—or at least a means of asserting the existence of such a framework—that could smooth over contradictions and disjunctions between the streams that came together in Neo-Impressionism. For Charles Henry, for example, the "science" of psychophysics was part of a trend that would destroy naturalism and "every realist school." He remarked, "I believe on the contrary in the arrival of an art that will be very idealist, even mystical, based upon absolutely new techniques."[7] A mystical element was never entirely absent from the art of several of the Neo-Impressionists, most notably Henri Edmond Cross and Hippolyte Petitjean.

But Signac's contrast between the instinctive Impressionists and the scientific Neos proved overconfident for reasons besides the blurred demarcation of the scientific. In 1895, Maximilien Luce wrote to Cross that the new approach "does not prevent me from thinking, nor from contemplating, but there is no more instinct." Cross demurred that "in creation, next to instinct the question is, in large part, one of will, and will can support itself only on a precise foundation. This precision troubles me."[8] The frequently repeated call for *synthèse* in Neo-Impressionism evinced the determined effort to find a balance between polarities—between the real and the ideal, the fugitive and the permanent, the scientific and the instinctive.

The quest for synthesis carried individual Neo-Impressionists in dramatically different directions. In itself, that is scarcely surprising: the Neos came from a variety of backgrounds and joined the movement at different times under varying conditions. Even the generalization that they represented a second generation of Impressionists is misleading: Camille Pissarro was from the first generation, and many of the others had had no ties to Impressionism at all. Signac had painted for a time in the manner of Monet, whom he also sent dunning letters for money, and Pissarro's sons—especially Lucien, the oldest—had a solid grounding in Impressionist techniques and concepts. Of the others, Albert Dubois-Pillet had exhibited fairly traditional academic works at the Salons

7. *Ibid.*, 414. Henry added, "Therefore, yes, I believe in the future of an art that would be the opposite of any method, logical or historical, precisely because the brain, fatigued by purely rational endeavors, needs to be redeceived through states of an absolutely opposite nature" (pp. 414–15).

8. Philippe Cazeau, *Maximilien Luce* (Paris, 1982), 105.

of 1877 and 1879; Charles Angrand's early work, exhibited at Rouen in 1880, wavered between academic orthodoxy and a timid flirtation with Impressionism; Louis Hayet was a largely self-taught watercolorist in the Barbizon tradition; Luce had been trained as a commercial printmaker; and both Seurat and Cross were products of conventional academic training at the Ecole des Beaux-Arts.[9] The heterogeneity of background and interests was never wholly submerged. The Neo-Impressionist circle ranged from Pissarro, who insisted on the need to paint directly from nature, to Signac, who prided himself on doing precisely the opposite; from Luce, whose alienation from French dominant society was the product of exposure to the slaughter of the defeated Communards in 1871, to Dubois-Pillet, who had served in the army that had done the slaughtering; from the Pissarros, who were dedicated to scenes of peasant life, to Cross, who came to dismiss peasant subjects as of no intrinsic plastic interest. Luce's careful studies of working-class life in the Belgian industrial belt were painted at the same time as Théo van Rysselberghe's portraits of a languid and contented Belgian bourgeoisie. Cross was personally close to the Symbolist painters and sometimes exhibited with them; Pissarro detested them; Signac seems at times to have done both.

Age also divided the group. Camille Pissarro came to France to make his career as a painter in 1855—three years before Luce's birth, and nine years before Hayet's. In 1886, Pissarro was fifty-five years old, Dubois-Pillet was forty, Seurat twenty-seven, and Hayet only twenty-two.

Still, the group had some things in common. Their family fortunes were widely disparate, but the first wave of Neos were overwhelmingly from the lower middle class: many of their fathers were employed in crafts and trades directly threatened by France's belated industrialization. Signac's father was a saddler, Cross's a tinsmith, Angrand's a schoolmaster, Luce's a bookkeeper, van Rysselberghe's a building contractor, Hayet's the manager of a

9. Lily Bazalgette, *Albert Dubois-Pillet: Sa vie, son oeuvre, 1846–1890* (Paris, 1976), 41–48; Jean Sutter, "Albert Dubois-Pillet," in *The Neo-Impressionists,* ed. Jean Sutter, trans. Chantal Deliss (Greenwich, Conn., 1970), 94; Bogomila Welsh-Oncharov, *The Early Work of Charles Angrand and His Contact with Vincent van Gogh* (Utrecht, 1971); Jean Sutter, "Louis Hayet," in *The Neo-Impressionists,* ed. Sutter, 113; Cazeau, *Maximilien Luce,* 15–22; Jean Sutter, "Maximilien Luce," in *The Neo-Impressionists,* ed. Sutter, 153; John Russell, *Seurat* (New York, 1965), 24–30; Richard Thomson, *Seurat* (Oxford, 1985), 14–22; Isabelle Compin, *H. E. Cross* (Paris, 1964), 17–24.

painting and glazing shop, Petitjean's a barber who did odd jobs as a fiddler and a crafter of musical instruments. Some of their families enjoyed economic success and rose in the social pyramid: Cross's father moved up to manage a dye works, and Angrand's became mayor of the village of Criquetot. Others suffered financial ruin: the Hayets' shop went bankrupt in 1869. None of the group—with the possible exception of Pissarro through his in-laws—had solid ties to the new financial or industrial wealth of the country. Even Seurat's family had been farmers, though his father became a court official in what was then the independent village of La Villette. On the other hand, none were from proletarian families. Nearly all grew up in the floating, unstable social stratum of tradesmen and white-collar workers, reaching into the middle ranks of the bourgeoisie at one end and the ranks of a marginalized layer of ruined shop owners at the other.

The Neo-Impressionists shared a political orientation as well. All could be placed left of center in the politics of their era. With the possible exception of Seurat and Dubois-Pillet, for whom the evidence is suggestive but inconclusive, the Neo-Impressionists had an identification with the anarchist movement, particularly with the communist wing associated with Peter Kropotkin and, in France, Jean Grave and Elisée Reclus. Their anarchist affiliation was sufficiently well established that Luce was rounded up in the mass arrests following the assassination of President Sadi Carnot in 1894, and Camille Pissarro, who had to flee the country to avoid the same fate, had his name listed in police files.[10] Both anarchist and artistic commentaries on Neo-Impressionism took the sympathies of the Neos for granted; in 1890, an issue of *Les Hommes d'aujourd'hui* that was devoted to Luce described him matter-of-factly as "this Neo-Impressionist, this man with a deformed hat, attentively reading *La Révolte,* an anarchist journal."[11] It took twentieth-century connoisseurship and modern scholarship to efface that affiliation, treating the anarchism of the Neos as a psychological quirk or a product of genial confusion, when not omitting it altogether.[12] Only in 1960, with the pioneering work of

10. Archives Nationales, Paris, Box F7, 12506.

11. Jules Christophe, "Maximilien Luce," *Les Hommes d'aujourd'hui,* VIII (1890).

12. Scholars have developed several strategies for minimizing the Neos' political affiliations. Benedict Nicolson has stressed that "sociology" does not "help us to answer the question why, during Pissarro's period of greatest revolutionary activity, he should have lost the inspiration and vitality of his earlier years" ("The Anarchism of Camille Pissarro," *The Arts,* II [1947], 51). Nicolson looks to Freud for a possible answer. Donald Drew

Robert L. Herbert and Eugenia W. Herbert, was anarchism reinstated as an integral facet of Neo-Impressionist art and theory.[13]

The anarchism of the Neo-Impressionists was rooted in a common alienation from the dominant society and its values, though their alienation stemmed from divergent sources. Signac was comfortably well off even after the death of his father in 1880. He was repelled, however, by the academic art his conservative father favored, and he moved deliberately to the lumpen-Bohemianism of the early Chat-Noir: he wrote for its journal, helped organize its soirees, and even masqueraded as a nun at a mock funeral for Rodolphe Solis, the owner of the club.[14] For others in the Neo-Impressionist circle, alienation was more deeply rooted. The Hayets' shop went bankrupt when Louis was only five years old. The Hayets lived perpetually on the verge of starvation, surviving in 1881 and 1882 on two francs a day for the five surviving family members. (Eight of twelve children died in infancy.)[15] Hayet was repeatedly forced to interrupt his painting to work in construction or other trades to support his family; he developed an acute sense of persecution that made him a perennial outcast. If Signac's anarchism stemmed from a defiance of authority, Hayet's was of a more visceral and pragmatic sort: his major political cause was the *pain gratuit* movement that the writer Victor Barrucand launched to campaign for recognizing food as a basic right of all.[16]

Luce was from a less destitute plebeian family. He grew up in a working-class faubourg in Paris; his views were shaped by his ex-

Egbert, in *Social Radicalism and the Arts—Western Europe: A Cultural History from the French Revolution to 1968* (New York, 1970), maintains that well-known artists found it essential to preserve their art by moving toward the conception of "art for art's sake." See, for example, Egbert's discussion of the Neos, pp. 247–48.

13. An exception must be made for a handful of socialist and radical critics. Compare Nicolson's "The Anarchism of Camille Pissarro" with Millicent Rose's "Letters of Camille Pissarro," *Modern Quarterly,* n.s., III (1948), 23–54. See also Adolphe Tabarant, *Camille Pissarro* (Paris, 1924); Adolphe Tabarant, *Maximilien Luce* (Paris, 1928); and Francis Jourdain, "Paul Signac, peintre et logicien," *La Pensée,* September–October, 1955, pp. 18–23.

14. On the Chat-Noir, see Alvan Sanborn, *Paris and the Social Revolution: A Study of the Revolutionary Elements in the Various Classes of Parisian Society* (Boston, 1905), 284–86; Jerrold Seigel, *Bohemian Paris: Culture, Politics, and the Boundaries of Bourgeois Life, 1830–1930* (New York, 1986), 216–41; and Charles Rearick, *Pleasures of the Belle Epoque: Entertainment and Festivity in Turn-of-the-Century France* (New Haven, 1985). On Signac's actions, see Jean Sutter, "Paul Signac," in *The Neo-Impressionists,* ed. Sutter, 47–48.

15. Sutter, "Louis Hayet," 107.

16. The manifesto of the *pain gratuit* movement, drafted by Barrucand, appears in Sanborn's *Paris and the Social Revolution,* 329–31. On Hayet's involvement, see Sutter, "Louis Hayet," 112.

periences during the *semaine sanglante* of 1871, when the victorious Versailles troops slaughtered as many as thirty thousand Parisians after the fall of the Commune. The Commune and its martyrs continued as a theme in Luce's art through his career, and he sought to perpetuate its example of intransigent opposition to the state and social order. His father allowed him to study painting on condition that he learn a manual trade, and at fourteen he was apprenticed to a wood engraver. In the 1880s, he studied painting briefly under Carolus Duran, and his ties as an artist had been not to self-proclaimed avant-garde circles but to the anarchist and socialist political left until he came into contact with the budding Neo-Impressionist circle through Pissarro, who shared his political views.[17]

Among the older converts the Neos attracted, Dubois-Pillet departs from the "typical" profile in a number of ways. He was a career army officer from a comfortable family, a graduate in 1867 of the elite Saint-Cyr military academy, and a participant, however reluctant, in the suppression of the Commune. The French army of the late nineteenth century, however, had its own fractures and schisms, with its own patterns of alienation. This was, after all, an army under officers from a toppled Empire, who had proved much better at slaughtering French civilians than at defeating foreign enemies. Within the officer corps, secret Masonic cells provided a sort of counterleadership, providing the republican regime with information about the political affiliations of fellow officers, as a means of hobbling those hostile to the republic. French Freemasonry was an element within Georges Clemenceau's Radical party, but it was, more broadly, the refuge of those in the military with anticlerical and republican inclinations, ranging from the ruling Opportunist Republicans to the socialists.[18] Dubois-Pillet joined a Masonic cell some time in the late 1870s.

The tensions between Dubois-Pillet and the army high command in the 1880s stemmed from both his vaguely radical views—possibly including a loose sympathy for anarchism or socialism—and his efforts to make a name for himself as a nonconformist artist while still on active duty.[19] He exhibited two safely academic

17. See Cazeau, *Maximilien Luce*, 9–22. Luce's own tastes ran to Poussin, Corot, and Daumier.

18. Theodore Zeldin, *Politics and Anger* (Oxford, 1979), 323–24, 356, Vol. II of Zeldin, *France, 1848–1945*.

19. There are few specific references to Dubois-Pillet's politics. For the suggestion that he was "revolutionary" beyond aesthetic radicalism, see Jules Antoine, "Dubois-Pillet," *La*

works at the Salons of 1877 and 1879. From 1880 to 1884, though, his submissions were rejected by every Salon jury. In 1884, he turned to the new Salon des Indépendants, exhibiting *The Dead Child,* made notorious by Zola's novel *L'Oeuvre.* Dubois-Pillet became president of the Société des Artistes Indépendants in 1884 and guided the new organization until his death from smallpox, in 1890. The Société was founded at a mass rally similar to that with which Gustave Courbet had launched the Commune's Fédération des Artistes in 1871; like its Communard predecessor, the Société was open to all artists on a democratic basis, with no juries or awards. That similarity did not go unnoticed at the time—and it may well have been the impetus for two unsuccessful attempts by the army high command, in 1884 and 1887, to purge Dubois-Pillet from its ranks.[20]

The strain of attempting to conduct himself as concurrently a radical painter and a career army officer was unique to Dubois-Pillet. By contrast, Camille Pissarro's difficulties in the 1880s were all too familiar. He was the best-known and best-established of the Neo-Impressionists at the inception of their movement, but he suffered new economic difficulties in the depressed environment that followed the bankruptcy of the Union Générale bank in 1882.[21] Pissarro's long-held anarchist views led him consistently to tie the distress of artists, his own and others', to the general crisis affecting the country. In a letter to his son Lucien, Pissarro in 1886 wrote,

> From all sides—the bourgeois, professors, merchants—I hear it said that France is lost, is in a state of decadence, that Germany has won the land, that artistic France has been conquered by mathematics, that the future belongs to the mechanics, to engineers, to the *big* German and American financiers. As if we could foresee the surprises of the future! Indeed, yes, France is ill, but from what? . . . That is the question. She is ill from transformation; she can get through it, this is certain, but much depends upon the other parties of Europe, if they have also suffered from the same path: we will see new things. . . . Obviously, this cannot last.[22]

Plume, LVII (1891), 299; and the interview with the socialist *L'Egalité,* reprinted in Bazalgette's *Albert Dubois-Pillet,* 135–39.

20. Jean Sutter, "Albert Dubois-Pillet," in *The Neo-Impressionists,* ed. Sutter, 89–92.

21. See Tabarant, *Camille Pissarro,* and Ralph E. Shikes and Paula Harper, *Camille Pissarro: His Life and Work* (New York, 1980), 180–84.

22. Camille Pissarro to Lucien Pissarro, March 3, 1886, in Camille Pissarro's *Correspondance,* I, 30.

The half-fearful, half-envious references to mathematics and engineers are anything but casual. It was in this very year that Pissarro joined with the Neo-Impressionists to advance a technique that held out the promise of wedding art to mathematics and science—all in the cause of enlightenment and human emancipation. For Pissarro, in a country he saw as sick from change, from a generation of uninterrupted social and political dislocation, Neo-Impressionism obviously offered the prospect of stability, as part of a universal—or at least a pan-European—reign of social justice.

Alienation alone did not account for the decision of artists in the mid- to late 1880s to affiliate with the new Neo-Impressionist circle, for Neo-Impressionism was only one of a number of competing attempts to fuse aesthetic forms with a global political and ethical vision. Other remnants of the Impressionist milieu found harbor in the Pont Aven school, which promised integration of aesthetic and social ideals through a militantly conservative and sometimes avowedly feudal Catholicism. But Neo-Impressionism held out a manifold promise to alienated artists. It furnished them with a group identity, new comrades with whom to share concerns, and a common artistic project. It opened an avenue for marshaling their frustrations over the reigning social and economic order, through the group's developing linkages with anarchocommunism. Finally, it gave them a body of theory around which to structure their art, one that held out the promise of an integral synthesis of form and content.

The attractive power of Neo-Impressionist theory must not be underestimated. The Neos occupied a commanding position within the ranks of the Indépendants far in excess of their numbers. From the establishment of the Société des Artistes Indépendants in 1884 until 1941, the organization's official leader was a Neo-Impressionist. After Dubois-Pillet died, in 1890, he was succeeded by Signac, who was followed by Luce, from 1934 until his death. The Neos had a powerful enough presence that a satirical cartoon of the Indépendants' exhibition of 1890 in the *Courrier français* showed puzzled viewers standing in the midst of a sea of pointillist works: the legend read, "Full stops, commas, and semicolons."[23] A number of the artists in the vanguard—including Vincent van Gogh, Henry van de Velde, Louis Anquetin, and Henri Matisse—experimented briefly with the technique, though all eventually found it too constraining.

23. The cartoon is printed in *The Neo-Impressionists,* ed. Sutter, 215.

Neo-Impressionism had the ability to attract and influence artists during some two decades, though it proved unable to hold
most of them for very long. As a self-defined movement, Neo-
Impressionism long survived the death and defection of many of
its founders. By 1891, two of them, Seurat and Dubois-Pillet,
were dead, Hayet had resigned altogether, and Camille Pissarro
had moved rapidly toward severing his association. Nevertheless,
the Neos continued to grow and prosper. Cross formally joined
the group only after Seurat's death. The first Neo-Impressionist
group show came in 1892; the Neos' cooperative opened in 1893.
The theoretical attractions of the circle were clearly independent
of the participation or contribution of a single individual, even
long after Seurat's death.[24]

Still, as a movement, Neo-Impressionism was in many cases
only a way station for artists. The continuing attraction of the
circle was more than balanced in the long run by the ultimate rejection of its fundamental premises by some—the Pissarros, Petitjean, Hayet, van de Velde—and its modification from within,
for greater intelligibility or marketability. Paul Signac, in *D'Eugène Delacroix au néo-impressionnisme,* offered the great diversity of
Neo-Impressionist painting and painters as proof of the group's
breadth and depth.[25] His private journals from the same period,
however, are filled with denunciations of his colleagues for their
departures from Neo-Impressionist orthodoxy.[26]

It has been common in the twentieth century—as it was, to
be sure, in the nineteenth—to account for the schisms in Neo-
Impressionism through its encumbrance by theoretical complexity
and a rigor that is often described as rigidity.[27] Yet, from the out-

24. This is underscored by the concurrent development of Divisionism in Italy, which
grew out of the same optical theories and a comparable situation of political and social crisis
and communist anarchism. See Annie Paule Quinsac, *La Peinture divisionniste italienne: Origines et Premiers Développements, 1880–1895* (Paris, 1972), esp. 63–90, 131–55; and Annie
Paule Quinsac, "Italian Divisionism: An Overview," delivered at the symposium "Justice
in Society, Harmony in Art," Smart Gallery, University of Chicago, January 30, 1988. See
also Sandra Berresford, "Divisionism: Its Aims and Its Relationship to French Post-
Impressionist Painting," in *Post-Impressionism: Cross-Currents in European Painting* (London,
1979), 218–26. For Divisionist theory, see Gaetano Previati, *Les Principes scientifiques du
divisionnisme,* trans. V. Rossi-Sacchetti (Paris, 1910).

25. Signac, *D'Eugène Delacroix au néo-impressionnisme,* 113–14,

26. Signac attacked van Rysselberghe and Luce in his entry for March 15, 1899. See
Signac, "Extraits du journal inédit," 46.

27. See, for example, H. R. Rookmaker, *Synthetist Art Theories: Genesis and Nature of
the Ideas on Art of Gauguin and His Circle* (Amsterdam, 1959), 91.

set, it was precisely the claim of a rigorous, disciplined approach that set Neo-Impressionism apart from its predecessors and rivals and that must have played a role in attracting dissident artists. The problem seems rather that Neo-Impressionism promised something many artists came to feel it could not deliver, that its reach exceeded its grasp. The simultaneous attraction and disintegration that mark Neo-Impressionism lay in both the nature of its claims and the climate in which such claims could provide a banner for discontented artists.

"La Science délivre de toutes les incertitudes"

Signac's contrast between an instinctive, spontaneous Impressionism and a disciplined, scientific Neo-Impressionism is problematic in itself. A recent study of Neo-Impressionist theory concludes that Seurat misread and then systematically misapplied the scientific studies on which he based his approach, that Neo-Impressionism was never more than a pseudoscience posing problems for Seurat "that were beyond his capacities."[28] Much of what that criticism sees as misinterpretation can better be viewed as reappropriation, but it is evident that the "scientific" focus of Neo-Impressionism had ideological implications of a sort a modern reader might not fully anticipate. In that regard, it closely resembled the "scientific" basis Balzac and Zola claimed for their novelistic depictions of French society, or René Ghil for his poetry. The appeal to "science" cannot be dismissed as mere rhetoric. Pierre Macherey has argued in an examination of Balzac's novels that their "scientific" and ideological components amount to an interrelated core, by which Balzac sought to translate his views and studies into an art form that could capture an "essential" basis of social reality so as to transform it. Macherey writes, "The transformist novel is not a scientific novel: the myth of science gives only an image of objective reality, and thus lends a form to the writer's general project. The symmetry proposed between science and the novel is obviously false: it serves to justify, by means of whatever theory, a pre-existing anthropological project . . . ; it

---

28. Alan Lee, "Seurat and Science," *Art History,* X (1987), 203–26, esp. 203–204, 222–23. Lee charges repeatedly that Seurat's images were not "naturalistic"—a term he treats as if it were self-defining and necessarily commendatory. See the rebuttal by Dana Freeman in *Art History,* XI (1988), 150–55.

does not establish an authentically new content, but provides the means of realising an already given project—by analogy with . . . natural science." Macherey adds, "Science is not Balzac's path to new realities; rather it supplies a *style,* in the most general sense of the word. But this new instrument implies that the novel has been penetrated by a *doctrine,* an unscientific doctrine which will eventually be inverted: the process of variation is used to portray a certain conception of man."[29]

Plainly, Neo-Impressionism's attempt to enlist contemporary optical theory gave it a scientific core far more rigorous than Balzac's, yet Macherey's general argument applies with equal strength to the Neos. "Science" for the Neo-Impressionists was a necessary fiction, giving equal weight to both words. It helped provide, as Macherey asserts, both a distinctive style—a means to distinguish itself from rival movements—and a sustained programmatic basis upon which that distinctive style could be justified and explained.

The assertion that the Impressionists were spontaneous and instinctive is equally dubious. Recent studies have stressed that Monet's work—the seemingly most spontaneous of Impressionist oeuvres—was in practice anything but unplanned.[30] The claim that Impressionism was spontaneous and instinctive was clearly an ideological pronouncement, with implications not only for how Impressionists were seen to treat nature but even for how nature itself was conceived to operate.

A prevailing opinion was that by knocking down old schools of art with all their formal rules, conventions, and privileged subjects the Impressionists made it possible to experience and record nature directly, without mediation. In Zola's novel *L'Oeuvre,* the writer Sandoz (a rather transparent surrogate for Zola himself) walks through the Salon and observes that "open air" art had not only permeated the exhibition but had eroded its stale old subjects and techniques from within: abandoned were "the old academic subjects, with their dreary traditional coloring, as if the rejected doctrine had carried with it its shadowed people, . . . the cadaverous

29. Pierre Macherey, *A Theory of Literary Production,* trans. Geoffrey Wall (London, 1978), 259–60.

30. See, for example, John House, *Monet: Nature into Art* (New Haven, 1986), focusing on formal—stylistic and technical—considerations, and especially Robert L. Herbert, "Method and Meaning in Monet," *Art in America,* LXVII (1979), 98–108. The attribution of an "intuitive, spontaneous" origin to Berthe Morisot's art has also come under scrutiny in recent years. See, for example, Tamar Garb, *Women Impressionists* (New York, 1986), 15; and Kathleen Adler and Tamar Garb, *Berthe Morisot* (Ithaca, N.Y., 1987), 57–64.

nudes of mythology and Catholicism, the legends without faith, the anecdotes without life, all the Ecole bric-a-brac, employed by generations of villains or imbeciles." The sweeping-away of the old mythologies and their subjects and styles became in Zola's account a metaphor for the abolition of the institutions that generated them: "The influence was obvious even among those, young or old, who clung to the ancient recipes; the sun was dawning there, too. From afar, at every step, one could see a canvas pierce the wall itself, open a window upon the world outside." He concluded that soon even "the walls will crumble and nature will enter; for the breach was large, the assault had swept away the routine, in the joyous battle waged by temerity and by youth."[31] Across the Atlantic, another radical republican from a Latin Catholic culture independently offered the same prognosis. When José Martí, the exiled leader of Cuba's independence movement, reviewed the show of French Impressionist paintings in New York City in 1886, he saw the exhibiting painters as products of the "advanced countries, where man is free," as artists who had grown up in an "epoch without altars" and had therefore replaced an antiquated piety with a "virile and enriching love for mankind." For Martí, Impressionism was an effort not merely to identify the external effects of nature but to recapture the identity between human substance and existence and that of the universe as a whole. "The dust of the earth, the bones of men, and the light of the stars," he stressed, "are all made from the same substance." Without seeking to do anything more than "paint as the sun does," the Impressionists had achieved paintings transcendent in both form and purpose.[32]

Léon Bazalgette wrote in a similar vein about Monet's studies of Rouen Cathedral. He held that Monet had opened himself to nature, discarding dogmas and preconceived notions in order to experience nature directly: "Entirely free from remembrances, from any cult or religious tradition, the painter considered the edifice only as a fragment of nature, following reality rather than dogma." He went on, "For him it was not a matter of liturgy nor of symbolism: no mystery of deciphering, no doubt of interpre-

31. Emile Zola, *L'Oeuvre* (Paris, 1886), 399.

32. José Martí, "Nueva exhibición de los pintores impresionistas," *La Nación* (Buenos Aires), August 17, 1886, translated as "A New Exhibition of Impressionist Painters," in *On Art and Literature by José Martí: Critical Writings,* trans. Elinor Randall, ed. Philip S. Foner (New York, 1982), 118–24, quoted from pp. 120–21.

tation, no theological debate could reach him. *Reality was there in front of him, without any uncertainty: he saw and interpreted it.*"[33]

French republicanism had traditionally valued antique forms; the heritage of Jacques Louis David and eighteenth-century rationalism made Periclean Greece and republican Rome natural sources of imagery. In the 1870s, however, the republican drive for power sometimes supplemented its leanings toward classicism by a contrasting valorization of spontaneity, of unplanned, popular acts that demonstrated the living, modern nature of republican beliefs and practice. To celebrate old battles was essential, but it held the danger of binding republicanism to the past; a living movement, it was argued, should celebrate its victories in new ways, as proof of its continuing vitality. Léon Gambetta's *La République française* declared in 1872 that "a free nation needs national celebrations. But in order that these celebrations have a morality and meaning, that they be worthy of liberty, they must be spontaneous. It is not fitting that a respectable people adopt prescribed solemnities."[34]

The decade of the seventies was also marked by an asserted—and in part real—mood of enthusiasm and optimism at the top, an expression of the republican victories of 1876 and 1878 and the heady confidence of a young and aggressive echelon of bankers and industrialists who were consolidating their fortunes and power. Impressionism had congruences and affinities with that class, in both its avoidance of old subject matters (and historic subjects) and its celebration of change, modernization, and flux.[35] Some republicans continued to defend the Neo-Classicism of David,

33. Léon Bazalgette, *L'Esprit nouveau* (Paris, 1898), 376. My emphasis. My discussion of both Bazalgette's and Clemenceau's writings is indebted to Robert L. Herbert in "The Decorative and the Natural in Monet's Cathedrals," in *Aspects of Monet: A Symposium on the Artist's Life and Times,* ed. John Rewald and Frances Weitzenhoffer (New York, 1984), 162–79.

34. "Paris, 14 juillet," *La République française,* July 15, 1872, p. 1. On spontaneity in republican fetes and republican thought under the Third Republic, see Charles Rearick, "Festivals in Modern France: The Experience of the Third Republic," *Journal of Contemporary History,* XII (1977), 435–60.

35. See Richard Brettell, "The Impressionist Landscape and the Image of France," in *A Day in the Country: Impressionism and the French Landscape,* ed. Andrea P. Bellioli (Los Angeles, 1984), 27–49; Paul Tucker, "The First Impressionist Exhibition and Monet's *Impression, Sunrise:* A Tale of Timing, Commerce, and Patriotism," *Art History,* VII (1984), 465–76; Paul Tucker, *Monet at Argenteuil* (New Haven, 1982), esp. 57–87; and T. J. Clark, *The Painting of Modern Life: Paris in the Art of Manet and His Followers* (New York, 1984), 147–204.

with its attendant cult of the antique, as the only properly "republican art," but others praised the work of Monet and Pissarro for the combination of spontaneity and enthusiasm they saw mirroring their own hopes and confirming their successes.[36] A reviewer in the republican journal *Le Rappel* praised Impressionism as an art that could render an "intense, emotional impression, like Delacroix' *Session of 2 Prairial* (*Boissy d' Anglas at the Convention*), in which the tumult of a surge of humanity is rendered by means of an extraordinary simplicity." The reviewer singled out two paintings by Monet of the republican *fête nationale* of June 30, 1878, as works "of truth, of force, of an absolutely remarkable reality."[37]

The equation of spontaneity with truth runs particularly strong in the radical republican approval of Impressionism. There is a celebration of the movement's destruction of the traditional, academic ideal of a static, serene world of perfect tranquillity. Rather, Impressionism is taken to show the world as changing and dynamic; by an adroit sleight of hand, that depiction of the world in turn becomes a trope for education and social enlightenment. Truth is contrasted against old dogmas and superstitions; to embrace the flux of nature is to discard all the old beliefs and institutions which had been obscuring that truth.

The Radical leader Clemenceau devoted almost the entire front page of his daily, *La Justice,* to a treatment of Monet's paintings of Rouen Cathedral. Clemenceau wrote, "The wonder of Monet's way of sensing things is to see the stone vibrate and to have it given to us vibrating, bathed in luminous waves that collide and break into twinkling sparks. *It is the end of the immutable canvas of death.*"[38] Like Bazalgette and other republican defenders of Impressionism, Clemenceau saw the movement as presenting not a fictive construct, or a way of depicting the world, but reality itself: what it portrayed was "life itself, just as the sensation of it can be given to us, in its most living reality." He concluded, "Thus art,

---

36. Among defenders of David, see, for example, Henry Havard, "L'Exposition des artistes indépendants," *Le Siècle,* April 27, 1879, p. 3. Havard expresses his fierce detestation of Impressionism; he defends his preferences in starkly political terms: "A republican, I love antiquity for its philosophy, for its literature, and for its arts. I love it because of its simplicity, its purity, its logic, which are precisely the objective to which the contemporary spirit is developing."

37. Ernest d'Hervilly, "Exposition des impressionnistes," *Le Rappel,* April 1, 1879, p. 2.

38. Georges Clemenceau, "Révolution des cathédrales," *La Justice,* May 20, 1895, p. 1.

in trying to express nature with an ever more perfect precision, teaches us to regard, to perceive, to feel." Like Martí, Clemenceau maintained above all that Monet revealed a world pulsing with both life and light, evolving in a manner that defies any lasting attempt at stability, in favor of continuous motion: "It is the unstable vibration of life that animates the sky and the earth and the sea, and all of nature, whether swarming with life or 'inert.' . . . This moving wonder of each hour, which leaps to our eyes, and all the spectacles of the luminous planet, this ever-changing miracle, which never ceases except to give birth to still more miracles, this intensity of life which emanates from man or beast but which comes as well from herbs, from trees, and from stones—the earth lavishes upon us this feast without end."[39]

Bazalgette too had believed that Monet's work was proof that an enlightened humanity could fuse with nature: "The individual, whom Christian dogma has isolated from nature, sensed increasingly that between her and himself there existed an indestructible and most profound of bonds." Monet grasped that the individual and the world were "eternally united, consubstantial, and interdependent." The ability to discard all ossified belief and face nature directly meant for Monet the ability to conquer every secret of nature: "He faced reality, that of yesterday, today, and always: and it is with the vision of modern man that he compelled it to reveal its secrets—life robbed of its screens, stripped of every symbol, every artifice, every lie."[40]

On that interpretation, the Impressionist celebration of light became an analogue to the process of enlightenment and education. Clemenceau wrote, "With the Impressionist school, the sovereignty of light is affirmed. It explodes, invades the being, imposes itself in conquering, dominates the world, supported by its glory, instrument of its triumph."[41] In such accounts, light is never a neutral force. As in Zola's *L'Oeuvre,* it serves as a symbol for the dispelling of darkness and ignorance. In Zola's *Travail* and *Vérité,* sunlight in particular is a dominant motif in the later chapters, as science and reason triumph over ignorance and stupidity.[42]

39. *Ibid.*
40. Bazalgette, *L'Esprit nouveau,* 384–90.
41. Clemenceau, "Révolution des cathédrales," 1.
42. "Men might well continue stupidly to devour one another in their blind struggle, religions might continue to pile error upon error to defend their domination, but every day invincible science advanced yet another step, creating more light, more fraternity, more happiness. And by the irresistible force of truth, it will finally sweep away the darkness and

In such attributions of Impressionist spontaneity, ideology poses as its own absence, and social and political theory masks itself as the negation of theory. The world is viewed as comprehensible by any individual who discards old routines and binding beliefs. The world becomes self-evident, change self-justifying, truth a matter of opening oneself to the flux—the festival, as Clemenceau said, without end.

Neo-Impressionism retained only two central traits of Impressionism: its worship of light and its conceit that it captured and represented reality. It reversed the means by which the representation of reality was to be attained, however, and drastically altered the entire conceptual framework of representation. In place of *change* and *flux,* the new catchwords were *permanence, harmony, synthesis.* In place of spontaneity, the emphasis was on science and rigor. Where Impressionism—or its defenders—could envision the achievement of comprehension once an individual had discarded dogma and embraced nature itself, Neo-Impressionism interposed a complex set of operations to analyze and re-create the entire process by which the individual sees and comprehends.

What matters most is not whether either avowed approach corresponded to the actual practice of the movement associated with it. Rather, it is that in Neo-Impressionism the whole conceptual framework of Impressionism was turned on its head and a radically different paradigm was proposed.

Thomas Kuhn's *Structure of Scientific Revolutions* rebutted the notion that scientific theory develops as a simple accretionary process, in step with the testing and falsification of hypotheses. He argued that scientific paradigms instead tend to withstand even what might seem like damning refutations, either by casting doubt upon the new data or by undergoing just enough adjustment to encompass the new information. Eventually, however, there comes a point when the complications needed to span the accumulating lacunae and to account for the contradictory data become excessive and a new general theory is advanced.[43]

Aesthetic theories are not falsifiable even in the limited manner of those in the physical sciences; in the modern world, there are apt concurrently to be competing ways in which artists look at and

---

the hatred, liberate minds so as to bring hearts together under the great and beneficent sun, the father of us all" (Emile Zola, *Travail* [Paris, 1927–29], 574–75).

43. Thomas Kuhn, *The Structure of Scientific Revolutions* (Chicago, 1962).

interpret the world.[44] But there are definable moments in the history of artistic production when the previous ways of conceiving and depicting the world no longer serve, when the gap between what viewers experience in their own lives and what is presented becomes so great that it can no longer be bridged. The Impressionist movement arose on one such occasion, as a break with academic norms and their underlying conceptualization of a tranquil, unchangeable world solidly, and necessarily, anchored to traditional institutions and historical faith.[45] To an art that privileged pastoral myths, hierarchy, tradition, and stability, Impressionist artists counterposed one that celebrated change, thc new, the modern, and the urban.

Superseding paradigms inevitably begin by employing the vocabulary and conceptual apparatus of those they supplant, which they sharply redefine, however. The socialist leader Rosa Luxemburg pointed out in an essay in 1898 that every new movement "begins by finding support within the preceding movement, though it may be in direct contradiction with the latter." She enlarged, "It begins by suiting itself to the forms found at hand and by speaking the language spoken hitherto. In time, the new grain breaks through the old husk. The new movement finds its own forms and its own language."[46] That pattern largely prevailed in the break from Impressionism to Neo-Impressionism. Clemenceau quoted Monet in a typical avowal of an intuitive praxis: "While you examine the world itself philosophically, I simply exert myself toward a maximum of appearances, in direct correlation with unknown realities. When we are on the plain of concordant

44. This period also saw the rise of theories denying that art's office was to interpret the external world at all. See, for example, Oscar Wilde, "The Decay of Lying," in *Complete Works* (London, 1930), 970–92, esp. 978, 987. The impact of this essay on French Symbolism is discussed by Jean Pierrot in *The Decadent Imagination, 1880–1900,* trans. Derek Coltman (Chicago, 1981), 19–24.

45. It was not, of course, the first attempt to undermine that official view. Daumier and Courbet had made a frontal assault, while the Barbizon school had subverted many of its assumptions. Within the Salon, by the mid–nineteenth century the prestige conferred on history painting was undercut by the overwhelming preference of the marketplace for landscape and genre scenes. See Cynthia White and Harrison White, *Canvases and Careers* (New York, 1965), 90–93. See also Patricia Mainardi, *Art and Politics of the Second Empire* (New Haven, 1987), 154–93.

46. Rosa Luxemburg, "Reform or Revolution," in *Rosa Luxemburg Speaks,* ed. Mary-Alice Waters (New York, 1970), 37. See also Kuhn, *The Structure of Scientific Revolutions,* 148.

appearances, we cannot be far from reality, or at least what we can know of it. I have done nothing but observe what the universe has shown me, and then testified to that with my brush."[47] For Signac, Monet's distinction between ways of knowing the world demonstrated the superiority in practice of Neo-Impressionism over its predecessor. He contended that "the Impressionists are the definitive masters whose glorious task has now been completed; the Neo-Impressionists are still in the period of research, and they understand just how much is left for them to do." The difference between the two movements, he decided, lay not in talent but in technique, and only Neo-Impressionism could truly guarantee the "integrity of luminosity, of coloration, and of harmony." As the logical successor to Impressionism, Neo-Impressionism was, he concluded, above all guided by the search for "integral purity and complete harmony."[48]

Little remained there of the idea of a spontaneous comprehension of a changing world. In Signac's account, external reality must be researched, studied, and very deliberately and methodically translated into pictorial terms capable of ensuring the integrity and harmony of the canvas as a whole. Indeed, any attempt to compose an image by this procedure will be removed from a spontaneous response by not one but two separate mediating frameworks: "Guided by *tradition* and by *science*," Signac wrote, the Neo-Impressionist "will harmonize the composition with his conception." Both tradition and science are essential for producing art of a "unified and moral harmony" and a precision beyond the Impressionists' resources.[49]

"Harmony" in Neo-Impressionism

The word *harmony* bears two distinguishable, if often overlapping, references in Neo-Impressionist writings—the first more or less close to purely aesthetic, the second social.

Seurat clearly mapped the first reference in a statement he made on August 28, 1890. He wrote, "Art is harmony. Harmony is the analogy of contraries, the analogy of similarities, of *tone*, of *tint*, of *line*, examined in terms of a dominant and under the influence

47. Georges Clemenceau, *Claude Monet: Cinquante ans d'amitié* (Paris, 1965), 145–46.
48. Signac, *D'Eugène Delacroix au néo-impressionnisme*, 105.
49. *Ibid.*, 104.

of a system of illumination in gay, calm, or sad combinations."[50] Seurat drew upon two categories of scientific (or "scientific") studies of the arts. The first involved optics, primarily as explained in the writings of Ogden Rood and Ernest Chevreul and particularly as summarized in the writings of Charles Blanc. The second, a "science of forms," included attempts to identify inherent meanings in combinations of lines and shapes, consonant with the theories of Humbert de Superville and especially Charles Henry.[51] Seurat combined the two kinds of "science" to come up with specific combinations intended to engender a consistent dominant mood. For gaiety, the combination included luminous colors, warm tints, and upward-directed lines; for sadness or melancholy, somber tones, cold tints, and downward-directed lines. A dominant mood of calmness required the "equality of light and dark," an equal mix of warm and cold tints, and a predominance of horizontal lines.[52]

Aesthetic harmony also presupposed the detailed study of color itself. Only pure colors were to be used; like the Impressionists, the Neos banned black, which does not occur in nature. To heighten luminosity, they *divided* the colors. That did not signify breaking green down into yellow and blue and expecting the eye to mix them. But small strokes or dots of yellow and blue, carefully introduced, could heighten a green and make it seem brighter. Moreover, the dominant colors in one section of a painting could be played off their complements: red against green, orange against blue, yellow against violet. In Seurat's *Grande Jatte,* the brilliant green of the lawn contains flecks of red throughout; in the painted border surrounding the canvas, the color mix is always the reverse of that in the adjoining strip of the painting.

The Neos' division of color immediately earned them the name of pointillists. None were ever fond of the appellation or employed it themselves: Luce complained to Cross that even the most intel-

---

50. Henri Dorra and John Rewald, *Seurat* (Paris, 1959), lxxii.

51. Among the most important works here: Charles Blanc, *Grammaire des arts du dessin* (Paris, 1867); Ogden Rood, *Théorie scientifique des couleurs et leurs applications à l'art et à l'industrie* (Paris, 1881); Charles Henry, *Introduction à une esthétique scientifique* (Paris, 1885); Michel Eugène Chevreul, *Des couleurs et de leurs applications aux arts industriels, à l'aide des cercles chromatiques* (Paris, 1864); David Sutter, *Les Phénomènes de la vision* (Paris, 1880); and Charles Henry, "L'Esthétique des formes," serialized in *Revue blanche* from August, 1894, to February, 1895.

52. Dorra and Rewald, *Seurat,* lxxii. See also Charles Henry, "Harmonie des couleurs," *Revue indépendante,* 3rd ser., VII (1888), 458–78.

ligent critics, though, persisted in using it. "They talk to you about pointillism," he wrote. "Nothing exasperates me more than that word."[53] Signac emphasized that Neo-Impressionism had never insisted on the use of the point: "*Division* is a complex system of harmony, an aesthetic more than a technique. The *point* is but a means." Division, he admonished, entailed "searching for the power and harmony of color by representing the light colored by its pure elements and by employing the optical mix of these pure elements, separating and measuring them according to essential laws of contrast and of degradation." Pointillage was useful only to a modest degree and in its appropriate role: "It merely makes the surface of the canvas more vibrant, but it does not assure either luminosity nor the intensity of color, nor of harmony." The *touche divisée* was essential: "Changing, living, 'light'—that is not the *point,* which is uniform, dead, material."[54]

Why, then, did critics go on characterizing the new movement as pointillism? Signac's objections provide a strong clue. The *touche divisée* was in fact rendered on most Neo-Impressionist canvases by something resembling points, by small "dots" of divided color that yielded a particulate surface utterly unlike that of the Impressionists. Although the Italian Divisionists sometimes resorted to a combination of small strokes and thin lines, giving their canvases a stippled effect, the early Neo canvases were striking to the first viewers—as they are today—for the absence alike of the academic "licked surface" and the loose, overlapping brushstrokes of Monet or Morisot.

The particulate surface was not accidental. It is notable that the one occasion in Signac's account when he departed from a vocabulary of harmony, permanence, method, and reflection was in speaking of divided color, for which he made a sudden, if unextended, return to the vocabulary of Impressionism: "changeante, vivante, 'lumière.'" There, constrained by the carefully regulated parameters of the overall canvas, the tiny, individual dots of color play the role assigned to the entire canvas in Clemenceau and Bazalgette's critiques of Monet's paintings. Clemenceau spoke of "this furor of living atoms" in Monet's cathedral paintings, finding there the basis for his own appropriation of Impressionism into a republican cosmogony.[55] Henry wrote of both atoms and

53. Cazeau, *Maximilien Luce,* 57.

54. Signac, *D'Eugène Delacroix au néo-impressionnisme,* 116–22.

55. Clemenceau, "Révolution des cathédrales," 1.

organic molecules in a similar vein, to the extent that one of his followers developed the notion of the *atôme de vie* or *atôme biologique* as an analogue to the atoms of chemistry. Like Clemenceau's "living atoms," they were the essential particles of life and motion, changing constantly but in accordance with physical laws that could track and analyze them in order to delineate how color, form, and motion could affect the psyche of the individual. In the words of the writer, "It is possible to say, therefore, that the atom of life is at the same time the atom of sensibility and the psychic atom."[56] Through the particles of divided color—acting and interacting, heightening one another as they worked on the mind and eye of the viewer, never quite fused but always in fusion—Neo-Impressionism sought to reclaim the life and motion that it otherwise constrained through deliberation and rigor.

For Signac, the harmony attained by the *touche divisée* was not simply aesthetic—but was ethical as well. With the exception of Seurat, the Neos pursued "harmony" in its complete dual reference. When, in a journal entry, Signac denounced Petitjean for disharmonious colors, the criticism was purely aesthetic.[57] More often, though, harmony had manifest social connotations. Cross wrote in a letter to Signac, "Art seems to me to be simply an intellectual vision of harmony, a vision composed of characteristic elements, through which reality is strewn." Pissarro deprecated Gauguin's work for being out of harmony with the march of humanity, and Signac summarized the social implications of art in a terse equation: "Justice in sociology, harmony in art: the same thing."[58]

There is, to be sure, a rather considerable conceptual leap from the first reference of *harmony* to the second. It is one thing to describe a harmonious relationship within the confines of a canvas, and quite another to bind an approach in painting to an external, social harmony—whether one discoverable in society or nature or

---

56. Robert Mirabaud, *Charles Henry et l'Idéalisme scientifique* (Paris, 1926). On the significance of atomic theory and the particulate surface to Neo-Impressionist theory, see Robyn S. Roslak, "The Politics of Aesthetic Harmony: Neo-Impressionism, Science, and Anarchism," *Art Bulletin*, LXXIII (1991), 381–90.

57. "The pictures are absolutely inharmonious. . . . His drawing is precise but banal" (Rewald, ed., "Extraits du journal inédit de Paul Signac," 111; the entry is for December 14, 1894).

58. Cazeau, *Maximilien Luce*, 4–5; Camille Pissarro to Lucien Pissarro, April 20, 1891, in Camille Pissarro's *Correspondance*, III, 65–66; Robert L. Herbert, "Les Artistes et l'Anarchisme," *Le Mouvement social*, XXXVI (July–September, 1961), 9.

one that can be brought to exist only by contrivance. There is little in Neo-Impressionism's technique by itself that would impel the leap to a concern for social harmony. Signac's casual phrase about the modern artist's being "guided by tradition and by science," however, allows some insight into Neo-Impressionism's transition to social preoccupations. His own *D'Eugène Delacroix au néo-impressionnisme* sets out one possibility, presenting the Neos as heirs to a progressive tradition in French art beginning with Delacroix. The scientific sources cited by Signac, however—from Blanc to Henry to David Sutter—show another, even stronger sort of tradition that shaped the sort of "science" Neo-Impressionism was to be.

French republicanism was filled with references to unity and harmony as the goal of the arts. Republican theorists viewed their concepts of harmony as gaining a foothold in art in direct consequence of the harmonious *social* order they claimed to have founded.[59] The theorists appropriated by Seurat and the other Neo-Impressionists were themselves part of that republican tradition. Blanc borrowed at will from the quasi-socialist utopian writings of his brother Louis, yet Charles Blanc was also a full professor at the Collège des Arts and director of the arts under the conservative regime of Adolphe Thiers in the early 1870s. Henry, a professor at the Sorbonne, was less directly involved in the institutional art hierarchies of republican France, but his definitive *L'Education du sens des formes,* with illustrations by Signac, was published in 1891 by the Ministry of Commerce, Industry, and the Colonies as a training aid for technical schools.[60]

The writings of Sutter exemplify the rationalist theme of moral uplift evident in these scientific writings. In an essay from 1880 circulated by Seurat to his friends, Sutter proclaimed, "Science delivers us from incertitudes and permits us to move in total freedom, in a well-understood circle; therefore it is a double injury to art as well as to science to believe that the one necessarily excludes the other. As all the rules follow the same laws of nature, nothing

59. Miriam R. Levin considers the writings of Victor Hugo, Antonin Proust, Edouard Lockroy, and Jules Ferry in *Republican Art and Ideology in Late Nineteenth-Century France* (Ann Arbor, Mich., 1986). See especially pp. 77–113, 210–22.

60. Levin, *Republican Art and Ideology,* 149; José A. Argüelles, *Charles Henry and the Formation of a Psychophysical Aesthetic* (Chicago, 1972), 120. On the French state's use of the theories of Sutter and Henry, see Albert Boime, "The Teaching of the Fine Arts and the Avant-Garde in France During the Second Half of the Nineteenth Century," *Arts Magazine,* LX (1985).

is easier than to recognize by principle, nor more indispensable. In art, all must be willed." Sutter commended the reciprocal relationship between art and science as a guarantor of individual freedom within a scientifically determined matrix. The laws and rules he described bound and limit art, he argued, just as science defines the working boundaries of nature; the laws and rules are objective and fixed. Within them, though, the individual imposes a specific message in virtue precisely of having a thorough knowledge of how sight and interpretation operate. Sutter was not claiming a scientific art only on the grounds of its technique but wished to use science to make art serve humanity. In his words, "Painting must concur with the fine arts in the moral perfection of society."[61]

Henry similarly conceived the science of forms as issuing in a program of enlightenment and emancipation. Control of forms to yield the right message was both necessary and sufficient for encouraging social harmony: "What science can and must do is expand the agreeable within and outside us, and from that point of view its social function is immense in this time of oppression and blind conflicts. Science must spare the artist hesitations and useless attempts by assigning the path along which he can locate ever richer aesthetic elements."[62]

Henry, far more than Sutter, placed the collaborative emancipatory mission of science and art in the unrolling of a social evolution: great art historically, he wrote, had been produced by "brilliant social states" such as those of classical Greece or the Italian Renaissance; art also played a role in aiding evolution, in assisting humanity toward a distant goal of universal harmony.[63]

Far from valorizing spontaneity and individual union with nature, these writings returned to an earlier tradition of evaluating existing society and its output against a glorified past: tradition was seen as the bedrock that liberty and knowledge require. This

61. Dorra and Rewald, *Seurat,* xxxvi.

62. Charles Henry, *Le Cercle chromatique* (Paris, 1888), 442.

63. Charles Henry, "Rapporteur esthétique et Sensation de forme," *Revue indépendante,* 3rd ser., VII (1888), 16. See also Levin, *Republican Art and Ideology,* 204–205. The poet Paul Valéry argued that Henry's unified systems of human actions and sensibilities had a special application to and a special appeal for young artists. See Françoise Cachin, *Paul Signac,* trans. Michael Bullock (Greenwich, Conn., 1971), 31. An analogous utopian strand exists in the writings of Henry's predecessor Humbert de Superville. See Barbara Maria Stafford, "'Les Deux Edifices'—The New Areopagus and a Spiritual Trophy: Humbert de Superville's Vision of Utopia," *Art Quarterly,* XXXV (1972), 50–73.

appeared particularly acultely in the writings of Blanc, for whom art had an essentially transformative mission. It could accomplish what official education and even morality could not: "Since painting is not burdened with the task of official education, it slowly reforms and improves us. The law would be less obeyed because it orders; morality would be less heeded because it obligates; art knows how to persuade us because it pleases us."[64]

For Blanc art had the goal of restoring the universal harmony that had existed in Eden before humanity corrupted it and was expelled. In a modern and enlightened world, humanity was marching to reclaim its lost golden age and art had a central role in the recuperation of the earlier paradisiacal state:

"Humanity, guided by a star that is the memory of a former grandeur, will march to the conquest of paradise lost—the conquest of truth, of good, and of beauty—and humanity must recover these three forms of happiness by means of science, industry, and art. Science will dissolve the errors; industry will vanquish the world of matter; art will discover beauty." Aesthetics was to have an important part in the march. From being the lowest of philosophies, the study of beauty would "regain its natural place: first. Once located in the glimmers of sentiment and spirit, across the shadows which envelop it, the synthesis will finally flame in its turn."[65]

It was that sociopolitical aesthetics, the grafting of republican notions of moral uplift upon the period's studies of optics and Henry's "psychophysics," that Signac invoked as the central essence of Neo-Impressionism: science and tradition yoked to produce an integral art. Old tradition and new science were melded to form a strong matrix within which the artist could regain what the theoreticians of Impressionism had thought could be simply observed and spontaneously recorded.

64. Blanc, *Grammaire,* 515.

65. *Ibid.,* 6–7, 712. See also Charles Blanc, *Les Beaux-Arts à l'Exposition universelle de 1878* (Paris, 1878), 40. Albert Boime asserts, "For Blanc . . . modern science promised on the one hand to liberate the working classes from the yoke of animal labor and on the other to cultivate in the emancipated proletariat a taste for the industrial and fine arts" ("Seurat and Piero della Francesca," *Art Bulletin,* XLVII [1965], 268). See also Misook Song, *Art Theories of Charles Blanc, 1813–1882* (Ann Arbor, Mich., 1984). Song views the sociopolitical aspects of Blanc's writings as inimical to his aesthetic concerns (p. 12); she also contends that the "totalitarian" aspects of Blanc's attempt to unite form and signification "seem to have demeaned the intrinsic value and independent growth of individual art," preventing him from an "objective evaluation of painting [*sic*]" (p. 49). If Boime seems to conflate Blanc with Jean Jaurès, Song would have preferred him to be Clive Bell.

Commentators have remarked that the scientific progenitors of Neo-Impressionism—apart from Henry—lent themselves to a thoroughly traditional art practice.[66] That would scarcely have been news to Seurat, a former student at the Ecole des Beaux-Arts. Plainly, Seurat sought to reappropriate those scientific writers—to draw on them to legitimate and win a place for his own artistic theories. For the anarchist militants among the Neo-Impressionists, it was natural to add a second layer to this, to appropriate not only traditional techniques but also the vestigial utopian elements of the writers' thinking, as part of a strategy of asserting Neo-Impressionism as a totalizing theory.

Seurat's personal ties to anarchism remain murky. Félix Fénéon asserted that Seurat shared the anarchist views of his colleagues. He was certainly aware of anarchist ideas and availed himself of a wide variety of sources for his theories and imagery, many of which had special resonance for the anarchist movement.[67] But there is no evidence of the kind of organizational affiliation Luce, the Pissarros, and Signac had with anarchism. Seurat's attitude seems to have been predominantly aloof and skeptical; that attitude can certainly be fitted with late-nineteenth-century French anarchism but not with the much more specific anarchocommunism with which the Pissarros, Signac, Luce, and even Angrand and van Rysselberghe were affiliated.

There is a paradox in anarchist artists dwelling on the importance of tradition and discipline. It is to be expected that the Pont Aven painters—especially Maurice Denis and Paul Sérusier—would trace the development of the arts through ancient Egypt, the Babylonians and Chaldeans, or Hindu India. Denis' Neo-Traditionism demanded the weight of centuries to validate its claims in behalf of a transcendent, spiritual art. Even Seurat's rigorous Ecole training can account for his fascination with classical forms. But why did anarchist artists—who might readily

66. See Lee, "Seurat and Science," 204, 206. The implication is that Seurat would have been startled to learn this.

67. Félix Fénéon to John Rewald, in Rewald's *Seurat* (New York, 1943), 47. The most detailed and ambitious attempt to examine Seurat's work in light of anarchist theory and in connection with the anarchist milieu remains Sally Medlyn's "The Development of Georges Seurat's Art with Special Reference to the Influence of Contemporary Anarchist Philosophy" (M.A. thesis, University of Manchester, 1976); a more cautious appraisal, which nonetheless recognizes the issues raised by Medlyn, is Thomson's *Seurat,* esp. 94–95. A contrary assessment of Seurat's views and approach can be found in John House's "Meaning in Seurat's Figure Paintings," *Art History,* III (1980), 345–55.

have identified with the asserted spontaneity and individuality of Impressionism—find themselves comfortable with a corpus of art theory grounded in a parallel tour of Periclean Athens, republican Rome, and Renaissance Florence? (Both tours made stops at the Middle Ages, though the rival movements appear to have stopped at different inns.) How can the anarchists' traditionalism be squared with their equal insistence on the scientific basis of Neo-Impressionist art?

In part, the answer lies in the gradual acceptance by anarchist leaders—most notably Peter Kropotkin and Jean Grave—that anarchist theory should base itself on the physical, not the social, sciences; social evolution became equated with the evolution of species, and an anarchist victory was deemed guaranteed by the very nature of human existence. Historical periods of artistic and cultural innovation were judged times of maximum individual freedom and a pantheon of the past's thinkers and rebels was assembled to provide anarchism with a powerful heritage.[68]

By the 1880s, the underlying optimism that had fed the Impressionist world view was breaking down. It had never really had relevance for Degas' work, in any case; by mid-decade, Renoir had retreated into a make-believe world where industry was absent, faith and order reigned, and women were without exception happy and ignorant.[69] Mary Cassatt's art—and to a lesser extent that of Morisot—came not so much to celebrate the new life of the bourgeoisie as to seek a way to assert the contribution and the potential of middle-class women within the modern world and to map out the space within which they lived and worked.[70]

Seurat's own work is a product of the collapse of the Impressionist celebration of bourgeois life. He toured where the Impressionists had declined to go, through the new industrial suburbs; he turned a jaundiced eye on new forms of mass recreation and on the leisure activity of the middle class. His detached irony and

68. Concerning an anarchist art "tradition" based on the theory of intellectual resistance to tyranny, see Charles Malato, *Philosophie de l'anarchie, 1888–1897* (3rd ed.; Paris, 1897), 138–56.

69. This is explored by John House in "Renoir's Worlds," in the Arts Council of Great Britain's *Renoir* (London, 1985), 11–18; and by Tamar Garb in "Renoir and the Natural Woman," *Oxford Art Journal,* VIII (1985), 3–15.

70. See Susan Fillin Yeh, "Mary Cassatt's Images of Women," *Art Journal,* XXXV (1976), 359–63; Sally Webster, "Mary Cassatt's Allegory of Modern Women," *Helicon 9,* I (1979), 39–47; Griselda Pollock, *Mary Cassatt* (London, 1980); and Griselda Pollock, *Vision and Difference: Femininity, Feminism, and the Histories of Art* (London, 1988), 50–90, 208n43. On Morisot, see Adler and Garb, *Berthe Morisot,* esp. 80–102.

skepticism are in some respects reminiscent of Edouard Manet's, as though the intervening generation of Impressionists had never existed—but with the crucial difference that Manet looked askance at the beginnings of a process of social change whereas Seurat lived and painted in the midst of it. Seurat's skepticism was born from experience, and his art constantly poses questions—about societal norms, about artistic conventions of all types. His art probes and unsettles.

The self-assigned task of most of his followers, I will argue, was altogether different. It is not that they "misunderstood" Seurat; they had far more opportunity to explore his views than do contemporary scholars. Nor is the question whether they lived up to a challenge Seurat set for them; the point is that they had, by and large, something else to say and that the different messages inevitably shaped, and changed, the form of the delivery. The Neos' art sought to sew up the seams Seurat had ruptured, to reassure where he questioned and undermined. Their art attempted to reestablish some of the confidence of the Impressionist era, but by different methods, as a result of deliberation and artifice rather than a supposed spontaneity and lack of a priori theories.

Peter Bürger takes stock of the shift in this period from what he terms courtly art—which was based on forms that originated for an aristocratic audience—to bourgeois art, and he examines the transition as part of a process of privatization of purpose, production, and reception. The effect was an atomization of something that had been seen as a stable and unified system, leading to a disjunction between art and social life as a whole. Each artist was forced to deal—alone—with dealers and negotiate with the various bodies organizing exhibitions. The modern avant-garde was intended, he concludes, to reintegrate the arts, and the artist, into the totality of social existence, to reinvest art with purpose and function.[71] Neo-Impressionism sought precisely that. The task in the following chapters will be to understand the nature of the crisis, as perceived by the artists of the time, and the nature and purpose of the proposed solution.

71. Peter Bürger, *Theory of the Avant-Garde,* trans. Michael Shaw (Minneapolis, 1984), 47–50.

2

Anarchism and the Search for Solid Ground

> All are awaiting the birth of a new order of things; all ask them-
> selves, some with misgiving, others with hope, what the morrow
> will bring forth. It will not come with empty hands. . . . Industrial
> appliances, that by a single electric impulse make the same thought
> vibrate through five continents, have distanced by far our social
> morals, which are yet in many regards the outcome of reciprocally
> hostile interests. The axis is displaced; the world must crack that its
> equilibrium may be restored.
>
> —Elisée Reclus (1884)

What did it mean to call oneself an anarchist in late-nineteenth-century France? The use of the term was fiercely contested by both opponents and adherents; it could be precisely descriptive or a mere term of abuse. It linked at some level back-to-nature faddists and dynamiters, fierce individualists and self-proclaimed communists, gentle intellectuals and at least one grave robber. It encompassed dedicated militants who endured years in prison as well as dilettantes for whom anarchism was briefly chic.

For the French government, anarchism was a disease both of the individual intellect and of the social organism—to be extirpated in either case without giving quarter. For the business leaders and middle-class professionals of the Third Republic, the political and social order they led was the logical culmination of centuries of progress, education, and enlightenment. If it was not yet the best of all possible worlds, it was at least the indispensable foundation for that. Anarchism seemed to them at best an incomprehensible folly, at worst a deceptive child of dark plots to subvert social cohesion and harmony.[1]

---

1. Some anarchist circles were funded by the French police to justify repression. The first anarchist journal in France was set up in 1880 with funds provided by Louis Andrieux, the prefect of police in Paris. Andrieux knew of—and perhaps helped plan—an attempt in June, 1881, to blow up a statue of the late President Thiers. See George Woodcock, *Anarchism: A History of Libertarian Ideas and Movements* (2nd ed.; Harmondsworth, Eng., 1986), 246–48. See also Richard David Sonn, *Anarchism and Cultural Politics in Fin-de-Siècle France* (Lincoln, Nebr., 1989), 31–48.

Across both Europe and North America the dominant image of the anarchist was of the terrorist. The *attentat*—the "propaganda of the deed"—involved bombings and assassinations that pitted lone anarchists against the world's rich and powerful. The targets were sometimes specific: an American businessman in 1892, a Spanish general in 1893, a French president in 1894 or a Spanish premier in 1897, an Austrian empress in 1898 or an American president in 1901. The targets could also be frighteningly undifferentiated, as earlier, in 1881, when the French anarchist Emile Florian was unable to get close enough to kill the republican leader Léon Gambetta and accordingly resolved to shoot the first bourgeois he met. In 1893, bombs were flung into a Spanish performance of *William Tell;* in 1896, anarchists hurled bombs into a Corpus Christi procession in Spain and a session of the Chamber of Deputies in France. Bourgeois cafés proved tempting targets on several occasions. Asked why he had selected a café full of innocent citizens, the French anarchist Emile Henry responded flatly, "There are no innocent bourgeois."[2]

In France alone, no fewer than eleven bombings were attributed to anarchists between 1892 and 1894. On June 24, 1894, President Sadi Carnot (dubbed Sadi-Crétin by the anarchist periodical *Le Père Peinard*) was stabbed to death by an Italian anarchist, in retribution for the execution of Emile Henry. (The succession of actions and counteractions can be dizzying: Henry's bombings were in retaliation for the execution of Auguste Vaillant, whose bombing of the Chamber of Deputies had been a response to the execution of François Claudius Koenigstein, the infamous Ravachol.)[3]

The image of the anarchist bomber fascinated—as it terrorized—French society. Novel after novel took up the subject, ranging from serious works to potboiler thrillers and written from a welter of competing perspectives: Emile Zola's *Germinal* in 1885, Jane de La Vaudère's *L'Anarchiste* in 1893, Augustin Léger's *Journal*

2. Concerning the era of the *attentats,* see Jean Maitron, *Le Mouvement anarchiste en France* (Paris, 1983), I, 206–50; James Joll, *The Anarchists* (2nd ed.; Cambridge, Mass., 1979), 99–129; and Barbara Tuchman, *The Proud Tower: A Portrait of the World Before the War, 1890–1914* (New York, 1966), 63–113. For anarchist critiques, see Charles Malato, "Some Anarchist Portraits," *Fortnightly Review,* n.s., LXII (1894), 315–33; Elisée Reclus, "Anarchy: By an Anarchist," *Contemporary Review,* XLV (1884), 627–41; Gabriel Mordod, "The Political Situation in France," *Contemporary Review,* XLVII (1895), 592–608; and J. H. Rosny, "Anarchy in Paris," *Harper's Weekly,* XXXIX (1895), 967–69.

3. Tuchman, *The Proud Tower,* 93.

d'un anarchiste in 1895, Zola's *Paris* in 1896, J. H. Rosny's *Les Ames perdues* in 1899, Victor Barrucand's *Avec le feu* in 1900, Camille Pert's *En anarchie* in 1901, and Adolphe Retté's *Le Règne de la bête* in 1907.[4] For social reformers such as Zola, Rosny, and Barrucand, the anarchist bomber was tragic proof of the futility of individual violence.[5] For rightists such as Retté—himself a former anarchist—the bomber incarnated the evil unleashed by republican free thought. Retté's protagonist is destroyed by an act of God as he is about to toss a bomb into a church during mass.

The French upper classes lived in fear of the anarchists. The collapse of a piece of scenery at a play was sometimes enough to send the audience screaming into the street, panicked by an imaginary bomb. Ford Maddox Ford recalled in his memoirs that in 1892, Paris—his Paris, the Paris of a comfortable social elite—was "absolutely paralyzed" by dread of the anarchists. He recalled a particularly ludicrous rumor that anarchists had hidden bombs under the seats of the tiny *fiacres* that traversed the streets.[6] Authorities proclaimed that even verbal support for anarchism was proof of a mental pathology; various European governments demanded international cooperation to repress an alleged secret international terrorist brotherhood.[7]

4. For a detailed critique of French novels about anarchists, see Marius-Ary Leblond, "L'Anarchiste dans le roman français," *Revue socialiste,* XXXVII (1903), 185–213. See also Alvan H. Sanborn, *Paris and the Social Revolution: A Study of the Revolutionary Elements in the Various Classes of Parisian Society* (Boston, 1905), 313–58. Anglo-American novels that relate to the same anarchist scare include Henry James's *Princess Cassamassima* (1886), Joseph Conrad's *The Secret Agent* (1907), Charlotte Teller's *The Cage* (1907), Frank Harris' *The Bomb* (1908), and G. K. Chesterton's *The Man Who Was Thursday* (1908). Novels about anarchism by anarchists of the period include John Henry Mackay's *The Anarchists* (1891, translated into French as *Les Anarchistes* in 1892) and Jean Grave's *Malfaiteurs! Roman* (Paris, 1903). Olivia Rossetti and Helen Rossetti, who had been anarchists, wrote *A Girl Among the Anarchists* (Paris, 1903) under the pseudonym Isabel Meredith.

5. Barrucand was a sometime anarchist sympathizer himself and founder of the *pain gratuit* movement. His anarchist hero in *Avec le feu: Roman* (Paris, 1900), when unable to steel himself to commit an *attentat,* kills himself.

6. Ford Maddox Ford, *Return to Yesterday* (New York, 1932), 107–108.

7. On anarchism as pathology, see Cesare Lombroso, *Les Anarchistes,* trans. M. Hamel and A. Marie (Paris, 1898); and Charles Calmeilles, *Quelques Considérations sur l'anarchie: Ses causes, ses effets, le remède* (Tours, 1895). For a strong rebuttal, see Augustin Hamon, *Psychologie de l'anarchiste socialiste* (Paris, 1895). The call for international collaboration to combat anarchism is discussed by Richard Bach Jensen in "The International Anti-Anarchist Conference of 1898 and the Origins of Interpol," *Journal of Contemporary History,* XVI (1981), 200–225, and especially by Daniel Pick in "The Face of Anarchy: Lombroso

The French state imposed increasingly sweeping laws against the anarchists; if, to Henry, there were no innocent bourgeois, to the government of the Third Republic there were no innocent anarchists. A series of new laws—promptly despised as the *lois scélérates* by the anarchists and socialists—made it a criminal offense for the press to defend criminal acts, and for the press or others to show support in any way for "associations of evildoers" or to support *propagande anarchiste* in any way.[8] In 1892, the Chamber of Deputies voted 471 to 30, with only the socialists opposed, that anarchism was in and of itself a criminal conspiracy to be wiped out at the root: "The acts as well as the doctrines of anarchy constitute a danger for the fatherland, an obstacle to social progress, and a disgrace for the Republic."[9] In August, 1894, hundreds of anarchists were rounded up for a series of show trials designed to prove the existence of and at the same time to crush the anarchist *association des malfaiteurs.* Thirty defendants went to trial first—a grab bag of anarchist theoreticians, simple militants, and robbers who had cited "anarchism" as a reason for their acts. The goal of the trial was to demonstrate the existence of a conspiracy whereby intellectuals planned, activists incited, and criminals carried out violent acts. The state prosecutor maintained that "the accused belong to a sect that establishes a fellowship [*compagnonnage*] among all of its adepts, whose goal is the destruction of all societies and whose means are theft, pillage, arson, and assassination."[10]

The Procès des Trente marked the apogee of the war against the French anarchists. Among those in the dock were the editors of

---

and the Politics of Criminal Science in Post-Unification Italy," *History Workshop Journal,* XXI (1986), 60–86. The idea of anarchism as a literal pathology defines a subset of late-nineteenth-century horror fiction: unusual only in the sheer relentlessness of the obsession is Sabine Baring-Gould's "A Dead Finger," in *A Book of Ghosts* (London, 1904).

8. For a critique of the laws from an anarchist perspective, see Emile Pouget and Francis de Pressensé, *Les Lois scélérates de 1893–1894* (Paris, 1899). For the socialist position, see Jules Guesde, *Contre les lois scélérates* (Lille, 1894). Less sympathetic was Paul Laffitte in "Le Loi contre les anarchistes," *Revue bleue,* 4th ser., II (1894), 129–30. R. Garraud, in *L'Anarchie et la Répression* (Paris, 1895), was a strong opponent of the anarchists and a vigorous defender of the laws. For a summary of the laws and their impact, see Sonn, *Anarchism and Cultural Politics,* 9–29.

9. *Journal officiel,* May 22, 1892, pp. 599–600.

10. Extracts from the trial are reprinted in Albert Bataille's *Causes criminelles et mondaines de 1894: Les Procès anarchistes* (Paris, 1895). See also Maitron, *Le Mouvement anarchiste,* I, 251–61; and Jeanne Humbert, *Sebastien Faure: L'Homme, l'Apôtre, une Epoque* (Paris, 1949), 91–148.

the three major Parisian anarchist journals—Emile Pouget, of *Le Père Peinard;* Jean Grave, of *La Révolte;* and Sebastien Faure, of *Le Libertaire*—along with the young scholar Paul Reclus (a stand-in for his more famous father, the social geographer Elisée Reclus) and the sardonic art critic Félix Fénéon. In Mazas prison, waiting to be tried, was a larger bloc of prisoners, including the Neo-Impressionist painter Maximilien Luce. Others evaded arrest by leaving the country, including the painters Camille Pissarro and Théophile Alexandre Steinlen, the novelist and critic Octave Mirbeau, and the poet Paul Adam.[11] The anarchist press was largely eliminated: the number of anarchist periodicals fell from 247 in 1892 to a low of 39 in 1894. *La Révolte* and *Le Libertaire* ceased publication; *Le Père Peinard* temporarily exiled itself in London.[12]

Yet even in the wake of Sadi Carnot's assassination, the Procès des Trente proved a fiasco for the French government. The principal defendants were all acquitted; the major anarchist reviews began to reappear, sometimes under new names. By 1896, there were at least 350 anarchist periodicals published in France. One major study estimates that there were at least a hundred thousand anarchist sympathizers scattered across the rural areas and urban centers.[13]

The net cast by the French government proved too wide. It was one thing for variously impelled people to call themselves anarchists but quite another for the regime to try to bind them all together in the sort of conspiracy potboiler serials had impressed upon the popular mind. In another sense, however, the net was not wide enough. The French republican state was forced to confront the unpleasant reality that the more than a hundred thousand anarchist sympathizers included a disproportionate number of prominent writers, artists, and intellectuals. At precisely the mo-

11. Camille Pissarro to Lucien Pissarro, July 30, 1894, in Camille Pissarro's *Correspondance,* ed. Janine Bailly-Herzberg (Paris, 1980–), III, 469–70. Pissarro listed the other exiled artists and added, "I fear that I will be forced to remain abroad for a while. Since the last law voted by the French parliament, it is absolutely impossible for anyone to be safe."

12. Aline Dardel, "L'Etude des dessins dans les journeaux anarchistes de 1895 à 1914" (Thesis, University of Paris, n.d.), 2.

13. Maitron, *Le Mouvement anarchiste,* I, 130. Using somewhat different criteria, Augustin Hamon, a sociologist friendly to the anarchists, estimated that there were some sixty thousand anarchist sympathizers in France, mostly concentrated in the urban centers. He excluded individualist anarchists from his count. See his "The March of Socialism in France," *Free Review,* IV (1895), 392. For an accusation that Hamon was underestimating anarchist support, see "The Anarchists in France," *Rebel* (Boston), I (September 20, 1895), 6–7.

ment when anarchism was routinely described as a pathology and a vast conspiracy, the segments of the French intelligentsia openly proclaiming their sympathies for anarchism as a cause were multiplying. Hippolyte Fierens-Gevaert, in his gloomy *La Tristesse contemporaine,* described anarchism as permeating every outpost of French intellectual and artistic life. In addition to militant anarchists—whose doctrines, he said, were marked by the *instincts de brute*—there were, he warned, "legions" of unconscious or dilettante anarchists who were far more dangerous, because they provided the cause with a veneer of respectability: "They recruit from the most elevated classes of society. They make up the intellectual elite of their time." Fierens-Gevaert believed that the rot had spread everywhere: "Every philosopher, writer, poet, dramatist, artist is today a latent anarchist."[14] In the theater, every dramatist, he thought, espoused the "theories of Kropotkin and of Jean Grave."[15]

Fierens-Gevaert's account seems too exaggerated to be fully credible, but the attraction anarchism held for French artists and intellectuals was certainly real enough. The 1880s and 1890s saw the proliferation of a large number of politicoartistic journals that sought in varying ways and for differing lengths of time to combine the discussion of philosophical and aesthetic issues with anarchist ideals: *La Vogue, L'Enclos,* the *Revue indépendante, La Société nouvelle, L'Humanité nouvelle, La Plume, L'Art social, Entretiens politiques et littéraires, Le Plébéian,* the *Revue blanche.* Even writers hostile to anarchism were forced by political fashion to pay tribute to the beauty of the "anarchist ideal."[16] Journals that were neutral about or even averse to anarchism opened their columns to anarchist writers. In July, 1893, the literary review *L'Ermitage* polled artists and writers on the question "Which is the better condition of social good—a spontaneous and free organization, or an organization that is disciplined and methodic? Which of these conceptions should be the preference of the artist?"[17] Deliberately or not, the wording of the question cut across traditional left-right poli-

---

14. Hippolyte Fierens-Gevaert, *La Tristesse contemporaine: Essai sur les grandes courants moraux et intellectuels* (Paris, 1899), 102–104. Cf. Adolphe Tabarant, *Maximilien Luce* (Paris, 1928), 33–34; and Camille Mauclair, *Servitude et Grandeur littéraire* (Paris, 1928), 111–39.

15. Fierens-Gevaert, *La Tristesse contemporaine,* 104.

16. See Henri Mazel, "L'Anarchisme," *Essais d'art libre,* I (1892), 198–207.

17. "Un Référendum artistique et social," *L'Ermitage,* VII (July, 1893), 1–24. Of the 99 responses, the editors classified 23 as supporting "constraint," 24 as mixed, and 52 as coming from "partisans de la liberté," that is, anarchists.

tics. Of twenty-three artists the editors classified as "partisans of constraint" (out of ninety-nine polled), they identified six as aristocrats, ten as socialists, and seven as some variety of "authoritarian." More than half of those answering, however, unambiguously identified themselves as anarchists. The critic Camille Mauclair responded, "Logic glorifying sensibility, the exaltation of the being in harmony with natural laws, appreciating in others what one appreciates in oneself, oppressing neither oneself nor others—that is my ethical formula!" Oscar Wilde described himself as a former supporter of tyrants who had become simply an "artist and anarchist." The composer Ferdinand Hérold asserted that the free development of each individual would be best guaranteed by "economic communism, joined with political, intellectual, and moral anarchy."[18]

The influence of the anarchist movement on French intellectuals is apparent as well in the subscription lists of the major anarchist periodicals, seized by the police as part of the mass arrests of 1894. Among the prominent subscribers to Jean Grave's *La Révolte* were not only those most openly identified with anarchism as a cause—including Adam, Luce, Mirbeau, Signac, Bernard Lazare, Camille and Lucien Pissarro, and the poet Jean Richepin—but some of France's most prominent cultural and literary figures, among them Maurice Barrès, Alphonse Daudet, Anatole France, Remy de Gourmont, Joris Karl Huysmans, Jules Lemaître, Leconte de Lisle, and Stéphane Mallarmé.[19]

A narrow focus on the appeal of anarchism to this elite understates the support anarchism received, however. Most French anarchists were uncelebrated; their roots were most commonly in the plebeian soil under threat by industrialization and its attendant social dislocations.[20] But prominent anarchists themselves noted, in tones ranging from bemusement to irony, their sudden popularity

18. *Ibid.,* 10, 13, 21. A similar survey was published in several issues of the anarchist-oriented *L'Enclos* under the collective title "De l'art," beginning in November, 1896. The view of the editors themselves is expressed in "De nôtre art," *L'Enclos,* II (December, 1896), 35.

19. The subscription lists to *La Révolte, Le Père Peinard,* and *Le Libertaire* are all in the Archives Nationale, Paris, Box F7,12506. Journals subscribing to *La Révolte* included *La Plume,* the *Revue blanche, L'Art littéraire, L'Art et la Vie,* the *Revue d'art et de littérature,* and *Essais d'art libre.* See Eugenia W. Herbert, *The Artist and Social Reform: France and Belgium, 1885–1898* (New Haven, 1961).

20. At this time, *La Révolte* had a circulation of 8500 copies. See Félix Dubois, *Le Péril anarchiste* (Paris, 1894), 108.

among the intelligentsia. In Mirbeau's play *Les Mauvais Bergers,* the anarchist hero Jean Roule sarcastically describes the liberal son of a reactionary factory owner as "revolutionary and socialist . . . , anarchist, too, no doubt! That is very much the fashion, this year, with the bourgeois."[21] Writing three years later, Emile de Saint-Auban, a friend and colleague of Jean Grave's, was even more scathing. He remarked, "Today the *dynamitard* is a bit outdated, he has lost his allure"; but he went on to say that even so the anarchists had their share of phonies and hangers-on: "Like religion, politics, the toilette, like everything, anarchy has its dandies; in certain circles, to be an anarchist is in good taste, it is the authentic mark of a superior spirit."[22]

Peter Kropotkin later confessed to his colleague Max Nettlau that in the 1890s the ranks of "French bourgeois youth" had been briefly attracted to what they saw as the "'nihilism' of anarchy," developing a "narrow and selfish" concept of anarchism dedicated not to social betterment but to "liberation from the concept of good and evil."[23]

Prominent intellectuals drawn to anarchism were for their part combating a social order they found unacceptable. The poet and vitriolic critic Laurent Tailhade recalled, "I saluted anarchy as the dawn of a new era. Did the anarchists not present themselves as the builders of Salente [utopia] we dreamed of, during one of the most miserable epochs in our history?" The people had longed for something—anything—that would sweep away a reigning society of corruption, he wrote, and those of the elite who loved justice and liberty had had to side with the people in that desire.[24] But Tailhade also advanced another rationale for his interest in anarchism, connecting it not to popular desires but to his own needs: anarchism, he wrote, was the rational means by which a "cultivated and patriotic intelligentsia" could conserve its own individuality in the face of an increasingly conformist society.[25]

<hr>

21. Octave Mirbeau, *Les Mauvais Bergers: Pièce en cinq actes* (Paris, 1898), 17.

22. Emile de Saint-Auban, *L'Idée sociale au théâtre* (Paris, 1901), 29, 35. See also Sonn, *Anarchism and Cultural Politics,* 53–78.

23. Peter Kropotkin, *Selected Writings on Anarchism and Revolution,* ed. Martin A. Miller (Cambridge, Mass., 1970), 294–95. In *Malfaiteurs!* Jean Grave looked back with a certain wistful fondness, however, to a time when even the bourgeois press flirted with anarchism. See *Malfaiteurs!* 59.

24. Ernest Raynaud, *En marge de la mêlée symboliste* (3rd ed.; Paris, 1936), 127–29.

25. Max Nettlau, *Geschichte der Anarchie* (4 vols.; Vaduz, 1981), IV, 253.

The two strands present in Tailhade's reasoning help distinguish two partly if often ferociously competing currents in late-nineteenth-century French anarchism. In 1897, the Russian Marxist Georgi Plekhanov charged in a pamphlet that anarchism was stamped from its inception with two incompatible ideals, that it was an untenable amalgam of socialism and "Manchesterianism," that is, bourgeois liberalism, much as "Jesus is born of commerce between the Holy Spirit and the virgin Mary."[26] Though some anarchists dismissed the tensions between the populist and socialist and the individualist currents in anarchism as irrelevant, most favored one or the other and excoriated those with the contrary preference.[27] One wing of anarchism—the anarchocommunists associated with Kropotkin, Grave, and Elisée Reclus—argued that individual freedom could exist only within a historically evolved social matrix based on cooperation and mutual aid. The other wing—the individualists—rejected social responsibility in favor of absolute personal freedom. They drew upon often ill digested snippets of Friedrich Nietzsche and Max Stirner (the latter primarily by way of Stirner's French disciple Félix Le Dantec) to invoke a world of pitiless struggle in which all had the potential for freedom but only few superior individuals had the courage to seize it.[28] Gourmont exemplified the individualist anarchist. An inveterate opponent of both the anarchist and the socialist left, he asserted that for the gifted there were only two permissible forms of social organization: anarchism (which would leave them free to do as they liked) and a dictatorship by the gifted elite (which would have the same effect).[29] Kropotkin complained that individualist anarchists aimed "at the full development not of all members of society, but only those who would be considered the most gifted

26. Georges Plekhanoff, *Anarchisme et Socialisme* (Paris, 1897), 55–56. Plekhanov added, "The two natures of the anarchist ideal are also as difficult to reconcile as the two natures of the son of God." In practice, he argued, anarchism postponed its socialist goals indefinitely in deference to its individualism.

27. For a dismissal of the tensions between the socialist and individualist currents, see Voltairine de Cleyre, *Selected Works* (New York, 1914): "It no longer seems necessary to me that one should base his Anarchism upon any particular world conception" (p. 107). Sebastien Faure's journal, *Le Libertaire*, made a determined effort to avoid taking sides in this debate.

28. See Friedrich Nietzsche, *Thus Spake Zarathustra*, trans. Thomas Common (New York, 1960), 52: "There, where the State ceaseth—pray look thither, my brethren! Do ye not see it, the rainbows and bridges of the Superman?"

29. Eugenia W. Herbert, *The Artist and Social Reform*, 93. See Remy de Gourmont, "Pour l'individualisme (contre le communisme et le collectivisme)," *L'Action*, I (1896), 1.

ones, without caring for the right of full development for all."[30] Certainly the statements of the French individualists seldom evinced much concern for the great majority of the human race. Laurent Tailhade sparked a near-riot at an anarchist performance of Ibsen's *Enemy of the People* when in prefatory remarks he described the anarchist utopia as one in which "the pleb would kiss the footsteps of the poets."[31] The plebs in attendance seem to have had other ideas.

The French protofascist right of the late nineteenth century often portrayed anarchism as the logical, if demented, culmination of the French republican tradition. Edouard Drumont charged, typically, that "the bourgeois revolutionary [of 1789] who made the Republic according to his desires, who corrupted the People in order better to exploit them, finds before him the anarchist who expresses himself just like the bourgeois of eighty-nine. . . . Anarchists are no doubt guilty; but what has society given them by way of models?"[32] Retté argued in the preface to his antianarchist novel *Le Règne de la bête* that anarchists were merely inheritors of the traditional republican hostility to the elements that collectively constituted the historical "French Fatherland— . . . traditional religion, the family, solidly constructed, a taste for hierarchy and discipline, all of which have fallen to ruin."[33] To see in anarchism a continuation of republican values and social paradigms is perceptive, but only so far as it is anarchocommunism that is under inspection. The individualist ethos, with its rejection of social solidarity, and above all in its outright antagonism toward the republican creed of progress through enlightenment and science, was a sharp repudiation of the republican tradition. The individualists in their disdain for equality and their fascination with the mystical and the occult often stood closer to the French far right. Retté long before his conversion to the right described the duty of art as the safeguarding of beauty against the "folly of

<hr>

30. Peter Kropotkin, "Modern Science and Anarchism," in *Revolutionary Pamphlets,* ed. Roger N. Baldwin (New York, 1927), 161–62. Cf. "Communisme-Individualisme," *La Révolte,* V (January 4, 1892). For a cynical critique of the same debate, see Rossetti and Rossetti [Meredith], *A Girl Among the Anarchists,* 202–208.

31. Hamon, *Psychologie de l'anarchiste socialiste,* 124.

32. Edouard Drumont, *De l'or, de la boue, du sang: Du Panama à l'anarchie* (Paris, 1895), 114–15. See also Edouard Drumont, *La Fin d'un monde: Etude psychologique et sociale* (Paris, 1889), 171–72.

33. Adolphe Retté, *Le Règne de la bête* (Paris, 1907), vii. See also Léon Daudet, *Le Stupide XIXe Siècle* (Paris, 1922), 62–63.

progress" and the nineteenth century's resentment of natural intellectual and social hierarchies.[34] In that, he said little that the most impassioned royalist would have cared to dispute. It is scarcely surprising that many individualist anarchists became fascists in the early 1900s.[35]

Anarchocommunism, by contrast, flowed in large part from the same stream as bourgeois republicanism.[36] Its source was a faith in an inexorable evolutionary process, in accordance with immutable scientific laws, that would lead the way back to a world of enlightenment and individual freedom. For Kropotkin, Reclus, and Grave, unalterable scientific laws governed and defined every facet of existence. Several of the major theoreticians of anarchocommunism, most notably Kropotkin and Reclus, prided themselves on their scientific training and regarded their social theories as scientific in both form and content.[37] Their anarchism was to be grounded not on the "imprecise" and inexact social sciences but on the physical sciences. Kropotkin wrote, "Anarchism is a world-concept based upon a mechanical explanation of all phenomena embracing the whole of nature—that is, including in it the life of human sciences and their economic, political, and moral problems. Its method of investigation is that of the natural sci-

34. Adolphe Retté, "L'Art et l'Anarchie," *La Plume,* XCI (1893), 45–46. For a rebuttal by an anarchist writer, see Clement Rochel, "L'Art et la Vie," *L'Art social,* III (1893), 73–79. Retté seems never to have taken anarchy to imply equality, but rather he seems to have looked toward a removal of all restrictions on Adolphe Retté: "Anarchy implies the abolition of all constraints and, consequently, of all laws imposed in the name of a principle, of a tradition, or an interest" (*Réflexions sur l'anarchie* [Paris, 1894], 4–5).

35. See G. D. H. Cole, *Marxism and Anarchism, 1850–1890* (London, 1954), 355, Vol. II of Cole, *A History of Socialist Thought.* See also Sonn, *Anarchism and Cultural Politics,* 362–434. Memoirs of anarchists who turned fascist include Léon de Montesquieu's *De l'anarchie à la monarchie* (Paris, 1911) and Georges Valois' *D'un siècle à l'autre: Chronique d'une génération nouvelle* (Paris, 1921).

36. One small example: when Sebastien Faure published the *Almanach anarchiste pour 1892* (Paris, 1892), a furor resulted among anarchists because it employed the Gregorian calendar, with all its religious references and holidays. After the *Almanach anarchiste* failed, later anarchist almanacs—most notably the *Almanach du Père Peinard* and the *Almanach de la révolution*—were careful to use the calendar of the French Revolution. See Dubois, *Le Péril anarchiste,* 148, 150.

37. Both Kropotkin and Reclus were geographers by training. See Gary Dunbar, *Elisée Reclus, Historian of Nature* (Hamden, Conn., 1978), and George Woodcock and Ivan Avakumovic, eds., *The Anarchist Prince: A Biographical Study of Peter Kropotkin* (New York, 1950), esp. 49–91. On the hope of bringing the joy of scientific discovery to all, see Peter Kropotkin, *Memoirs of a Revolutionist* (New York, 1971), 226–27.

ences, and, if it pretends to be scientific, every conclusion it comes to must be verified by the method by which every scientific conclusion is to be verified." He concluded that the aim of anarchism "is to construct a synthetic philosophy comprehending in one generalization all the phenomena in nature and therefore also the life of societies."[38]

Individualist anarchism placed its highest value on the subjective will, especially in the supreme individual, the *ennemi des lois,* in Barrès' phrase. Its emphasis was on the need to struggle against anyone or anything hampering the individual's absolute freedom and independence.[39] By contrast, anarchocommunists sought to establish their individuality in a radical objectivism. It has been rightly affirmed that Kropotkin felt he could be an anarchist because his universe was determinist. His freedom and autonomy, he argued, depended upon nature's bedrock of stability, without which change would mean not evolution but chaos.[40]

Individualist anarchists frequently acted out their freedom, sometimes ostentatiously. Tailhade delighted in a relentless flamboyance: he strode about Paris in a long cape and sombrero; he greeted one group of young poets in a golden chasuble. He surrounded himself with the tokens of Catholic ritual, attracted not to the faith they represented but to their mystic character and aesthetic qualities.[41] Anarchocommunists looked to social evolution rather than personal eccentricity and individual will as the guarantor of human freedom. Against the reigning social Darwinism of the era, the anarchocommunists offered an evolutionary theory founded upon the ideas of mutual aid and solidarity. *Les Primitifs,* released in 1885, by Elie Reclus, Elisée Reclus' brother, and especially Kropotkin's *Mutual Aid: A Factor of Evolution,* first serialized in the 1890s, maintained that the survival of any particular species,

38. Kropotkin, "Modern Science and Anarchism," 150. See Emile Janvion, *Le Dogme et le Science* (Paris, 1897), and Jean Grave, *Les Scientifiques* (Paris, 1913). Valois wrote, "For Grave, anarchy and science were indissolubly united; he saw himself not as a propagandist but as a sort of man of science who had discovered the final social truths" (*D'un siècle à l'autre,* 121).

39. See Maurice Barrès, *Sous l'oeil des barbares* (Paris, 1888). Barrès denounced the "barbarians" who restricted him; the *barbares* were defined as the "non-moi," anyone who sought to impede or hinder him from realizing his desires.

40. Concerning the stability of nature as the basis for anarchism, see T. Gamp, "Why We Are Anarchists," *Torch,* October 31, 1894, pp. 1–2.

41. Raynaud, *En marge,* 117–19; Bernard Lazare, *Figures contemporains, ceux d'aujourd'hui, ceux de demain* (Paris, 1895), 213.

and therefore of humanity, rested primarily on the ability of the members of the species to cooperate for mutual protection and assistance. A species thus constituted a mutually supportive organism, in which each creature depended upon others for the essentials of existence. Though the growth of the modern state apparatus—and the domination of capitalism, with its ethos of private gain—had corrupted human existence, the ultimate triumph of anarchy was not only aided but guaranteed by the inborn nature of the human species.[42]

Individualist anarchists hailed the *attentats* of the 1890s for their sheer defiance of law and authority. Tailhade responded to Vaillant's bombing of the Chamber of Deputies with the quip "Qu'importe le reste, si le geste est beau?"[43] By contrast, anarcho-communist leaders gradually turned against the *attentats* as misguided and dangerous attempts to force the pace of social evolution. Such acts, they argued, though comprehensible given the miseries endemic in society, endangered the whole of the revolutionary movement.[44] Grave, in *Malfaiteurs!*—a novel based on a romanticized version of his own life—admitted that the bombings terrified the bourgeoisie; yet their only real effect, he concluded, was to strengthen the ferocity of the repression of the anarchist cause.[45] By the 1890s, Grave and his colleagues came close to arguing that virtually any action—apart from education—designed to quicken the pace toward an anarchist future was a serious error. It would be simple, Grave maintained—perhaps because he had never tried it—to incite the workers into rebellion by shouting, "Comrades, the owners are robbing us! The bourgeois are scoundrels! Governments are scum! We must revolt, kill the capitalists, burn down the factories!" But any revolt so instigated could lead only to new forms of slavery. Instead, Grave argued, the goal of anarchocommunists had to be to explain and educate, winning thereby not mere converts but fully informed cothinkers who un-

42. Peter Kropotkin, *Mutual Aid: A Factor of Evolution* (1902; rpr. Boston, 1914), 298–300. See also Jean Grave, *La Société future* (Paris, 1895), 17–42.

43. Maitron, *Le Mouvement anarchiste,* I, 236. Tailhade was injured by a similar "beau geste," when a café bombing left him scarred and sightless in one eye.

44. See, for example, "Le Terrorisme," *La Révolte,* V (April 23–30, 1892), 1; and "Revolution and Terrorism," *Torch,* November 18, 1894, pp. 3–5. In Ford's *Return to Yesterday,* there is a rather unlikely argument between Kropotkin and the union organizer Tom Mann in which Mann calls for destruction of the tyrants and the Russian responds, "No, we must build. We must build in the hearts of men. We must establish a Kingdom of God" (p. 110).

45. Grave, *Malfaiteurs!* 86.

derstood the totality of the anarchist cause. The process would take decades, even generations, to accomplish.[46]

The anarchocommunist concept of social change comes across in a lithograph, *Les Démolisseurs,* made by Paul Signac for Grave's *Les Temps nouveaux* in 1896 (Figure 1). Removed from the body of anarchist theory that generated it, the work seems at first glance to be a rather innocuous image of manual labor.[47] But Signac's image differs from that of the heroic workers who populate, for example, the prints and paintings of Théophile Steinlen and other socialist artists. Steinlen's *The Laborer,* an oil painting from about 1900 (Figure 2), depicts, much like Signac's lithograph, a muscular worker in the foreground, set off against a cityscape and illuminated by the first rays of the sun. Both works draw upon a tradition at least as old as the Paris Commune of displaying the rising sun as a metaphor for the approaching victory of the revolution. Steinlen's image is particularly clear: the dawn highlights the rippling muscles of the worker. It is his strength, his power—coupled with that of the factories in the background—that is stressed here.[48] In Signac's print, the emphasis is not on construction and working-class power but on destruction: the two workers are engaged in demolishing a building. The observation that it is the edifice of the state that is being torn down is no doubt correct; Signac had a fondness for the metaphor of the "blow of the pick."[49] The image of the *démolisseur* as agent of social change was also current in anarchist writings of the period. In 1896, *Le Plébéian* reprinted an essay by Amilcare Cipriani, a former Garibaldian, that helps illumine this aspect of Signac's image: Cipriani opened with the cry "Destructio est edificatio," placing social progress in the context of the need to destroy the entire edifice of bourgeois society. He concluded, "Because everything that our enemies have built is evil, immoral, and unjust, because everything must be

46. Grave, *Moribund Society and Anarchy,* trans. Voltairine de Cleyre (San Francisco, 1899), 16–20, quoted from pp. 16–17. See Louis Patsouras, *Jean Grave and French Anarchism* (Dubuque, Iowa, 1978), and Sanborn, *Paris and the Social Revolution,* 81. But Patsouras dates the shift of attitude much later.

47. See Eugenia W. Herbert, *The Artist and Social Reform,* 20. See also Annemarie Springer, "Terrorism and Anarchy: Late Nineteenth-Century Images of a Political Phenomenon in France," *Art Journal,* XXXVIII (1979), 264–65. Springer sees *Les Démolisseurs* as an evocation of the "working man's strength, endurance, and skill."

48. In this, Steinlen's painting differs from an earlier print on the same subject, in *Le Chambard socialiste* of December 30, 1893, in which the worker looks out at a row of question marks.

49. See Dardel, "L'Etude des dessins," 111.

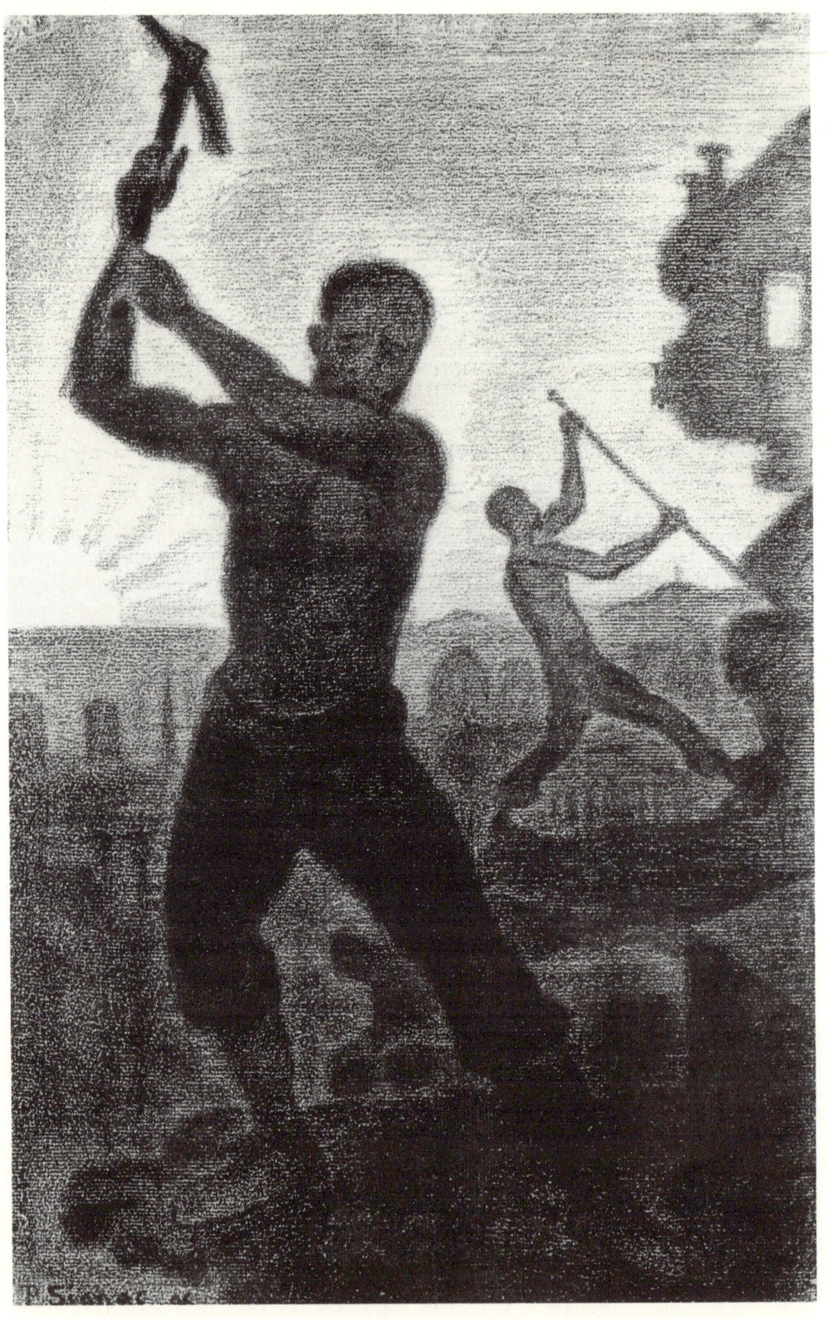

Figure 1   Paul Signac, *Les Démolisseurs*
Paul Signac, French, 1863–1935, The Wreckers (Les Démolisseurs), lithograph, 1896, 47 x 30.5 cm, Gift of Martin A. Ryerson, 1928.643, photograph © 1994, The Art Institute of Chicago, All Rights Reserved.

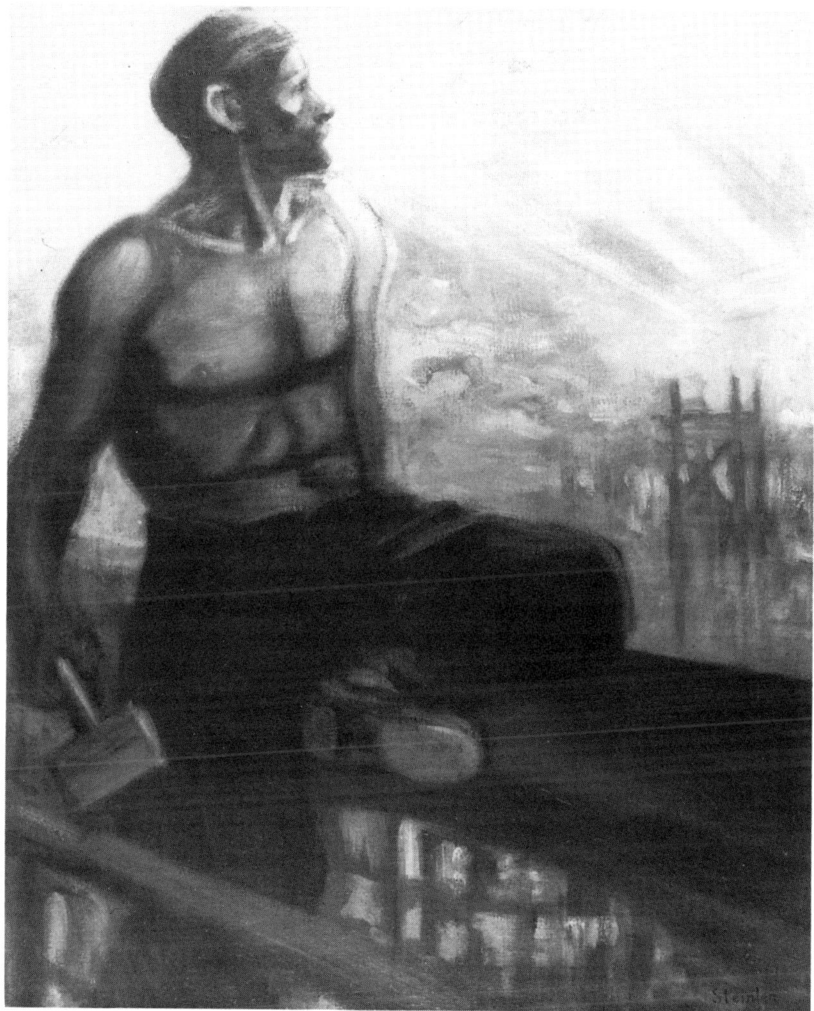

Figure 2   Théophile Steinlen, *The Laborer*
Le Charpentier au-dessus du port, oil on canvas, *ca.* 1900. Courtesy of Musée du Petit Palais, Geneva.

remade, well then! in the next social revolution the oppressed will have to march into combat to the cry of TEAR IT DOWN!"[50]

50. Amilcare Cipriani, "Démolissons!" *Le Plébéian,* II (September 1–15, 1895), 2–3. The founder of French anarchism, Pierre Joseph Proudhon, used the motto Destruam et Aedificabo. See Woodcock, *Anarchism,* 14.

This still leaves unexplained, however, the way in which Signac portrayed the two workers. Steinlen's image reflects the socialist emphasis on the power and muscularity of the male working class; it is part of an effort to create a sense of empowerment, to suggest the strength of the workers as a class. By contrast, Signac endows his workers with almost no detail at all. They are dark, shadowy, almost unmodeled; the sun rises, but its faint beams have yet to touch the workers and turn their world bright.

The anarchocommunist emphasis on education and enlightenment as the vehicle for human emancipation is to the point here. The cover of an undated French edition of Kropotkin's *Communisme et Anarchie* (Figure 3) shows a worker—shovel, rather improbably, in hand—sitting, reading, at a workbench, flanked by wife, child, and anarchist savant. Behind them, the sun rises in the sky. The link between the sunrise and anarchist education is explicit: the impeccably dressed gentleman, hand resting benevolently on the worker's shoulder, points out a useful passage in the bulky tome on the table. Revealing the unconscious condescension that underlay much anarchist thought—as well as the masculinist bias that made enfranchisement run from male thinker to male worker, with women and children as indirect beneficiaries—the picture seems relatively transparent iconographically.

Signac's print, derived from an oil painting of the previous year, can be read in the same light. To Kropotkin and Grave, human relations were naturally spontaneous, noncompetitive, and based on mutual aid, but modern society had suppressed the natural human bonds, keeping people divided to sustain the power of the rich. Consequently, a key anarchist task was to encourage the dismantling of artificial and repressive society, to allow the reforging of the natural bonds that normally govern human affairs.[51] Signac's print shows the workers engaged at that task, but they still work, and live, in darkness. It is the disassembly of the old social edifice—church and state—that allows the sun to shine in and dispel the darkness. Steinlen's voluntarist notion of socialism—as something to be grasped and taken—is countered by Signac's passive notion. Signac's workers merely pry open cracks to let in the light; the sun shines all by itself. The contrast between the two images of how the new social order will arrive prefigures the attacks socialists and syndicalists were to make on anarchocommunism by

51. See Cole, *Marxism and Anarchism*, 352–53.

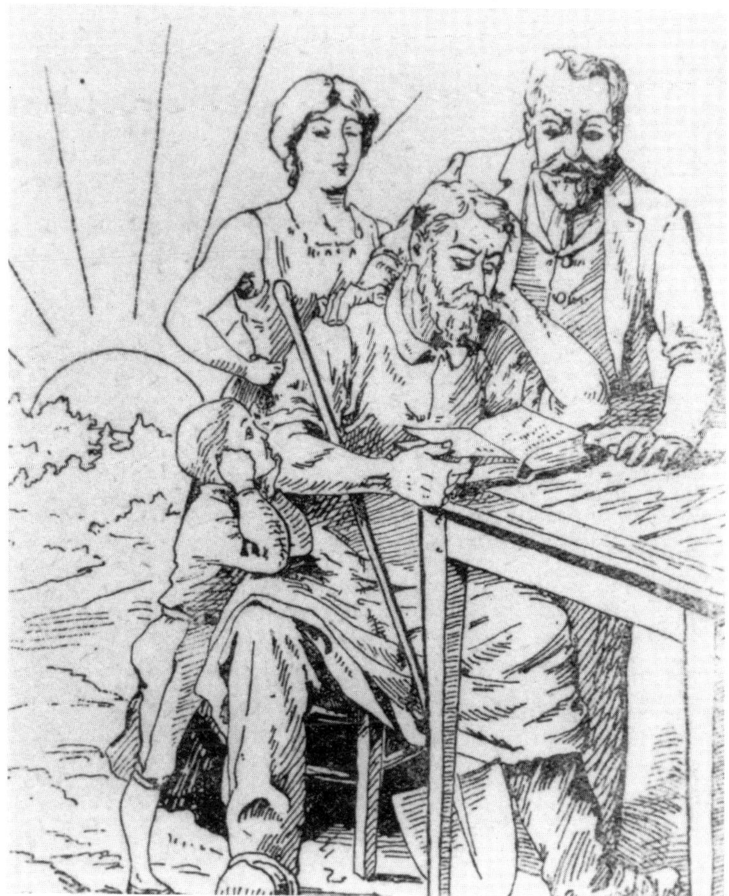

Figure 3   Cover illustration for Peter Kropotkin's *Communisme et Anarchie,* n.d.

the end of the century when they charged that anarchocommunism was an intellectual game in which no one ever had to do anything because science and knowledge would take care of everything.

Despite the evident divergences between anarchocommunism and individualist anarchism, there were important ways in which the two stood together. Both rejected what they saw as a corrupt and sordid bourgeois society; both saw the existing industrial world as implacably hostile to the arts. Both posed—in differing vocabularies—the alternative to existing society in terms of individual choice rather than mass movements. The individualists dared their listeners to act out their independence from society and to live as free agents answerable only to their own desires and needs.[52] The anarchocommunists spoke of *l'homme nouveau,* or more rarely of *la femme libre,* who internalized the values of the movement and offered the populace an example of what the world was bringing. The common strain about the heroic individual who dares to stand alone led to unexpected crossovers and overlapping contentions: the anarchocommunist Emma Goldman, for example, saw no contradiction between her call for human solidarity and her glorification of Nietzsche for his aristocratic spirit.[53]

Both wings of anarchism dismissed, or evaded, the matter of social class. The individualists did so in uncompromising terms: "For us," declared André Lorulot, "there are no classes; we recognize only individuals, some of whom are ready to help us in exchange for our help—these are the anarchists—and others who contribute to the functioning of the society that oppresses us." He added, "Whether they are workers or owners is unimportant. . . . Our propaganda is addressed to all."[54] Although the anarchocommunists more readily spoke—and claimed to speak—for *les ouvriers,* at base they too, unlike the protosyndicalists around Emile Pouget's *Le Père Peinard,* were at pains not to limit the appeal of their movement to any single class but instead to welcome everyone of goodwill. Anarchism was a means of liberating the worker, but it was to be achieved through the accretion of all "rebels," regardless of their origins, who rejected the commands and norms of the state.[55]

Both wings of the anarchist movement also rejected the socialist and syndicalist idea that the industrial working class was the mo-

52. This point dominates Maurice Barrès' *L'Ennemi des lois* (Paris, 1892).

53. "His aristocracy was neither of birth nor of the purse; it was of the spirit. In that respect Nietzsche was an aristocrat, and all true anarchists were aristocrats" (Emma Goldman, *Living My Life* [2 vols.; London, 1932], I, 194).

54. André Lorulot, "Syndicalisme et Organisation," *L'Anarchie,* October 12, 1905, quoted by Maitron in *Le Mouvement anarchiste,* I, 276–77.

55. Jean Grave, *L'Anarchie: Son but, ses moyens* (Paris, 1910), 42–43. This tenet of anarchocommunism came increasingly to the fore with the rise of an explicitly class-based syndicalist movement. See M. Pierrot, "Anarchistes et Syndicalistes," *Les Temps nouveaux,* XII (April 13, 1907), 2: "Whereas the anarchist-communist can address himself to all individuals of goodwill, syndicalism addresses itself only to workers."

tive force for a socialist transformation of society. On the contrary, anarchists often censured workers as conformist drudges and derided their strikes as exercises to negotiate the terms of their own enslavement.[56] Anarchists in both camps instead hailed as models the ranks of French society that had been marginalized and cast aside by industrial society. An article in *Le Libertaire* proclaimed that "those without trades, the jobless, vagabonds, bums, prostitutes, the declassed, are the revolutionaries of tomorrow."[57] In place of the icon of the worker, the anarchists held out as a model the *trimardeur,* the anarchist vagabond, ranging the world in search of work and spreading revolt from land to land. The vagabond—beholden to no one, defying both law and the elements—was seen as living proof that it was possible to slip through the cracks of dominant society.[58]

The emphasis on the sectors of French society marginalized by industrialization was coupled in both wings of French anarchism with a nostalgic view of the preindustrial era—especially the Middle Ages—as a time of relative stability, peace, and prosperity, free from the evils of centralized government, technology, and capitalism.[59] A sympathetic historical study of anarchism neatly summarizes the anarchist viewpoint as one according to which the individual "stands in an evil, government-dominated present, looking back to a lost paradise of primitive innocence and forward to a future whose civilised simplicity will rebuild the golden age of liberty."[60] Anarchocommunists, and even many individualists, presented the golden future in scientific garb, but in both cases

56. The anarchist protagonist of Raoul Henry's serialized drama "Les Vagabonds" states flatly, "I am no friend to the good workers and good servants—good servants to their masters. I am a renegade, a rebel." (*La Débâcle sociale,* I [January 25–February 8, 1896], 3). The German anarchist Gustav Landauer dismissed the worker as a "born philistine" and hopeless conformist. See Landauer's *Aufruf zum Sozialismus* (2nd ed.; Berlin, 1919), 53.

57. G. Paul, "L'Anarchie et les Sans-Travail," quoted by Maitron in *Le Mouvement anarchiste,* I, 275–76n26.

58. See Charles Flor [Flor O'Squarr], *Les Coulisses de l'anarchie* (Paris, 1892), 8–14. See also Sanborn, *Paris and the Social Revolution,* 40–43. Concerning the Neo-Impressionist treatment of the vagabond, see John Hutton, "'Les Prolos Vagabondent': Neo-Impressionism and the Anarchist Image of the *Trimardeur*," *Art Bulletin,* LXXII (1990), 296–309.

59. On the anarchist mythology of the Middle Ages, see André Reszler, *L'Esthétique anarchiste* (Paris, 1973), 10–15. Kropotkin tended to see in the medieval commune the basis for a new golden age. See his *Mutual Aid,* 153–222. See also G. M. Horner, "Kropotkin and the City: The Socialist Ideal in Urbanism," *Antipode,* X–XI (1979), 33–43.

60. Woodcock, *Anarchism,* 47. Woodcock ascribes the view to Tom Paine.

juxtaposed their vocabulary of science uneasily against references to dreams and visions.[61] Praising Kropotkin's *The Conquest of Bread* in a letter to Mirbeau, Camille Pissarro wrote, "It must be admitted that, if it is utopian, it is at any rate a beautiful dream."[62] In 1895, Signac lauded Emile Verhaeren's poem cycle *Les Villages illusoires* for the manner in which it invoked the world of the future, the "hope of a golden age, one that is calm, happy, sunny."[63]

The Search for Solid Ground

In May, 1889, the French president Sadi Carnot formally opened the International Exhibition in Paris with a mass fete at Versailles at which he extolled the glories of the French Revolution of 1789. The exhibition itself was intended to demonstrate the superiority of French industry and technology—epitomized by Gustave Eiffel's colossal monument to himself, an open-lattice iron tower demonstrating the capabilities of French metallurgy and engineering.

Just eleven years before, the newly victorious republican parties had with great skill availed themselves of a similar exposition to cement their claim to power and legitimacy as huge and enthusiastic crowds turned out to celebrate the glories of the republic. Only the small, nascent socialist movement had remonstrated that the observances of 1878 deliberately falsified French revolutionary history and were a "universal exploitation" covering up the realities of life for the vast majority of French citizens.[64] In 1889, the mood was altogether different, beneath a surface of gaiety and celebration. The socialists had turned from general reproaches about unfairness and inequality to prophecies of doom: Marx's son-in-law Paul Lafargue warned that after the glitter of the festivity faded away, "the discontent . . . will be redoubled by disillusionment, annoyances, and miseries left by the millionaires as souvenirs of their passage." He charged that the exposition, far from exhibiting the strength of the bourgeois republic, would only "precipitate economic crisis and deliver a mortal blow to the

61. Concerning a scientific theory of individualist anarchism, see Mackay, *The Anarchists,* 278–82.

62. Georges Lecomte, *Camille Pissarro* (Paris, 1902), 95.

63. John Rewald, ed., "Extraits du journal inédit de Paul Signac," *Gazette des beaux-arts,* 6th ser., XXXVI (1949), 116.

64. Un Prolétaire, "L'Exploitation universelle en 1878," *L'Egalité,* May 12, 1878, pp. 1–2, June 2, 1878, pp. 4–5.

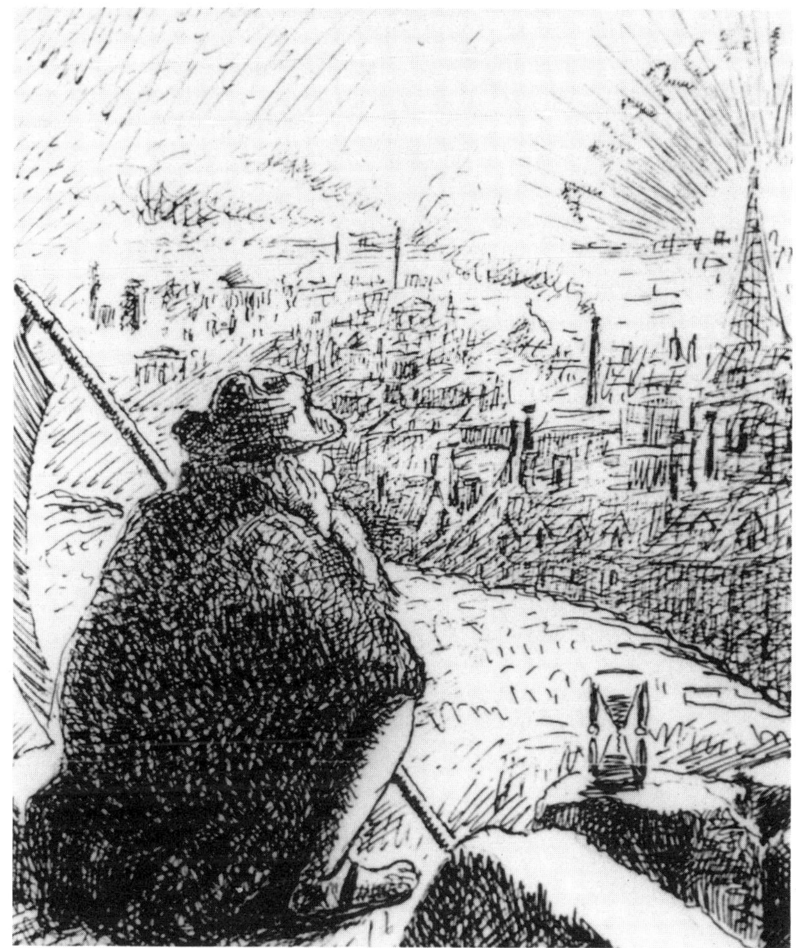

Figure 4   Camille Pissarro, frontispiece for *Turpitudes sociales*
Pen-and-ink drawing, 1889. Collection Skira.

parliamentary republic."[65] More dramatically, Mirbeau labeled the
fair "the final surge of a moribund society . . . the supreme cry of
a civilization in agony."[66] Camille Pissarro, in his *Turpitudes sociales,* drawn at the end of 1889, captured this mood (Figure 4): the
Paris of the exhibition, the Eiffel Tower featured prominently, is

65. Paul Lafargue, "L'Exposition," *L'Egalité,* March 1, 1889, p. 1. See also Défrance
[pseud.], "Fête bourgeoise," *ibid.,* May 2, 1889, p. 1.
66. Reg Carr, *Anarchism in France: The Case of Octave Mirbeau* (Montreal, 1977), 29.

menaced by Father Time, scythe in hand, while behind the city the first rays of an anarchist dawn are breaking.[67]

Across the French political spectrum in the 1880s and 1890s, a recurrent apocalyptic note sounded. A continuing cycle of scandals, riots, and bombings had a powerful impact on the morale of not only intellectuals and politicians but a much broader public. The unhappy career of Sadi Carnot had the flavor of the times. He became president in 1887, after two weeks of riots that brought down his predecessor, Jules Grévy.[68] Carnot's term of office encompassed the Boulangist crisis, the beginnings of the Dreyfus affair, and the massive financial scandals that followed the bankruptcies of the Union Générale and Ferdinand de Lesseps' Panama Canal Company. Under Carnot, French troops opened fire on unarmed youths and children at Fourmies in 1891; during his term, as well, an ill-advised attempt in 1893 to close the new syndicalist *bourse du travail* in Paris led to four days of fierce street fighting. Carnot saw the opening of the era of *attentats;* indeed, a lone assassin attempted to gun him down as he made his way to open the exhibition in 1889. He became France's most prominent victim of the *attentats* when he was stabbed to death by the Italian anarchist Santo Caserio in 1894.

Conditions in Paris caused visitors in the 1880s and 1890s to remark on the expectation of imminent catastrophe, though they seldom agreed about the cause or nature of the looming disaster. To the American police reporter Michael Schaack, France appeared threatened by the "Red Terror," a socialist, anarchist revolt that could "only be a wild and bloody riot, followed by a wild and bloody retribution, by a nation frightened out of freedom back into the arms of a strong government." The English reporter William Henry Hurlbert, on the other hand, foresaw only a reactionary coup. He wrote that France was menaced by a resurgent royalist, Bonapartist right that was on the eve of seizing power: "The Third Republic is in much more imminent danger of a crash today

---

67. On Pissarro and the exposition, see Richard Thomson, "Camille Pissarro, *Turpitudes sociales,* and the Universal Exhibition of 1889," *Arts Magazine,* LVI (April, 1982), 82–88; Fiona Fitzgerald, "The Prints of Lucien Pissarro from 1886 to 1896" (M.A. thesis, University of East Anglia, 1981), 3–5; and Ruth Forley, "Camille Pissarro's *Turpitudes sociales:* Documents of History" (M.A. thesis, Adelphi University, 1981). See also Camille Pissarro to Lucien Pissarro, September 9, 1889, in Camille Pissarro's *Correspondance,* III, 291–93.

68. See Susanna Barrows, *Distorting Mirrors: Visions of the Crowd in Late Nineteenth-Century France* (New Haven, 1981), 12–13.

than was the Second Empire after the plebiscite of May 1870."[69]

The word *crash* had begun to recur in essays and articles as early as the mid-1880s. In 1884, an article in the quasi-anarchist *Revue indépendante* opened with the words "The *crash,* the great social *crash,* is at our doors." The piece continued, "It hovers like a menace above all civilized nations, but, in France, in this extremely nervous country of rapid progress, where the example of the debacle is always before us, one can say that bankruptcy, 'hideous bankruptcy,' is no more than a question of months, weeks, or perhaps days."[70] The anarchist *L'Idée ouvrière,* of Le Havre, similarly asserted in 1887, "The social edifice trembles upon its henceforth very unsure foundations; the harbingers of rapid dissolution manifest themselves every minute." Capitalist society, the journal prophesied, had enfolded humanity like a giant chrysalis and the human race was about to burst forth into freedom. The first issue of the literary and artistic review *La Vogue,* established in 1886 by Gustave Kahn and Félix Fénéon, editorialized that "the social revolution will come; all the coalitions [against it] will only serve to bring it about."[71]

What the socialist and anarchist left saw as approaching revolution the right perceived as collapse and degradation. Charles de Mazade, writing in the conservative *Revue des deux mondes,* argued in 1889 that that was the "decisive crisis of the republic." He believed that France was menaced by the alternative of chaos or dictatorship; its social fabric was unraveling in the face of widespread doubts over the efficacy and even legitimacy of its values and principles. Josephin Péladan, self-styled Sâr of the quite extinct Chaldeans, was still more pessimistic, asserting bluntly, "I believe in the fatal and imminent putrefaction of a Latinity lacking both God and symbol. . . . I judge that the end of France is no more than a question of years."[72]

France was repeatedly compared to a critically—often mor-

69. Michael J. Schaack, *Anarchy and Anarchists: A History of the Red Terror and the Social Revolution in America and Europe* (Chicago, 1889), 688; William Henry Hurlbert, "A Republic *in Extremis," Fortnightly Review,* n.s., XLVI (1889), 642.

70. G. Chevrier, "Banqueroute," *Revue Indépendante,* I (1884), 91. See Lucien Weil, "Vive la banqueroute!" *L'Attaque,* II (June 15–22, 1889), 1.

71. "Fin," *L'Idée ouvrière,* I (September 17–24, 1887), 2; Gustave Kahn and Félix Fénéon, "Le Courrier social," *La Vogue,* I (April 4, 1886), 27.

72. Charles de Mazade, "Chronique de la quinzaine," *Revue des deux mondes,* XCI (1889), 226–36; interview with Péladan, in Jacques Huret's *Enquête sur l'évolution littéraire* (Paris, 1891), 37.

tally—ill patient. In 1892, Camille Lemonnier wrote in his novel *La Fin des bourgeois* that "the corruption having become gangrenous at every point, the rot began to germinate." By 1896, Emile Zola was comparing France to a cancer patient, in his novel *Paris:* "The filth overflowed, the hideous sore, bloody and voracious, spread shamelessly, like the cancer that eats away at an organ, conquering the heart. And what disgust, what nausea at this spectacle, and what longing for a vengeful knife that would bring health and joy!"[73] In 1888, Senator Paul Challemel-Lacour compared France to Frederick III on his deathbed: "If it is rid of the cancer, it will die of the cure. If it shrinks from the cure, it will die of the cancer." Edouard Drumont held that France had already died, though he conceded that most of its citizens had failed to notice.[74]

If France was not already dead, however, what could be done to save it? If it was on the verge of collapse, what could avert the catastrophe? If it could be saved by a new revolution, who would make it? The answers were as effusive as they were vague: Zola's invocation of the "vengeful knife" was exceptional only for the bloodthirsty note he struck. To a writer in the *Revue indépendante,* hope for national redemption seemed to lie in a spontaneous, if not yet visible, solution—an "X factor" that "could not be accommodated by the denials of our skeptics."[75] A recent study of the Third Republic suggests that from the 1880s a large segment of the French lower middle class in particular became politically "unattached," with no long-standing affiliation but swinging wildly between a number of political perches, from that of the moderate republicans in the 1870s to that of Clemenceau's Radicals, to General Boulanger in the 1880s, to the anarchists or—especially from the mid- to late 1890s—to the socialists.[76]

The support for Boulanger peaked in early 1889, after his triumphant election to a Paris parliamentary seat. A hundred thousand followers rallied in the city center, fanning fears of a coup d'etat.[77] Boulanger drew support broadly from the disaffected:

73. Camille Lemonnier, *La Fin des bourgeois* (Paris, 1892), 335. See also Emile Zola, *Paris* (Paris, 1929), 70.

74. Hurlbert, "A Republic," 649; Edouard Drumont, *La Fin d'un monde: Etude psychologique et sociale* (Paris, 1889), 111.

75. Chevrier, "Banqueroute," 95–96.

76. Jean Marie Mayeur and Madeleine Rébérioux, *The Third Republic from Its Origins to the Great War, 1871–1914,* trans. J. R. Foster (New York, 1984), 125–37.

77. For two sharply conflicting interpretations of the events of this period, see James Harding, *The Astonishing Adventure of General Boulanger* (London, 1971), 181–91; and Fred-

from disgruntled Blanquists, frustrated republicans, self-styled socialists, and die-hard monarchists. Barrès, in the midst of his own swing from anarchist to fascist, remarked, "The Royalists saw in Boulanger their king; Republicans saw their republic; Imperialists, their Caesar; patriots, the return of Metz and Strasbourg; peaceful folk saw order; and those who were restless saw an adventure which would solve all their problems."[78] The very formlessness of Boulangism gave it a certain strength: whatever one opposed in France, Boulanger could pose as its eradicator.

The Boulangist movement collapsed after the general fled France in April, 1889, to avoid arrest, but the discontents that had engendered his movement did not dissipate. Séverine (Caroline Remy Guebhard), editor of the independent radical *Le Cri du peuple,* wrote to a conservative republican senator that popular support for Boulanger had not meant a repudiation of republicanism but only of the existing republic dominated by the wealthy few ruling in their own interest.[79] Tailhade wrote later, "The regime was so compromised that the people turned enthusiastically to General Boulanger to overthrow the government. The undertaking of the fractious general having failed, the people did not cease to appeal for a radical change of the constitution." He recognized that many turned to the anarchists as the force that seemed most determined in opposing the entrenched regime.[80]

That a significant portion of the French public could swing from a would-be Caesar to a movement calling for an end to government altogether may astonish. Many anarchists themselves found the shift puzzling. The leading anarchist militants and journals had never wavered in combating Boulanger; Signac's first political cartoon was a cover illustration for a satirical pamphlet discussing Boulanger's "funeral."[81] Still, the anarchist milieu in the broadest sense proved entirely receptive to Boulanger, just as the

erick H. Seager, *The Boulanger Affair: The Political Crossroads of France, 1886–1889* (Ithaca, N.Y., 1969), 203–10. On the breakup of the movement, see Barrows, *Distorting Mirrors,* 13–14.

78. Harding, *The Astonishing Adventure,* 162. See Zeev Sternhell, *Maurice Barrès et le Nationalisme français* (Paris, 1972), esp. Chaps. 2–4. Sternhell emphasizes the role of a nationalist left in the formation of Boulangism.

79. Caroline Remy Guebhard [Séverine], *Notes d'une frondeuse: De la Boulanger au Panama* (Paris, 1894), 18. The letter was to Arthur Ranc, a senator and close ally of Gambetta.

80. Raynaud, *En marge,* 127–28.

81. For the attitude of *La Révolte* to Boulangism, see "Mouvement social: Le Boulangisme," *La Révolte,* III (September 20–26, 1890), 2–3. Boulangism is described there as a fusion of "clericalism, Orleanism, Bonapartism, Russian absolutism, and high finance."

collapse of Boulangism proved a windfall for the anarchist move-ment.[82] The explanation goes in large measure to the social tensions inherent in France's belated industrialization in the latter half of the nineteenth century. France had lagged far behind not only England but also Germany and Belgium; as late as 1914, 40 percent of French women and men were still peasants. France remained, according to one study of European socialism, basically a "country of small enterprise and luxury production, of independent peasants, of shopkeepers, and of skilled artisans who worked in small shops rather than in factories."[83] In 1896, the 575,000-odd firms in a French census averaged only 5.5 workers apiece; only 151 companies in the whole of France employed more than a thousand persons.[84] As late as 1906, only 12 percent of the French work force was employed in plants with a thousand or more workers.[85]

Nonetheless, the industrialization of France had a major, growing impact on the economic, social, and political life of the country. A small industrial working class developed and expanded. With a more concentrated work force came trade unions—not legalized in France until 1884—and, inevitably, strikes. By the standards of other European countries these were infrequent, short, and rarely violent.[86] Even so, they caused near-hysteria within the regime. The press treated the occasional violent confrontations between workers and *patrons*—among them those at Anzin in 1884 and Decazeville in 1886—as outbreaks of an infectious rage that afflicted the "dangerous classes." Zola's *Germinal,* of 1886, portrays the fears labor unrest sparked, while letting it be seen that even a reformer of Zola's stripe shared not a few of them himself.[87]

During the 1880s and 1890s, the French government routinely banned or censored plays depicting strikes. The theatrical adaptation of *Germinal* was not licensed for performance until 1888,

82. On ties between the anarchist group and the Boulangists, see Sonn, *Anarchism and Cultural Politics,* 31–48.

83. Albert S. Lindemann, *A History of European Socialism* (New Haven, 1983), 138–39.

84. John Clapham, *The Economic Development of France and Germany, 1815–1914* (Cambridge, Eng., 1921), 258.

85. Roger McGraw, *France, 1815–1914: The Bourgeois Century* (London, 1983), 233.

86. In 1890, fewer than 140,000 workers were unionized, in some thousand local syndicates; as late as 1902, only 17 percent of the industrial work force was organized. Strikes increased from 261 in 1892 to 386 in 1898, but only one-tenth of them involved any public demonstration and fewer than 4 percent involved even minimal violence. See Edouard Dolléans, *Histoire du mouvement ouvrier* (Paris, 1947), I, 20–21. See also Michelle Perrot, *Les Ouvriers en grève, 1871–1890* (Paris, 1974).

87. Emile Zola, *Germinal* (Paris, 1978), esp. 406–407, 585.

when it was presented stripped of its "incendiary" moments, in particular the scene where troops fire on the striking workers; Zola disowned the expurgated version.[88] A French adaptation of Gerhart Hauptmann's *The Weavers* was banned outright in 1893, as was the play *L'Automne* by the anarchist writers Paul Adam and Gabriel Mourey.[89] In each case, the ban was on grounds of the sensitivity of the subject during times of unrest.

The government of the Third Republic acted promptly—and savagely—at any sign of independent action on the part of workers. The massacre at Fourmies, in 1891, which rallied the socialists and anarchists, began with a local trade union's request for a permit to hold a legal demonstration, to be followed by a dance. The mayor banned the event; troops were summoned to enforce the ban. A crowd of children and teenagers assembled to heckle the troops; when the youths began to throw stones, the soldiers opened fire. Of the fourteen dead, only three were over twenty-one. The government commended the leader of the detachment and arrested local and national socialist leaders for incitement to riot.[90]

Events in Belgium heightened fears about France's industrial work force. In 1886, a series of unconnected local strikes and protests blossomed into a spontaneous insurrection, encompassing the whole of Belgium's industrial belt. The socialist Parti Ouvrier sought to channel the protests into a strike for universal suffrage, but anarchists and an insurgent splinter from the party demanded all-out revolution. The turmoil subsided only in 1890, with the failure of a general strike against the regime.[91] French republicans,

88. James Sanders, "*Germinal,* mis en pièce(s)," *Cahiers naturalistes,* LIV (1980), 68–86; F. W. J. Hemmings, *The Life and Times of Emile Zola* (New York, 1977), 107.

89. The published script for *L'Automne* (bearing the prominent cover label Interdit par la censure le 13 février 1893) also contains a lengthy, bitter exchange between Maurice Barrès and Charles Dupuy, the minister responsible. See Paul Adam and Gabriel Mourey, *L'Automne: Drame en trois actes* (Paris, 1893), i–xv. See also Emile Portal, "Les Théâtres," *L'Ere nouvelle,* II (1894), 541–44. There is sarcastic reference to the banning of Hauptmann's play in Camille Pissarro to Lucien Pissarro, December 15, 1893, in Camille Pissarro's *Correspondance,* III, 409.

90. Barrows, *Distorting Mirrors,* 28–29; Dolléans, *Histoire de mouvement ouvrier,* II, 36–37. For anarchist reactions to the events, see "Le Massacre de Fourmies et nôtre 'noble armée,'" *La Révolte,* IV (May 9–15, 1891), 1; and "Le Massacre de Fourmies," *La Révolte,* IV (May 16–22, 1891), 3.

91. See Jules Destrée and Emile Vandervelde, *Le Socialisme en Belgique* (Paris, 1898), 62–63; Louis Bertrand, *Histoire de la démocratie et du socialisme en Belgique depuis 1830* (2 vols.; Brussels, 1907), II, 394–460; and G. D. H. Cole, *The Second International* (London, 1954), Part II, 617–23, Vol. III of Cole, *A History of Socialist Thought.* For an anarchist view, see "Le Commencement de la fin," *La Liberté,* I (May 29, 1887), 1.

full of the lore of 1789, had not forgotten that their own revolution was preceded by unsuccessful insurrections in what later became Belgium and the Netherlands.

Above all, the French state sought to control and incorporate the industrial workers into the social and political order. When Léon Gambetta's fiery rhetoric about an alliance of the bourgeoisie and the proletariat against the aristos began to fray around the edges, new projects emerged to take its place. Georges Clemenceau's Radical party sought to unite the "common people" into a single front led by the petite bourgeoisie and white-collar professionals. Clemenceau warned that a failure to give workers a stake in the status quo would lead to new revolutions. Léon Bourgeois proposed the theory of *solidarisme:* to Bourgeois, class distinctions were acceptable so long as education opened up access to all levels of society and the state to the gifted of every origin.[92]

Less immediately obvious than the problems of the industrial working class were those of the strata just above them: the lower middle classes—small shopkeepers, skilled laborers, artisans, and petty producers. They found themselves awkwardly situated in late-nineteenth-century France. On the one hand, they thought of themselves, and were often saluted by the state, as the historic backbone of the French revolutionary tradition and the republican movement. On the other, they were gradually being squeezed out—the artisans and skilled laborers by industrial labor, the small shopkeepers, bakers, shoemakers, and the like by the new department stores and larger shops catering to the nouveau riche.[93] They often detested the upper classes who were squeezing them and feared the new industrial workers who were replacing them, and into whose ranks they might eventually be forced.[94]

The political ideals of the lower middle classes were as complex and contradictory as their social status. One history of the Third Republic asserts, "Whether he was a shoemaker, a tailor, a

92. For Georges Clemenceau's views, see his *Question ouvrière* (Bordeaux, 1884), a reprint of a speech he made in the Chamber of Deputies in January, 1884. Only by defusing worker anger, he argued, could the state "pacify spirits . . . in the country of violence, revolutions, and bloody reactions" (p. 15). For Bourgeois' views, see Theodore Zeldin, *Politics and Anger* (Oxford, 1979), 290–307, Vol. II of Zeldin, *France, 1848–1945.*

93. Michael B. Miller, *The Bon Marché: Bourgeois Culture and the Department Store, 1869–1920* (London, 1981), 33–34, 206–208.

94. See Heinz Gerhard Haupt, "The Petite Bourgeoisie in France, 1850–1914," in *Shopkeepers and Master Artisans in Nineteenth-Century Europe,* ed. Geoffrey Crossick and Heinz Gerhard Haupt (London, 1984), 95–119.

cabinet-maker or a printer, the small craftsman liked to be a revolutionary. He had been an internationalist, a communard, and he was tempted by anarchism, but as a small independent producer he did not like the idea of collectivism; without ever being familiar with them, he hit upon the libertarian intuitions of Proudhon." According to this account, the small producer vacillated between several fixed political constellations: anarchism, Radicalism, the "independents," "French socialism," and a "certain degree of nationalism."[95] Grave and Kropotkin, Proudhon, Barrès, Clemenceau, and General Boulanger—these formed the outer perimeter for the political aspirations of the small craftsman.

Anarchism was firmly rooted in precisely this milieu. At the anarchist trial of 1883 in Lyon, most of the 64 condemned by the court owned or were employed by small shops; of 152 anarchists cited in Lyon's police registers in 1894, artisans accounted for 55 percent.[96] A more detailed study of an anarchist circle in Toulouse from 1880 to 1900 reveals that the members were essentially "artisans in sedentary trades, such as the cobbler's or hatmaker's, as well as workers employed in small workshops of the same type." Almost all were from trades that required "great professional competence and often a lengthy apprenticeship."[97]

Boulanger, whose calls for order and justice seemed to promise a cementing of the status quo, offered the artisan class the hope of preventing further social dislocation. It is more difficult to see what hope a movement whose very nomenclature appeared to envisage the obliteration of organized society offered. Local anarchist circles routinely bore such bloodthirsty names as Les Insurgés, La Panthère, Le Revolver à la Main, Les Terribles, La Guerre Sociale, L'Affamé; the Toulouse circle dubbed itself *Les Vengeurs*. But behind the rhetoric, anarchism—and most especially anarchocommunism—promised not further upheaval but an amelioration of unrest, the soothing of discontent, and the painless achievement of a radiant future.

Karl Marx made the same point in 1846 in his attack on Pierre

---

95. Mayeur and Rébérioux, *The Third Republic,* 53. See also Haupt, "The Petite Bourgeoisie," 108. Haupt notes that from the 1840s, tailors, shoemakers, and others were forced to work for larger "merchant capitalists" and that from around 1880 small shopkeepers had to do so as well. By the late 1880s, crises had "violently shaken the petite bourgeoisie's traditional allegiance to republicanism and set them off in search of a new political home."

96. Alain Pessin, *La Rêverie anarchiste* (Paris, 1982), 45–46.

97. *Le Mouvement anarchiste à Toulouse à la fin du XIXe siècle,* without recorded editor (Paris, 1971), 98–99. Pessin summarizes the findings briefly in *La Rêverie,* 46.

Joseph Proudhon, the founder of French anarchism. Marx accused Proudhon of thinking that every economic category could be split into a good side and a bad, with the task simply that of preserving the good while eliminating the bad. Marx held that in practice such an idea was a blind alley: by attempting to explain the "successive appearance of social relations," Proudhon denied in fact that anything could appear at all. For Marx, Proudhon's real goal was not so much to advance history as to stop it dead in its tracks, not to overcome and replace existing social and economic systems but to patch them up. He asked, "If, during the epoch of the formation of feudalism, the economists, enthusiastic over the knightly virtues, the beautiful harmony between rights and duties, the patriarchal life of the towns, the prosperous conditions of domestic industry in the countryside, . . . had set themselves the problem of eliminating everything that cast a shadow on the picture—serfdom, privileges, anarchy—what would have happened?" It would have meant, Marx concluded, that the entire modern world—with its vastly greater economic and social possibilities— would have been stillborn.[98] In 1848, Marx and Engels described Proudhon's anarchism as "reactionary and Utopian." They looked upon it as a movement aspiring "either to restoring the old means of production and of exchange, and with them the old society, or to cramping the modern means of production . . . within the framework of old property relations."[99]

The anarchocommunism of Kropotkin, Grave, and Reclus explicitly abandoned Proudhon's defense of small-scale private ownership as the basis of society, though it is sometimes unclear how deeply rooted that change was within French anarchist circles. Grave himself, at the Procès des Trente, in 1894, told the court that his idea of communism was that of Proudhon, whom he acknowledged as his "doctrinal inspiration."[100] French anarchism had, in any case, held on to its goal of reconciling and reordering society by nurturing the good in the present while shucking off the dross. French anarchocommunist critiques of society occasionally have some of the flavor of an accountant's ledger, with the

98. Karl Marx, *The Poverty of Philosophy* (New York, 1963), 116–22. See also Paul Thomas, *Karl Marx and the Anarchists* (London, 1980), 214–23. According to Thomas, Proudhon understood a contradiction as an "opposition inherent in *some* of the forms of constituting society, *which will tear it apart unless we understand them*" (p. 215; my emphasis).

99. Karl Marx and Friedrich Engels, "The Manifesto of the Communist Party," in *Birth of the Communist Manifesto,* ed. Dirk J. Struik (New York, 1971), 115–16.

100. Bataille, *Causes criminelles,* 202.

positive marked off on one side and the negative on the other.[101]

That aspect of anarchocommunism also came across in its unstinting praise for the Middle Ages. Kropotkin and Grave never went so far as the German anarchist Gustav Landauer—for whom civilization was one uninterrupted decline since a medieval golden age—but they consistently cited the Middle Ages as the closest in spirit to the world to come. Much of the attraction of the English socialist William Morris and his arts-and-crafts movement for French anarchists lay in his love, too, for a mythified medieval past.[102]

In the disparate movements that appealed to French petty producers and small owners, the world *integral* crops up again and again: Integral Nationalism (with its own mythology of a heroic, medieval past to be rewon); the even more emphatically pseudo-medieval Integral Catholicism; the Integral Socialism of Benoît Malon and the other Independents; the integralism of anarchocommunism. All claimed to be global theories, not only describing but integrating and organizing knowledge and practice at every level, and bringing together everything from the nature of the cosmos to the bases of everyday life. Malon, a former anarchist, affirmed that his Integral Socialism was the "synthetic result of all the progressive activities of contemporary humanity." Still less modestly, Kropotkin asserted that anarchocommunism sought to become "*the* philosophical thought of the civilized world."[103] Each theory attempted to reintegrate not only the myriad severed strands of human thought but even fragmented humanity itself. Malon wrote that one would seek in vain through the "individualistic desert of bourgeois society" for a "general conception of the world and the common principles of individual and social morals."[104] Kropotkin insisted that the goal of a renewed sense of community could come only through a restoration of social harmony. "There is no more communion of ideas," he observed. "The town is a chance agglomeration of people who do not know one another, who have no common interest, save that of enriching themselves at the expense of one another. The fatherland does not ex-

101. See, for example, Elisée Reclus, "The Progress of Mankind," *Contemporary Review,* LXX (1896), 761–83.

102. See Woodcock, *Anarchism,* 23–24.

103. Eugène Fournière, "Le Socialisme intégral," *Revue socialiste,* XII (1890), 258; *Les Temps nouveaux: Conférence faite à Londres* (Paris, 1894), 7.

104. Benoît Malon, "La Civilisation bourgeoise et ses aboutissants," *Revue socialiste,* XI (1889), 54.

ist." He concluded that only when "cities, territories, nations or groups of nations, will have renewed their harmonious life, will art be able to draw its inspiration from ideals held in common, . . . deriving their power of execution from the same vital source, and gloriously marching all together towards the future."[105]

Anarchocommunism in particular took up the burden of reversing the drive under capitalism toward specialization and fragmentation in what had been skilled crafts and labor. The concern was that skilled labor was being replaced by monotonous, unskilled toil in which the worker no longer had time for anything but a single task, hour upon hour. Craftwork had been a form of art, rewarding and enriching both those who made it and those for whom it was produced; industrial labor, on the other hand, was enervating and dehumanizing. In 1899, Kropotkin, in *Fields, Factories, and Workshops,* wrote, "Skilled artisanship is being swept away as a survival of the past, condemned to disappear. For the artisan who formerly found aesthetic enjoyment in the work of his hands is substituted the human slave of an iron slave." Human beings were thereby becoming "mere servants to some machine . . . ; mere flesh and blood parts of some immense machinery, having no idea how and why the machinery performs its rhythmical movements." In place of division and specialization of labor, Kropotkin called for a new integration, "a society of integrated labor; a society where each individual is a producer of both manual and intellectual work; where each able-bodied human being is a worker, and where each worker works both in the field and in the industrial workshop." In that society, the ability of each person to perform a variety of tasks was to be promoted by the creation of decentralized communes, each with its own fields, small factories, ateliers, and schools.[106]

Anarchocommunism allotted a central role to the forms of craft and artisanal small production that were being steadily eroded by

---

105. Peter Kropotkin, *Fields, Factories, and Workshops* (1899; London, 1974), 23–29. See Augustin Hamon and Georges Bachot, *L'Agonie d'une société: Histoire d'aujord'hui* (Paris, 1889), 147. Myrna Breitbart appraises Kropotkin's views in "Impressions of an Anarchist Landscape," *Antipode,* VII (1975), 44–49. Kropotkin's views echo uncannily those of the Ligue Syndicale pour la Défense des Interêts du Travail, de l'Industrie, et du Commerce, an association of small shopkeepers and people from the petty trades founded by supporters of the Radical party, with some Boulangists, in 1888. See Miller, *The Bon Marché,* 209–12; and Philip Nord, "The Small Shopkeepers' Movement and Politics in France," in *Shopkeepers and Master Artisans,* ed. Crossick and Haupt, 175–94.

106. Kropotkin, *Fields, Factories, and Workshops,* 153–58.

French industrialization. It built upon the pride small owners and skilled artisans felt in their crafts; it promised that the coming golden age would be artisanal in character. In that world, petty production would no longer be threatened by new technologies but would rather be enhanced by them. It reassured the small producers that the erosion of power and prestige they had suffered would be only temporary. Kropotkin conceded that "petty trades" were beset by recurrent crises and frequent ruin of both employers and employees. The crises, however, had proved unable to eliminate the petty trades altogether—even in industry: "Far from showing a tendency to disappear, [small trades and industries] show . . . a tendency towards making a further development." Municipal ownership of electrical plants, for example, was enabling small shops to electrify and modernize. Given that petty production was marked by conditions "superior in every respect, material and moral, to the condition of factory hands," Kropotkin saw the future of social production not in giant urban or suburban factories but in small, decentralized industries and trades dotted across the countryside.[107]

Beneath the revolutionary rhetoric—in fact, beneath the evolutionary analogies—anarchocommunism in France enshrined a concept of progress with strong affinities to stasis. For Kropotkin, social evolution produced not better systems, merely more complicated ones; the ideals of mutual aid and libertarian communism were immanent in humanity, as powerful and real at the dawn of history as in the 1890s. Statism, religion, and capitalism were all mere overlays, incrustations that hid but did not change the reality of human potential. They had distorted human values but could not destroy them; the proof lay, it was argued, in the very survival of peasant communes and small shops.

The anarchism of Kropotkin and Grave spoke directly to the fears and needs of a declining, dispirited, and sometimes desperate middle stratum in French society. The small, independent producers were a residual tier, increasingly compressed by a newer bourgeoisie; tied to the market, they were also its victims. Their "revolutionism" was in large part an avowal of a mythologized past against the reality of a perilous present.[108]

Joseph Déjacque's anarchist utopia *L'Humanisphère*, issued in 1858–1859 and republished by Grave in 1899, seemed to fuse lib-

107. *Ibid.*, 125–126.
108. Mayeur and Rébérioux, *The Third Republic*, 53.

eral humanism with the conservatism of Edmund Burke, anchoring human existence at once in classless solidarity and human tradition. "Man is no longer alone, isolated, feeble," Déjacque wrote, "he is a race; he thinks and he acts, and he participates by thought and by act in everything that thinks and acts in other men. . . . Solidarity reveals itself to him. His life is enlarged by this; he no longer lives only as an individual, no longer solely in the present generation, but in the generations that precede him, as in those which follow."[109] In such a vision, revolution never meant the new but hung on the ability to retain the old: "Revolutions are conservations. Revolutionize yourself, therefore, in order to conserve yourself."[110]

Of the several competing social and political options that appealed to the disaffected in the name of social peace and harmony, such as Bourgeois' *solidarisme,* Alfred Naquet's *socialisme libéral,* and Barrès' *socialisme nationaliste,* each provided a somewhat different mix of revolutionary verbiage, individualism, and social solidarity. Ultimately, many artisans found a home within the new socialist party (SFIO), many master artisans and small merchants affiliated with the Parti Radical, and many petty merchants drifted into the nationalist far right. Radicalism in particular claimed to speak for the "common citizen," to be the champion of the "petty bourgeois, small employers, small tradesmen, small landowners, small civil servants," the buffer between the haute bourgeoisie and the workers.[111] In Radicalism, the anarchist call for individual freedom became an attenuated demand for "free choice," the anarchist hostility to the state devolved into the Radical call for decentralization, the anarchist hope for a transcendence of class in favor of the free man and woman was translated into the cheery assurance that, with the proper educational climate, everyone would find a proper niche in society.

In the 1890s, however, the Radicals were still far from the ramshackle mass party they would become in the twentieth century—though they were no longer just the small coterie of white-collar

109. Joseph Déjacque, *L'Humanisphère* (Brussels, 1899), 23. In keeping with Grave's emphasis on peaceful change, the book was censored to eliminate sections advocating violence. See Woodcock, *Anarchism,* 233.

110. Déjacque, *L'Humanisphere,* 85. For ambiguities in the anarchist view of progress, see Woodcock, *Anarchism,* 23–25.

111. Zeldin, *Politics and Anger,* 353; see also pp. 319–60. The rightward drift of many small shopkeepers past Radicalism to the nationalist right is the focus of Nord in "The Small Shopkeepers' Movement."

professions in the Chamber of Deputies that they had been in the 1880s. In an atmosphere of social crisis and upheaval, Radicalism did not yet seem a credible alternative among those whom recurrent crises had left unsettled and desperate. Some lines in Grave's *La Révolte* transcended generic anarchist disgust to capture the prevailing mood in the wake of the Panama Canal Company scandals: "Thieves in government, thieves in the presidency, thieves in the Senate, thieves in the Chamber, thieves in the palace of injustice . . . The fleet, the army, the administration. Thieves in the boudoirs, thieves in the commissions, thieves in the press, thieves everywhere!" From England, Kropotkin's organ, *Freedom,* was issuing warnings that no party could pose any longer as savior; all were enmeshed in the scandals.[112] Antiparliamentary solutions seemed the order of the day: in the 1893 elections, only some 50 percent of the eligible voters bothered to participate.[113] For significant sections of the French populace, for whom socialism was still unthinkable and the republican parties no longer tenable, anarchism seemed a safe haven—an ideological solid ground on which they could weather the turmoils of the day.

Artists and the Social Crisis

To a large degree, artists shared in the mood of crisis; many shared as well the abhorrence of the reigning social and political order. In 1889, the novelist and critic Joris Karl Huysmans wrote that repugnance toward the failures of the present had led artists into a form of retrograde revolt: "Exceptional beings retrace their steps down the centuries and, disgusted by the promiscuities they must bear, throw themselves into the abyss of bygone ages, into the tumultuous spaces of nightmares and dreams." The syndicalist theoretician Edouard Berth advanced a similar interpretation, with a focus on arts patronage: artists, he held, were dependent materially upon a bourgeoisie in whom they reposed no trust; lacking faith in the workers as well, they "no longer know which social reality to attach to their dreams; they turn with desperate envy to

112. "Le Régime parlementaire," *La Révolte,* VI (December 4–10, 1892), 1; "What Next?" *Freedom,* VII (March, 1893), 9.

113. Jacques Bainville, *The French Republic, 1870–1935* (London, 1940), 122–24; Barrows, *Distorting Mirrors,* 13–14. On the antiparliamentary mood of the petite bourgeoisie, see Patrick Dumont, *Etude de mentalité de la petite bourgeoisie vue à travers les contes quotidiennes de journal, 1894–1895* (Paris, 1895), 55–56.

happy centuries, where art had a public capable of understanding and sustaining it."[114]

Certainly, there were artists who were perfectly secure and comfortable in their support for the reigning order in society and the arts.[115] But a younger generation of artists—and older artists such as Pissarro—found that order contemptible and, perhaps worse, undependable. Not a few saw their artistic affiliations in terms of their politics: the Pont Aven painter Maurice Denis, a founding member of the protofascist Action Française, was merely blunter than most when he insisted that an artist must choose between total social revolution—which he tied to syndicalism—and total reaction, in the form of corporatist monarchism.[116]

It is common to think of professional artists and writers as middle-class professionals.[117] But they meet the most basic criteria for being considered artisans: they are independent producers of a specific commodity, owning their own tools, contracting individually for commissions or producing on speculation, and being paid for piecework. The growth of academies that began in the seventeenth century had partly masked the artisanal character of artistic production for a relative handful of elite artists, who had deliberately repressed such remnants of feudal craft traditions as the Guild of Saint Luke.[118] In the nineteenth century, William

114. Joris Karl Huysmans, *Certains* (Paris, 1929), 20, Vol. X of Huysmans, *Oeuvres complètes;* Edouard Berth, *Dialogues socialistes* (Paris, 1901). See Sebastien Faure, *La Douleur universelle: Philosophie libertaire* (Paris, 1895), 55–56.

115. Daniel M. Fox calls the artists of the era "businessmen-idealists." He agrees that some were fascinated by bohemia but argues that "most artists knew they produced a commodity . . . hard to market and that they engaged in activities demanding worldly abilities." He adds, "They were often as conscious of supply and demand as middling farmers or manufacturers." His list of prosperous and successful artists would be more convincing if he did not include Théodore Rousseau among artists who "appeared regularly" in the Salon between 1830 and 1848. See Fox's "Artists in the Modern State: The Nineteenth-Century Background," *Journal of Aesthetics and Art Criticism,* XXII (1963), 135–48. Albert Boime offers a similarly benign reading of the relation between art and the market in "Entrepreneurial Patronage in Nineteenth-Century France," in *Enterprise and Entrepreneurs in Nineteenth- and Twentieth-Century France,* ed. Edward C. Carter II, Robert Forster, and Joseph N. Moody (Baltimore, 1976), esp. 184–91. See also I. L. Zupnick, "The Social Conflict of the Impressionists," *College Art Journal,* XIX (1959–60), 146–53.

116. Maurice Denis, "De Gauguin et de van Gogh au classicisme," in *Théorie, 1890–1910, du symbolisme et de Gauguin, vers un nouvel ordre classique* (4th ed.; Paris, 1920), 267.

117. See Harrison White and Cynthia White, *Canvases and Careers: Institutional Changes in the French Painting World* (New York, 1965), 130: "A painter is a learned professional—and a learned professional is middle class."

118. Thomas Crow, *Painters and Public Life in Eighteenth-Century Paris* (New Haven, 1985), 1–22.

Morris—and in a different context, Gustave Courbet—had challenged the assumptions of an upper-class art by invoking the craft traditions of the Middle Ages; Courbet's use of the terms *maître* and *atelier* was not random or accidental but stemmed directly from his desire to assert a powerful link between his own art and popular traditions.[119] With the erosion, disestablishment, and finally the fragmentation of the French Salon (1880–1906), and with the concurrent passage of the private dealer system from being a fringe phenomenon concerned largely with art supplies to occupying the center of the Parisian art world, artists once again had to rethink their relation to an uncertain, shifting, and elusive market.

The problem extended beyond the plastic arts. Writers found, for example, that traditional "quality" newspapers and journals were increasingly crowded out by the mass circulation, popular press. The *Petit Journal,* founded in 1863, set the pattern for the new papers: mass-oriented, avowedly apolitical but actually quite right-wing, distributed not by mail but by twelve hundred paid vendors, it set out unashamedly to capture every popular prejudice. Writers for the paper, its publisher said, had to "be bold enough to appear stupid." By 1880, the *Petit Journal* had a circulation of nearly 600,000—more than four times its nearest competitor's.[120] Théodore Duret complained to Camille Pissarro that commerce had degraded writing; even Zola was collaborating with Busnach to earn a few sous. Duret foresaw no improvement: "I am retiring, I will never write anywhere. The papers have an atrocious fear of everything that is not banal, stupid." He vowed to retire to Cognac.[121]

Novelists faced a similar situation, created especially by the potboilers serialized in the mass press. By 1852, popular novels, along with how-to books and almanacs, dominated the market. Lurid detective stories vied with gothic horror tales and accounts of heroic outlaws for public esteem. "Serious" novelists commanded

---

119. A basic source for this aspect of Courbet's work remains Meyer Schapiro's "Courbet and Popular Imagery: An Essay on Realism and Naïveté," *Journal of the Warbourg and Courtauld Institutes,* IV (1941), 164–91. See also T. J. Clark, *Image of the People: Gustave Courbet and the 1848 Revolution* (2nd ed.; London, 1982), esp. 155–61. Anarchist writers frequently equated artists with craftworkers. See, for example, Charles Albert, "Art et Société," *Les Temps nouveaux,* I (November 23–29, 1895), 1–2.

120. Theodore Zeldin, *Taste and Corruption* (Oxford, 1980), 178–79, Vol. IV of Zeldin, *France, 1848–1945.*

121. Camille Pissarro, *Lettres à son fils Lucien,* ed. John Rewald (Paris, 1947), 144.

prestige but precious little remuneration. Flaubert received only four hundred francs for *Madame Bovary;* by the 1880s, most novels were earning their author only four or five hundred francs.[122]

Visual artists, however, were confronted most directly by the drastically altered commercial climate. The newly dominant private dealer system has been described—most thoroughly by Harrison White and Cynthia White—as more flexible and decentralized than that of the state-supported Salon, and as capable of managing careers rather than having to focus exclusively on individual canvases. They document the change in considerable detail and point to convincing advantages the new system possessed.[123] The experimental artists of the era—the self-described avant-garde—could scarcely have come into their own without private dealers able to identify and target specific audiences and buyers.[124]

The private dealer system incurred social costs, however, that ran to a deeper source than the system's growing pains. Private dealers were indeed concerned with careers more than canvases, but in practice their primary concern, after all, was their own careers, not those of the artists they represented. Journals and letters testify to the grievances many artists felt against those Signac called "ces sots de marchands."[125]

The complex and contradictory relationship between even a prominent and relatively successful artist and a major dealer is evident in the letters of Camille Pissarro. Pissarro often came to the defense of the dealer Paul Durand-Ruel, standing by him as an

122. Zeldin, *Taste and Corruption,* 23–33. Zeldin adds that a reasonably successful "serious" author could expect to earn about ten thousand francs a year.

123. White and White, *Canvases and Careers,* esp. 94–98. Since 1965, this judgment has become even more positive. See Jerrold Siegel, *Bohemian Paris: Culture, Politics, and the Boundaries of Bourgeois Life, 1830–1930* (New York, 1986), 306–307. See also Boime, "Entrepreneurial Patronage," 137–207. For a more detailed and less benign verdict, see Nicholas Green, "Dealing in Temperaments: Economic Transformation of the Artistic Field During the Second Half of the Nineteenth Century," *Art History,* X (1987), 59–78; and Nicholas Green, "Circuits of Production, Circuits of Consumption: The Case of Mid-Nineteenth-Century French Art Dealing," *Art History,* XII (1989), 29–34.

124. On the conversion of the concept of the avant-garde into a purely aesthetic one from one referring to a struggle to transform society, see Peter Bürger, *Theory of the Avant-Garde,* trans. Michael Shaw (Minneapolis, 1984). See also Linda Nochlin, "The Invention of the Avant-Garde," in *Avant-Garde Art,* ed. John Ashberry and Thomas B. Hess (London, 1967), 3–24; and Nicos Hadjinicolaou, "On the Ideology of Avant-Gardism," *Praxis,* VI (1982), 39–70.

125. Paul Signac to Camille Pissarro, December, 1893, in Camille Pissarro's *Lettres à son fils Lucien,* 320.

honest man doing his best for those whose work he sold.[126] More often, however, his letters betray a deep resentment of the need to depend so heavily on the mercantile maneuverings of a single person. Pissarro sometimes lurched between praise and abuse in the same letter. He began a note to Lucien Pissarro with an attack on Durand for holding paintings off the market, charging the dealer with hoarding them for his children to sell later. Though Durand might appear angelic, Pissarro wrote, he was guided only by the calculations of a jackal. The artist wrote of his wish that there could be more enlightened dealers, of the caliber of the late Théo van Gogh: "Here is the man we must find. But such men cannot be ordered up." Pissarro thought that perhaps only a later generation, "freed from religious, mystical, mysterious ideas, returning to more modern ideas, could have the qualities necessary to admire this road."[127] What is striking here is the way anarchist utopianism collides with the immediate hope of an enlightened patron. The sense of desperation is constant, but Pissarro's answer oscillates from the hope of a liberated future to the purely individualist aspiration for someone—anyone—to admire and buy his work.

An uncomfortable juxtaposition of social revolution and private patronage has, to be sure, a venerable tradition in French anarchism: Courbet's vaunted revolutionary independence was kept afloat by the francs of Alfred Bruyas, a wealthy, middle-aged, and rather conservative art collector. Nor is it at all odd for artists to be concerned about their source of income. But artists whose work placed them outside the traditional, if decaying, network of state and church commissions were especially dependent on the private dealers and their clientele. The result was often a mixture of truculence and despair, defiance and self-pity. Attempts to bypass the *sots de marchands,* through group shows and artists' cooperatives, consistently foundered, reinforcing the dependence they were intended to eliminate. In a study of Camille Pissarro, Michel Melot points out that "what is usually called an avant-garde in art really exists only in a liberal economy." A competitive market system pits various artists against one another, with the victor retro-

---

126. Camille Pissarro to Lucien Pissarro, December 30, 1886, in Camille Pissarro's *Correspondance,* II, 93.

127. Camille Pissarro to Lucien Pissarro, April 13, 1891, in Camille Pissarro's *Correspondance,* III, 61–63.

actively recognized as belonging to the avant-garde. Melot writes, "The artist must produce unique objects and endlessly renew them. He must do so within the framework of a mode of production that remains intangible: his is the exuberant freedom of a moth circling a flame. The avant-garde endlessly runs up against the limits of the economic and social system. In a society that claims to be free, limits are not placed on the form of the product but its function. The avant-garde, with all its insecurity and risk-taking, consists of volunteers to act out freedom, with all its ambiguities."[128]

Dependence on the pressures of a commercial market predated, of course, the dominance of the major private dealers. Charles Blanc declared in 1872 that the Salon was intended to be a means of social uplift, not an art market: "An exposition opened by the state ought not to have as its purpose the creation of a commercial outlet for artists." Nonetheless, in a market economy, it could scarcely avoid such a role; in 1892, in a review of Pissarro's work, Mirbeau called the Salon the Bon Marché of art and praised Durand's private gallery as a discreet salon in which the viewer could revel in the thoughts of the works' creator, "his enthusiasm, his transformations, his progressive conquests over the material realm."[129] Ironically, it was the private galleries that were able in practice to borrow effectively, if selectively, from the techniques of the Bon Marché to market art in a burgeoning consumer society. Remy Saisselin has argued persuasively that the department stores so effectively blurred the distinction between a consumer object and an objet d'art that bourgeois art lovers came increasingly to see the art in museums simply as commodities out of their immediate price range.[130] The galleries of Durand-Ruel or Alfred Petit served as the ideal mediator between the mass-produced goods of the Bon Marché and the art in the Louvre.

Pressures on artists to sell were constant. The dealers were mer-

128. Michel Melot, "Camille Pissarro in 1880: An Anarchistic Artist in Bourgeois Society," trans. Alan Wallach and Carol Duncan, *Marxist Perspectives,* II (Winter, 1979–80), 35. See Robert L. Herbert, "Impressionism, Originality, and Laissez-Faire," *Radical History Review,* XXXVIII (1987), 7–15.

129. Robert Allen Jay, "Art and Nationalism in France, 1870–1914" (Ph.D. dissertation, University of Minnesota, 1979), 5; Octave Mirbeau, "Camille Pissarro," *Le Figaro,* February 1, 1892, reprinted in Mirbeau's *Des artistes: Peintres et Sculpteurs* (1922–24; Paris, 1986), 145–46. See Martha Ward, "Impressionist Installations and Private Exhibitions," *Art Bulletin,* LXXIII (1991), 599–622.

130. Remy G. Saisselin, *Bricobracomania: The Bourgeois and the Bibelot* (London, 1985), 41.

chants, not altruists, and art that failed to sell consistently would lose its berth in their shops. The result was that the pressure on artists to conform to certain molds and styles was reminiscent of the old Salon system—though the pressure had become economic rather than aesthetic or ideological and the artist typically had a choice among the styles and models that sold well. The dealers did not develop a rigid hierarchy of genres or other classifications for the works they handled. But it would have been of little import to artists whether their works were rejected by a Salon jury for deviating from classical norms or by a dealer for deviating from his notions of what would sell. At worst, the artist simply had more places to go to be rejected. New limits were always being drawn: Durand-Ruel, champion of the Impressionists, was far less taken with their successors. In 1890, Durand's son explained why his father had declined to mount even a posthumous show of Vincent van Gogh: he had to be very careful because the "public always held him responsible whenever some people guffawed."[131]

Harrison White and Cynthia White stress that the painter nonetheless had more options under the new system, because "dealer-patrons were in competition with one another and each critic was eager to be spokesman for his own artistic movement."[132] Many of the Impressionists became quite skillful at playing off dealers against one another, especially Durand-Ruel against Petit. But for a younger painter—and even for many an older one—the benefits the Whites perceive would scarcely have been evident. Van Gogh wrote to a friend in 1887, "Trade is slow here. The great dealers sell Millet, Delacroix, Corot, Daubigny, Dupré and a few other masters at exorbitant prices. They do little or nothing for young artists. The second-class dealers sell those, but at very low prices."[133]

Artists were often trapped between their aims and their economic needs. A vocal hostility to the bourgeoisie was commonplace. In a letter to the restaurateur Eugène Murer, Camille Pissarro in 1884 wrote, "[I] am quite convinced, thinking of Paris, that we are once more like lepers, like beggars, no? It is impossible that an art that disrupts so many old convictions would win approval . . . no, the bourgeois . . . are bourgeois from their toe-

131. John Rewald, *Post-Impressionism from van Gogh to Gauguin* (3rd ed.; New York, 1978), 383.

132. White and White, *Canvases and Careers*, 98–102.

133. Rewald, *Post-Impressionism*, 17.

nails to the hair on their heads." In a letter to Lucien Pissarro, he was even more emphatic, developing the image of a bourgeoisie in a state of total decay. "Look at all the bourgeoisie," he exclaimed. "See how stupid the true bourgeois have become, see how they sink step by step—in a word, they are losing the idea of the beautiful, they are wrong about everything." He lamented, "Where there should be praise, they shout it down, they disapprove. Where they should turn away from the dreariness of their alcoves, they swoon or jump for joy!" In a shift of metaphor, his invective drew on the colonialist stereotype of the "savage" that even progressive circles still accepted: the bourgeoisie were "Zulus with straw-yellow gloves, top hats and magpie tails." Finally, he had the artist become Sisyphus, the bourgeoisie the massive stone Sisyphus has to roll: "They are the rock that falls, rolls, that we must constantly push back so we will not be crushed."[134]

Occasionally, though, there is also a recognition in such exchanges that the artist has some connection—however tenuous or grudging—in life-style (desired or real) with the detested bourgeois. Pissarro touched on the relationship delicately in another letter to Lucien: "What a joke! A nice business, being bourgeois . . . without a penny." But he immediately rejected that self-description in favor of another. "The bourgeois," he pointed out, "is inconceivable without unearned income." Rather, the artist is a worker: "All who work with their hands or brains, who create, *when they depend upon intermediaries,* become proletarians! . . . with or without overalls."[135] Thus, Pissarro took the class of the artist to be established by the artist's relationship with an intermediary—the dealer. He sidestepped the question of patronage, of the market and intended audience of the art itself.

Pissarro depicted the marketing of art as an essential, if rather dismal, obligation. He dismissed his wife's complaints about the difficulties of raising a large family on an erratic income, asking rhetorically, "Does Mama believe that you take care of your affairs by beating your own drum? Does she believe that it amuses me to run in the snow, in the slush, from morning till night, without a penny in my pocket?" In another letter, he evinced his distrust of those—notably Gauguin—who had entered too wholeheartedly

134. Camille Pissarro to Eugène Murer, August 8, 1884, in Camille Pissarro's *Correspondance,* I, 310–11; Camille Pissarro to Lucien Pissarro, December 28, 1883, in Camille Pissarro's *Correspondance,* I, 267.

135. Camille Pissarro to Lucien Pissarro, June 5, 1887, in Camille Pissarro's *Correspondance,* II, 183.

into the commercial side of the art world: "Gauguin worries me a lot; he, too, is terribly commercial, at least in his preoccupations." Pissarro blamed that on Gauguin's family background of wealth, and struggled to reach his own truce with the mercantile aspects of art: "Not that I think one mustn't try to sell, but I think it is wasted time to think only of that; you lose sight of your art, you exaggerate your worth." Signac wrote in his private journal that "proud and innovative artists do not have the immediate success of the cowardly artists who follow fashions."[136]

The artists of the time devised several schemes to combat the dealer system, from Alfred Meyer's abortive Société de l'Union, of 1874, to van Gogh's envisioned artist's commune in southern France, in the 1880s. Essentially, these were to be artists' cooperatives, not unlike those other craftworkers contrived in the same period. The Impressionist nucleus around Monet and Pissarro responded enthusiastically to Paul Alexis' call for such an "association" in 1874; Pissarro's first draft of a charter for the Impressionists was copied directly from the constitution of a Parisian craft association, the bakers' union.[137] All these mechanisms were to let artists address the art-buying public directly, bypassing the Salon—by the 1880s, the Salons—as well as the private dealers.

The Neo-Impressionist "boutique" in the rue Laffitte, which opened in December, 1893, was one of the most elaborate of the projects. As Signac described the shop, it was intended to be an anarchist enterprise: for a suggested fee of one franc per year, participants would have a rotating opportunity to exhibit inside and be featured in the shop window. Out of the sale price of any work, 20 percent would go toward rent and other expenses; the works were to be promoted through a monthly bulletin or catalog the press and prospective customers would receive. "We would be proud," Signac wrote Pissarro, "to have among us your precious canvases which those fools, the dealers, didn't want!"[138]

---

136. Camille Pissarro to Lucien Pissarro, October 31, 1883, in Camille Pissarro's *Correspondance*, I, 245; Rewald, ed., "Extraits du journal inédit de Paul Signac," 106–107.

137. For the various drafts of the charter, see John Rewald, *Histoire de l'impressionnisme* (Paris, 1955), 358–64.

138. Paul Signac to Camille Pissarro, in Camille Pissarro's *Lettres à son fils Lucien*, 320. Signac's words were not gracious when he heard the first rumors that Antoine de La Rochefoucauld, "sponsor" of the boutique, was about to shut it down: "I knew very well that the enthusiasm of this neophyte would be quenched by the urine of the first passerby who pissed in front of our shop! . . . This is the only compensation I claim: not to have banal and easy success" (Rewald, ed., "Extraits du journal inédit de Paul Signac," 106–107).

Much like other comparable alliances—workers' savings banks, housing cooperatives—the artists' attempts to bypass the dealers did not directly challenge the market system but rather aimed at winning a niche in that system while simultaneously planting the seeds of a more satisfactory social order. In a letter to Théo van Rysselberghe, Signac wrote that the Neo boutique was already beginning to play a transformative role: "It sings already the good dynamogenic song of gaiety, of light, of strength, of health, . . . of triumph."[139] But inevitably underfinanced, the cooperatives were dwarfed by their competition and as a rule lacked access to the markets and the economies of scale of their well-financed and entrenched rivals.

The artists' cooperatives faced major problems beyond those of the other alliances. The very commercialism artists deplored in the private dealers had an inherent advantage from an economic point of view: it carried with it a sensitivity to the market and an unsentimental attitude toward changing moods—a willingness to back what sold and desert what did not. The integrity upon which Signac and Pissarro prided themselves could only make the marketing of their work more difficult in a competitive market. It is a safe assumption, too, that for many wealthy collectors an anarchist artists' cooperative was not the first place to look for new acquisitions.

Nor for the most part did even radical artists yet seek a different form of patronage in a new class. Studies of patronage conducted during this period have shed light on the mechanics of art production. But attention exclusively to which specific buyer bought which artist or which work can sometimes obscure the impact of the system as a whole. The Belgian socialist Emile Vandervelde, who attempted a survey of the entire system, argued that, of necessity, art and artists had constantly orbited around that segment of *la classe riche* which found the arts interesting. Those who made art for a living had to conform to bourgeois prejudices and tastes or face ruin; artists with the means to survive without the approbation of buyers were themselves the products of a bourgeois upbringing, with its own cumulative impact on their interests, tastes, and views. Although Vandervelde was conscious that not all art comformed completely with his schema, he concluded that so long as the workers lacked sufficient social and economic weight to let them constitute a pole of attraction themselves, the subjec-

139. Guy Pogu, *Théo van Rysselberghe: Sa vie* (Paris, 1963), 18.

tion of the worker meant in practice the domination of artistic and intellectual life as well.[140]

There were few cases in Vandervelde's day of dealers or patrons openly dictating or censoring what artists produced, but that was because overt demands were seldom necessary. The impression that comments by the artists give is rather of a continuing pressure to produce what would find favor. A number of Lucien Pissarro's letters to his father in the mid- to late 1890s were shadowed by the specter of buyers who no longer believed in the precepts or practices of Impressionism. Thus, in September, 1896, he wrote of his worry that art buyers, in England at least, were beginning to favor a Neo-Catholic art that would take support away from him; he began to defend Pre-Raphaelite art to his father, as part of his turn toward the Catholic Revival art of Charles Ricketts and the so-called Vale group in England.[141]

Art was for the rich—at least until times changed. For the political right, art was necessarily for a small elite with the taste, leisure, and "breeding" to appreciate it. Artists of the left—including the Neo-Impressionists—often looked to the workers, but always the workers of the future, of the *âge d'or* to come. Henri Edmond Cross wrote that his art was produced for the "moral and physical beauty of humanity" in a utopian future when "the masks Daumier made will have completely disappeared."[142] Signac, in notes apparently made for addressing a working-class audience, wrote, "When the society we dream of exists, when the worker, freed from the exploiters who brutalize him, has the time to think and instruct himself, he will appreciate all the diverse qualities of the work of art."[143]

But until a liberated future arrived, Neo-Impressionists and their colleagues saw no alternative to the existing patronage systems. Lucien Pissarro reacted scornfully to a call in Grave's *Les Temps nouveaux* for an art aimed at workers. He demanded to know just how that would be possible. "Produce for the masses,

140. Emile Vandervelde, "L'Art en régime bourgeois," in *Essais socialistes* (Paris, 1906), 201–206. For a comparable anarchist critique, see Jean Grave, *La Société future* (Paris, 1895), 362–68. Grave, however, saw no possible palliations before the triumph of anarchism.

141. Lucien Pissarro to Camille Pissarro, September, 1896, in Camille Pissarro's *Lettres à son fils Lucien,* 418. See also Lucien's letters of November 6 and 26, 1896, in the Pissarro Archives, Ashmolean Museum, Oxford University.

142. Isabelle Compin, *H. E. Cross* (Paris, 1964), 53.

143. Robert L. Herbert, "Les Artistes et l'Anarchisme," *Le Mouvement social,* XXXVI (July–September, 1961), 9.

you say? The masses today have been kept in complete ignorance, the inequalities among men are too great. Should not those who have cultivated their intellectual faculties make use of them?"[144]

Socialist writers of the era made similar points. In a lecture in 1833, William Morris pointed out that artists "were obliged to express themselves, as it were, in a language not understood by the people." He added, "Nor is it their fault." Artists who watered down their work to appeal to a working population too brutalized to appreciate genuine art "would be traitors to the cause of art, which it is their duty and glory to serve." Karl Marx's daughter Eleanor wrote to protest against the staging of inferior theatrical and musical performances for workers.[145] The socialists of the last two decades of the nineteenth century also attempted to remedy the situation, however, by conducting classes and above all by pressing demands that were designed to correct the ignorance and exhaustion of the workers. The goal of an eight-hour day was premised in part on the need for rest and leisure time sufficient to enable working people to learn about history, society, and the arts.

Anarchists—including anarchist artists—tended, though, to dismiss efforts of this sort as meaningless and self-defeating attempts to make capitalism less oppressive. In 1895, Pissarro responded negatively to a proposal by Gustave Geffroy to create publicly funded museums, open in the evenings, to educate the workers about art and culture—in Pissarro's words, "to develop good taste in the workers so as to lead them to abandon their unfortunate taste for trash." Geffroy's proposal was rather patronizing in tone and content, a typical attempt at middle-class moral uplift, but it was not with that aspect of it that Pissarro quarreled. His objection was that it was impossible for workers to learn to appreciate and love art at all, at least in the foreseeable future: "But I doubt whether this will bring about a taste and a love for art among the starving! The worker, as long as he has a capitalist and miserable salary, will not care about beauty." Until capitalism, somehow, someday, was abolished altogether, the workers were inevitably unable to gain from any project, no matter how "socially" inclined, of genuine artists. Nor did Pissarro shy from the

144. Lucien Pissarro, "Art et Société," *Les Temps nouveaux,* I (December 7–13, 1895), 1. Grave's collaborator Charles Albert made a similar point at greater length in *Qu'est-ce que l'art?* (Paris, 1909), 14–15.

145. William Morris, "Art Under Plutocracy," delivered in November, 1883, reprinted in *Political Writings of William Morris,* ed. A. L. Morton (London, 1979), 61; Yvonne Kapp, *Eleanor Marx: The Crowded Years, 1884–1898* (London, 1979), 108–109.

implications of his argument. He concluded that until that day, *"It is the buyers that one must educate."*[146]

Just as for Grave a bourgeois turned anarchist was no longer a bourgeois but a "rebel," for Pissarro a bourgeois who bought his work was a benefactor. In the middle of complaints about the misery of having to market his art, he added, "I ask for but one thing: for a man confident enough in my talent to provide me and my family something for us to live on."[147] The wealthy buyer, he believed, could be educated, taught not only to love art but to absorb its values, to be transformed by it.

To concede that possibility, however, unbares the reciprocal truth that "education" can work on the artist as much as on the buyer and that, in a situation where the livelihood of the artist is at stake, the buyer has a decided edge. It seems scarcely coincidental that those who in the next generation appropriated certain techniques and concepts from Neo-Impressionism abandoned without exception the underlying goal of social transformation. It is difficult to minimize the gap between Signac's hopes for an art that would serve the workers of the future and Henri Matisse's avowed goal of one that would help the tired bourgeois relax at the end of a hard day.[148]

Pissarro, Signac, and their confederates tried to fuse the concept of a socially transformative art with the notion of "high art" they inherited from the past, ultimately from Renaissance ideas as transmuted by the Enlightenment and then the nineteenth-century Salon. They wanted, as Pissarro said of Daumier, to be both revolutionaries and "true artists." In search of a synthesis that could explain how the high art associated with a wealthy art-buying public was to aid in the gestation of a new, more just social order, the Neo-Impressionists turned not only to theories that sprang from the dominant notions of art but also to theories of an *art social* which had evolved in the 1880s in artistic and literary circles influenced by the anarchist and socialist movements.

146. Camille Pissarro to Lucien Pissarro, February 14, 1895, in Camille Pissarro's *Correspondance,* IV, 31. My emphasis. Gustave Geffroy's proposal is in his *Musée du soir aux quartiers ouvriers* (Paris, 1895).

147. Camille Pissarro to Lucien Pissarro, February 17, 1884, in *Correspondance,* I, 287.

148. John Russell quotes Matisse: "What I dream of is an art of equilibrium, of purity, of tranquility; an art free from disquieting or bothersome subject matter, an art which will calm and soothe the man who works with his head, be he businessman or man of letters" (*The World of Matisse* [New York, 1969], 79). Matisse here echoes Charles Baudelaire in "Salon de 1846," in *Oeuvres complètes* (2 vols.; Paris, 1976), II, 415.

3

Art Social: A Blow of the Pick?

> Anarchists do not base their organizations upon *forms,* but upon
> conscious *ideas.* Forms only enslave, but conscious ideas lead the
> way to liberty. . . . We do not wish for premature action, we wish
> that each and all of us may well discuss what is necessary to make
> life enjoyable for him, we wish that this may go on until action is
> the irresistible outcome of intense, conscious and earnest desire.
> —C. T. Quinn (1894)

Anarchist writers often stressed that anarchism would triumph as an idea, gradually taking root in existing society until the great moment of social transformation, the return of the golden age. For artists, that belief posed the special question of how their art played—or could play—a role in the transformative process. Was their role agitational, to produce overtly didactic works to advance the process of social evolution, or were their works simply reflections of the process? Did images of social harmony offer hope for those dissatisfied with existing society? Could art play a decisive role in toppling the old order, delivering, in the words of Paul Signac, a "solid blow of the pick to the old social edifice?"

The argument that the arts had a vital role to play in social and moral betterment had deep roots in the French Enlightenment of the eighteenth century.[1] In the nineteenth century, Claude Henri de Saint-Simon recruited the arts as an essential component in his strategy for social change. Saint-Simon adroitly transferred the myth of an idyllic golden age from a prehistoric past to a realizable future: "The golden age of the human race is no longer behind us, it is before us, it is in the perfection of the social order; our fathers have not seen it, our children will reach it one day; it is up to us to show them the way."[2] Saint-Simon allotted artists a leading part

---

1. See James A. Leith, *The Idea of Art as Propaganda in France, 1750–1799* (Toronto, 1969); and Warren Roberts, *Morality and Social Class in Eighteenth-Century French Literature and Painting* (Toronto, 1974).

2. Claude Henri de Saint-Simon, *Textes choisis* (Paris, 1951), 99.

in the social transformation. In a three-part "dialogue" published in 1825, featuring an artist, a scientist, and an industrialist, he had the artist proclaim, "We, the artists, will serve as your vanguard. The power of the arts is in reality the most immediate and rapid of all. . . . We address ourselves to the imagination and feelings of man; therefore, we always have the liveliest and most decisive effect."[3]

Although Saint-Simon's writings—and especially the movement he left behind him—played a fundamental role in French republican and socialist thought, it is important to remember that Saint-Simon was himself neither republican nor socialist. He was a technocratic idealist and a supporter, however pragmatic, of the monarchy. The you of "your vanguard" are not the poor, nor even French society as a whole, but industrialists, whom Saint-Simon saw as the "sole class of society in which we would like to see political ambition and courage grow, the only one in which this ambition can be useful, where this courage will be necessary." In the dialogue, his goal is to disarm the prejudices of business leaders and savants against the utility of artists; he urges the industrialists—among whom he singles out bankers—to impose their views on society, employing artists to give their visions force.[4]

Saint-Simon's enlistment of the arts produced two distinguishable though interacting lines of development in nineteenth-century French writings on art and society. The first kept alive the insistence upon an alliance between art and industry as a precondition for social betterment; typically it conflated industry and science with the interests of industrialists and private business, as guarantors of a modern, socially just society.[5] The second tradition absorbed and built upon the idea of a vanguard role for the arts in social change but linked it to socialist projects, from those of Charles Fourier to the anarchist undertakings of Pierre Joseph

3. Claude Henri de Saint-Simon and Léon Halévy, *L'Artiste, le Savant, et l'Industriel: Dialogue* (1825), reprinted in Saint-Simon's *Oeuvres* (6 vols.; Paris, 1964), V, 210.

4. Saint-Simon and Halévy, *L'artiste, le Savant, et l'Industriel,* 217–19. See also the series of lectures delivered to the Saint-Simonian cadre between 1828 and 1829: *The Doctrine of Saint-Simon: An Exposition, 1828–1829,* trans. Georg G. Iggers (Boston, 1958), 240–41; and *Aux artistes—Du passé et de l'avenir des beaux-arts: Doctrine de Saint-Simon* (Paris, 1830), 73–84. See Marguérite Thibon, *Le Rôle social de l'art d'après les Saint-Simoniens* (Paris, 1926).

5. See Alexandre Decamps, "Les Arts et l'Industrie au dix-neuvième siècle," *Revue républicaine,* III (1834), 27–52, IV (1835), 175–94; Charles Baudelaire, "Salon de 1846," in *Oeuvres complètes* (2 vols.; Paris, 1976), II, 415–17.

Proudhon and then Peter Kropotkin.[6] Unlike Saint-Simon, the early proponents of a socialist art generally downplayed or even neglected the question of who would pay for the art produced. Their focus was instead on the shape artists could give to the ideals of movements for social change.[7] Proudhon exhorted mid-nineteenth-century artists to fuse the ideal and the real in order to expose the baseness of their epoch. Art, he wrote, had to participate actively in the evolution of society, both by provoking reactions by baring injustices and by responding to changing social conditions.[8] By the end of the century, Kropotkin was even more definite about the didactic role for art and artists: "Show the people what is ugly in contemporary life and make us understand the causes of this ugliness; tell us what a rational life would have been if it had not been blocked at every stage by the ineptitudes and vileness of the present social order."[9] Kropotkin did not argue that the arts should be purely agitational. He suggested elsewhere

6. The extensive literature is weighted toward the disjunction between the artistic avant-garde and social movements. See, for example, Linda Nochlin, "The Invention of the Avant-Garde," in *Avant-Garde Art,* ed. John Ashberry and Thomas B. Hess (London, 1967), 3–24; Donald Drew Egbert, "The Idea of 'Avant-Garde' in Art and Politics," *American Historical Review,* LXXIII (1967), 339–66; George T. Noszlopy, "The Embourgeoise-ment of Avant-Garde Art," *Diogenes,* LXVII (1969), 83–109; and John Tagg, "The Idea of the Avant-Garde," *Artery,* XII (Summer, 1977), 4–10. Nicos Hadjinicolaou ("On the Ideology of Avant-Gardism," *Praxis,* VI [1982], 39–70) can serve as a corrective to the others; he argues that the whole notion of an artistic avant-garde is based on an obsolete and reactionary positivism. By contrast, Robert Spertus attempts to establish a continuing radical tradition in avant-garde art. See his "Toward a Socialist Perspective on the Avant-Garde," *Socialist Revolution,* September–October, 1972, pp. 51–77.

7. Gabriel Desiré Laverdant, a follower of Fourier, called on artists both to depict the ideals of the cause and to expose the miseries of the modern world. See his "Salon de 1842," *La Phalange,* 3rd ser., V (1842), 691–700, esp. 697–98. Laverdant wrote that artists had only two real options: "the critique of evil and odious things; the glorification of good and desirable things." Indifference or neutrality was forbidden. See also his "Souvenir de Salon de 1846," *La Phalange,* n.s., III (1846), 558–88. Here he emphasized the need for artists to act to build the socialist movement: "Artists, the time has come to change all this, to transform this backward world; the time has come to give you the scepter and crown, to organize your reign, O chiefs who do not dominate by destruction and death, O master creators, O kings of intelligence and feeling, whose empire is beauty! Come, come to the science of justice, to the law of association and of universal unity; come to this new world where everything is luxury, splendor, beauty, love, happiness, exquisite harmonies!" (p. 588).

8. Cf. Pierre Joseph Proudhon, "De l'idée du progrès," in *Philosophie du progrès,* in *Oeuvres complètes* (15 vols.; Geneva, 1982), XII, 94. For an examination—sometimes problematic—of Proudhon's artistic theory, see Jean G. Lossier, *Le Rôle social de l'art selon Proudhon* (Paris, 1937).

9. Pierre Kropotkine, *Paroles d'un révolté* (Paris, 1885), 66–67.

that the right of everyone to art would come into its own in the golden age.[10] Until then, though, he viewed art as an extension of the slogans and demands of the cause.

From such a vantage point, many anarchist militants saw as irrelevant the debates within the art world over style and form. In a review of Zola's *L'Oeuvre,* Jean Grave complained that though the reigning social order had provoked a rebellion by young artists, their revolt was not in pursuit of social justice. He asserted, "Under this regime, the rebel artist is not a revolutionary who seeks liberty for all but an adventurer who cultivates the principle, Get out so I can replace you!" He held that the ideals of solidarity would find true expression only with the advent of a libertarian society.[11]

The artistic attitude that Grave evinced here was in part a continuation of his own earlier, more voluntarist suppositions about social change. But as Grave's convictions about an evolutionary transition to a stateless communism grew, they inevitably influenced his conception of the arts as well. Increasingly, Grave, Elisée Reclus, and their colleagues argued not only that anarchism was scientific but that science and education were inherently anarchist. In 1895, Reclus asserted in a speech delivered at the inauguration of the socialist Université Nouvelle in Brussels that science did not serve the interests of any one party, class, or sovereign.[12] If it was pursued honestly, it had to lead to the insights of anarcho-communism.

In 1887, Grave established a literary supplement to *La Révolte* in direct expression of his certainty that anarchism and knowledge were essentially one. The literary supplement was grounded on the premise that anyone not totally blinded by dogma or superstition would, in seeking the truth, confirm essential tenets of anar-

10. See Peter Kropotkin, *The Conquest of Bread* (London, 1985), 108–20. The book was compiled from essays written in the 1880s.

11. Jean Grave, "L'Art dans la société bourgeoise: L'Oeuvre par M. Emile Zola," *La Révolte,* VIII (July 19–25, 1886), 4, (July 17–23, 1886), 3–4; (August 21–27, 1886), 3–4. The idea that a truly social art would be born only with the attainment of a libertarian communism was not unique to Grave; see "Réponse à quelques objections," *L'Etendard révolutionnaire,* I (October 8, 1882), 3; Emile Massard, "L'Art et le Socialisme," *L'Attaque,* I (June 20–27, 1888), 2; and "A propos d'art," *Le Père Peinard,* I (September 29, 1889), 10–11.

12. Elisée Reclus, "Sur l'éducation," reprinted in *Les Frères: Elie et Elisée Reclus,* ed. Paul Reclus (Paris, 1964), 193–202. See also J. Routaled, "Science et Autorité," *Les Temps nouveaux,* III (July 24–30, 1897), 2–3; and Marie Fleming, *The Anarchist Way to Socialism: Elisée Reclus and Nineteenth-Century Anarchism* (London, 1979), 124–25.

chist theory. Even the most reactionary thinkers could be mined for unwitting confirmations of anarchist theses. Anarchocommunist theory remained for Grave the global truth against which all other affirmations and world views were to be weighed and measured. He expected that as society evolved and ignorance and superstition were overcome, bits and pieces that even the enemies of anarchism were obliged to credit would gradually accumulate, and eventually the fragments of truth would coalesce with the core of anarchist knowledge, clearing the way to the *âge d'or.*

As the term *literary supplement* intimates, knowledge for Grave included poetry and literature. He mentioned Zola and the Goncourt brothers as exemplifying social vision in practice. He explained that, though the Goncourts were political reactionaries, "their books are a cry of revolt."[13]

A comparable theory of literature and society appeared concurrently on the French left, among the Independent Socialists grouped around Benoît Malon's *Revue Socialiste.* Malon, a former anarchist, established the Société pour l'Economie Sociale in 1885 as the direct counterpart of Britain's Fabian Society. His *socialisme intégral* attracted a diverse following, from nonparty radical intellectuals to aspiring cabinet members, most notably Alexandre Millerand and René Viviani. The Independent Socialists were as a group uncompromisingly hostile to anarchism, but they shared with the anarchocommunists the ideal of fostering a gradual social evolution through education and enlightenment.[14] Both anarchocommunism and *socialisme intégral* beckoned radical intellectuals who felt philanthropic impulses toward the poor and a disgust at the fragmentation and banality of social existence, and who were wary of control by organized parties and suspicious of what they deemed philistine tendencies within the socialist parties of the day.[15] Like the anarchocommunists, the Malonists saw around

<hr>

13. Jean Grave, *La Société future* (Paris, 1895), 359–60.

14. See, for example, the writings of Malon's close ally Georges Renard: *Socialisme libertaire et Anarchie* (Paris, 1895); and "Le Socialisme séparé de l'anarchisme," *Revue socialiste,* XXIV (1896), 1–7.

15. G. D. H. Cole, *The Second International* (London, 1954), Part II, 330–31, Vol. III of Cole, *A History of Socialist Thought;* Leslie Derfler, *Alexandre Millerand: The Socialist Years* (The Hague, 1977), 36–37. On Malon's attitude toward anarchism, see Jean Carrère, "Entretiens sur l'anarchie: Benoît Malon," *Le Figaro,* April 25, 1892, p. 2. Malon distinguished between anarchist aspirations, with which he agreed, and anarchist doctrines, which he termed absurd. For an anarchist critique of Malon's faction, see Charles Malato, "Les Fractions socialistes: Les Socialistes indépendants," *L'Idée ouvrière,* I (February 25–

them continuous proof of the power of socialist ideas among even socialism's most bitter enemies. If Grave cited Zola and the Goncourts, Tabarant offered readers of the *Revue socialiste* Zola and Balzac.[16]

The educing of political ideas was at first almost exclusively from literature. The visual arts went largely unmined. Nor would Grave's first attempt to draw upon the visual arts have favorably impressed many artists. In 1886, he sought unsuccessfully to make a deal with the journal *L'Illustration* to purchase their plates of current events. With deftly composed captions, he felt, the pictures would do nicely for *La Révolte.* For example, a plate depicting the miners at Decazeville passing in review before their employers fortified Grave's confidence that even enemies of anarchism could not help strengthening it: "Never have I seen an image more expressive of inequality or shame. And this picture represents the triumph of banality, the abjection of labor—and it is our enemies who publish this! We must always keep them under watch." Artists had to infer that Grave took art to be merely a visual extension of political agitation; his use of the term *propagande de l'image* reinforced that assessment.[17] As it turned out, *La Révolte* was not the first French anarchist journal to employ graphic artists: Emile Pouget's insurrectionary *Le Père Peinard* began running satirical cartoons on its back page in 1889.

The Genesis of Art Social

Among radicalized and alienated artists, a somewhat different debate about the role of the arts was under way. Their discussion was over how to align art as art—apart from ancillary didactic elements and intents—with social progress. Increasingly, this debate focused on the new forms art should take so as to express new ideas.

In 1886, Max Sulzberger, a Belgian, deplored that even progressive artists confined themselves to forms copied from the past:

March 25, 1888), 2–3. Fernand Pelloutier's "Benoît Malon" (*L'Art social,* III [1893], 279–80) is a very friendly obituary.

16. Adolphe Tabarant, "Le Club de l'art social," *Revue socialiste,* VIII (1890), 103.

17. Félix Dubois, *Le Péril anarchiste* (Paris, 1894), 143–44; Alvan Sanborn, *Paris and the Social Revolution: A Study of the Revolutionary Elements in the Various Classes of French Society* (Boston, 1905), 74.

Gustave Courbet merely took over stylistic elements from the Flemish primitives, and Charles De Groux' paintings were reminiscent of Gothic art. Because the old styles and techniques the artists borrowed had long since lost their power, Sulzberger thought it essential to create new ones that could "crystallize the democratic idea" in the way Christian art had strengthened the early church.[18] Edmond Picard, a Belgian socialist, editorialized in the same vein in his influential *L'Art moderne:* contemporary art, he argued, had remained aristocratic in form and content. As the old elites were swept away, the question arose, "Which art will replace the art abolished? What form will it take in the democracy that is opening up today, replacing the one that flowered, rare and morbid, in an aristocracy? The atmosphere, the light of inspiration, the whole climate changes, even the vegetation will certainly be different. Which? Which?"[19] Sulzberger wanted the new art to resemble a humanistic pantheism, worshiping the divine in nature rather than some external, anthropomorphic deity. Picard's goal was a "new Middle Ages," an attempt to build a new world from the ruins of the old, just as, on his interpretation, the Middle Ages had reunited and rebuilt Europe in the wake of barbarian invasions. The art of the future was to be in the "common tongue, . . . no longer . . . some hermetic dialect destined for a college of Brahmins."[20]

The mid-1880s brought a number of groups that attempted to meet the need for a new art in each step with new—often radically different—visions of society. In 1886–1887 alone, the Neo-Impressionists made their debut at the final Impressionist exhibition, Jean Moréas published his "Symbolist Manifesto," and five erstwhile followers of Zola took the occasion of the publication of his *La Terre* to break away in protest of what they called his *note ordurière.* Their Manifeste des Cinq envisaged an art that would be

18. Max Sulzberger, "La Démocratie et l'Art," *La Société nouvelle,* IV (1888), 256–57. See also Henry Bérenger, "L'Art, la Science et la Démocratie," *Essais d'art libre,* I (February, 1892), 1–10. The anarchist Amédée Catonné tied the persistence of archaic forms to official art training by the state, with its "unrepentant Academicism, in the obstinate fidelity to the forms of the past, to the most questionable traditions" ("L'Árt et l'Etat," *Les Temps nouveaux,* X [January 21–27, 1905], 1–2).

19. Edmond Picard, "Un Nouveau Moyen-Age," *L'Art moderne,* X (1890), 9–10.

20. *Ibid.,* 10–11; Sulzberger, "La Démocratie et l'Art," 258. The idea of a "scientific pantheism" was a staple of humanist culture, especially among the followers of Malon. See Jules Baissac, "Pantheisme scientifique," *Revue socialiste,* IV (1886), 644–47; and Benoît Malon, "Morales pantheistes," *Revue socialiste,* IV (1886), 730–36.

realistic but animated by a conscious idealism, whether political, social, or religious. The manifesto did not prescribe the idealism, inasmuch as the five signatories had allegiances ranging from anarchism to a conservative Catholicism.[21] In 1889, the claim of the Neo-Impressionists to be the logical inheritors of the Impressionist mantle was challenged by the first exhibition of the "Impressionists and Synthetists," a forerunner of the Pont Aven group.

The term *art social* gained currency among artists and writers who, at whatever level, proclaimed a link between their art and the goal of social justice. In 1889, six writers and intellectuals, all closely linked to Malon's *Revue socialiste,* announced the formation of the Club de l'Art Social. The club grew quickly, expanding to include other Independent Socialists, including Malon himself, as well as a number of anarchocommunists, among them the Neo-Impressionist painter Camille Pissarro, the novelist Lucien Descaves, and the venerable Communard Louise Michel. One of its founding members, the socialist critic Tabarant, wrote that the phrase *art social* was meant to provide the club with "an orientation, a solid beacon," based on the shared ideals of "science, light, justice, humanity."[22] The statutes of the club declared that the ideal of republicanism was not open for discussion. The club was to adhere to no political faction, though its members were free to act as they chose.[23] The organization met weekly at the offices of the *Revue socialiste* to debate literary and artistic theories and works, as in its open discussion of Descaves' antimilitarist novel *Sous-Offs.*[24]

21. On the Manifeste des Cinq, see Léon Deffoux and Emile Zavie, *Le Groupe de Medan* (Paris, 1920), 223–29; Eugenia W. Herbert, *The Artist and Social Reform: France and Belgium, 1885–1898* (New Haven, 1961), 62–63; and Lucien Descaves, *Souvenir d'un ours* (Paris, 1926), 87–96.

22. Tabarant, "Le Club de l'art social," 101. See also Adolphe Tabarant, *Camille Pissarro* (Paris, 1924), 57–58.

23. "Club de l'art social: Statutes," *Annales artistiques et littéraires,* II (1889), 288. The founding members of the club, besides Tabarant, were Robert Bernier, a literary critic for the *Revue socialiste;* Léon Cladel, a novelist and "socialist aesthetician" and a former protégé of Baudelaire's; Henry Fèvre, the writer and critic; Georges Renard, a professor at the University of Lausanne; and J. H. Rosny, in reality the novelist Joseph Henri Boex. The "Impressionist poet" Jean Ajalbert was an active member, as was Auguste Rodin.

24. The meeting of December 15 was announced in "Club de l'art social," *Annales artistiques et littéraires,* II (December 1, 1889), 320. For attacks on the notion of *art social,* see Charles Marki, "Art social," *Mercure de France,* VII (1893), 370–73; and Albert Mockel, "L'Art social: Les Symbolistes," *La Wallonie,* I (1886), 142–49.

Conflicts between the Malonists and the anarchocommunists eventually tore the Club de l'Art Social apart.[25] The anarchocommunists gradually appropriated the term *art social* in a series of new projects. The anarchist poet Gabriel de La Salle founded the review *L'Art social* in 1891, and an anarchist Théâtre d'Art Social was established in 1892. *L'Art social* suspended publication in 1894 because of problems with funding, but in 1896 it was reconstituted as the organ of the new Groupe de l'Art Social, which held regular public forums on art and revolutionary politics.

All of these collaborations emphasized the need for creative freedom. "Social art," La Salle wrote, "does not repudiate any literary or artistic form."[26] Resisting the demand for a baldly agitational art, the various circles promoting *art social* asserted that it was precisely through a free and open creative process that art could lend itself to the evolution of society. That was reaffirmed by the anarchist theoretician Reclus in an open letter to the editors of the review *Entretiens politiques et littéraires* in 1892. Six years before, Reclus' friend and colleague Jean Grave had rejected any artistic rebellion that did not have a clear social goal, but Reclus asserted that it was crucial to be free to create in accordance with each artist's "interior mirror." By striking down official canons of taste and style, artists—whether they knew it or not—were acting as part of the anarchist struggle, Reclus suggested. Few artists and writers recognized that, he said, but they were already in fact "ardent, instinctive socialists, impelled by the poetry of the struggle."[27]

Anarchist artists and writers sought to lodge their work within this conception of social change. La Salle wrote in the preface to an anthology of his poems that "the smallest scientific, philosophical, or industrial progress is a manifestation of Art, of Art generalized, of human Art as it must be understood." Art, he

25. Adolphe Tabarant blamed the breakup on quarrels sparked by the anarchists. See his "Chronique: A la maison du peuple," *La Petite République,* July 9, 1894, p. 1. An article in the *Revue socialiste* ridiculed the anarchist *L'Art social*'s pretension to be the club's successor. See "Théâtre social," *Revue socialiste,* XXXI (1895), 501. By the early 1890s, the Malonists' ideas had already shifted to a Belgian-style *maison du peuple* as the cornerstone of progressive art and literature.

26. "L'Art social," *L'Art social,* I (1891), 1. Compare "Statutes de la Théâtre d'Art Social," printed on the back cover of *L'Art social* for February, 1892. On the theater, see Xavier Durand, "L'Art social aux théâtre: Deux Expériences, 1893, 1897," *Le Mouvement social,* XCI (April–June, 1975), 13–33.

27. Elisée Reclus, "Aux compagnons rédacteurs des *Entretiens,*" *Entretiens politiques et littéraires,* IV (1892), 3–6.

contended, could not be limited to the "puerile" notation of sensations; sensation was only the bedrock on which art rested. A genuine art had to encompass, and work in concert with, the entire march of science, education, and industry: "the trains, industrialism, the Eiffel Tower" were all far more significant and worthy of attention than ancient legends or compilations of *poèmes barbares.*[28]

Neo-Impressionists made a determined effort to position their art within such discussion, refining the idea that art is determined by the social circumstances of its production. In 1887, Camille Pissarro wrote a letter in which he advanced the view that debates over whether the peasant painter Jean François Millet had been a socialist were irrelevant. Millet's art was progressive not because of his subjective intentions, Pissarro maintained, but because of the pressure of social evolution. "Another one of those blind men, soldier or general," he said of Millet, "unconscious of the march of modern ideas, who defends the idea without knowing it!! . . . Isn't this curious? For a long time I have been struck by the unconsciousness of men of the elite."[29]

In 1891, Paul Signac published an unsigned essay, "Impressionnistes et Révolutionnaires," that included a precise and ambitious attempt to define and defend Neo-Impressionism in relationship to anarchocommunist theories. The essay was a landmark because of the sheer scope of Signac's argument, and its publication in Grave's *La Révolte* took on significance in virtue of his determined effort to extend Grave's own theories to encompass the visual arts. The discussions of *art social* had been framed before Signac's article almost exclusively in literary terms; the Club de l'Art Social was dominated by writers and political theorists.

Signac began by asserting that at the most recent Salon des Indépendants the popular—as opposed to the bourgeois—public had received the art of the Neos with interest. That was due, he decided, to the "revolutionary tendency of the Impressionist painters."[30] The tendency was evident in their art's formal innovations as well as in their moral example ("too rare in our epoch") in painting according to their ideals rather than for "beautiful gold coins . . . honors . . . decorations." The Neos had earned a "sym-

28. Gabriel de La Salle, *Les Révoltes: Luttes stériles* (Paris, 1892), 14–21.

29. Camille Pissarro, *Correspondance,* ed. Janine Bailly-Herzberg (Paris, 1980–), II, 157.

30. Paul Signac [Un Impressionniste Camarade], "Impressionnistes et Révolutionnaires," *La Révolte,* IV (June 13–19, 1891), 3–4. Throughout the essay, Signac uses *Impressionist* where *Neo-Impressionist* is clearly meant.

pathetic salute from everyone who applauds the collapse of all prejudices and routines." Of even greater importance was the way the Neo-Impressionists modeled a basic principle of the anarchist movement. Though they painted in answer to the purely aesthetic impulses "produced by the picturesque quality of things and beings," their art was attended by an insistent "social, unconscious dimension that has already marked contemporary literature." Like Grave and Tabarant, Signac cited several novelists—Flaubert, the Goncourt brothers, Zola—for works that "have served the revolutionary cause much more potently than all those novels in which political preoccupations take precedence over the literary aspect." He considered Zola's *Germinal* and Flaubert's *L'Education sentimentale* far more penetrating and truthful in their critique of modern society than the novels of George Sand or Eugène Sue, much less the "vast joke entitled *Les Misérables*."[31]

In expanding the company of soldiers unconsciously serving the revolutionary cause to include painters, Signac followed Pissarro by dwelling on the case of Millet. Millet, painting as a peasant, had produced art in which Signac discovered a more pronounced social character than he could find in Courbet, a "painter and thinker." More provocatively, Signac also summoned the example of Ernest Meissonier's *The Barricade,* of 1850 (Figure 5). To anarchists and socialists, Meissonier was best known as the persecutor of Courbet. Signac acknowledged that the painter had been an archreactionary, yet insisted that his painting constituted a "terrible accusation against the social state established one hundred years ago by the bourgeoisie." The painting, produced solely in aesthetic response to "the strangeness of the scene, the effect of colorations," had the power of inspiring a powerful emotive response in the viewer.[32]

Signac was not arguing that the moral and political character of art can be divorced from content. Rather, the question he canvassed concerned the process by which that content is produced. Proudhon had been in error, Signac judged, in demanding a precise socialist tendency in art works. What was labeled "socialist art" could be both artificial and hypocritical.[33] By contrast, artists

31. *Ibid.,* 3.

32. *Ibid.,* 4. This point may well have been suggested by Charles Blanc in *Grammaire des arts du dessin* (Paris, 1867), 514: "Such a scene of the Inquisition, where Granet would have seen but the somber poetry of a subdued light, teaches us tolerance."

33. In this connection, Signac cited the example of a "melodramatic composition representing an 'unhappy family.'" See the Appendix, Signac's "Impressionists and Revolutionaries," p. 249 below.

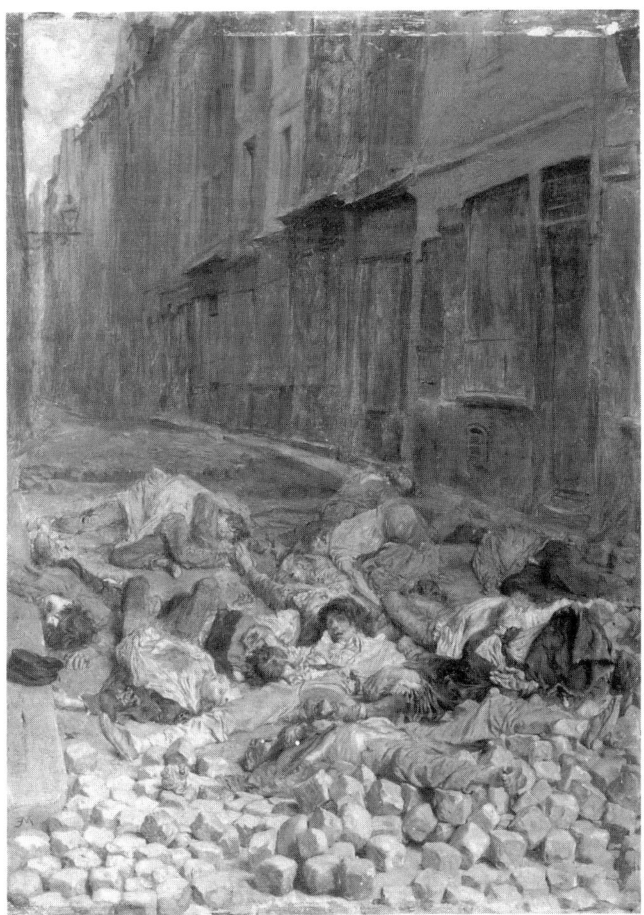

Figure 5   Ernest Meissonier, *The Barricade*
La Barricade, rue de la Mortellerie, juin 1848, oil on canvas, 1850. Courtesy of Musée du Louvre, Paris. © PHOTO R.M.N.

devoted to "pure" art, especially those whose technique was the "negation of old artistic routines," had by striking down old styles and prejudices opened the road to an art in harmony with human social evolution. Instead of replicating a contrived and fossilized official art, the Neos rendered the unfolding world in all its vitality, from the workers' blocks of Saint-Ouen and Montrouge to the "pleasures of decadence" characteristic of a transitional epoch in which there is a "great social trial under way between workers and capital." In the artistic production of "revolutionaries by temperament," honesty and openness to the course of social evolution enabled the unconscious delivery of a "solid blow of the pick to the old social edifice that, worm-eaten, cracks and crumbles like an old deconsecrated cathedral." Signac was certain that "sooner or later one will find the true artists on the side of the rebels, united with them in an identical idea of justice."[34]

The insight that the content, or significance, of art is largely independent of the subjective intent of the artist is a vital one, and it appears in a wide range of radical critiques of art from the period. Friedrich Engels esteemed the novels of the monarchist Honoré de Balzac as being qualitatively superior as social critiques to the writings of Zola or Sue.[35] For Engels, however, the "truthfulness" of Balzac's novels arose from the conjunction between the author's ideological preconceptions, the course of capitalist development in France during his lifetime, and the impact of the specific aesthetic form within which he worked. As Terry Eagleton has remarked, there is no acceptance by Engels of the "notion of a direct, spontaneous relation between text and history," which Eagleton denominates a naïve empiricism.[36] Anarchocommunist writers, on the other hand, credited precisely that "direct, spontaneous relation" between text and history. For Grave and his colleagues, there was an unmediated bond between the artist and the historical moment. As André Girard asserted, "A new art responds to a new age, . . . for, of all the emanations of the human spirit, Art characterizes the psychological state of an era with the most precision. . . . The artistic heritage of the past offers us an assured criterion for the evolutionary reconstitution of vanished civilizations."[37] Another anarchist writer held that "art is a sublimation, a crystallization of human thought; it gives to perpetuity a definitive form of the conceptions of the century."[38]

34. *Ibid.*

35. Friedrich Engels to Margaret Harkness, April, 1888, in Karl Marx and Frederick Engels, *Literature and Art* (New York, 1947), 41–43.

36. Terry Eagleton, *Criticism and Ideology: A Study in Marxist Literary Theory* (London, 1976), 69–70. See also, however, Peter Demetz, *Marx, Engels, and the Poets,* trans. Jeffrey L. Sammons (Rev. ed.; Chicago, 1967), 173–77. Demetz, who conflates Engels' views with those that prevailed in Stalin's Russia, sees potential insights in Engels' critique but argues that the German socialist missed the point of Balzac's works.

37. André Girard, "Art nouveau," *Les Temps nouveaux,* I (May 11–17, 1895), 2.

38. "L'Art," *L'Idée,* 2nd ser., I (September 15, 1894). 47. See the essay by Walter Crane in a special issue of *La Plume* on art and anarchism: "L'Art et les Artistes," *La Plume,* IX (1893), 212. The view of art as a direct expression of the historical moment had its roots in French utopian thought and formed a major theme in the movement of Charles Fourier. Reviewing the Salon of 1842, Gabriel Desiré Laverdant wrote, "Let us allow artists in all freedom to draw their motifs from every epoch, from every country, so long as, in all these

If, however, an epoch produces its art—if the late nineteenth century produced revolutionary art because of the period's inner essence—what is the point of being an anarchist artist at all? If the novels of the Goncourt brothers were a "cry of revolt," why suffer the privation of being an anarchist instead of enjoying the rewards of becoming successful and prominent writers of the day? Are there no breaks in the linkage between the artist and historical pressures? Is all art revolutionary? Some anarchists responded affirmatively to the last question. André Veidaux reasoned that "anarchism englobes art in its synthesis. The anarchism of art is Art itself." Veidaux was an individualist anarchist with no inclination toward *art social,* but André Girard, a colleague of Jean Grave's, made much the same point. Girard too asserted that all art is anarchist by nature. "It is not regimented under any banner," he wrote, echoing Reclus on science, "it does not enclose itself in any formula, it does not bow before any symbol."[39] Among the Neo-Impressionists, Lucien Pissarro proclaimed that all art is social, since even the rejection of society or progress is by definition a social choice. He implied that Grave's journal was hypocritical in praising some artists or artistic circles over others, since Grave himself called for "absolute liberty for the artist in the society to be." Lucien Pissarro persisted, "Then why not admit it in any era? The true is always true."[40] Most anarchocommunists—and most Neo-Impressionists—drew back from Lucien Pissarro's discrimination-liquidating logic. The letters of Camille Pissarro and the private journals of Signac are filled with attacks on rival artistic groups, particularly on the Symbolists and Pont Aven painters, as reactionary in both form and essence.[41] In "Impressionnistes et Ré-

---

varied forms, their faithful brush always reproduces that which never varies, the soul and its passions" ("Salon de 1842," 691).

39. André Veidaux, "Le Néant de l'art bourgeois," *Revue libertaire,* II (1894), 69; André Girard, "L'Art du peuple," *Les Temps nouveaux,* IV (July 2–8, 1898), 1. Even Camille Pissarro sometimes expressed himself in these terms. In a letter to Octave Mirbeau in 1892, he exclaimed, "All the arts are anarchist! When it is beautiful and good!" (Cabinet des Dessins, Louvre, Paris). See also "Aux artistes," *La Révolte,* VII (December 9–16, 1893), 1–2; there art is termed the "negation of all authoritarianism."

40. Lucien Pissarro, "Art et Société," *Les Temps nouveaux,* I (December 7–13, 1895), 1. The essay, signed "L. P.," is a letter responding to Charles Albert's "Art et Société," *Les Temps nouveaux,* I (November 23–29, 1895), 1–2. See also Adophe Retté's remarks in "De nôtre art," *L'Enclos,* II (December, 1896), 58: "Art—social or not—is always the expression of the life of a people, of a group, or of an individual." He attacks the term *art social* as detestable pedagoguery.

41. For Pissarro's attacks on the Symbolist and Pont Aven painters, see his *Lettres à son fils Lucien,* ed. John Rewald (Paris, 1947), 234–35, 259, 317–18, 360, 398, 420–21, 437. For

volutionnaires," Signac raised barriers: "I exclude the Impressionists/Symbolists [that is, Paul Gauguin, Emile Bernard, Maurice Denis, and others of the Pont Aven circle], who, confining themselves to retrograde subjects, fall back into vagaries and forget that art consists much more in searching into the future than in disinterring the legends of the past, no matter how golden they might be."[42] Although many of the Symbolist poets—and some of the Belgian, if not French, Symbolist painters—had anarchist sympathies, anarchist writers and militants, prominently the writer Octave Mirbeau, a close friend of Pissarro's, and Paterne Berrichon, the editor of *Le Libertaire* and Rimbaud's brother-in-law, frequently denounced the Symbolists even more vigorously.[43]

Thus the debate swung back to subject matter. Revolutionary art again had to make a revolutionary point, however that art might be generated, or had to deal with social subjects. Signac and Pissaro repeatedly reached the point of calling their opponents reactionary because their art and subjects were retrogressive, mystical, and superstitious. It must have been difficult to feel comfortable, however, with an argument that seemed to ignore the manner in which the art was produced. Two additional arguments were summoned to distinguish a truly social art: one focused on how an artist lived and worked; the other emphasized the techniques shaping the art.

Anarchocommunists saw the growth of their movement as accretionary—a convert here, a few more there, as individuals chose to accept the ideals of the cause and live, so far as possible, free from oppressive rules and values. Through the examples of *l'homme nouveau* and *la femme libre,* others would see in practice the superiority of the anarchist mode of existence and be won over. For the anarchists, being did not determine consciousness; rather, consciousness determined being. An anarchist novel from the late twentieth century summarizes the view Kropotkin's movement

---

Signac's views, see John Rewald, ed., "Extraits du journal inédit de Paul Signac," *Gazette des beaux-arts,* 6th ser., XXXVI (1949), 116–19; and Signac, "Fragments du journal," *Arts de France,* XI (1947), 102.

42. Signac, "Impressionnistes et Révolutionnaires," 4.

43. A particularly scathing attack on Symbolism as a reactionary, antianarchist art can be found in P. Flaustier's "Le Symbolisme pseudo-libertaire," *Le Plébéian,* II (September 1–15, 1895), 1. For Mirbeau's reactions, see the essays collected in his *Des artistes: Peintres et Sculpteurs* (1922–24; Paris, 1986), 194–208, 219–25, 234–50. See also Paterne Berrichon, "Sur le peinture," *Le Libertaire,* II (January 4–11, 1896), 4. Grave rejected the idea that all "antibourgeois" art was progressive. He held that partisans of *l'art pour l'art* in particular were "as well, without a doubt, basically reactionary" (*La Société future,* 357–58).

held as well: "You cannot take what you have not earned, and you must give yourself. You cannot buy the Revolution. You cannot make the Revolution. You can only be the Revolution. It is in your spirit, or it is nowhere."[44]

Signac asserted this point for himself and his fellows. They were artists, he argued, who lived out their freedom, passing up chances for fame and fortune to live simple and honest lives in accordance with their ideals. In a draft speech intended for a working-class audience, he argued that "the anarchist painter is not the one who paints anarchist pictures but the one who, without concern for profit, without desire for recompense, struggles with all his individuality against official and bourgeois conventions by his personal contribution."[45] An anonymous artist wrote in Grave's *La Révolte,* "Is the mission of the artist not to persevere in his route toward the ideal he has glimpsed, indifferent to criticism, listening only to the voice of his heart, happy if, at his death, he is conscious of having, by his work, contributed to the education and liberation of humanity?"[46]

Here there was at least partial agreement with a point made by the Cuban revolutionary José Martí in his review of the New York Impressionist exhibition in 1866: "All rebellion of form involves a rebellion of essence."[47] The assertion is that a new way of living contributes to a new way of expressing values and beliefs. Beyond that, however, there is also the point that a harmonious art is the product of a harmonious life. In an article in the *Revue blanche,* an anarchist writer described the goals of his movement as "life triumphant in harmony with its emancipated organism, the march without further hindrance toward natural civilization, reason glorifying the laws of instinct."[48] Georges Beaume, a founding member of the Club de l'Art Social, perceived the purpose of art similarly when he said that art expresses humanity's search for the "door of light," in order to reclaim "human justice, security, and

44. Ursula K. Leguin, *The Dispossessed: An Ambiguous Utopia* (New York, 1971), 262. The subtitle hints at differences between nineteenth- and twentieth-century utopianism.

45. Robert L. Herbert, "Les Artistes et l'Anarchisme," *Le Mouvement social,* XXXVI (July–September, 1961), 9. See Aline Dardel, "Catalogues des dessins et publications illustrées du journal anarchiste *Les Temps nouveaux*" (Dissertation, University of Paris IV, 1980), II, 43–46.

46. "Réponse d'un artiste," *La Révolte,* VII (December 31, 1893–January 5, 1894), 1–2. The response was to "L'Art communiste," *La Révolte,* VII (December 25–31, 1893), 1–2.

47. José Martí, "A New Exhibition of Impressionist Painters," in *On Art and Literature by José Martí,* trans. Elinor Randall, ed. Philip S. Foner (New York, 1982), 121.

48. Ludovic Malquin, "L'An-archie," *Revue blanche,* I (1891), 106.

harmony." He added, "The idea ferments in the soul of the people. A creation is readying itself. No one knows what earth will emerge, but it will be a sweeter and more fertile one. Once again the people will be God."[49]

For anarchocommunists—including the Neos—living in harmony with their beliefs meant being in harmony with inexorable laws of history. If a Goncourt or a Zola—much less a Meissonnier—could catch glimpses of where the world had to head, how much clearer it must be to those who opened themselves to it and internalized it in their daily lives and work.

Arguments about technique had their roots in the ideal of social harmony. Some defenders of *art social* sought to negate the scope of intentionality almost entirely.[50] For most, however, there was a delicate balance between the imperatives of history and the possibilities of individual innovation. Charles Albert Daudet, who under the name of Charles Albert became Grave's chief writer on the arts, thought that the new golden age would be more propitious for a planned and methodical approach. "Popular art of past epochs was an unconscious art," he wrote, "produced by personal instinct, whether the recreation of an isolated individual or of weak partnerships, as consolation for a bad life." The future, he believed, would be quite different: "The popular art of tomorrow will be produced by conscious intelligence, by the feeling of social solidarity and the enthusiasm of a rational life." What until then? Charles Albert saw that time as an uneasy juncture between the two distinct epochs, with their qualitatively divergent forms of art: "Between the two forms of popular art, one of which is irremediably dead and the other not yet born, it is not surprising that a chaotic period has opened up in which the sense of beauty has almost disappeared."[51]

In gathering momentum, enlightenment was expected to have an enormous impact on society. The possibilities of the new era

49. Georges Beaume, "L'Art social," *Revue socialiste,* XIV (1891), 732. See Gustave Geffroy, "La Vie artistique," *Les Temps nouveaux,* I (1895), Literary Supplement, 196.

50. See, for example, the preface by the socialist reformer and poet Clovis Hugues to Léon Cladel's *Kerkadec: Garde barrière* (5th ed.; Paris, 1884), xvii–xxix: "This petrification of the republic in the bourgeois spirit does not prevent literature from being socialist—which it is, perhaps, unconsciously, but it is so and this is the essential thing for the future. . . . Did the author feel a responsibility to the revolution in writing his work? Not in the least. He has yielded to the enormous pressure of events, he has submitted to the historic fatalities of his time, the permanent influence of humanity in labor."

51. Charles Albert, "L'Art et la Société," *L'Art social,* n.s., VI (1896), 173.

would thus be dramatically extended, the vision of the world to come would be clearer, the unconscious advance would become increasingly a conscious one. *Science* becomes a key term here, permitting the demarcation of the new art from the old: the artists of the past had ideals, but their vision of humanity and its potential had not been scientific. The new art would combine ideals and science—ideals to motivate and give it purpose, science to define and delimit and ensure the greatest possible impact. The critic Arsène Alexandre, writing in Grave's literary supplement, predicted that a social art would employ science in the same way that Christian art had once used the church's credo to galvanize people to action. Science would rejuvenate art, suffusing it with an idealism which was capable of concrete application, which would point the way forward, rather than back to antiquity: "The art of tomorrow will be idealist and scientific, or it will not be at all."[52] The anarchocommunist André Girard maintained that science would provide art with a powerful vision of human solidarity, teaching art to be both optimistic and profound, motivated by the vision of an emancipated humanity.[53] Zola's last novel cycles—the *Trois Villes,* of the 1890s, and the unfinished *Les Quatre Evangiles,* of the early 1900s—abandoned the "objectivity" of his Naturalist works and openly propagandized for a society in which superstition, religion, and capitalism are peacefully abolished by the workings of science, education, and human solidarity. In *Travail,* which was deeply influenced by Kropotkin's writings, a leading character states simply, "Science and truth will alone liberate man and, more, will make him master of his destiny, will give him sovereignty over the world, reducing natural forces to the role of docile servants."[54]

Signac's first boast for Neo-Impressionism in "Impressionnistes et Révolutionnaires" was that its technique was revolutionary because it was "more logical and scientific." Neo-Impressionist principles were viewed as copying the natural laws that govern all existence: they delved into the substance of the external world

52. Arsène Alexandre, "L'Art de demain," *L'Eclair,* reprinted in *La Révolte,* V (1892), Literary Supplement, 251.

53. "This ideal of a society harmoniously constituted by the free play of individual initiatives concurring in the common good seems to him to be the goal of human evolution" (Girard, "Art nouveau," 2).

54. Emile Zola, *Travail* (Paris, 1927), 639. The influence of Kropotkin's theories on Zola's novel is discussed by Frederick Ivor Case in *La Cité idéale dans "Travail" d'Emile Zola* (Toronto, 1974), esp. 28–38.

by conforming to the invariable physical laws that rule that substance.[55]

Science, it was expected, could achieve a synthesis not only between the real and the ideal but also between disparate movements in art. The conviction was that neither Naturalism nor Symbolism could provide an adequate synthesis of that sort. To Girard, Naturalism was at best capable of producing "documents"; it was pessimistic, offering no cure for the evils it depicted. According to the anarchist writer Bernard Lazare, Naturalism was incomplete. Even Zola was paralyzed in the face of "brutal fact." Naturalism saw humanity as flawed, life as abject and hopeless. It encouraged passivity and resignation, not struggle for a better life.[56] Symbolism stood accused of incurring the opposite error: a detached mysticism that led to a hermetic isolation from the outside world. Symbolism struck the Neos as atavistic and superstitious, having only a "sterile èlan, without a positive basis, which leaves behind only despair and inane sentiment."[57] In one especially vitriolic critique, an anarchist writer presented Symbolism as an eclectic and neurotic product of decaying capitalism, of the general "social bankruptcy." Its major characteristic, he said, was its incoherence: it was a movement "gravitating from deism to fatalism, atrophying the will to act, leaving neither hope nor certainty nor regret—bizarre, vulgar, crude, reducing our anarchist consciences to simple recording devices registering facts without reacting against them." The courtesies Symbolism offered anarchism were only the praise vice renders to virtue. He concluded, "The same

55. See John Adkins Richardson, *Modern Art and Scientific Thought* (Urbana, Ill., 1971), 67: "Not content with Impressionism's fabricated copies of the phenomenal world, [Seurat] aimed at constructing a phenomenal image first hand, an image that would possess all the brilliance and variability of the world and light itself, because it was constructed with regard to the laws governing the visual mechanics of that world."

56. Girard, "Art nouveau," 2; Bernard Lazare, "L'Ecrivain et l'Art social," *L'Art social,* n.s., I (1896), 12. Lazare argued that artists had been trapped between an art for and about the aristocracy and a Naturalism that "consisted of pulling them as often as possible into debauchery" (p. 12). See Edouard Berth, *Dialogues socialistes* (Paris, 1901), 213–14. For another view, more sympathetic to Naturalism, see Marcel Batilliat, "Le Naturalisme et l'Art social," *L'Art social,* II (1892), 84–86.

57. Freddis [pseud.], "Notes sur l'art," *Revue socialiste,* XV (1892), 458. See Alexandre, "L'Art de demain," 250–51; and Girard, "Art nouveau," 2. Bernard Lazare, no stranger to Symbolism, accused it of having evolved into the province of a "cast of scribes" using a Nietzschean myth of the Superman to justify privilege and power. Posing as antibourgeois, Symbolist art only mirrored the "bourgeois doctrine of free competition, of the struggle to the limit for the possession of the grandest property and the greatest pleasures" ("L'Ecrivain et l'Art social," 10–11).

difference exists between the state of mind called Symbolism and anarchy that exists between a syphilitic canker eating away an organism and the surgeon's scalpel."[58]

The brunt of this attack was against Symbolism as a literary, rather than a visual, movement. But many anarchist artists and militants denounced Symbolist painting with like contumely. A reviewer in Malon's *Revue socialiste* alleged that Symbolist art was the terrain of what an elegant public judged to be "pretty, eccentric, very droll." He called Symbolist *cénacles* the "Boulangism of art"—surely the ultimate insult. Camille Pissarro and Mirbeau waged an unrelenting attack on mysticism in art, condemning it as atavistic and reactionary. A reviewer in the nonparty socialist review *L'Escarmouche* compared Gauguin to a "sort of Tahitian Bastien-Lepage."[59]

The fusion of the ideals of anarchism with the rigors of science would help to yield a new art, it was asserted, a "social symbolism" or "idealistic realism" that could work toward transforming human consciousness. Lazare wrote, "The work of the writer, the work of the artist, the work of social art is to make today's man understand other forms of beauty but also to make him suitable to inhabit the cities of tomorrow."[60]

The goal of *art social* was to aid in the transition to a new age, but not primarily through an active agitation of the kind Proudhon or even Kropotkin had demanded. *Art social* was to mirror

58. Flaustier, "Le Symbolisme pseudo-libertaire," 1. See the vigorous rebuttal by Henry Zisly in "La Littérature libertaire," *Le Plébéian,* II (October 6–20, 1895), 3. See also Flaustier's accompanying reply, "Travestissement symbolique." Camille Pissarro attacked Symbolism as a trap by capitalists trying to turn back the clock: "The bourgeoisie, worried, surprised by the immense clamor of the disinherited masses, by the immense demands of the people, feels the need to return the people to their superstitious beliefs." He added that this explained the "confusion of religious symbolists, religious socialists, *idéiste* art, occultism, Buddhism, etc., etc. Gauguin has sensed this movement" (Camille Pissarro to Lucien Pissarro, May 13, 1891, in Camille Pissarro's *Correspondance,* III, 81–83). The same sentiment—with an almost identical list of isms—occurs in A. Delon's "Pessimisme et Socialisme," *Revue socialiste,* XII (1890), 681–82. For opposing views concerning the relationship between anarchism and Symbolism, see Stuart Merrill, "Chroniques," *L'Ermitage,* VI (1893), 370–72; and Gustave Kahn, *Symbolistes et Décadents* (Paris, 1902), 295–307.

59. Freddis, "Notes sur l'art," 457–59; "Opinions d'artiste," *L'Escarmouche,* I (November 19, 1893).

60. Lazare, "L'Ecrivain et l'Art social," 12. The faith that science, in alliance with a profound idealism, would produce a transformative art clearly distinguishes Lazare's view from that of many bourgeois republicans of the era. Havard, for example, argued that it was a sure sign of decadence when art began to repudiate "originality" in favor of scientific approaches. See Henry Havard, *L'Art à travers les moeurs* (Paris, 1882), 127.

the existing state of social evolution and to advance the process of enlightenment. Lazare wrote, "To transform ideas, to develop a more generous and more human morality must be the role of philosophers, poets, novelists, and artists." He added, "This will also be ours, and the combined effort of the proletariat working toward its own emancipation and the writer down from his ivory tower for good will suffice to create the new world."[61]

In the writings of Proudhon, Grave, and Kropotkin, artists had been called upon both to denounce the injustices of their time and to depict the idyllic future. The supporters of *art social* tended overwhelmingly to concentrate on portraying the better world that was possible. Their message was one of calming and ameliorating the evils of the present. A writer in *L'Art social* called artists advance sentinels who could see past the sordid present to a brighter world: "Holy mission: *to improve, to render a society more beautiful—that is to do social art.*"[62] René Ghil wrote, "Scientifically, in morals, we have achieved our duty and arrived at an altruism without sacrifice, at an unceasing tendency toward improvement at the intersection of balancing egoisms, which are the durable survivors of the primordial instinct of [self-]conservation."[63]

The focus on amelioration and soothing calm was not accidental, since an essential strand in the fabric of anarchocommunism itself was the effort by the displaced and marginalized to rejoin—verbally, if it was no longer possible to do so physically—the center of contemporary existence. Inevitably, the pressure to present a positive, utopian image of the world to come began to shape and mold Neo-Impressionism.

61. Bernard Lazare, "Ce que nous pensons," *L'Action,* I (1896), 1. See Pascal Forthuny, "L'Art et la Vie sociale," in *Almanach de la question sociale* (Paris, 1902), 111–12; and René Ghil, "L'Organisme-Humanité," *L'Enclos,* I (April, 1895), 6–7.

62. Ernest Museux, "Mission," *L'Art social,* I (1891), 26. My emphasis.

63. Ghil, "L'Organisme-Humanité," 6–7. David Sutter had called for a spirit of calm as essential in observation. Sutter argued that calm did not mean insensibility. Rather, "sweet affections and generous sentiments refresh, rest, and fortify the mind; serene thoughts arise from the purity of the soul" (*Philosophie des beaux-arts appliquée à la peinture* [Paris, 1858], 85).

4

Utopianism and the Retreat from the *Grande Jatte*

Georges Seurat's *Sunday Afternoon on the Isle of Grande Jatte* (Figure 6), painted originally in 1884 and reworked in 1886, became the cornerstone of the Neo-Impressionist movement from its debut at the final Impressionist exhibition in 1886. Maurice Hermel called the work a "manifesto painting." A recent biography of Seurat says that the painting forced the avant-garde artists of the day to respond to it, and Fred Orton and Griselda Pollock have examined the painting as the one "every vanguard artist . . . had to come to terms with." They argue that "vanguard painters had to situate their practice in relation to Seurat's current preoccupations; they had to develop along similar lines, take up the issues raised, or challenge his dominance." They examine Emile Bernard's *Breton Women at a Pardon*, produced in 1888, as a work that both appropriates and challenges Seurat's painting.[1]

If the *Grande Jatte* served as a manifesto for Neo-Impressionism, however, its legacy for the movement is ambiguous. As a technical springboard for the new movement, the painting represented an essential ground zero from which the group proceeded. Yet the Neos as a circle no less than the Catholic reactionary Bernard modified—even reversed—the *implications* of Seurat's painting. The *Grande Jatte* is a multivalent questioning or undermining of both form and subject matter in the dominant artistic discourses of the day: Impressionist images of bourgeois leisure fuse with Pierre Puvis de Chavannes' idylls, and then both are turned on their heads in a dizzying blend of deadpan irony and visual puns, many turning on slang terms for prostitution.[2]

---

1. Richard Thomson, *Seurat* (Oxford, 1985), 126; Fred Orton and Griselda Pollock, "Les Données brétonnantes: La Prairie de représentation," *Art History,* III (1980), 314–44.

2. See Thomson, *Seurat,* 97–126.

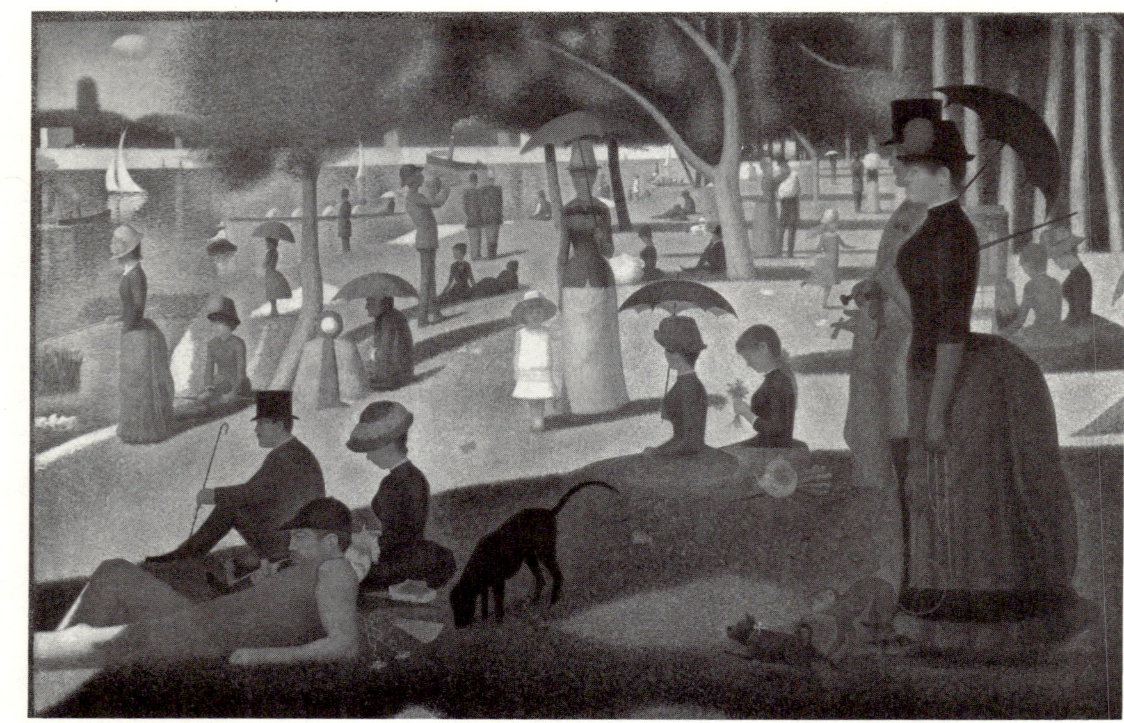

Figure 6   Georges Seurat, *Sunday Afternoon on the Isle of Grande Jatte*
Georges Seurat, French, 1859–1891, A Sunday on La Grande Jatte—1884, oil on canvas, 1884–86, 207.6 x 308 cm, Helen Birch Bartlett Memorial Collection, 1926.224, photograph © 1994, The Art Institute of Chicago, All Rights Reserved.

Critics allied with the socialist or anarchist movements noted the manner in which Seurat lampooned his subjects. For the socialist Henry Fèvre, a supporter of Benoît Malon and a founding member of the Club de l'Art Social in 1889, Seurat's work depicted the "stiffness of idling Parisians, at once starchy and flabby, where even recreation itself is a pose."[3] The poet Paul Adam, still involved in his long flirtation with the anarchist cause, commented in his review of the Impressionist exhibition for the *Revue contemporaine*, "Even the stiffness of these folk, their cutout forms, contribute to the modern tone, remind us of our too small clothes glued to our bodies, the reserve of our gestures, the British cant we all imitate. We strike attitudes like people in a Memling [painting]." He declared, "Monsieur Seurat has seen that perfectly."[4] Alfred Paulet, in *Paris,* took the *Grande Jatte* to portray the "banal promenade" of Parisians in their Sunday best, marching about like automatons.[5]

That the satirical implications of Seurat's painting occurred to Fèvre and Adam, however, does not mean that such an interpretation came easily. Indeed, many critics found the work incomprehensible. Even Fèvre, a proponent of social art, confessed in his review of the 1886 exhibition that he had to study the painting over and over to grasp what Seurat had done. "It is the grandest canvas of the exposition," he decided, "and the layman who looks at it from the side remains quiet, dumbstruck, tempted to cry, 'Hey! What sort of painting is this?'" Fèvre mentioned the abuse and coarse jests the *Grande Jatte* had elicited, but he argued that repeated viewing made both the subject and the manner of the painting clear: "And one closes one's eyes upon it, partly because one is dazzled—and then opens them, shading them with a hand; blinking, one allows a peek through two fingers and then *understands;* one understands the intentions of the painter, that the dazzling and the desired blindness are intentional, and little by little, one familiarizes oneself with it, one guesses, then one sees and loves the great yellow spot of grass eaten by the sun, the golden dusty haze in the treetops, the details the retina, blocked by the light itself, cannot distinguish." Part of the reason Fèvre had difficulty in interpreting the *Grande Jatte* may have stemmed from the

3. Henry Fèvre, *Etude sur la Salon de 1886 et sur l'Exposition des Impressionnistes* (Paris, 1886), 43–44.

4. Paul Adam, "Peintres impressionnistes," *Revue contemporaine,* IV (1886), 550.

5. T. J. Clark, *The Painting of Modern Life: Paris in the Art of Manet and His Followers* (New York, 1984), 264.

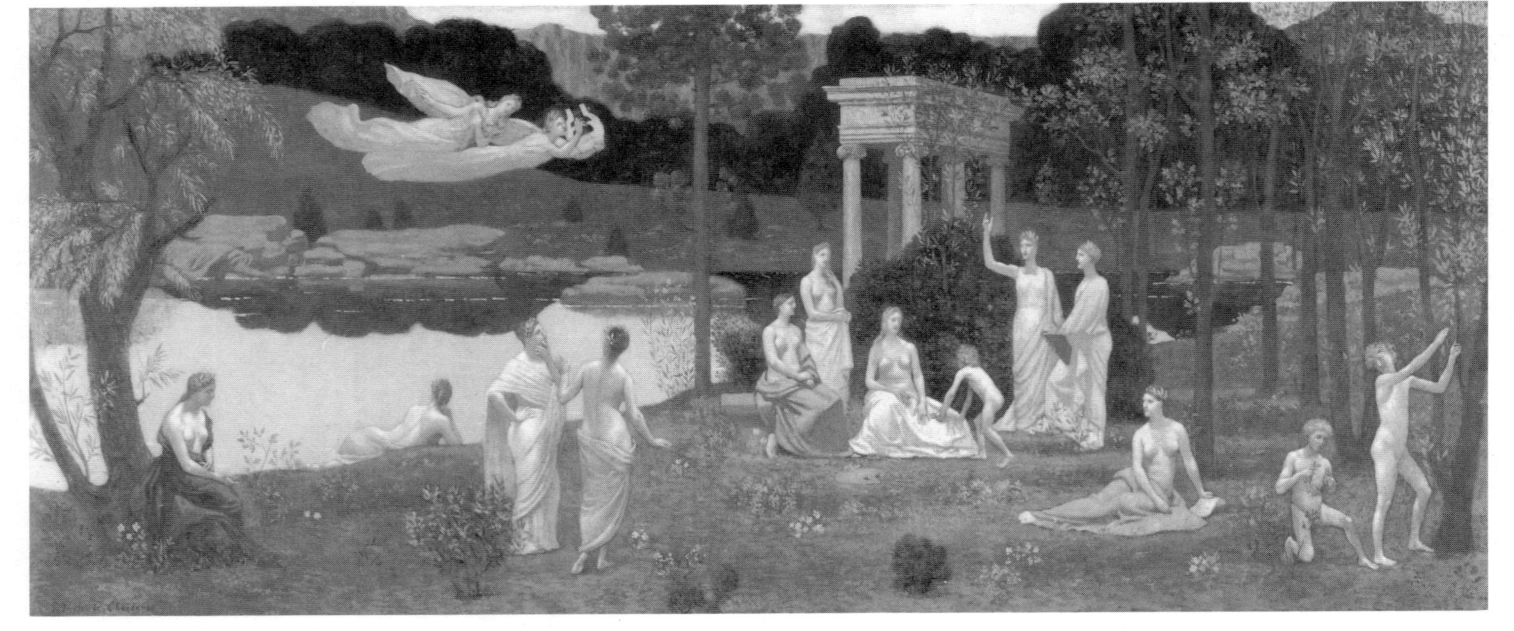

Figure 7   Pierre Puvis de Chavannes, *The Sacred Grove*
Pierre Cécile Puvis de Chavannes, French, 1824–98, The Sacred Grove (Le Bois Sacré cher aux Arts et aux Muses), oil on canvas, *ca.* 1884, 92.6 x 231 cm, Mr. and Mrs. Potter Palmer Collection, 1922.445, photograph © 1994, The Art Institute of Chicago, All Rights Reserved.

comparisons he saw with Puvis de Chavannes: "It is a bit like a materialist Puvis de Chavannes, a *grossomondo* of nature, savagely colored."[6] Puvis occurred to others too when they looked at the *Grande Jatte*. Félix Fénéon thought of Seurat as a "modernizing" Puvis. But what might a materialist Puvis or a modernizing Puvis be? How can Puvis' name gain entrance to the same sentence as *materialist* or *savagely colored?* What might a comparison of Seurat and Puvis signify—and to whom?

The Neo-Impressionists—much like the anarchists and even the socialists generally—were divided in their appraisal of Puvis and his works. In the 1880s, his admirers ranged from the far right to the far left. Vincent van Gogh wrote in a letter to his sister Wilhelmina in 1890 that Puvis' *The Sacred Grove,* of 1884 (Figure 7), seemed to promise a "complete but kindly rebirth of all things that one had believed in and desired, a strange and happy meeting of very remote antiquities with crude modernity."[7] It is not difficult to find remote antiquities in Puvis' classical landscape. Crude modernity, however, seems present only in the eye of the viewer, for Puvis ruthlessly expunged it from the painted canvas. Indeed, Puvis' world of art—the painting's full title is *The Sacred Grove, Dear to the Arts and the Muses*—is all but completely sealed off from our own. Puvis contended that *The Sacred Grove* must be surrounded "by high mountains that close off access to this favored place."[8] His world was necessarily a world without modern referents. One critic praised his paintings for their "eternal and immutable" character, and another, Théophile Gautier, wrote—in 1865, to be sure—that "his paintings have for their only date the golden age." Much like Ingres' *Golden Age,* from the years 1842–1849, Puvis' pastoral scenes spring from a profoundly reactionary antipathy to the modern world. In an essay in the *Revue de Paris* in 1871, Puvis wrote, "I do not exaggerate when I say that we are very, very sick. There is an immense poisoning of the moral sense. . . . How can [we] bring back religious faith, faith in politics, the respect of hierarchy, and the family spirit?"[9] Immediately after the suppression

6. Fèvre, *Etude sur la Salon de 1886,* 43–44.

7. Robert L. Delevoy, *Symbolists and Symbolism* (New York, 1982), 67.

8. Miriam R. Levin, *Republican Art and Ideology in Late Nineteenth-Century France* (Ann Arbor, Mich., 1986), 157.

9. Claudine Mitchell, "Time and the Idea of Patriarchy in the Pastorals of Puvis de Chavannes," *Art History,* X (1987), 188–202. On the political program and implications of Ingres' *Age d'or,* see Carol Ockham, "Astraea Redux: A Monarchist Reading of Ingres' Unfinished Murals at Dampierre," *Arts Magazine,* LI (October, 1986), 21–27.

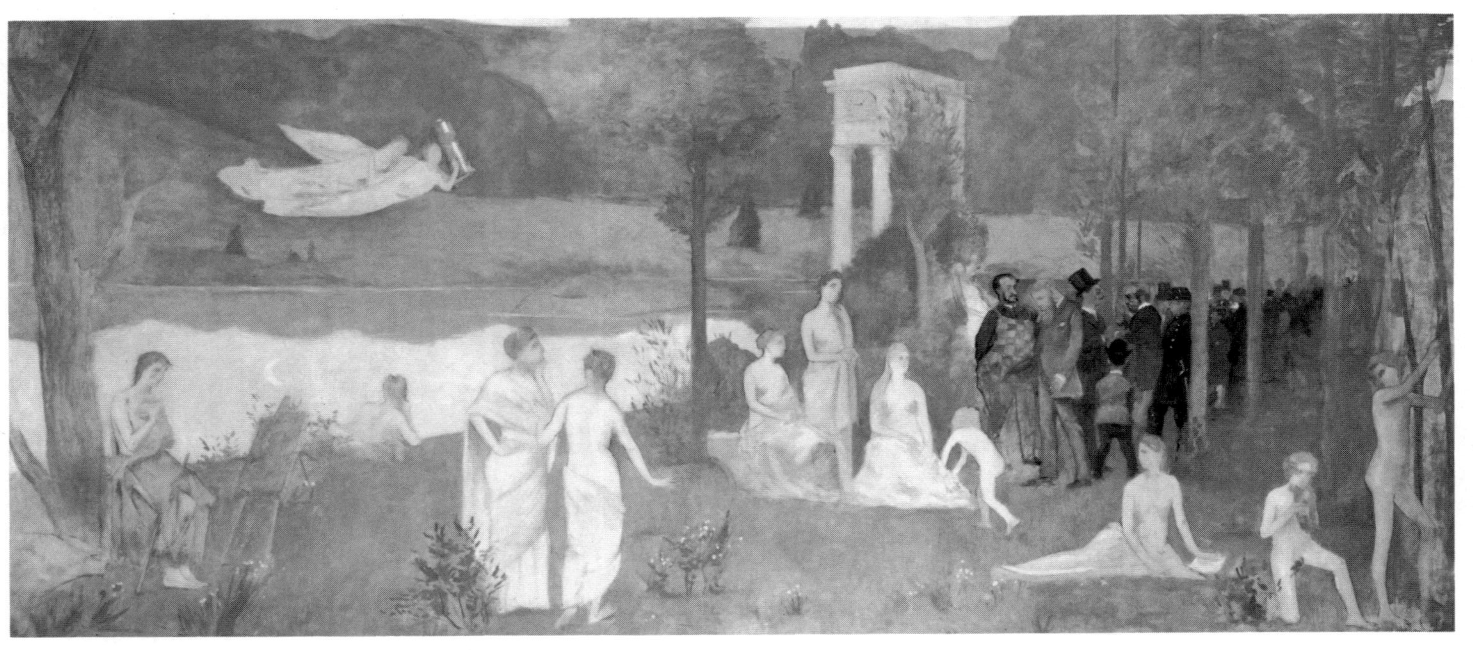

Figure 8   Henri de Toulouse-Lautrec, parody of *The Sacred Grove*
"Le Bois Sacré" Parodie du Panneau de Puvis de Chavannes du Salon de 1884, oil on canvas, 1884. The Art Museum, Princeton University. Lent by the Henry and Rose Pearlman Foundation.

of the Paris Commune, with the blood of as many as thirty thousand still staining Père Lachaise and the Lobau Barracks, *religious faith* and *respect for hierarchy* were anything but neutral phrases: they had framed and justified the slaughter itself.

Some anarchists nonetheless found merit in Puvis' art, at times exactly because of his elitism. Fénéon hailed his paintings as accessible to "thinkers alone."[10] French republican theorists, however—and even more clearly many socialists and anarchists—praised Puvis' work only in spite of its political subtext, for capturing on canvas the perfectibility of humanity and the social order. The socialist leader Jean Jaurès detected in the paintings a demonstration of the coming reconciliation of humanity with itself and with nature. In Puvis, he found a "sweet and white milky way that crosses, from the origin of the centuries, the disorder of the times and the brutality of things."[11] Bourgeois republicans such as Antonin Proust discovered the integrated, seamless reflection of social harmony they believed wanting in the paintings of Manet.[12]

The appeal of Puvis' lethargic utopias escaped others. Henri de Toulouse-Lautrec and a team of his friends worked for two days straight to complete a biting parody of *The Sacred Grove* (Figure 8). Here the crude modernity glimpsed by van Gogh assembles to invade the grove. A long line of bohemians led by Toulouse-Lautrec and Adolphe Willette marches in from the right, startling Puvis' placid nymphs. A modern clock graces the central structure in Puvis' grove—a sort of classicized gazebo—while the nikes who float overhead lug oversized paint tubes.

The insurgent anarchists of Emile Pouget's *Le Père Peinard* commended Toulouse-Lautrec for tearing apart the safe, gauzy world of official art. They considered the peaceful glades of Puvis' art merely an artificial gloss over a sordid present. For Pouget and his colleagues, Toulouse-Lautrec's art—regardless of his personal politics—was a powerful indictment of a smug and heartless society, and it was Toulouse-Lautrec who preeminently revealed the essence of the *capitalos gagas* who dominated French society.[13]

---

10. Levin, *Republican Art and Ideology,* 157.

11. Jean Jaurès, "L'Art et le Socialisme," *Le Mouvement socialiste,* III (1900), 587–88. See Edouard Berth, *Dialogues socialistes* (Paris, 1901), 214–15. See also Aristide Pratelle, "Vulgaraisons la beauté," *Les Temps nouveaux,* XII (February 9, 1907), 2; and Léon Deshairs, "Chronique artistique: Puvis de Chavannes," *Le Mouvement socialiste,* II (1899), 178.

12. Levin, *Republican Art and Ideology,* 184–86.

13. The article "Chez les barbouilleurs, les affiches en couleurs"—by the same Félix Fénéon who praised Puvis' *Sacred Grove,* which Toulouse-Lautrec mocked—appeared in

Toulouse-Lautrec's parody of *The Sacred Grove* not only attacked the form of Puvis' painting but punctured its nostalgic utopianism, in keeping with the way Toulouse-Lautrec's scenes of the underside of urban Paris were the negation of Puvis' anemic Classicism. Toulouse-Lautrec's art was neither utopian nor dystopian; it neither evoked a golden past nor anticipated a better future. Bound to a permanent present, it was an art of empathy rather than hope—an endless, often lacerating rendering of a world without any expectation of escape or release, much less social transformation. To a "timeless" art of rest and repose, Toulouse-Lautrec counterposed a relentless art inextricably bound to social reality as he experienced it.

The regularity of the references to Puvis' art in critical reviews of Seurat during the period should not divert attention from the qualifications offered whenever Puvis' name came up. A "modernizing" Puvis, a "materialist" Puvis, a Puvis of "savagely colored" nature is not Puvis at all: the restrictions yield an anti-Puvis in whose work key concepts and forms are inverted and reversed, reinvented for a new art in a new cause. Paul Alexis' description of Seurat's *Bathers at Asnières* as a "false Puvis" sensed the inversion.[14] In Seurat's paintings, Puvis' atmosphere of calm is replaced by an exaggerated rigidity and a distinct critical edge. Toulouse-Lautrec parodied Puvis directly, showing the clash between the allegorical figures and the invading bohemians; in the *Grande Jatte,* the bourgeoisie has made the grove its own. The policeman from Toulouse-Lautrec's work has been sent home, but there is a military band.

Reviews of the *Grande Jatte* were sprinkled with references to the hieratic qualities of the painting, but remarks about the painting's classical qualities do not efface the avidity with which critics sought to pin down the precise mixture of classes depicted in the work. Jules Christophe, writing in the *Journal des artistes* in 1886, discriminated a broad range of social classes. He inferred that Seurat had tried to capture the "diverse attitudes of age, of sex, and of social class: elegant men and women, soldiers, nurserymaids, bourgeois, workers."[15] Paulet identified maids, clerks, and sol-

---

Le Père Peinard for April 30, 1893; it is reprinted in Fénéon's *Oeuvres plus que complètes,* ed. Joan Halperin (Geneva, 1970), I, 229.

14. Paul Alexis [Trublot], "A minuit: Les Indépendants," *Le Cri du peuple,* May 17, 1884, p. 3.

15. Jules Christophe, "Chronique:. Rue Laffitte No. 1," *Journal des artistes,* June 13, 1886, quoted by Clark in *The Painting of Modern Life,* 263.

diers among the crowd, and Hermel observed the presence of wet nurses, conscripts, and *canotiers.*[16]

Recent scholarship has further extended the debate over the class composition of the painting, as well as the relationship between the *Grande Jatte* and the slumped plebeian figures in Seurat's earlier *Bathers at Asnières,* painted in 1883–84 (Figure 9).[17] But the crux is not the exact delineation of the status of the figures—who broadly number the *haute bourgeoisie,* together with its satellites, servitors, and parasites—but what Seurat does with the mix. Toulouse-Lautrec's images of the Parisian netherworld cling to some vestige of Impressionism's claimed spontaneity and objectivity; Seurat's group image of bourgeois Paris at leisure, by contrast, is all deliberation and predetermination—a deadpan vivisection of time, place, and milieu. Nothing in the *Grande Jatte* seems "natural"—no more than Neo-Impressionism claimed to continue the "natural spontaneity" of Impressionism. The stiff, overdressed figures standing or sitting in mute isolation exist in an openly unreal environment, where a tree can have two shadows and a lurking prowler hides in the darkness of a copse.

The venom of Seurat's image is partly coded: the pet monkey belonging to the large woman at the right seems clearly to serve as a signifier for prostitution.[18] The painting also employs more straightforward elements of caricature, however. The dress of the woman with the monkey, for example, seems a clear target: the grotesque dimensions of the bustle are all the more apparent from the rigid profile in which she is shown. Of course, even with the extra few inches of "hump" Seurat added to the bustle after he initially painted it, the woman's dress is scarcely more exaggerated than those presented in fashion illustrations of the time. There were, though, established techniques by which the figure could be smoothed out and the dimensions of the bustle minimized. Artists from Camille Corot to James Tissot—or for that matter, the Neo

16. Thomson, *Seurat,* 122.

17. For the details of this discussion, see Sally Medlyn, "The Development of Georges Seurat's Art with Special Reference to the Influence of Contemporary Anarchist Philosophy" (M.A. thesis, University of Manchester, 1976), 54–66; Clark, *The Painting of Modern Life,* 265–67; Thomson, *Seurat,* 121–23; John House, "Meaning in Seurat's Figure Paintings," *Art History,* III (1980), 345–46; and Mary Martha Ward, "The Rhetoric of Independence and Innovation," in *The New Painting: Impressionism, 1874–1886* (San Francisco, 1986), 434–36. More recently, other aspects of the social relations in the painting have come under investigation, particularly those involving gender and the family. See Hollis Clayson, "The Family and the Father: The *Grande Jatte* and Its Absences," *Museum Studies,* XIV (1989), 155–64.

18. Thomson, *Seurat,* 123–24.

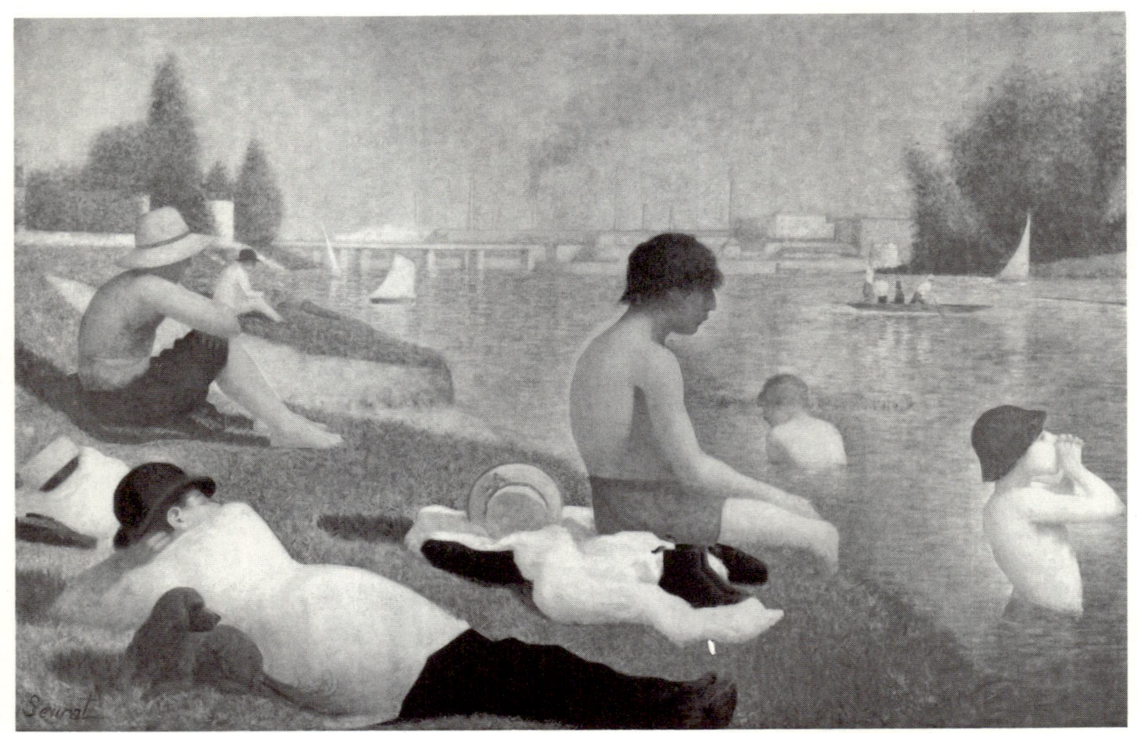

Figure 9   Georges Seurat, *Bathers at Asnières*
Oil on canvas, 1883–84. Reproduced by courtesy of the Trustees, The National Gallery, London.

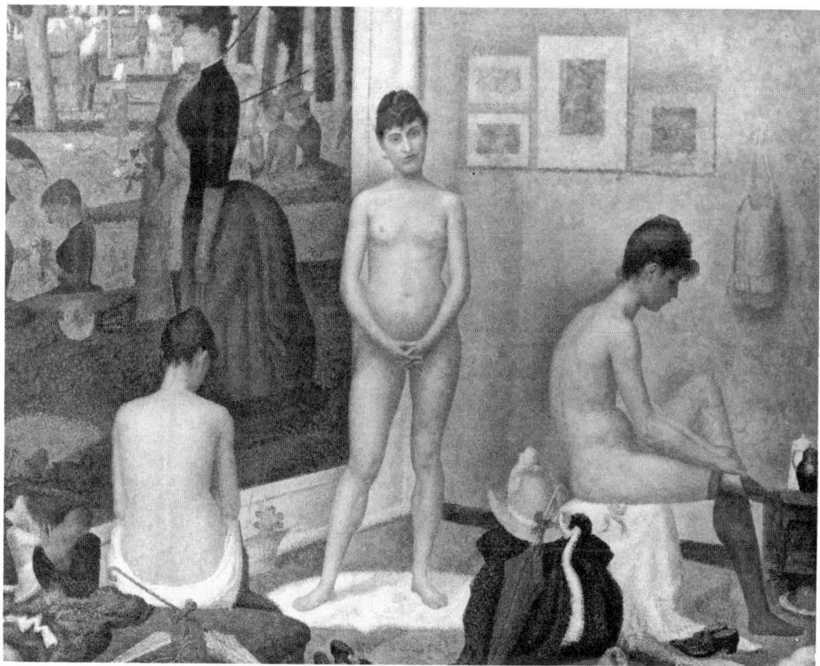

Figure 10   Georges Seurat, *The Models*
Oil on canvas, 1887–88. Photograph © copyright 1994 by The Barnes Foundation.

Henri Edmond Cross—commonly placed the woman at an angle
to the viewer, slanting her either toward or away to diminish the
sense that the subject had some large artifact strapped to her bottom. Seurat deliberately does the opposite: the woman is rendered
in painfully precise silhouette, stiffened and flattened and juxtaposed to her equally stiff companion and the absurd monkey.

Two other works in Seurat's oeuvre are linked to the *Grande
Jatte* thematically as well as in size and scale: *Bathers at Asnières,*
and *The Models,* of 1887–1888 (Figure 10). One recent study of
Seurat's work dismisses the idea that the *Grande Jatte* and the *Bathers* are pendants; they do not share a common horizon line and the
figures in the two works are not to the same scale.[19] Seurat was
not Hans Memling, however, and the juxtaposition of two class
groupings, engaged in two radically divergent forms of recreation
on opposing banks of the same river, possibly on successive days

19. *Ibid.,* 125.

(Sunday, Monday) rewards attention.[20] John House has argued persuasively that the two paintings together convey a sense of warring social spheres: the story of the Horatii and the Curatii—to use Seurat's own example—transformed in keeping with modern social class.[21] We can even infer a certain one-sided interaction between the two tableaux, as a young boy of the *Bathers* standing in the river, uncomfortably close to the ominous green effluent, cups his hands above his mouth to shout across the river to the opposite bank.

The relationship between the *Grande Jatte* and *The Models* poses analogous questions of class juxtaposition. In *The Models,* the right corner of the *Grande Jatte,* which is shown bisecting Seurat's studio diagonally, forms the backdrop to a scene of three young women, apparently auditioning as models. The motif of the auditioning model was developed also by Oswald Heidbrinck in *The Reception of the Model,* in an issue of the *Courrier français* from 1892 (Figure 11). Heidbrinck, attuned to the *Courrier'*s predilections, seized on the scene as a way of portraying a large amount of female flesh; his nudes are more robust than Seurat's and are provocatively posed. Though some viewers from the period—including Paul Signac's pupil Lucie Coustourier—found the nudes of *The Models* to be a "sort of triptych of feminine beauty," others found the counterposition of the *Grande Jatte* backdrop and the would-be models particularly significant.[22] Adam underscored the contrast between the "natural" simplicity of the models and the unnatural and exaggerated clothing and pose of the figures from the earlier painting.[23] The critic Gustave Geffroy, writing in Clemenceau's *La Justice* when that journal could still pose with some credibility as the voice of a "socialist" opposition, saw the models as working-class women whose thin build bespoke the "truth of the towns and of arduous toil." He perceived an odd mixture of cruelty and gentleness in the painting's treatment of the models' clothing and

20. Clayson, "The Family and the Father," 162.

21. House, "Meaning in Seurat's Figure Paintings," 348–49.

22. Lucie Coustourier, *Georges Seurat* (Paris, 1922), 21. Jules Christophe described the central woman similarly in "Georges Seurat," *Les Hommes d'aujourd'hui,* No. 368 (1890).

23. Paul Adam, "Les Impressionnistes à l'Exposition des Indépendants," *La Vie moderne,* April 15, 1888, p. 229. Adam's critique is deeply embedded in a masculinist discourse in which women equaled—or should equal—nature, in contrast to culture. The problematic aspects of defining what is natural with regard to clothing or the lack of it are discussed by Elizabeth Wilson in *Adorned in Dreams: Fashion and Modernity* (London, 1985). See especially pp. 234–35 of that book.

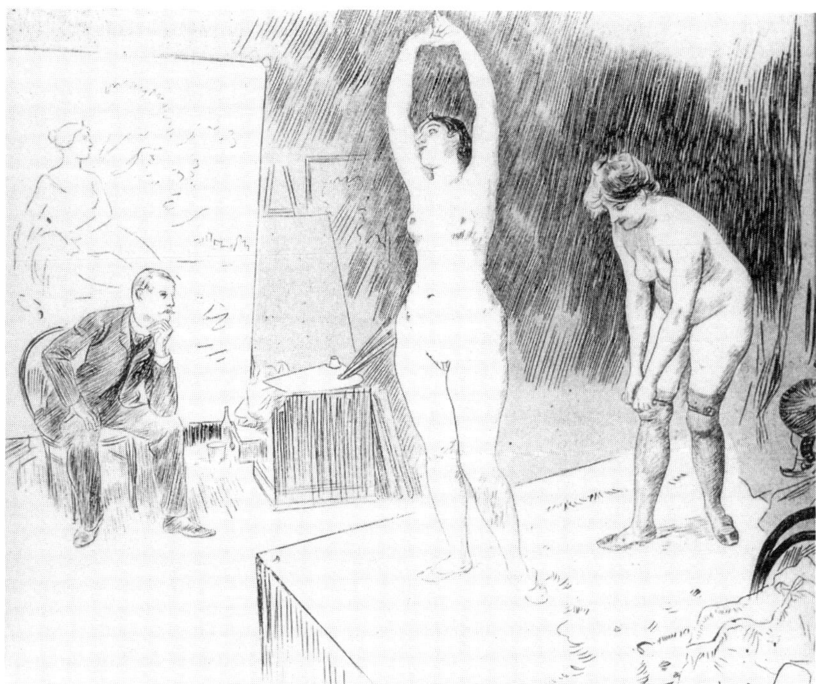

Figure 11   Oswald Heidbrinck, *The Reception of the Model*
In *Courrier français,* May 29, 1892

physiques. Geffroy felt that a certain affectionate empathy was dominant in the painting; he added that the painting "is perhaps the sign of the dreaming vision and the caress by M. Seurat of the things he adores."[24] *The Models,* although slightly smaller than the *Grande Jatte,* forms not so much a pendant to it as an *extension* into a different space, a different set of class relations.[25] Both the contrast noted by Adam between nude, "natural" modesty and clothed artificiality and Geffroy's invocation of class are applicable. The foreground world of young women from the working class in this interpretive framework would indicate simplicity and modesty; the prospective models are nude, but simple and un-

24. Gustave Geffroy, "Pointillé-Cloissonnisme," *La Justice,* April 11, 1888, p. 1. For a similar, if harsher, reading, see Ernest Varlant, "Le Salon des XX," *La Jeune Belgique,* XI (1892), 189.

25. Before its added painted border, the *Grande Jatte* was 207 cm. × 308 cm. *The Models* measures 200 cm. × 205 cm.

adorned.[26] The clothed, fashionable figure from the *Grande Jatte* is the prostitute, her rigidity contrasting with the models' thin contours. If the juxtaposition was intended to illustrate the contrast between a natural world and the unpleasant artificiality of bourgeois life, Seurat was breaking with the clichéd oppositions of male and female, and culture and nature, that were dominant in his time; *both* sides of the polarity are of the same gender, making class rather than gender the criterion of differentiation.[27]

Unlike Impressionist scenes of urban life, Seurat's works make no pretense of capturing a candid, spontaneous glimpse of reality. Seurat's paintings form an interconnected series of deliberate, conscientious efforts to freeze, analyze, and essentialize modern life. His deliberation, with its attendant return to careful preliminary studies, made Camille Pissarro suspicious of Seurat—if only fitfully—from the outset of the Neo-Impressionist movement. However "primitive" the result seemed to most critics—in the stiff friezes of partly flattened figures which reminded Adam of Memling and others of the Pan-Athenaic procession—the result was grounded in a complex matrix of scientific, and "scientific," theories. Charles Henry argued that "the progress of social organization will have the effect of simplifying and improving our social psychology." It would be possible, he maintained, to fix and freeze the essence of the psychology of modern life.[28]

Neo-Impressionism and Utopianism

In theory, anarchocommunist analyses of art provided for just the sort of social critique Seurat essayed in the *Grande Jatte*. In practice, however, proponents of *art social*—above all, the anarchocommunists and the reform socialists around the *Revue socialiste*—heavily

26. See Medlyn, "The Development of Georges Seurat's Art," 109–14; and Thomson, *Seurat,* 146. House argues similarly that the return to "more supple contours" in *The Models* demonstrates that the stiffness of the *Grande Jatte* figures is a deliberate part of the picture's program. In other words, the rigidity of the men and women of the *Grande Jatte* must be discussed in terms not just of style but of significance.

27. For an examination of the equation of the female with nature and of the male with culture, see Sherry B. Ortner, "Is Female to Male as Nature Is to Culture?" in *Woman, Culture, Society,* ed. Michelle Zimbalist Rosaldo and Louise Lamphere (New York, 1974), 67–87.

28. See the interview with Henry in Jules Huret's *Enquête sur l'évolution littéraire* (Paris, 1891), 413–19. Henry added, "It is certain that one will arrive at a certain *stable state* in language, which will tend toward a certain immobility in the evolution of psychological factors" (p. 417).

emphasized the need for art to calm, to soothe, to embody the beautiful dream of a dawning golden age. The anarchist poet Paul Napoléon Roinard typically linked political anarchism and social art as necessary complements, so that there were "anarchists of the act or the dream."[29] It is no coincidence that Fèvre, when defending the *Grande Jatte* against its detractors, could level no more damning accusation against them than that they were "pro-fane"—enemies of a sacred world of beauty.

It has been argued that Kropotkin and his fellows rejected uto-pianism.[30] It is certainly true that anarchocommunist writings em-phasized their scientific basis. But, like the English Fabians and the French Independents, the anarchocommunists believed that it was essential to exhibit in detail the shape of a future classless so-ciety. Kropotkin's followers held that the failure of Marxian so-cialism to prepare a detailed blueprint for the future proved that Marxism only pretended to work for a thoroughgoing social revo-lution.[31] They believed that concrete visions of a golden future were essential to anarchists and utopian socialists because they gave a solid form to yearnings for a better, alternative society.[32] The plethora of anarchist utopian novels at the turn of the century testifies to the prevalence of the notion that through an awakening of the dream of a better world, the cause would be advanced.[33] Both anarchocommunists and Malon's followers would have con-curred with Malon's friend and colleague Georges Renard that so-cialism was to come about as "Eden regained, peace descending from the sky 'strewing gold, flowers, and ears of corn,' as in the songs of one of our old *chansonniers,* . . . concord reigning from one end of the globe to the other."[34]

29. P. N. Roinard, "Anarchie d'art," *L'Art social,* II (1892), 131. On Roinard and his views, see Jeanne Lambert, "Le Poète Paul-Napoléon Roinard, 1856–1930," *La Rue,* XXI (1976), 97–99.

30. See George Woodcock, *Anarchism: A History of Libertarian Ideas and Movements* (2nd ed.; Harmondsworth, Eng., 1986), 21–22.

31. "Marx advances no fundamental theory of future society: for him, the term *com-munism* is only a trompe l'oeil" ("Le Congrès international à Bruxelles," *La Révolte,* IV [September 19–25, 1891], 2).

32. See Benoît Malon, "L'Utopie dans l'histoire," *Revue socialiste,* XVIII (1893), 129–57. "The act of hoping is not illusory" (p. 130).

33. Among the novels are Joseph Déjacque's *L'Humanisphère,* republished by Grave in 1899, and Grave's own *Terre-Libre,* of 1908. Sebastien Faure's *Le Bonheur universelle,* of 1920, was a late entry into this category. William Morris' *News from Nowhere,* of 1890, with its depiction of a quasi-medieval, rural, decentralized future, was widely acclaimed by French anarchocommunists.

34. Georges Renard, *Paroles d'avenir* (Paris, 1904), 80–81.

The Neo-Impressionists themselves most commonly responded to anarchocommunist theoretical statements not as guides to actions but as lovely dreams. In April, 1892, Camille Pissarro wrote in a letter to Lucien that he had received a new book by Kropotkin.[35] The book—most likely Kropotkin's *The Conquest of Bread*—impressed him greatly.[36] He wrote to Octave Mirbeau the same month, "I have just read Kropotkin's book. *It may be that it is utopian, but in every way it is a beautiful dream.*" He went on, "And as we have had plenty of examples of utopias becoming realities, nothing prevents us from believing that it will be possible one day, unless man founders and returns to complete barbarism."[37] In 1892, Cross wrote to Maximilien Luce that he received Grave's *La Révolte* regularly. "What a generous and powerful philosophy!" he exclaimed.[38]

Such attitudes were clearly predisposed to accept Puvis de Chavannes as the harbinger of a new *âge d'or;* even the syndicalist Edouard Berth saw in Puvis' work a "harmonious and serene form, freely social."[39] Many anarchist critics were remarkably eclectic in their appreciation of art and artists; they acclaimed works and artists for subject matter and emotional impact. The praise for Puvis could move swiftly to praise for Claude Monet: an anarchist critic commended Monet for capturing not mere reality but "reality enchanted."[40] Puvis and Monet alike could be admired for their consistent eschewing of the ugly and the sordid.

Hence, it is to be expected that when anarchist critics praised Neo-Impressionism, it was rarely if ever for the multivalent ironies of Seurat's images. Rather, Neo-Impressionism's anarchist supporters hailed the movement for capturing the certainty of a radiant and beautiful future. One of the most detailed and enthusiastic critiques of Neo-Impressionism in an anarchist journal was the one in Jean Grave's *Les Temps nouveaux* in which Charles Albert employed Signac's *D'Eugène Delacroix au néo-impressionnisme*

35. Camille Pissarro to Lucien Pissarro, April 26, 1892, in Camille Pissarro's *Lettres à son fils Lucien,* ed. John Rewald (Paris, 1947). See Lucien's response of May 5, 1892, also included there.

36. The identification of the book is from Robert L. Herbert and Eugenia W. Herbert's "Artists and Anarchism: Unpublished Letters of Pissarro, Signac, and Others," *Burlington Magazine,* CII (1960), 480n40.

37. Georges Lecomte, *Camille Pissarro* (Paris, 1902), 95. My emphasis.

38. Isabelle Compin, *H. E. Cross* (Paris, 1964), 51.

39. Berth, *Dialogues socialistes,* 216.

40. Jean Denauroy, "Exposition Claude Monet," *Les Temps nouveaux,* X (May 21–27, 1904), 6.

as the theoretical framework for an examination of the movement. Albert congratulated the Neos for the way they captured the "beauty of tomorrow: not the harsh and fugitive beauty dear to unhealthy souls of our time *but essential beauty, refreshing and pure.*" For Albert, the key to understanding Neo-Impressionism lay in recognizing Signac's goal of "complete harmony" in "integral purity." Conscious of the passion with which Neo-Impressionism had been debated by artists, intellectuals, and the public, Albert argued that he found in its works a "deeply uniform impression of restful serenity, of peaceful harmony, of innocent and pure freshness."[41] It was clear to him that Neo-Impressionism looked forward to the day when the workers would be liberated from the struggle for bare necessities, when in a "regenerated society," Neo-Impressionism would be employed "for our railway stations and our factories, for our schools and *maisons de santé,* for our meeting halls and our playhouses, for our baths and gymnasiums, as well as for the beauty of our streets and our towns."[42] Mirbeau was satisfied with Pissarro's landscapes for conveying the essence of the "great terrestrial harmony," and an article in *Les Temps nouveaux* saluted the landscapes of Luce as embodying the "image of the harmonious and free life we desire."[43]

Anarchist criticisms of Neo-Impressionism were often—taken together—contradictory. Mirbeau criticized Signac's art for its immobility: "He ignores movement, life, the very soul of things. M. Signac renders nature immobile and static."[44] Within anarcho-communist circles, however, it was widely argued that Mirbeau gave priority to aesthetics—the idea of beauty in particular—over the analysis that was the basis for a comprehensive, essentializing art.[45] The essence that art pursued was by definition beautiful, just as the essence of life and humanity was beautiful. The anarchist

41. Charles Albert, "La 21° Exposition des Artistes Indépendants," *Les Temps nouveaux,* X (April 8–14, 1905), 6–7. My emphasis.

42. *Ibid.,* 7.

43. Jean Denauroy, "Exposition Maximilien Luce et Notes sur le paysage," *Les Temps nouveaux,* XII (March 2, 1907), 7. See Octave Mirbeau, "Camille Pissarro," *L'Art dans les deux mondes,* VIII (January 10, 1891), 84. See also Pierre Dhure, "Art," *Journal du peuple,* April 7, 1899, p. 2. Edmond Coustourier ("Notes d'art," *Entretiens politiques et littéraires,* VI [1893], 331–33) is unusual in praising Pissarro for his cityscapes as well as his rural scenes.

44. *L'Echo de Paris,* January 23, 1894, reprinted in Camille Pissarro's *Lettres à son fils Lucien,* 327–28.

45. See Charles Albert, "Entreprendre une définition de l'art," *Les Temps nouveaux,* X (September 17–23, 1904), 4–5.

Jacques Brieu, writing in *La Plume,* defined "integral art" in such a way as to make art part of a trio of unresolved antinomies existing in separate but equal spheres: science, he said, searches for truth, ethics for the good, and art for the beautiful, with each needing the others but unable to be substituted for them.[46]

When anarchist militants or writers attacked Neo-Impressionism, it was often for a perceived inability to capture the essential beauty of the golden age; Neo-Impressionism was sometimes taken to task for being too "cold" and unemotional. Occasionally the critique was only implicit: one anarchist writer briefly summarized and examined the bases of Neo-Impressionist theory, then cited as his own ideal a maudlin evocation of motherhood from the Salon of 1888.[47] Others were more specific in their criticisms: the poet P. N. Roinard classified the Neos as Neo-Realists (a grouping so broad that he could list Toulouse-Lautrec, Louis Anquetin, and Vincent van Gogh in it as well), in contrast to the "Neo-Mystic" symbolist artists. Roinard asserted that Neo-Impressionist theory was disastrous: "Pointillism . . . makes me rage," he wrote, "but it is dying." He conceded, "Certainly this formula, the last good idea of an analysis fallen into minutiae and shabbiness, is not altogether destitute of interest." But for him, Neo-Impressionism's claim to a scientific basis was a liability, as "science always produces bad art."[48] Roinard, it should be made clear, was not excluding science from anarchist theory—just from anarchist art, which he wished to see permeated with an overriding idealism. He rejected Neo-Impressionism's claim to provide a synthetic vision of life; he looked instead toward a coalescence of Neo-Realism and Symbolism to form an art "ideally real."[49]

A more detailed and incisive—if ultimately almost as hostile—attempt to examine the same division of contemporary art and its implications for the anarchist movement came in a two-part review in *Le Libertaire* by the editor Paterne Berrichon, who, in concord with Roinard's classification, began, "Springing from Impressionism, two groupings of painters can be distinguished from all others," namely the "chromo-luminarists" (Neo-Impressionists) and the Symbolists.[50] Berrichon expressed no sympathy for the

46. Jacques Brieu, "L'Art intégral," *La Plume,* C (1893), 263–64.

47. Charles Jacques Ehrly, "La Nature et la Vie dans la peinture," *Le Libertaire,* VII (February 3–9, 1901), 13–14.

48. Roinard, "Anarchie d'art," 126.

49. *Ibid.*

50. Paterne Berrichon, "Sur la peinture," *Le Libertaire,* II (December 28, 1895—January 4, 1896), 2, (January 4–11, 1896), 4.

Symbolists whatever: "As opposed to the Neo-Impressionists, the Symbolists want everything of the subject and nothing of the object, but there are grounds for complaint against them for a subjective exaggeration, resulting sometimes in a superstitious monstrosity, indeed idiocy." Berrichon took Symbolism to be a by-product of the "aesthetic uncertainty of our time, of its general psychological state" marked by a nostalgic mysticism and a fondness for morbid emotion and a general embrace of "artistic barbarism."[51]

Berrichon conceded more space and sympathy to the Neos. He saw them as moral and philosophical comrades, but he found their theoretical and formal framework overrestrictive: it ended in "too much disciplined exclusivism based upon a too rigorous science where art loses its face." He added of the Neos that, "all analytics, their vision killed emotivity." Their study of color yielded only a "cold shock on the eye of the spectator, without repercussion in the nervous corridors attendant upon sensation."[52]

Unlike Roinard, Berrichon took some pains to expose what he saw as the fundamental problem inherent in the idea of a "scientific art." Like Brieu, he asserted that artistic truth is not scientific truth. The two kinds of truth must maintain a certain separation so that a global truth can be found in their continued interaction: "The one and the other . . . are but different aspects, poles, elements of a total Truth still to be discovered. . . . Neither Harmony nor Rhythm is capable of a litigious marriage of similar unities." (He asked, "But does this [unity] exist even in Nature?")[53]

Roinard and Berrichon struck at the heart not just of Neo-Impressionist theory but of the whole concept of *art social* as a perfect synthesis of the scientific and the ideal. They rejected the idea of synthesis as a fusion, in favor of a conception of it as a permanent oscillation between antinomial truths; Brieu saw synthesis as residing in a triangular field marked out by the separate claims of science, ethics, and art. Both interpretations denied that art could by itself serve as the seat of synthesis. It could only be one element of an aggregate, and an element bound more closely to the affirmation of ideals than to the critique of existing forms or institutions.

In accord with that conviction, the Neo-Impressionist circle tended to smooth out the deliberate ambivalences of Seurat's work,

---

51. *Ibid.* (January 4–11), 4.
52. *Ibid.* (December 28, 1895—January 4, 1896), 2.
53. *Ibid.*

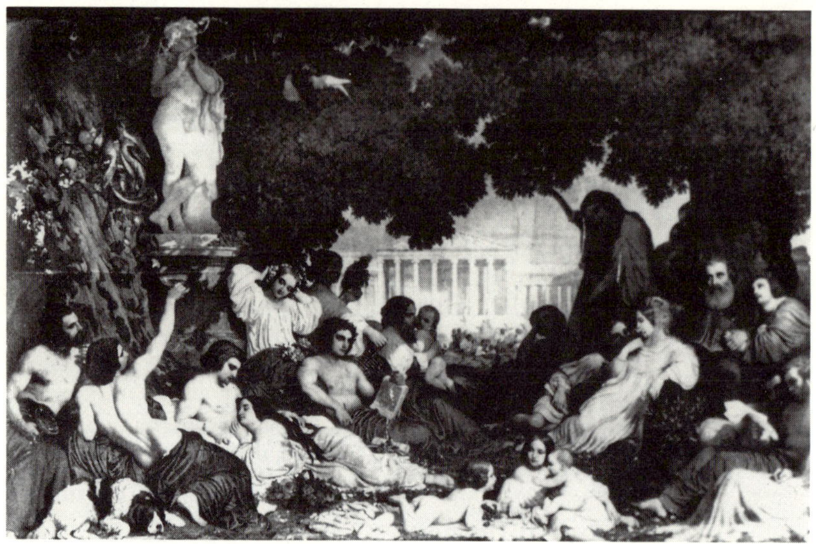

Figure 12   Dominique Papety, *Dream of Happiness*
Rêve de bonheur, oil on canvas, 1843. Musée Vivenel, Compiègne.

to deemphasize his detached irony in favor of a relatively unambiguous assertion of social harmony and the beauty of a return to a "natural" life.

In addition to drawing on Puvis' classical pastorals, the Neo-Impressionists could also tap a more explicitly utopian artistic tradition. Dominique Papety's *Dream of Happiness,* of 1843 (Figure 12), is a clear prototype from that tradition. Papety's painting is a rather crowded classical landscape, with a somewhat awkwardly conveyed Fourierist theme: idealized figures, including children, loll on what is apparently the lawn of a phalanstery, reveling in the abundance of the emancipated future. The costumes are classical; only the title and the word *harmonie* inscribed on the base of the statue at the left manifest the work's social theme.

Papety wanted to distinguish his work from the "timeless" but always antique world of such reactionary pastorals as Ingres' *Golden Age:* Ingres located the *âge d'or* in a distant past, whereas Fourier placed his in the future. Yet for the coming age to be truly golden, for it to depict humanity once more in harmony with the world of nature, the signs of industrialization—with all its tensions and dislocations—had to be minimized, even effaced. Papety intended at one point to include a railroad in his *Dream of Happiness,* but that symbol of the machine age could only have

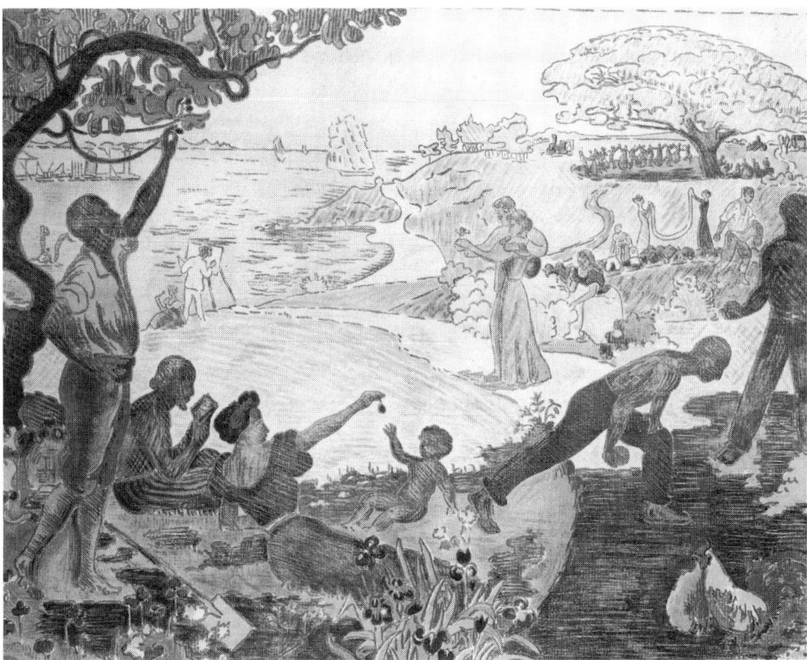

Figure 13   Paul Signac, *In Times of Harmony*
The Pleasures of Summer, colored lithograph, 1896. Cleveland Museum of Art, Dudley P.
Allen Fund, 25.1053.

been intrusive in Fourier's decentralized world of autonomous communities.[54]

Signac's *In Times of Harmony,* of 1895, is structurally and thematically linked both to Papety's *Dream of Happiness* and—more surprisingly—to Seurat's *Grande Jatte.* More exactly, it reworks the *Grande Jatte* to make it conform with the utopian thinking behind Papety's painting. Originating as an oil sketch for an anticipated major work, the painting in 1896 became the basis for a five-color lithograph produced for Jean Grave's *Les Temps nouveaux,* for which Signac received some hundred francs (Figure 13). The original painting was exhibited in 1895 at the Indépendants and in

54. Fourier's follower Gabriel Desiré Laverdant demanded that artists invoke the coming golden age in their art: "And you whose soul withdraws from those terrible scenes and lets itself be carried away irresistibly by radiant dreams and images of wealth and happiness, offer to our eyes ravished by luxury smiles, glorious feasts, voluptuousness and happiness" ("Salon de 1842," *La Phalange,* April 3, 1842, quoted by Nancy A. Finley in "Fourierist Art Criticism and the *Rêve de Bonheur* of Dominique Papety," *Art History,* II [1979], 328).

1896 at the Libre Esthétique: it bore its full title, *In Times of Harmony: The Age of Gold Is Not in the Past, It Is in the Future.*[55] Signac seems to have been pleased with the work. Viewing it at the showing in 1895, he wrote in his journal, "On the whole, I was happy enough with it. . . . The canvas certainly seemed well-colored, luminous, and harmonious. After the compliments that I got, I believe that it is a success with the painters."[56]

In Times of Harmony shares with *Dream of Happiness* a sense of calm and tranquillity; the figures in both occupy an untroubled setting. Traditional pastoral painting achieved its tranquillity by abstracting what it showed from any vexatious social or political ties: everything existed in a social void, the only ambience in which such beauty could exist. Papety and Signac have simply extended the make-believe island of tranquillity into surrounding society—Cythera on a global scale, open to everyone on a daily basis, gratis. The age of gold indeed.

Striking differences exist between Papety's painting and Signac's, however. Signac was able to present his golden age as a modern one by putting his figures in a simpler, more casual version of the garb of his day. Nor are his characters the indolent loungers of Papety's dream; they are fully active and interactive. Most of their doings relate to leisure and nurture. At the left, a man reaches for a fruit while a mother teases her infant child. At the right, a group plays at bowls. In the background, one man paints, a man and a woman admire a flower as they embrace, and a distant group of men and women dance in a long chain around a tree. Labor and industry are present, though, in the distant ship and train, as the backbone to and precondition for leisure. Labor and leisure are in balance, natural parts of a harmonious relationship between humanity, industry, and the environment, in which leisure is always foregrounded and industry always sits quietly and peacefully in the distance.

Sally Medlyn first called notice to the clear formal relation between *In Times of Harmony* and Seurat's *Grande Jatte.*[57] Signac's image shares with Seurat's the brilliantly lit riverbank, with contrasting pockets of shadow, across which small tableaux are

<hr>

55. *Signac: Musée du Louvre, décembre 1963–février 1964* (Paris, 1964), 57. The painting's subtitle is from the anarchist theoretician Charles Malato, himself paraphrasing Saint-Simon.

56. John Rewald, ed., "Extraits du journal inédit de Paul Signac," *Gazette des beaux-arts,* 6th ser., XXXVI (1949), 118. The entry is for April 26, 1895.

57. Medlyn, "The Development of Georges Seurat's Art," 65–66.

spread, each displaying a variety of leisure activities. Signac has transformed Seurat's deadpan mockery of bourgeois recreation by purging it of its stiffness and tension—the juxtaposed but isolated and alienated women and men self-absorbed and yet each supremely conscious of cutting a figure. Signac's men and women, by contrast, touch one another, dance together, interact, and embrace.

Signac labored to combine in one image virtually every facet of the anarchist *âge d'or:* little or nothing was omitted from the writings of Kropotkin or Jean Grave on the subject, from *amour libre* to the universality of art, from the need for leisure to the call for decentralized industry no longer at war with nature. In his *The Conquest of Bread,* which so impressed Pissarro, Kropotkin wrote, "A society thus inspired will fear neither dissensions within nor enemies without. To the coalitions of the past it will oppose a new harmony, the initiative of each and all, the daring which springs from the awakening of a people's genius." In Signac's hands, the resulting image resembles what Françoise Cachin has called a "marvelous Mediterranean picnic."[58]

Cross linked the fin de siècle to a liberated future in a different way in his *The Wanderer,* a lithograph created for Grave's *Les Temps nouveaux* in 1896 (Figure 14). *The Wanderer* was long seen as a simple composition of a vagabond and a group of peasants.[59] But in 1964, Isabelle Compin read its unhidden utopian message: while the vagabond sits in darkness in the foreground, a radiantly lit vision of future happiness blossoms around him. In that golden future, dancing youths cavort around a brazier containing such broken symbols of the oppressive modern world as a crown and a flag.[60] The device of the dream of the future was well established in utopian literature in the wake of such novels as Edward Bellamy's *Looking Backward,* of 1887, and—especially vital for anarchists—William Morris' *News from Nowhere,* of 1890.[61] Cross em-

58. Peter Kropotkin, *The Conquest of Bread* (London, 1985), 213; Françoise Cachin, *Paul Signac,* trans. Michael Bullock (Greenwich, Conn., 1971), 69. Medlyn argues that "Signac's *Temps d'harmonie* depicts an ideal anarchist society but is subject to a dual interpretation because he refuses to adopt overtly propagandistic imagery to convey his message" ("The Development of Georges Seurat's Art," 66). For a concurring judgment, see Catherine C. Bock, *Henri Matisse and Neo-Impressionism* (Ann Arbor, Mich., 1981), 74–75. That clearly applies to Signac's work as a whole, but in this case Signac has all but announced his message with drums and trumpets.

59. See Herbert and Herbert, "Artists and Anarchism," 470.

60. Compin, *H. E. Cross,* 52, 337.

61. William Morris, *News from Nowhere* (London, 1962), 300–301.

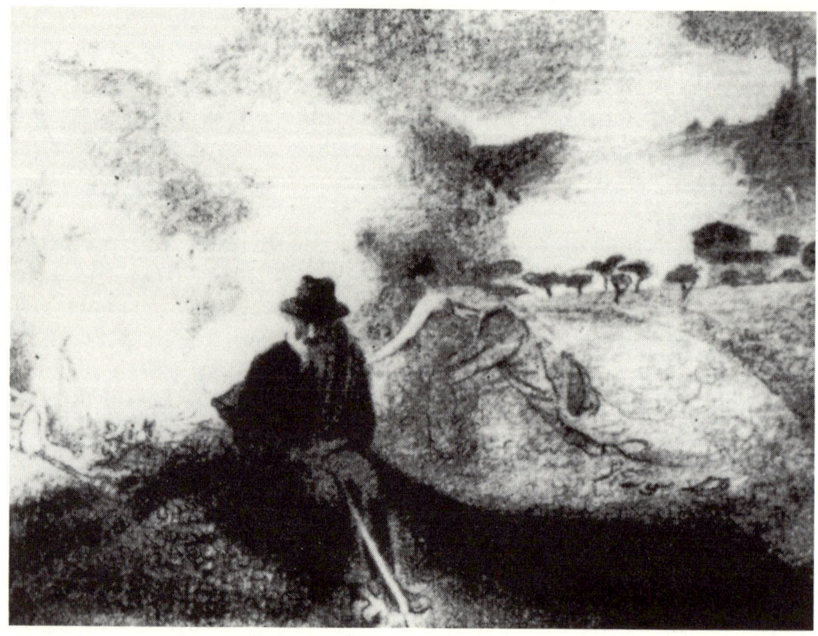

Figure 14   Henri Edmond Cross, *The Wanderer*
Lithograph, 1896. In *Les Temps nouveaux,* 1896

ployed the device to provide a link to the anarchist future: the tramp personifies the link, and is the medium through which the present segues into tomorrow. Here, as in anarchocommunist theory generally, consciousness determines being. The vagabond dreams of the age to come, and his dream thereby becomes reality. The emancipation of humanity is achieved through the vision of those excluded from or neglected by capitalist society.

Signac and Cross both depart from the traditional pastoral by attempting to bind their images—however tangentially—to their own time, by depicting the golden age as an outgrowth of the modern world rather than merely a nostalgic construct of a my- thologized past. Their candor about the modernity of the *âge d'or* was strictly limited, however. Signac marginalized what will be modern about the golden future: it is not so much that the signs of industry are compartmentalized and carefully tidied up—Kro- potkin did that—but that whatever readable indicators there are that the golden age takes place in the future rather than the past are reduced to tiny tokens in the corners and the background, as though embarrassed by their own existence. The future is leisure and play; somebody must work in Signac's "time of harmony," but the workers are anonymous and invisible. The harmony of the pastoral dream in the upper half of Cross's print is undercut only by the tramp at the bottom. The vagabond serves both as the victim of and the alternative to our society. He denies and negates the present just as the dancers of the future destroy its signs and emblems.

The dancers who appear in both the painting by Signac and the picture by Cross were to become a recurring motif in Cross's work. He explained later that his dancers in sylvan settings—inevitably nude, almost invariably female—were intended to portray the idyllic world of the future.[62] His paintings became increasingly dominated by the fairy-tale unreality that writers on the left often presented as an integral facet of the golden age, with its necessary destruction of the cynicism and jaded sophistication of the modern world. In Camille Lemonnier's *La Fin des bourgeois*, for example, one character objects that the protagonist's description of the utopian future sounds like myths for children. The protagonist responds, "Yes . . . you may be right. . . . Who knows? Regeneration by the infant, the return to the grand ages of the earth to the people . . ."[63]

The association of the ideal future society with scenes of pastoral beauty and serene, even static tableaux was inherent as well to the discussion of the *théâtre social* of the future. One socialist reviewer argued that the existing theater was decadent, even pornographic. The *théâtre social* of the coming social order, by contrast, would be truthful in its sentiment, marked by "its harmony, its luminosity, its serenity. Such a marvelous landscape, where the well-distributed air and light illuminate the lush prairies, the verdant hills, the dark forests, the bounding herds, the entwined young men and women—all this is seized by the piercing glance of a genial painter who perpetuates his sublime vision. And in this way socialist theater will reproduce new dawns, in an apotheosis of light."[64]

62. Herbert and Herbert, "Artists and Anarchism," 480.

63. Camille Lemonnier, *La Fin des bourgeois* (Paris, 1892), 331.

64. Gervaise [pseud.], "Tentative de théâtre social," *Le Socialiste*, February 8, 1894, p. 4. See the similar claim by Berth in *Dialogues socialistes*, 214–16.

In this vocabulary of serenity, calm, and harmony, entirely absent are the irony and deadpan mockery of Seurat. Perhaps the rest of what has been excluded is less evident: the future is entirely without politics, competition, strife, or struggle. Even the environment has somehow sensed the new social harmony and transformed itself. Charles Fourier had been fond of inventing new animals for his future world—vegetarian anti-lions and antifleas, all living together in peace with their former food. The utopians of the late nineteenth century were content also to eliminate gloom, storm, and natural disaster, so that the golden age appeared a world of green forests and eternal sunshine.

Cross's utopian pastorals diverge, however, from the dream of the socialist drama critic, as well as from Signac's image, at one crucial juncture at least. The reviewer spoke of embracing boys and girls, just as *In Times of Harmony* shows males and females dancing together. By contrast, Cross's images of the *âge d'or* included only females.

The pastoral imagery the Neos adapted for their utopian scenes was never neutral or value-free. It was the product of a complex web of patriarchal assumptions about women and men, and nature and culture. The anarchist reworking of the imagery did not dispel the long-standing assumptions. French anarchism was permeated by misogynistic and antifeminist values inherited from Pierre Joseph Proudhon and upheld by such close allies of Grave as Charles Albert.[65] The anarchist utopian pastoral welded the values together to reify the image of woman as "natural" earth mother. Even in Morris' *News from Nowhere*—seen by many French anarchists as a model because of the decentralized, antiurban future it projected—women of the future are "liberated" from outside jobs and public life to serve as mothers and homemakers.[66]

Men disappear altogether from Cross's later pastoral utopias in

65. On the misogynist strand in French anarchism, see John Hutton, "Camille Pissarro's *Turpitudes sociales* and Late Nineteenth-Century French Anarchist Anti-Feminism," *History Workshop Journal*, XXIV (Autumn, 1987), esp. 36–44. Major contributions to this current in French anarchism include Pierre Joseph Proudhon's *De la justice dans la révolution et dans l'église* (Paris, 1858) and his *La Pornocratie; ou, Les Femmes dans les temps modernes* (Paris, 1875). Charles Albert, in *L'Amour libre* (Paris, 1899), restates many of Proudhon's central ideas in a milder, less venomous tone. For an anarchist rebuttal, see Groupe des Etudiants Révolutionnaires Internationalistes de Paris, *Les Communistes anarchistes et la Femme* (Paris, 1900).

66. Morris, *News from Nowhere*, 232–36.

part because the signifying system he employed had no place for them: the goal was to show humanity at one with nature—the artificial constraints imposed by modern civilization dissolved, the boundaries and norms of industrial society obliterated. Signac's *In Times of Harmony* sought a fragile compromise in that regard: it depicted a return to nature but one that allowed carefully marginalized pockets of modern technology. Signac attempted a modernized pastoral, in much the way Seurat attempted to modernize Puvis. But Signac's compromise came at a price. He contrived for *In Times of Harmony* to allude to so many of the predicted attributes of a utopian society that the painting all but sank under their weight. As a composition, it is notably lacking in the harmony to which the title refers. It devolves into disconnected clots of people, all passionately engaged in acting out Kropotkin's dreams of the golden age. It illustrates, but it lacks the force or unity to evoke the dream it represents.

Cross ultimately rejected that compromise in favor of a return to the allegorical underpinnings of the nineteenth-century pastoral. His images echo Proudhon's assertion that "man is principally a power of action; woman, a power of fascination."[67] In *The Wanderer,* the dancers celebrate the destruction of the old social order; they actively cast aside the crowns and flags of the past. They are all male: they must be male if they are to celebrate the ideas of action and revolt. In that respect, the artistic vocabulary of Cross—out of Puvis and the pastorale—is impoverished even by comparison with that of Delacroix, who could embody the spirit of the Revolution of 1830 in a woman, a hybrid of a *poissarde* and the republican icon of Marianne. The dancers in *The Wanderer* are male because they act, because they triumph, just as the vagabond in the center, the incarnation of liberty, is also male. The dancers in the later works are all female because they no longer have to act or to triumph.

However awkward Signac's compromise, its significance—even the manner in which it sought to signify—lay in areas in which it broke from the tradition of the French utopian pastoral, in which it consciously reworked and reformulated material. By contrast, in Cross's idylls the most striking features are those which are retained. Cross's pastoral works are distinguished from their academic counterparts such as Joseph Wencker's *Summer,* shown at

67. Proudhon, *La Pornocratie,* 44.

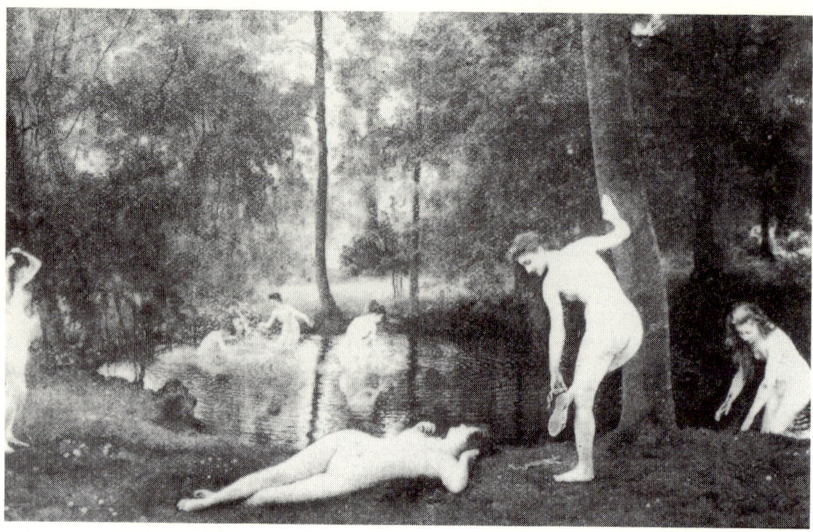

Figure 15 Joseph Wencker, *Summer*
Oil on canvas, 1896. In *Catalogue illustré du Salon* (Paris, 1896).

the Salon of 1896 (Figure 15), only to the extent that a portrait by Cross differs from an academic one: the choppy brushstrokes break up the glossy surface of the academic style, but the underlying structure and conception remain much the same. In paintings such as his *Landscape with Bathers,* of 1893–1894 (Figure 16) or his *The Shaded Beach*, of 1902 (Figure 17), Cross absorbs in full the academic format of nude females dancing eternally in perpetual sunshine.

In a close study of early-twentieth-century avant-garde painting, Carol Duncan remarks concerning the division between male and female, and nature and culture, "What is striking . . . about so many nineteenth- and twentieth-century vanguard nudes is the absoluteness with which women were pushed back to the extremity of the nature side of the dichotomy." Duncan underscores the way women came to serve as Other, existing somehow in "total opposition to all that is civilized and human." But the same insistence on total polarity already existed in Cross's pastorals, however more benign his nymphs seem in contrast to Symbolist evocations of women as vampires or medusas. As Duncan comments with regard to Matisse's *Joy of Life,* of 1905–1906, "Women simply

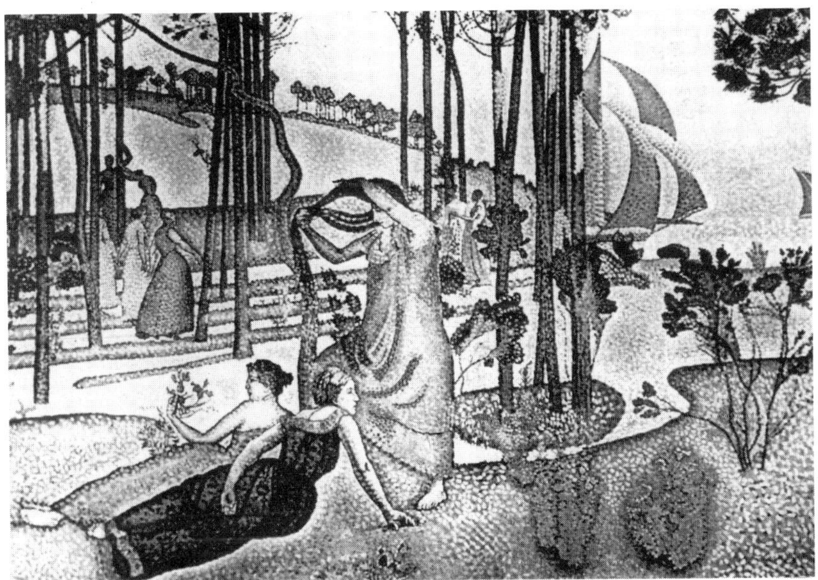

Figure 16   Henri Edmond Cross, *Landscape with Bathers*
Oil on canvas, 1893–94. Private collection, Paris.

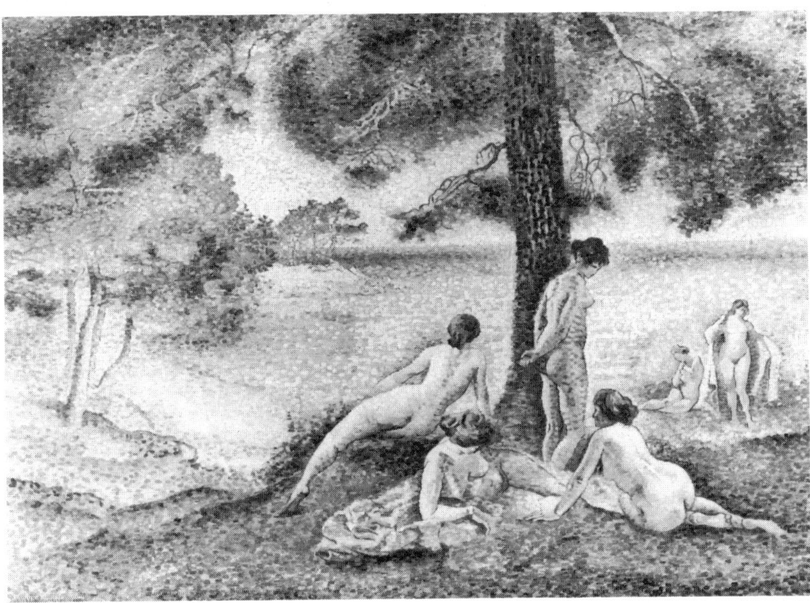

Figure 17   Henri Edmond Cross, *The Shaded Beach*
La Plage ombragée, oil on canvas, 1902. Galerie Schmidt, Paris.

exist as sensual beings or abandon themselves to spontaneous and artless self-expression."[68]

Born of an attempt to employ art to visualize the future and hence hasten its arrival, Neo-Impressionist utopian imagery was badly compromised from the outset by its conservative roots and implications. Cross's idylls became straightforward reifications of reactionary images with their concomitant values. In the end, Cross's pastorals of dancing nymphs succumbed to and in part reconstituted the forms of the patriarchal and mysogynistic classical model.

On the other hand, Cross's languid nymphs also seem caught between contrasting and antagonistic systems of representation, as a comparison of his work with that of Matisse can illustrate. Cross's images provide an obvious model for some early works by Matisse, especially his *Luxe, Calme et Volupté,* of 1904–1906 (Figure 18). Like several of Cross's paintings, this one by Matisse was inspired by a quasi-utopian pastoral, Baudelaire's "Invitation au voyage" from *Fleurs du mal,* published in 1857. The poem, possibly an evocation of the isle of Cythera, takes the form of a call to Baudelaire's lover to join him in a land of love and beauty: "There, all is but order and beauty, / Luxury, calm and voluptuousness."[69] Matisse' painting shares with Cross's works—especially his *Landscape with Bathers,* from which Matisse directly borrowed the image of the woman wringing out her long tresses—the framework of a sunny glade or shore, inhabited solely by women. In this, the poem has been stripped of its darker hints, in the service of a simple evocation of pastoral innocence. Experience was similarly edited: although *Luxe, Calme et Volupté* was based on a painting Matisse made in 1904 of his wife and son on the beach at Saint-Tropez, the artist replaced a sitting male child—his son Pierre—with a young, standing girl.[70]

68. Carol Duncan, "Virility and Domination in Early Twentieth-Century Vanguard Painting," *Artforum,* XII (December, 1973), 30–39, revised in *Feminism and Art History: Questioning the Litany,* ed. Norma Broude and Mary D. Garrard (New York, 1982), 303–304. Bram Dijkstra sees both academic and vanguard images of dancing women as attempts to depict "sex-crazed women. The hordes of girls who hopped about decorously in all those painted meadows . . . had a transparent secret: they were overheated hysterics letting off steam" (*Idols of Perversity: Fantasies of Feminine Evil in Fin-de-Siècle Culture* [New York, 1986], 244).

69. Charles Baudelaire, *Fleurs du mal/Flowers of Evil,* trans. George Dillon and Edna St. Vincent Millay (New York, 1962), 64–67.

70. See Jack Flam, *Matisse: The Man and His Art, 1868–1918* (Ithaca, N.Y., 1986), 116. But Nicholas Watkins asserts that the standing child is still Pierre. See his *Matisse* (Oxford, 1984), 55. That seems unlikely on both formal and thematic grounds.

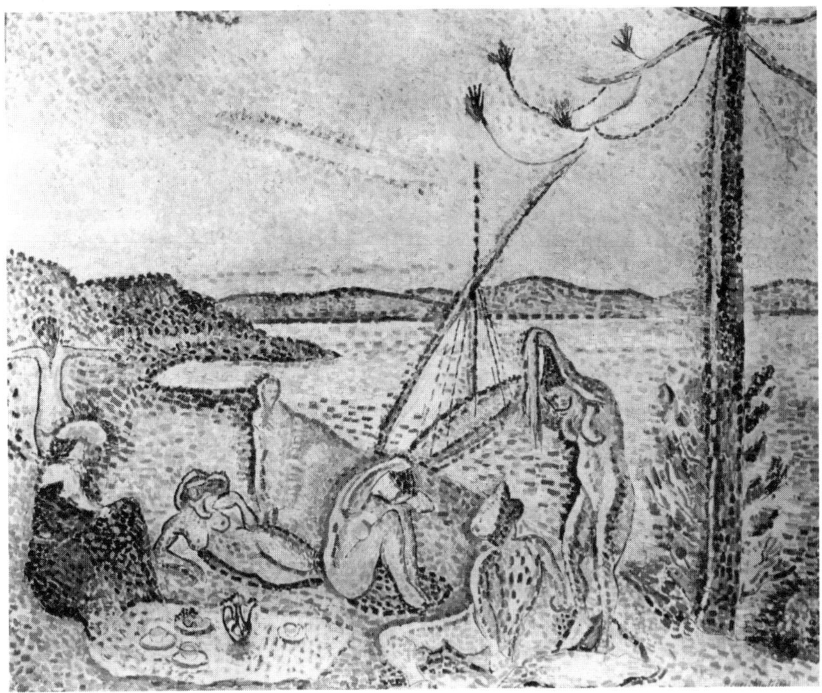

Figure 18   Henri Matisse, *Luxe, Calme et Volupté*
Oil on canvas, 1904–1906. Musée d'Orsay, Paris, Giraudon/Art Resource, New York,
© 1994 Succession H. Matisse/ARS, New York.

Both Baudelaire and Matisse were more concerned with the personal than the social. Baudelaire's land of sunshine is not an approaching golden age but—like Puvis' *The Sacred Grove*—a refuge, a place of sanctuary from a cruel outside world. By 1904, Matisse had abandoned any stray thoughts of social reform; instead, his art was increasingly aimed at providing a means of rest and pleasure for the weary rich.[71]

The very apoliticism of Matisse's work gave him, it would seem, a greater field for innovation and experimentation than Cross had. Matisse gradually eliminated background elements—foliage, landscape, details generally of time and place, all the "identifying" marks that could bind his works to traditional iconography and signification. Unquestionably, his imagery still carried a tremendous ideological charge in its depiction of women. Even in

71. See Watkins, *Matisse,* 58; and John Russell, *The World of Matisse, 1869–1954* (New York, 1969), 79. See also Flam, *Matisse,* 119–20.

his *Joy of Life* the only male in the picture is a gainfully employed shepherd; he tends to nature while the women in the painting embody it as they dance, play pipes, sun themselves, and loll about.[72] But at least a part of the effect of the flattening and stylizing of forms, of the final elimination of old emphases on the licked surface, on topography or skin tones, is less a dehumanization of the figure than a tautening of the message conveyed and an achievement of greater economy in expressing it. Matisse's twentieth-century dancers seek at least to communicate a specific sense of form and rhythm, disencumbered of accompanying details that would place the image squarely within a preconceived grid of ideas concerning women and men and their respective places in society.

Utopian imagery, with its emphasis on calm and harmony, must have seemed tailor-made for Neo-Impressionism. Utopian imagery suffers, however, from certain inherent difficulties, especially the necessity of making real a fictive time and culture lacking not only the tensions but even the essential hopes and fears of the time of the art's production. It is difficult to think of a utopian novel of particular interest apart from its program or historical impact; it is even more difficult to name a striking work of utopian visual imagery. Attempting to imagine an experience lacking in precedent or contemporaneous roots, the artist, as Kropotkin himself argued, tends to fall back on the sentimental and the clichéd.[73] The result is typically enervated and lifeless. It relates to the experienced world of the viewer only as its negation. It is both

72. Duncan, "Virility and Domination," in *Feminism and Art History,* ed. Broude and Garrard, 304. Duncan modifies the stance she took in the earlier version of her essay: she wrote in 1973 that *Joy of Life* is "one of the few images of nudity . . . in which a male attempted to transcend the assertion of virility and the male-female dichotomy it implies. It is one of those rare moments of imagination in which the male seeks to join the female without anxiety, ambivalence or loss of autonomy" (p. 35). Arguing that the work is unique in that "men as well as women relate to nature, to each other, and to their own bodies in harmony and freedom," she concluded that, "however tentative, the work remains a vision of social order without domination, a dream in which sensual beauty may be enjoyed without fear" (p. 35).

73. "The best canvases of modern artists are those that represent nature, villages, valleys, the sea with its dangers, the mountain with its splendours. But how can the painter express the poetry of work in the fields if he has only contemplated it, imagined it, if he has never delighted in it himself? If he only knows it as a bird of passage knows the country he soars over on his migrations? . . . The love of the soil and what grows on it is not acquired by sketching with a paint brush—it is only in its service; and without loving it, how paint it? That is why the best painters have produced in this direction is still so imperfect, not true to life, nearly always merely sentimental. There is no *strength* in it" (Kropotkin, *The Conquest of Bread,* 118–19).

escapist and reassuring, forward-looking and reactionary, reaffirming the anarchocommunist vision of a perfect world already in birth.

By the turn of the century, the calm faith such art reflected had begun to dissolve. There was a growing recognition among both socialist and syndicalist militants that a hard and bitter struggle lay between their own time and any golden age. The dystopian novel was born—works that consciously borrowed the format of the utopian tale to invert the theme and significance. In Ignatius Donnelly's *Caesar's Column,* published in the United States in 1891 and quickly translated into the major European languages, a visitor from Uganda discovers that the shining cities of a future America are built upon an undercity of the most appalling brutality and exploitation. The novel ends with a nihilist revolt in which both oppressors and oppressed are completely destroyed. In Jack London's *The Iron Heel,* of 1907, workers confidently expecting a gradual and peaceful evolution to socialism are instead crushed by "the Oligarchy," a brutal class dictatorship.

At least one novel from the period drew so clearly upon the fin-de-siècle image of a pastoral *âge d'or* that it seems to have been consciously intended as a bitter parody. The protagonist of H. G. Wells's *The Time Machine,* which appeared in 1905, and was translated into French in 1907, voyages to a seemingly idyllic, pastoral world of A.D. 802,000, a "tangled waste of beautiful bushes and flowers, a long-neglected and yet weedless garden" inhabited by the childlike Eloi: "I saw mankind housed in splended shelters, gloriously clothed, and yet I found them engaged in no toil. There were no signs of struggle, neither social nor economical. . . . The shop, the advertisement, traffic, all that commerce which constitutes the body of our world, was gone. It was natural on that golden evening that I should jump at the idea of a social paradise."[74] Here the world of the future recalls Cross's portrayal of it in his utopian works: a worldwide garden where the Eloi dance and sing in the sunshine.[75] But their dance proves to be a sign not of liberation but of humanity's final collapse and decadence: "This

74. H. G. Wells, *The Time Machine; and, The Invisible Man* (New York, 1984), 27–34.

75. To be sure, the Eloi included both females and males, but without significant physical or cultural distinctions: "All had the same form of costume, the same soft hairless visage, and the same girlish rotundity of limb. . . . In costume, and in all the differences of texture and bearing that now mark off the sexes from each other, these people of the future were alike. And the children seemed to my eyes to be but the miniatures of the parents" (*Ibid.,* 31).

has ever been the fate of energy in security; it takes to art and eroticism, and then comes languor and decay." Wells's traveler concludes, "To adorn themselves with flowers, to dance, to sing in the sunlight: so much was left of the artistic spirit and no more. Even that would fade in the end into a contented inactivity."[76] Nor is that judgment harsh enough: the Eloi prove ultimately to be mere human cattle for the molelike Morlocks, who raise them as food.

The early twentieth century was not without its own utopian aspirations, linked to the rapid growth of the parties of the Socialist International and trade union movements. But in a period of rising conflict—strikes, riots, and revolutions—the *beau rêve* of Pissarro seemed increasingly remote from social realities. In a time of new urgencies, of mass calls for action, there was a growing sense that between the existing world and that of endless dancing would have to be one of marching—and dying—in the streets.[77]

76. *Ibid.*, 36. John Huntington concludes that *The Time Machine* is a "guide which leads us away from a delusive Utopian vision of pastoral simplicity towards a much more complex vision of antithetic balances; guilt and innocence, labor and ease, decline and triumph, change and stasis" (*The Logic of Fantasy* [New York, 1982], 143). Cf. Darko Suvin, *H. G. Wells and Modern Science Fiction* (Cranbury, N.J., 1977), 23.

77. The changeover to a more activist era sparked more than a little bewilderment and hostility. See Eric J. Hobsbawm, "Socialism and the Avant-Garde in the Period of the Second International," *Le Mouvement social,* CXI (April–June, 1980), 189–99. In one of the few early-twentieth-century socialist utopian novels, Alexander Bogdanov's *Krasnaya Zvezda* (1908; Red star), the protagonist asks why he has been chosen for contact by representatives of a communist Mars, of all the socialist leaders of his land. He is told that the "old Man of the Mountain" (that is, Lenin) is too "exclusively a man of struggle and revolution. Our order would not suit him at all. He is a man of iron, and men of iron are not flexible." Only a gentle poet-scientist-philosopher such as Bogdanov's Leonid—or, implicitly, Bogdanov himself—could fully appreciate the vision of the Martian utopia. See Alexander Bogdanov, *Red Star: The First Bolshevik Utopia,* trans. Charles Rougle, ed. Loren R. Graham and Richard Stites (Bloomington, Ind., 1984), 134.

5

Terrible and *Beau:* The Modern World

In "Impressionnistes et Révolutionnaires," Paul Signac argued that Neo-Impressionist theory enabled its adherents to capture and re-create the essence of the modern world. Yet it was in the Neo-Impressionists' depiction of contemporary existence that the tensions inherent in the movement became most apparent—particularly the need to marry the "ideal" and the "real," to capture in one harmonious image the essence of a world still far from harmonious. As with overtly utopian imagery, Neo-Impressionist renderings of modern France shifted steadily to affirmative prophecies of a coming golden age. The result, however ironically, was often to paper over the disorder and inequality of existing society. A fairy-tale land of prosperous and egalitarian communes was superimposed on rural existence; Neo-Impressionist images of French industrialization were less coherent, exposing the contradictory anarchist views of industry and urbanization.

Rural Life

Camille Pissarro told the anarchist writer Octave Mirbeau that "work is a marvelous regulator of moral and physical health. All the sadness, bitterness, pain—I forget them, even ignore them in the joy of labor."[1] Though Pissarro was commenting here on the labor of painting, he most frequently connected *travail* with the land and the peasantry. In a letter to Lucien Pissarro in 1891, he praised Pierre Joseph Proudhon for his perception that the revolution would grow out of love for the land. That echoed anarcho-communist theory: one writer championed an art that would reaffirm the "cult of the land," and Jean Grave's colleague Emile de

1. Octave Mirbeau, *Des artistes: Peintres et Sculpteurs* (Paris, 1922–24), II, 226. Consciously or not, Pissarro was here echoing William Morris' statement that "art is the expression by man of his pleasure in labor" (*Art of the People* [Chicago, 1902], 29).

Saint-Auban argued that "the true drama of the land is that of France. The land is the *patrie*." Saint-Auban considered the peasant the "land incarnate."[2]

In the 1880s and 1890s, however, the peasant was very much a contested figure. Saint-Auban commented sourly on the diametrically contrasting depictions of rural life: "Georges Sand or Zola, idyll or ordure; Virgil or Balzac, eclogues or nightmares; dreams of naïve and laughing poetry, people of delicious sweetness or happy farmers whose only vice is ignorance of their bliss, or horrible visions of shameful baseness . . . peasants who smell only of roses or others who smell of dung."[3]

The Third Republic meant to win the peasants by transforming rural communities into bastions of a modern, capitalist France. New roads, new homes, better sanitation, and new schools were to bind peasants to the regime and the social order it defended. Eugen Weber has noticed that "many grieved over the death of yesterday, but few of them were peasants. Thatched cottages and log cabins are picturesque from the outside; living in them is another matter." Weber quotes an observer about the outlook the people of Mazières had arrived at in 1914: "All, even the poorest, had a lively sense . . . of immense material progress. They had an equally lively sense of great social progress, of limitless evolution toward more liberty and more equality, thanks to the vote."[4]

The methods adopted by the republic to forge a stable class of rural property owners carried clear social costs. One was to force millions of poor peasants from the land. There were also concerns that the villages were in danger of being absorbed by the cities and new factory complexes. A history of French peasant life asserts that by about 1900 the image of the brutal, repulsive village given currency by Balzac and by Zola's *La Terre* was being replaced in essay and literature by one of the village encroached upon and menaced by the modern world.[5]

2. Camille Pissarro to Lucien Pissarro, July 8, 1891, in Camille Pissarro's *Correspondance*, ed. Janine Bailly-Herzberg (Paris, 1980–), III, 103; Jean Baffier, "L'Art c'est la vie," *L'Enclos*, III (June, 1895), 36; Emile de Saint-Auban, *L'Idée sociale au théâtre* (Paris, 1901), 392, 354.

3. Saint-Auban, *L'Idée sociale,* 341.

4. Eugen Weber, *Peasants into Frenchmen: The Modernization of Rural France, 1876–1914* (Stanford, Calif., 1976), 478.

5. See Maurice Agulhon, Gabriel Desert, and Robert Specklin, *Apogée et Crise de la civilisation paysanne, 1879–1914* (Paris, 1976), 529, Vol. IV of Agulhon, Desert, Specklin, *Histoire de la France rurale,* 4 vols.

By the 1890s, even the "orthodox Marxists" around Jules Guesde sought peasant votes by promising lower taxes and land to those who tilled it. The socialists combined the promises offered by the republic—modernization, better living conditions, stable prices—with vows to protect rural life from the predations of capital. Benoît Malon's Independent Socialists and reformers such as Jean Jaurès made especially vigorous efforts to win peasants to an alliance against big business.[6]

If both the government of the Third Republic and the socialists sought to win the peasantry to social change, the French far right and the anarchocommunists called for restoring what were seen as the virtues of an idyllic, precapitalist past. For Catholic royalists, the peasant was the chosen vehicle for a return to power, the model, Theodore Zeldin has remarked, "of a human unspoilt by progress."[7] The peasant was acclaimed the bedrock of the church, a remnant of the France that had flourished prior to the rise of the detested bourgeoisie and industrial working class.[8] The peasant seemed the embodiment of piety, devoted to the church and the virgin.

Anarchocommunists also sang the glories of medieval life. If the right saw precapitalist France as an era of absolute faith and unchallenged social hierarchy, French anarchists extolled its decentralization, its powerful craft guilds, and its cooperative village life.[9] In *Mutual Aid,* a study of human biological and social evolution, Kropotkin discerned in the rural village a major survival of instinctive human cooperation and a locus for resistance to the centralized modern state. The French rural commune had been

6. Concerning socialist policies, see Theodore Zeldin, *Politics and Anger* (Oxford, 1979), 386, Vol. II of Zeldin, *France, 1848–1945.* For typical socialist appeals to the peasantry, see Paule Mink, "La Terre," in *Almanach socialiste illustrée pour 1895* (Paris, 1895), 44–47; Georges Renard, *Lettre aux paysans* (Paris, 1896); and Jean Jaurès, *Socialisme et Paysans* (Paris, 1897).

7. Theodore Zeldin, *Ambition and Love* (Oxford, 1979), 133, Vol. I of Zeldin, *France, 1848–1945.*

8. See Léon Daudet, *Le Stupide XIXe Siècle* (Paris, 1922), 62–67; and Richard Griffiths, *The Reactionary Revolution: The Catholic Revival in French Literature, 1870–1914* (London, 1966), 59–60. The right's professed love for the peasantry did not always extend to the peasants themselves. Theordore Zeldin quotes a country priest in 1885: "I would love the peasants, if the peasants did not disgust me. [The peasant] is the least romantic, the least idealistic of men. . . . He is original sin. . . . The peasant loves nothing nor anybody but for the use he can make of it" (*Ambition and Love,* 132).

9. On the right's view of precapitalist France, see Griffiths, *The Reactionary Revolution,* 266–73, 280–81.

deformed by capitalism, Kropotkin wrote, but it still showed the way to a future communist social order: "[The communes] maintain in village life a nucleus of customs and habits of mutual aid which undoubtedly acts as a check upon the development of reckless individualism and greediness, which small land-ownership is only too prone to develop." To communist anarchists, the rural villages presented themselves as at once the final lists of precapitalist solidarity and the harbingers of a brighter future. Kropotkin asserted that peasant communes could survive even the fiercest attacks, "and as soon as the States relax the iron laws by means of which they have broken all bonds between men, these bonds are at once reconstituted. . . . They indicate in which direction and in which form further progress must be expected."[10]

For the anarchocommunists, a fundamental transformation of rural life was consequently unnecessary; rural life served as a model for the broader transformation of the modern world. Until then, it was essential to guard the villages against any threat from state or society. Elisée Reclus called on the peasants to "guard jealously your land, you who have a bit of it; it is your life and that of the wife and children you love." He summoned peasants to join together in free associations of all whose land was threatened by industrialization, hunters, and speculators: "Forget your petty quarrels between neighbors, and group yourselves into communities where all interests are interdependent, where every inch of grass has each member of the community as a defender." An alliance of "one hundred, one thousand, ten thousand" would be strong enough to hold off an army, he advised. "With them, you will attack, you will tear down the enclosing walls; with them, you will found the great commune of men in which each will work in concert with others to animate the soil, to beautify it and live happily upon the good land that gives us bread."[11] The anarchocommunists were accordingly enthusiastic in their support of the "peasant syndicates" that began to form in rural areas of

10. Peter Kropotkin, *Mutual Aid: A Factor of Evolution* (1902; rpr. Boston, 1914), 229–50. The book was assembled from essays Kropotkin began to publish in 1890.

11. Elisée Reclus, *A mon frère le paysan* (Paris, 1910), 2. See Enrico Malatesta, *Entre paysans* (Paris, 1910). Other anarchocommunist writings on the peasantry sometimes added a discussion of the exploitation of peasant life under capitalism; see, for example, "Les paysans," *L'Idée ouvrière,* I (January 7–14, 1888), 1; "L'Agriculture," *La Révolte,* III (December 12–19, 1890), 1–2, (December 27, 1890–January 2, 1891), 1–2, (January 10–16, 1891), 1–2, (January 31–February 6, 1891), 1–2, (February 7–13, 1891), 2, (February 14–20, 1891), 1.

France in the late 1880s, though Kropotkin cautioned that they were estimable purely as moral and ethical reminders of the continuing power of mutual aid.[12]

The Visual Imagery of Rural Life

One of the first acts of the February Revolution of 1848 was to embrace—on paper—the idea of the *droit de travail.* A decree of the provisional government proclaimed that "the question of labor is of supreme importance; . . . there is no more lofty, more dignified preoccupation of a republican government."[13] Still, the official celebration of *travail* did not prevent the regime from slaughtering some six thousand Parisian *travailleurs* in June of the year it came to power. The cult of labor survived, however, not only the massacre but also Louis Bonaparte's coup d'etat in 1851. Napoleon III had, after all, published a vapid pamphlet in his youth vowing to abolish poverty and provide each citizen with the "possibility of raising himself by his merit and his labor."[14]

The leaders of the Third Republic spoke often and eloquently of their respect for the dignity of labor. Jules Simon wrote that art was to celebrate labor, for it is art that "ennobles work and crowns it." Though Simon's words seem a reprise of the language of William Morris and Camille Pissarro, his operating definition of *travail* was altogether different: he defined work as a "sustained activity to which the individual was committed in order to produce a useful result." By that definition, virtually everyone in France became a worker: rich and poor, business leaders and laborers were all *travailleurs,* cooperating for the benefit of all. The ideas of class, inequality, power, and privilege were blurred.[15]

Jules Breton recalled that the Revolution of 1848 had a powerful impact on the depiction of the urban and rural poor: "The causes and consequences of that revolution . . . had a strong influence on our spirits. . . . There was a great upsurge of new efforts. . . . We studied the streets and the fields more deeply; we associated our-

12. Kropotkin, *Mutual Aid,* 246–50. On the peasant unions, see Agulhon, Desert, and Specklin, *Apogée et Crise,* 527–28.

13. William H. Sewell, Jr., *Work and Revolution in France: The Language of Labor from the Old Regime to 1848* (New York, 1980), 243–76.

14. Louis Napoléon Bonaparte, *The Extinction of Pauperism* (London, 1849), 21–22.

15. See Miriam R. Levin, *Republican Art and Ideology in Late Nineteenth-Century France* (Ann Arbor, Mich., 1986), 10, 25–28.

selves with the passions and feelings of the humble, and art was to do them the honor formerly reserved exclusively for the gods and for the mighty." [16]

The desire to exalt the humble in art encompassed sharp antagonisms. Albert Boime has called the favored art of the Second Empire a myopic realism "verisimilar in its painstaking detail, but ringing false in the whole." [17] Breton, Jules Bastien-Lepage, and William Bouguereau were among the artists who presented a world—especially a rural one—of calm and tranquillity, in which a wealth of detail masked the underlying theatricality and relentless excision of any features apt to give offense to influential patrons. The peasants were invariably noble and pious, the men tall and strong, the women graceful and spiritual. Farm labor was treated as a sort of fete.

Under the Third Republic, a politicized image of the peasant was joined to the genial portrayal of peasant life. The peasant was transformed from Other to fellow citizen. Aimé Perret's *The Prizes,* of 1890 (Figure 19), shows peasant children receiving awards from the village mayor, under a trinity of tricolor banners. The village curé has been enlisted as a witness to the events, sharing the dais with the village officials, in a wistful homage to the peaceful church-state relations so rare during that era. His role is subordinate, however, in the secular ceremony under the banners of the state.

The academic vision of rural life amounted to an antibourgeois myth—albeit one to be sold to the bourgeoisie itself. As T. J. Clark has said of the presentation of rural existence in the 1840s, such a mythology is "shot through with an uneasy sense of those very social realities it tries to mask." In contrast to the increasingly disharmonious social life of urban and industrial France, rural society could be—and needed to be—presented as a "unity, a one-class society in which peasant and master work in harmony, . . . a world in which social conflicts are magically resolved, in which the tensions and class divisions of the city are unknown." [18]

There were, of course, disaccords in this project from the outset. Some on the left hoped that Gustave Courbet's uncompro-

16. Jules Breton, *La Vie d'un artiste* (Paris, 1890), 177.

17. Albert Boime, "The Second Empire's Official Realism," in *The European Realist Tradition,* ed. Gabriel P. Weisberg (Bloomington, Ind., 1982), 85.

18. T. J. Clark, *Image of the People: Gustave Courbet and the 1848 Revolution* (Princeton, 1973), 151. For a rather less pointed discussion of the same material, see Hollister Sturges, *Jules Breton and the French Rural Tradition* (New York, 1982).

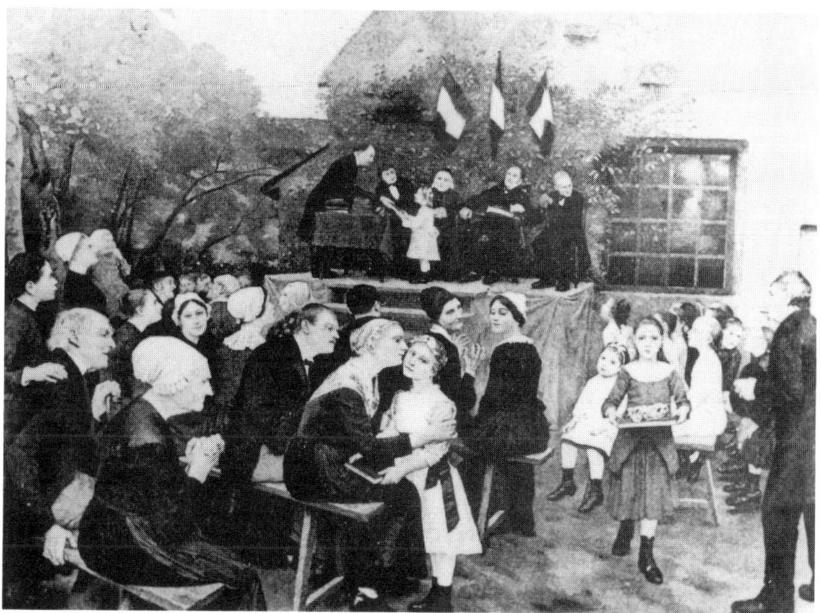

Figure 19   Aimé Perret, *The Prizes*
   Oil on canvas, 1890

mising *Stonebreakers,* from 1849, would become the nineteenth-century social revolution's equivalent of Jacques Louis David's *Oath of the Horatii*—a prototype for a new style and subject matter.[19] More looked to Jean François Millet's images of rural life as the most powerful critiques of peasant existence. Millet's subject matter—peasants at work, rest, or prayer—did not differ qualitatively from that of his contemporaries. Nor were his politics inclined to the left, as he was to make all too clear in his angry denunciations of the Paris Commune. Instead, paintings such as his *The Sower,* of 1849 (Figure 20), differed decisively from most contemporaneous works in their determined effort to convey the rigors of peasant life and labor. In a letter to his most prominent patron, the critic Alfred Sensier, in 1863, he wrote, "I see very well the haloes of the dandelions and, far away, beyond the land, the sun, whose glory is in the clouds. But I also see the steaming,

19. See, for example, Max Sulzberger, *Le Réalisme en France et en Belgique: Courbet et de Groux* (Brussels, 1874), 7–8. The anarchist theoretician Pierre Joseph Proudhon praised *Casseurs de pierre* as a masterly study of human exploitation and the basis for a new socialist art.

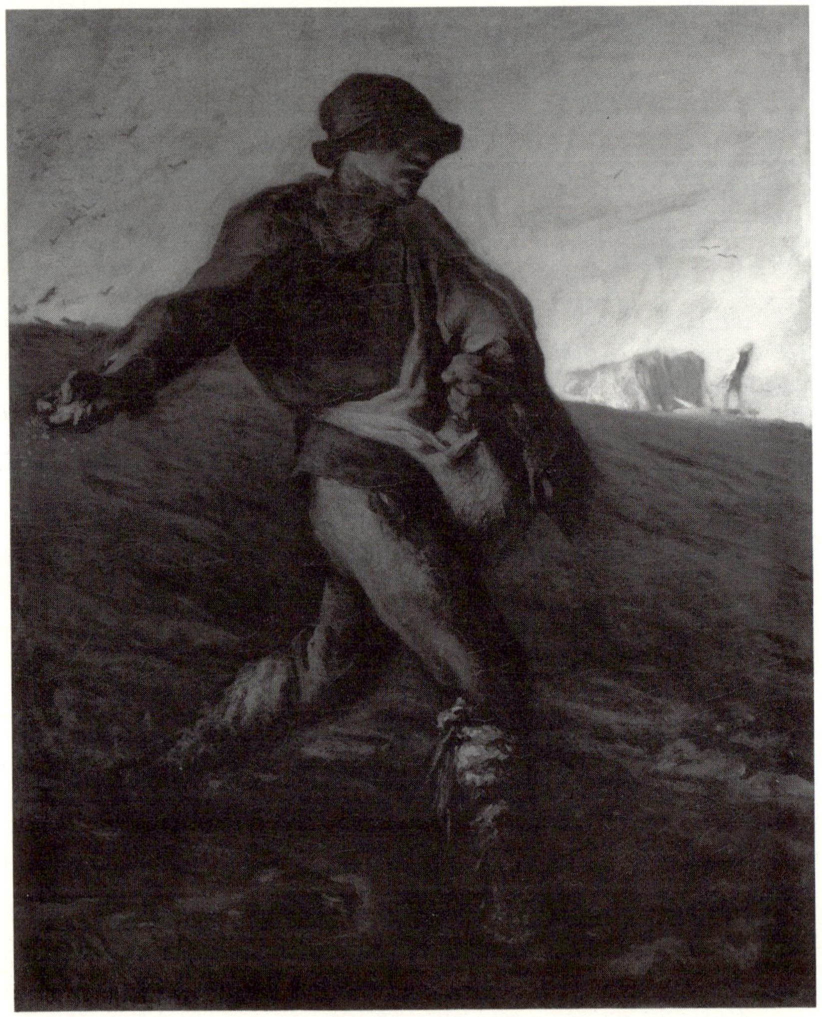

Figure 20   Jean François Millet, *The Sower*
Oil on canvas, 1849. Gift of Quincy Adams Shaw through Quincy A. Shaw, Jr., and Mrs. Marian Shaw Haughton. Courtesy, Museum of Fine Arts, Boston.

toiling horses—and the rocky place where a man, laboring and panting all morning, tries to straighten up for a moment to catch his breath. The drama is enveloped in splendors."[20]

20. Jean François Millet to Alfred Sensier, May 30, 1863, in Robert L. Herbert's *Jean-François Millet* (London, 1975), 138. On Millet's attitudes and those of Sensier, see Chris-

Many conservatives detected in Millet's peasant scenes a conscious effort to repel. Senator Challemel-Lacour denounced the artist for showing the "animalization of men." Another critic complained, "For M. Millet, art aims at slavishly copying ignoble models. He lights his lantern and searches for a cretin; he must have searched a long time before finding his 'Peasant Resting on His Hoe.' "[21] A cartoon by Cham showed Millet's *Man with the Hoe* wondering what happened to the back of his head. On the other hand, the nascent socialist movement of the 1840s and 1850s seized upon Millet's paintings—especially his *The Sower*—as emblems of social protest and exposés of the degradation of peasant life.[22] His *Man with the Hoe* met with a similar response from the French left in 1863.[23] It was only upon Millet's angry repudiation of his election to the national committee of the Paris Commune's Fédération des Artistes that the myth of the socialist Millet was put to rest.

The Use and Abuse of Millet

Millet's depiction of the peasantry was frequently looked to in the 1880s and 1890s by artists of the right and left alike. Increasingly, though, artists of both leanings stripped his imagery of its emphasis on the hardships of a life of toil. That transition is quite visible in Vincent van Gogh, perhaps the most intent to build upon Millet's imagery in delineating the life of the peasantry. Robert Herbert has argued that van Gogh's work acquires vitality from the strong tension between its determination not to blink the grueling labor of the peasantry and its disposition to place the peasant in a symbolic framework accordant with the artist's Dutch Calvinist faith.[24] Van Gogh numbered himself among the "landscape and peasant painters" that ranged from Millet to Corot and even Delacroix; he saw the land as a revivifying force in French life and

topher Parsons and Neil McWilliam, " 'Le Paysan de Paris': Alfred Sensier and the Myth of Rural France," *Oxford Art Journal,* VI (1983), 43–44. See also T. J. Clark, *The Absolute Bourgeois: Artists and Politics in France, 1848–1851* (Princeton, 1973), 72–98.

21. Parsons and McWilliam, " 'Le Paysan de Paris,' " 42; Clark, *The Absolute Bourgeois,* 82–96.

22. See Robert L. Herbert, *Jean-François Millet,* 78.

23. *Ibid.,* 138.

24. Robert L. Herbert, "City vs. Country: The Rural Image in French Painting from Millet to Gauguin," *Artforum,* VIII (February, 1970), 52.

wrote to his brother Théo in satisfaction over the "health and for-tifying power that I see in the country."[25] For van Gogh, peasants embodied a natural and healthy rural existence, bound inseparably to labor. In 1878, he observed to Théo in a letter, "For who are those who show some sign of higher life? They are those to whom may be applied the words: 'Laboureurs, votre vie est triste, labou-reurs, vous êtes bienheureux,' they are those who bear the signs of 'toute une vie de lutte et de travail soutenu sans fléchir jamais.' It is good to try to become as such."[26]

Van Gogh in his early work gave an emphasis much like Millet's to the rigors of rural labor. In 1885, he wrote that he was pleased to be attacked for not producing academically "correct" images of toiling peasants. He asked Théo to inform one of his detractors that "my great longing is to learn to make those very incorrect-nesses, those deviations, remodellings, changes of reality, so that they may become, yes, untruth if you like—but more true than the literal truth." The proportions would be wrong, the anatomies uncouth, but the figures would live and they would convey the real sense of what it meant to be a peasant laborer.[27]

In time, though, the symbolic won out over van Gogh's yearn-ing to translate the feel of peasant misery. In 1888, in one of many variations van Gogh did on Millet's *The Sower* (Figure 21), he joined the image of the sower with a brilliant setting sun that formed a halo over the peasant's head and with the dominant fore-ground image of an apparently dead tree sending out green shoots. The emphasis is on the cyclic pattern of death and new life in an implicit reaffirmation of Christian doctrine.

Pissarro and Signac had hailed Millet as an "unconscious" social

25. Vincent van Gogh to Théo van Gogh, April, 1885, July, 1890, in *The Letters of Vincent van Gogh,* ed. Mark Roskill (New York, 1982), 226, 338. See Griselda Pollock, "Artists' Mythologies and Media Genius, Madness, and Art History, *Screen,* XXI (1980), 81–89.

26. Vincent van Gogh to Théo van Gogh, April 3, 1878 in *Letters,* ed. Roskill, 109. Griselda Pollock interprets van Gogh's peasant images as simply "civic, mercantilist bour-geois" reactions to "progress and modern urban society" ("Artists' Mythologies," 86). Her interpretation is plausible, but it needs to be taken with caution: the options of embracing and of rejecting urban life and industrialization in the 1880s were both taken up by various ruling circles, by far right and anarchist left. Van Gogh's reaction to urbanization falls somewhere between the "back to feudalism, back to the Church" response of the Catho-lic Revival artists, including Bernard and Denis, and the utopianism of the Neo-Impressionists. See Pollock, "Stark Encounters: Modern Life and Urban Work in van Gogh's Drawings of the Hague, 1881–1883," *Art History,* VI (1983), 346–53.

27. Vincent van Gogh to Théo van Gogh, July, 1885, in *Letters,* ed. Roskill, 230–39.

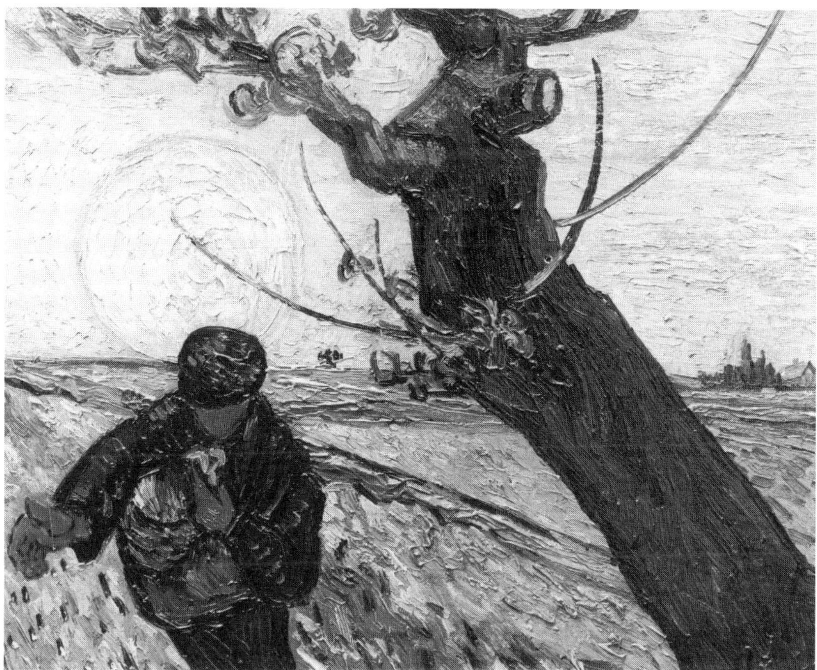

Figure 21   Vincent van Gogh, *The Sower*
Oil on canvas, 1888. Vincent van Gogh Foundation/Van Gogh Museum, Amsterdam.
Art Resource, New York.

artist—one who captured the era, Signac argued, far better than the consciously political Courbet did (see above, p. 104). But over time, the Neos deliberately revised Millet to make their own statement. Charles Angrand's *The Sower,* printed in Grave's *Les Temps nouveaux* in May, 1907 (Figure 22), clearly derives from Millet, but Angrand's sower is in tighter focus than Millet's and the background, the land itself, has been almost totally expunged. Yet Angrand's *The Sower* lacks the immediacy and aggressiveness of Millet's. Angrand's sower is anonymous, generalized, and abstracted—far more a symbol of the productivity and fecundity of the land than an actual, observed peasant.

Angrand's *The Sower* was from a period when Neo-Impressionism was in disintegration. All the same, the general tendencies it illustrates were present in Neo-Impressionist art from its gestation. In a comparison of Millet's *Man with the Hoe* and Seurat's

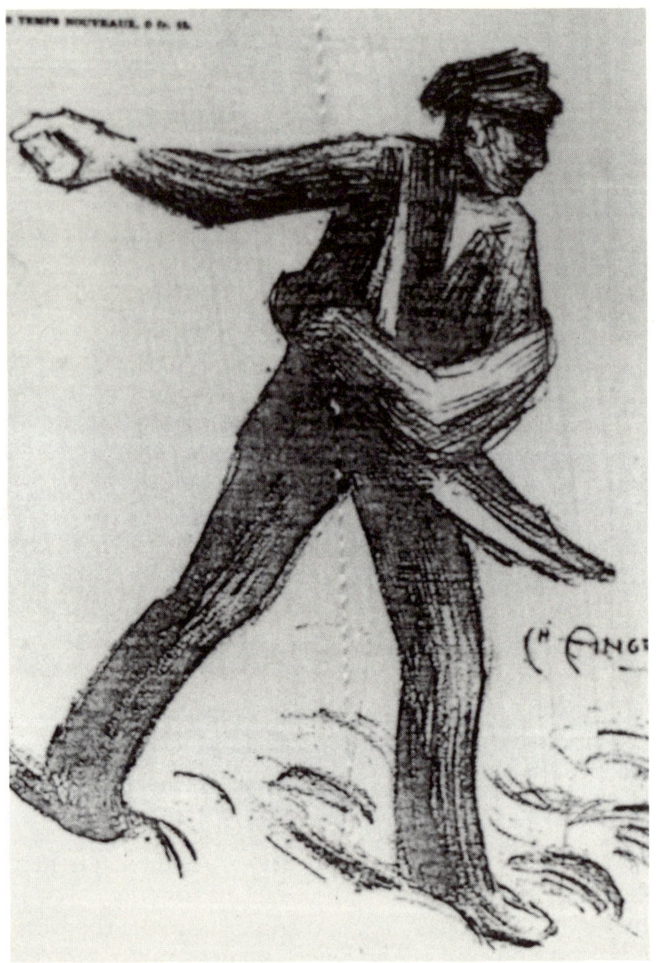

Figure 22   Charles Angrand, *The Sower*
In *Les Temps nouveaux,* May 4, 1907

The Stone Breaker, from 1883 (Figure 23), or of Millet's *The Gleaners,* from 1857 (Figure 24), and Seurat's *Farm Women at Work,* from 1883 (Figure 25), it stands out how Seurat focused on formal relationships—textures, color patterns, the simplification and patterning of the painted forms—more than on any idea of labor or toil.[28]

Formal values play a role in Seurat's painting they never did in

28. See John Russell, *Seurat* (New York, 1965), 107.

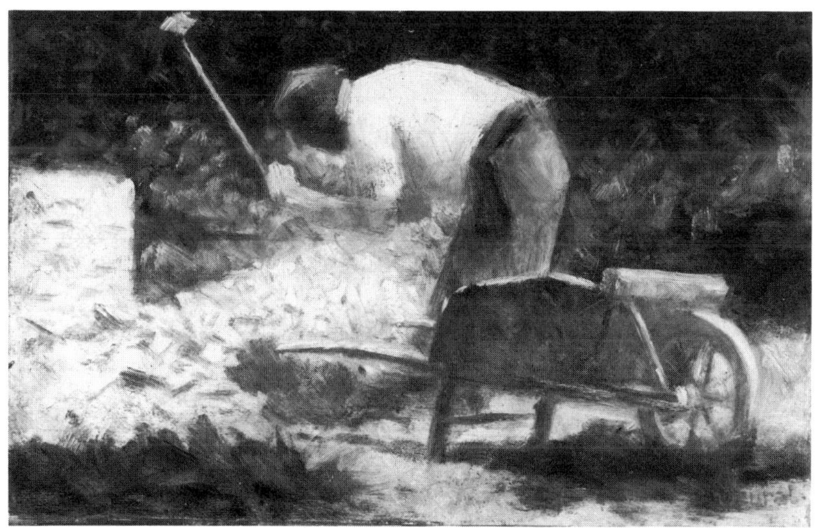

Figure 23   Georges Seurat, *The Stone Breaker*
  Oil on canvas, 1883. Courtesy of The Phillips Collection, Washington, D.C.

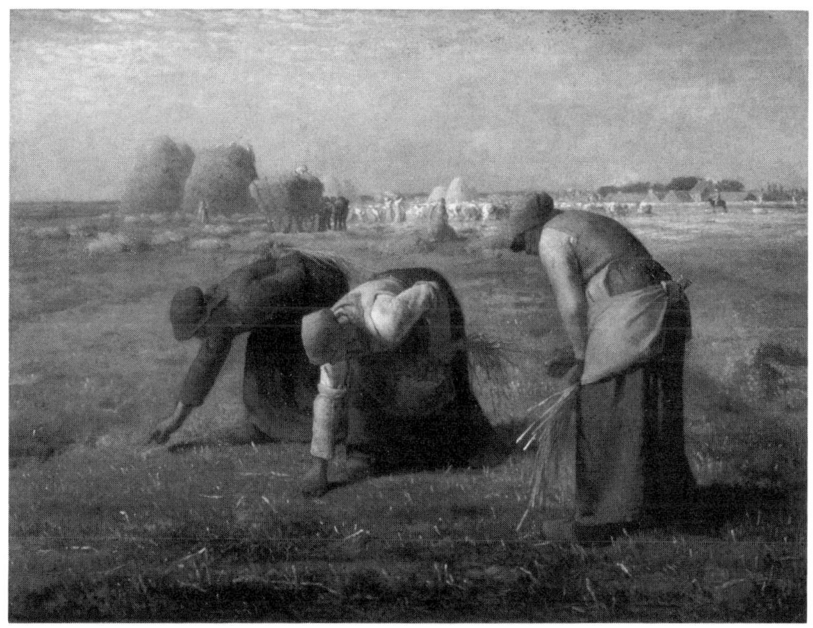

Figure 24   Jean François Millet, *The Gleaners*
  Les Glaneuses, oil on canvas, 1857. Musée d'Orsay, Paris. © PHOTO R.M.N.

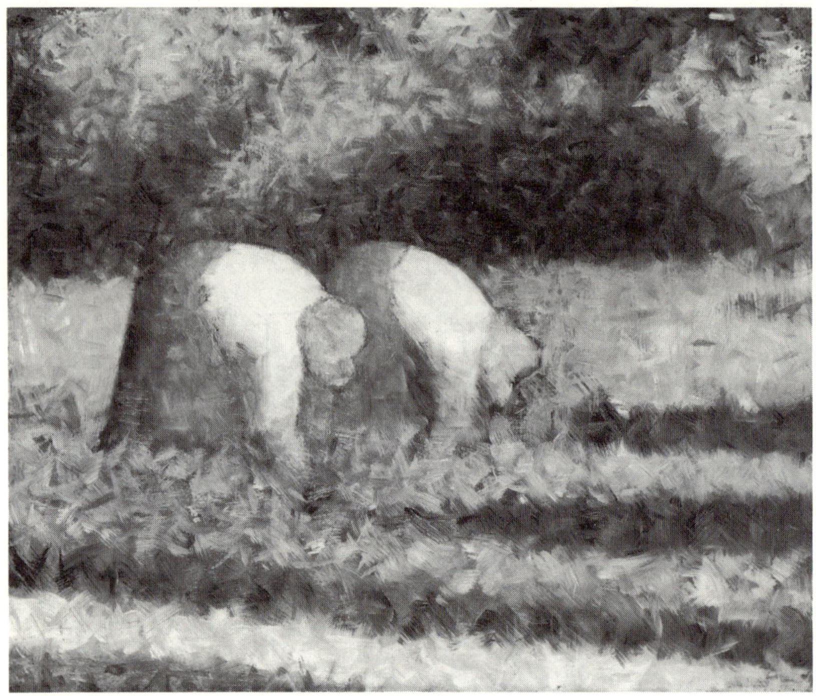

Figure 25   Georges Seurat, *Farm Women at Work*
  Oil on canvas, 1883. Photograph by Robert E. Mates, copyright Guggenheim Foundation, New York.

Millet's. At the same time, the shifts from Millet's art to Seurat's demonstrate both a changed relationship of the artist to the subject—Millet experienced peasant life from both observation and direct experience—and a weakening of the mythology of the peasantry and the land.

Many of the other Neos proclaimed their intent to *reinforce* the centrality of peasant life for the symbolic interpretation of voluntary, collective labor in harmony with nature. Camille Pissarro, in a letter to his son Lucien, commended Proudhon for stressing that "the love of the land links itself to the Revolution, and by consequence to the artistic ideal." Tying that love of the land to the Impressionist love of nature, Pissarro added, "We are on the true logical road that will lead us to this ideal."[29] The convergence he claimed between love of the land and the ideal in art is revealing.

29. Camille Pissarro to Lucien Pissarro, July 8, 1891, in Camille Pissarro's *Correspondance,* III, 102.

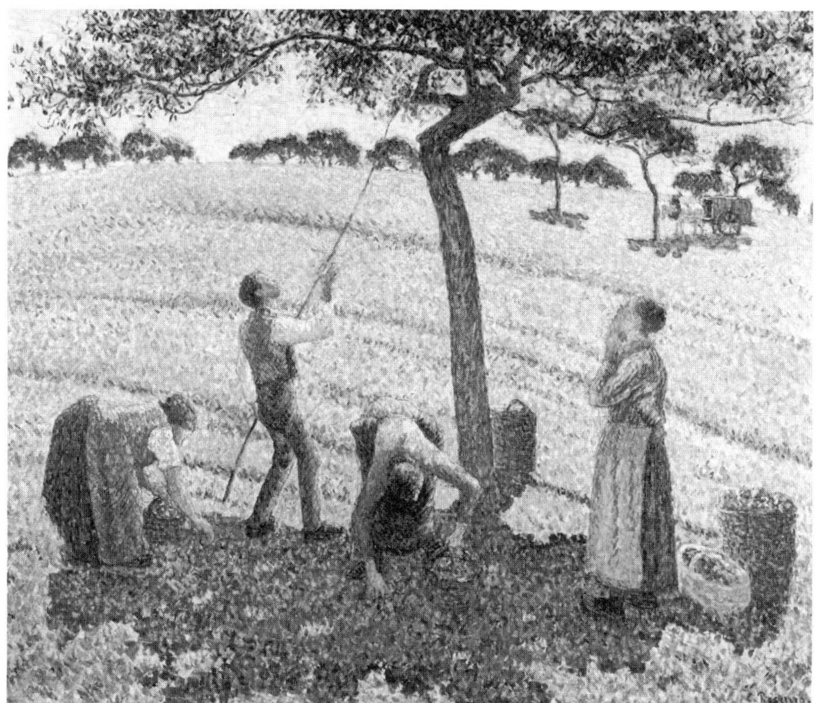

Figure 26   Camille Pissarro, *Apple Pickers, Eragny*
Apple Picking at Eragny-sur-Epte, oil on canvas, 1888. Dallas Museum of Art, Munger Fund.

The goal for Pissarro and his fellow Neos remained that of uniting observed reality with an idealizing essence—in particular, with the valorization Kropotkin, Grave, and Reclus imparted to the land and peasantry as the vital center of resistance to state and capital and as the nucleus of the social order to come.

Pissarro's *Apple Pickers, Eragny,* an oil painting from 1888 (Figure 26), Angrand's *Harvest Scene,* from 1892 (Figure 27), Henri Edmond Cross's *Vendanges (Var),* from 1892, and Maximilien Luce's *Summer at Bézincourt,* from 1897 (Figure 28), differ dramatically in size, scale, number of figures, and even execution, ranging from Luce's rather loose rendering to Angrand's utterly static composition. But the paintings are alike not only in their divided color and brilliant sunlight but also in their overwhelming emphasis on harmony, tranquillity, and collectivity. All four works depict labor, but without precisely what matters in Millet: the sweat and grit of the peasants and their world.

In a study of French peasant imagery, Herbert argues that what

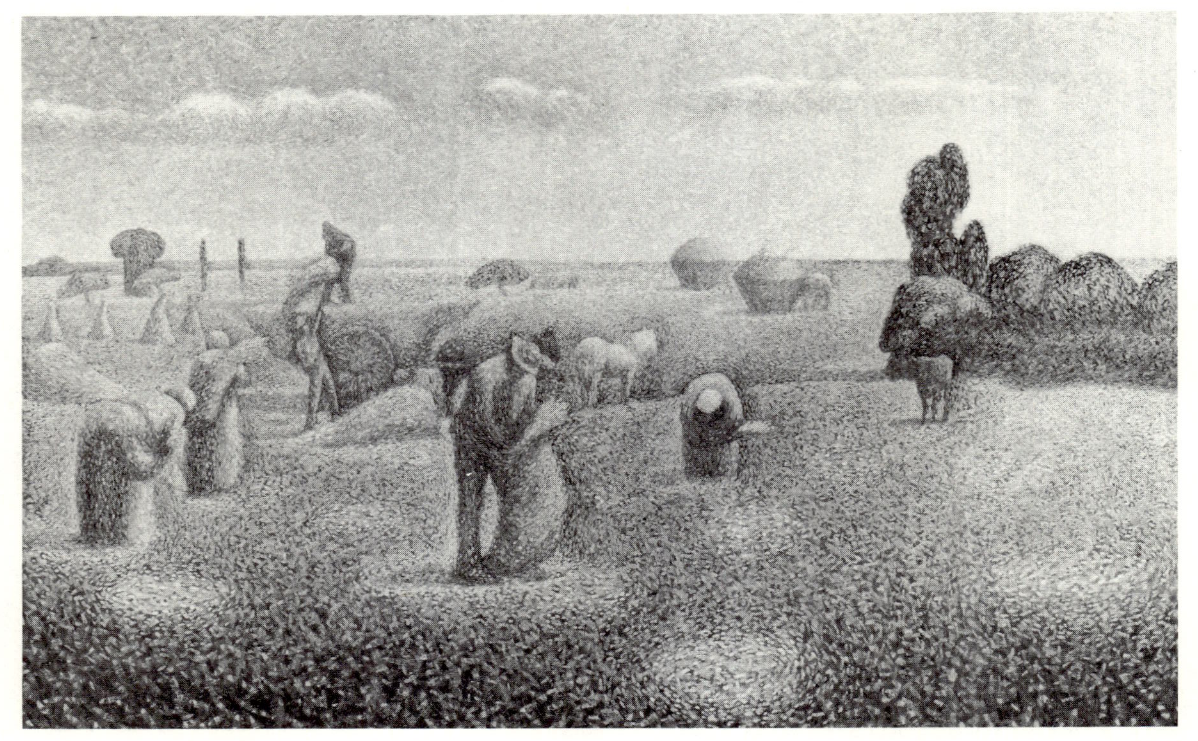

Figure 27   Charles Angrand, *Harvest Scene*
The Harvesters, oil on canvas, 1892. Museum of Fine Arts, Houston, The John A. and Audrey Jones Beck Collection.

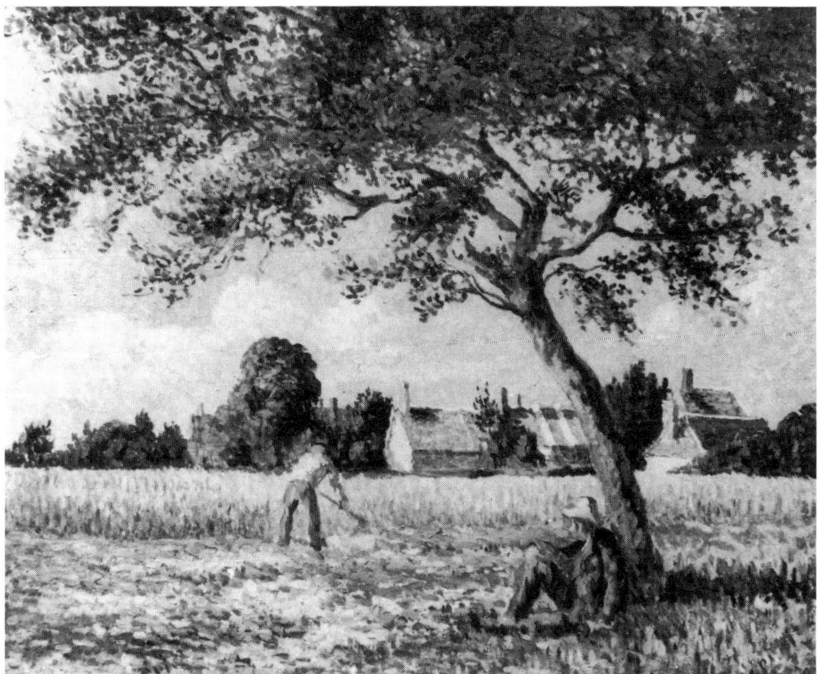

Figure 28 Maximilien Luce, *Summer et Bézincourt*
   Oil on canvas, 1897

distinguishes Pissarro from Millet is his inability to "endow his figures with a fully believable capacity for the work they are engaged in." They are obviously artist's models, not rural workers. The progression from Millet to Pissarro to Gauguin is marked by a "progressive decline in believable action, a slackening of an acceptable fiction of reality." Pissarro was "unable to accept peasant life as coequal with reality."[30]

For the Neo-Impressionists, reality always had to be melded with the ideal; essence always had to coexist with a potential, bet-

30. Herbert, "City vs. Country," 52–53. Compare Richard Brettell's argument that Pissarro's attitude toward the peasantry involved "as much detachment as familiarity, as much disgust as admiration" (*Pissarro and Pontoise: The Painter in a Landscape* [New Haven, 1990], 131). For an explicit contrast between the peasant imagery of Millet and Pissarro, see John House, "Camille Pissarro's Idea of Unity," in *Studies on Camille Pissarro,* ed. Christopher Lloyd (London, 1986), 29–32. A contrary argument is offered by Ralph E. Shikes in "Pissarro's Political Philosophy and His Art," in the same volume, especially on pp. 41–45.

ter state of affairs already present embryonically. Peasant imagery had, therefore, to be affirmative, to function much like utopian imagery. Thus, the labor the Neos portrayed was never back-breaking. This has looked to at least one scholar like a rejection of Millet's cult of toil.[31] But the Neos never shrank from acknowledging the importance of labor in human existence. Nor did they dwell on the idea, so common in socialist and even much anarchist literature, that the peasant is exploited and degraded by capitalism. There are no Neo-Impressionist analogues to Théophile Alexandre Steinlen's recurrent scenes of peasants being beaten or cowed. Rather, the Neos portrayed rural labor as ennobling and positive while increasingly peeling it away from any concrete physical or social space. They valorized the idea of peasant labor while shying from the physical reality of the peasant world in a manner not altogether removed from the bourgeois idealization of a Jules Adolphe Breton or a Bastien-Lepage.[32]

The Neo-Impressionist village was thus very much truncated, lacking both ends of the rural class spectrum, both the poorest and the wealthiest inhabitants. To project onto rural France the vision of harmony entailed that the brush not tell of class distinctions, inequality, and conflict—seemingly an odd set of ills for self-proclaimed communists to let pass uncommented, but the silence was firmly grounded in the needs and limits of anarchocommunist theory.[33]

The Neo-Impressionist image of the peasant stood in close counterpoint to that of the Pont Aven painters. The peasants of Paul Gaugin, Emile Bernard, Paul Sérusier, and Georges Lacombe are invariably clothed in the distinctive dark dresses and white caps so beloved of Parisian artists, the dress of the prosperous Breton upper peasantry.[34] They pray or stand transfixed by visions. Sometimes they labor, but as in Lacombe's *Women Gathering Chestnuts,* of 1892 (Figure 29), the effect is always stylized. Lacombe's

31. See, for example, Michel Melot, "Camille Pissarro in 1880: An Anarchistic Artist in Bourgeois Society," trans. Alan Wallach and Carol Duncan, *Marxist Perspectives,* II (Winter, 1979–80), 38–39.

32. Gabriel Weisberg argues forcefully for strong compositional and thematic ties between the art of Pissarro and the painting of Breton and Bastien-Lepage. See his "Jules Breton, Jules Bastien-Lepage, and Camille Pissarro in the Context of Nineteenth-Century Peasant Painting and the Salon," *Arts Magazine,* LVI (February, 1982), 115–19.

33. See Brettell, *Pissarro and Pontoise,* 39–45.

34. On the significance of Breton peasant dress in this era, see Fred Orton and Griselda Pollock, "Les Données bretonnantes: La Prairie de représentation," *Art History,* III (1980), 326–28.

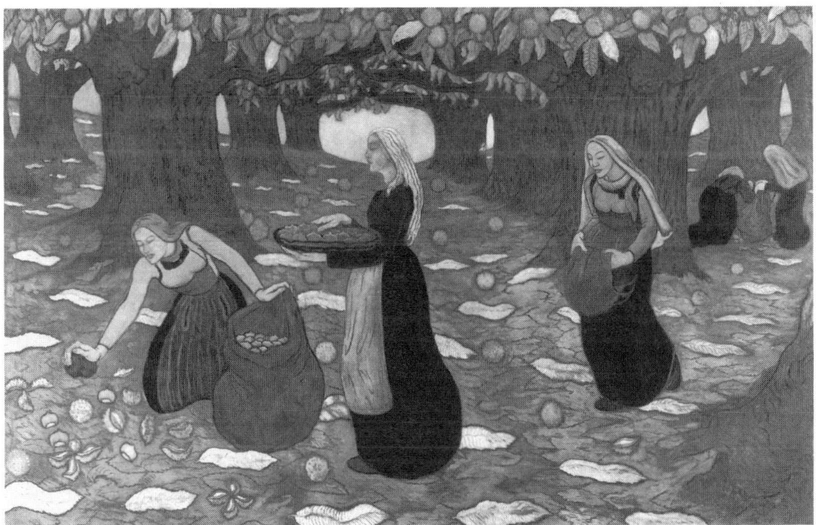

Figure 29   Georges Lacombe, *Women Gathering Chestnuts*
The Chestnut Gatherers, oil on canvas, 1892. Norton Simon Art Foundation,
M.1979.35.P.

peasant women are not sunk in drudgery; they scarcely exist in a
real space in which they can act at all. They become "timeless"
symbols corresponding to an anemic notion of the peasant, signi-
fiers in a representational system in which simplified, stylized figures people the space surrounding continuous miracles. For the
Pont Aven painters, physical reality was merely a skin over a mystical, otherworldly reality. Paul Sérusier's *Pont Aven Triptych,* of
1891 (Figure 30), shows Breton peasants at perfect ease with nature, living in an idyllic world of flowers and fruit, exempt from
toil and trouble. The Neo-Impressionist utopia was social rather
than mystical, but it shared this air of allegorized abstraction,
the tendency to transform the mundane into the transcendent. In
place of the Pont Aven group's scenes of worship and pardons, the
Neos showed harmonious toil and bustling village markets. The
images are wholly positive, from the brilliant colors to the fetelike
appearance. The Pont Aven peasants pray, the Neo peasants shop
and trade, but both live and work in an idealized, preindustrial
fantasy.[35]

35. Melot argued that the market was for Pissarro in particular an image of the rural
world as a "pure harmonious" society. See his "Camille Pissarro in 1880," 39–40. "There

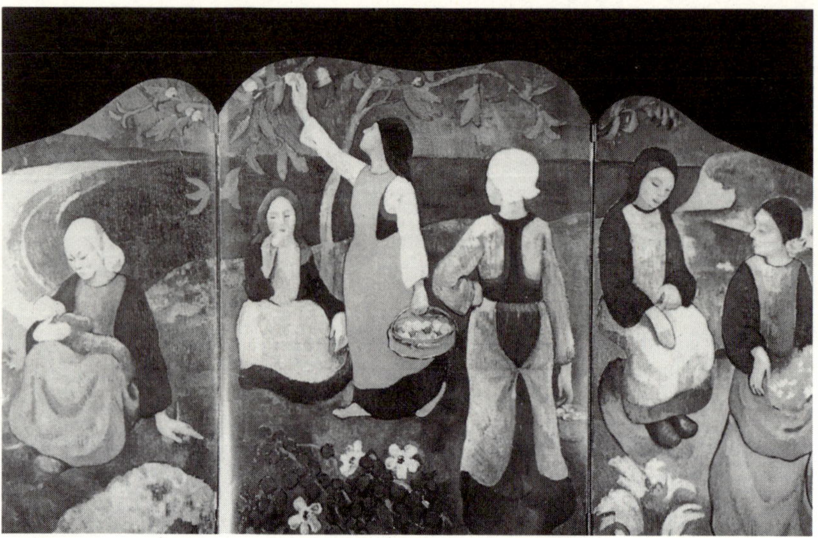

Figure 30   Paul Sérusier, *Pont Aven Triptych*
Oil on canvas, 1891. Courtesy of Jean Claude Bellier, Paris.

The Neo-Impressionist peasant scenes differ dramatically in this regard from those of their Italian counterparts, the Divisionists. In paintings such as Angelo Morbelli's *For Eighty Cents,* of 1895 (Figure 31), and *In the Rice Fields,* of 1901, the laboring peasants appear saturated by an almost painful blaze of light that heightens the intensity of the exertion depicted. The lighting focuses attention on the physical labor in a manner wholly alien to Pissarro or Angrand. The Divisionists could not obscure the reality of Italian peasant labor—in a country then far less industrialized than France. Their peasants are idealized, generalized, but the focus is still on day-to-day stoop labor.

In Neo-Impressionist rural scenes, harmony often means that the peasants are subsumed by the idyllic landscapes. Michel Melot has said that in Pissarro's peasant scenes "fieldhands blend into nature in a kind of degrading harmony."[36] That is even more clearly true in his colleagues' works. In Angrand's *End of the Harvest,* a Conté crayon drawing from 1905, the peasants are ab-

---

was little Pissarro could do to stop the development of modern society, but if he dreamed, it was surely of a simpler, more direct economy—of the kind he found at country fairs and markets" (pp. 39–40).

36. Melot, "Camille Pissarro in 1880," 38.

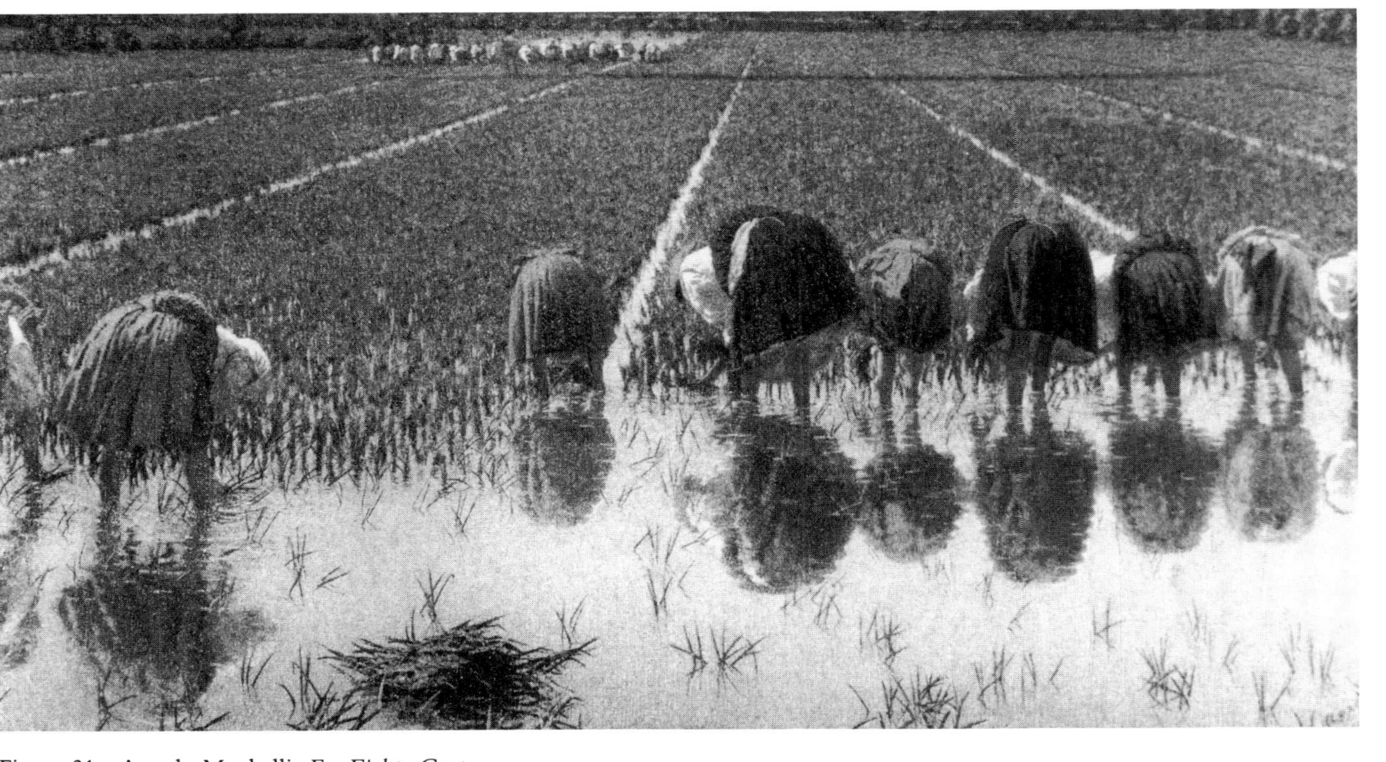

Figure 31 Angelo Morbelli, *For Eighty Cents*
Per ottanta centesimi, oil on canvas, 1895. Civico Museo Borgogna, Vercelli.

stracted into oddly angled shapes barely distinguishable from the hayricks around them.

After Pissarro left the Neo-Impressionists in the early 1890s, rural imagery played an increasingly peripheral role in the group's art. In a letter to Théo van Rysselberghe in 1905, Cross confessed, "A long time ago I discovered my insensitivity toward the peasant. I find him here [in the South] especially without plastic interest, and I would not know how to paint him." He added, "He only moves me as a spot, and he seems small and far away." For Cross, his personal fantasies alone seemed real: "On the rocks, on the sand of the beaches, under the clumps of pine, nymphs and naiads appear to me, a whole world born of beautiful light."[37] The synthesis of real and ideal had come unraveled; for Cross, at least, the real peasant could no longer hope to compete with the dream.

The Urban World

Anarchist writers wrote and spoke frequently of the love of the land; few if any would have spoken similarly of an *amour de la cité*. The anarchocommunist drive to utopianize the rural landscape had no parallel with respect to the urban scene. Instead, anarchist critiques of urban life and technology harbored deep contradictions. Anarchist rural imagery gave expression to one strand of anarchist thought in rendering the world as latently a seamless harmony. Anarchist urban imagery, on the other hand, ever devolved into a continuum of polar opposites that defied reconciliation.

The unresolved dichotomy in anarchist attitudes toward the city is evident in an essay by Reclus from 1895. The article began with vitriol: "To look at our enormous cities, expanding day by day and almost hour by hour, engulfing each year fresh colonies of immigrants, and running their suckers, like giant octopuses, into the surrounding country, one feels a sort of shudder come over one, as if in the presence of some strange social malady." Reclus wrote movingly of workers' suburbs "encumbered by stinking chimneys, where immense buildings skirt the blackened

37. Henri Edmond Cross to Théo van Rysselberghe, in the van Rysselberghe family archives, quoted by Robert L. Herbert in *Neo-Impressionism* (New York, 1968), 47. Brettell identifies a parallel development in Pissarro's work as early as 1874. See Brettell, *Pissarro and Pontoise,* 152–53.

streets, . . . where the air is almost unbreathable, where everything in sight . . . seems to sweat mud and soot." To the foulness of the industrial city, "where immense buildings skirt the blackened streets with walls either bare or blind, or pierced in sickening symmetry, with innumerable windows," Reclus counterposed a pastoral vision of harmony. "Will the time ever come," he asked, "when all men . . . shall breathe fresh air in abundance, enjoy the light and sunshine, taste the coolness of the shade and the scent of roses, and feed their children without fear that the bread will run short in the bin?" Reclus then switched directions. The growth of the modern city was a "sign of healthy and regular evolution." He added, "When the cities increase, humanity is progressing; where they diminish, civilisation itself is in danger." The only resolution of the contradiction—in which cities were a healthy sign of social development but also places of horror in which to live—would require anarchism, euphemized for middle-class readers as a society of "peace and good will." With anarchism, the "hopelessly sordid and unhealthy" aspects of the cities were to be gradually eliminated and the "delights of the town" finally harmonized with the joys of rural life.[38]

Anarchocommunism routinely asserted that cities were essential in the present but also detestable; ruined by technology that was a social good but misused; indicative of human progress in the modern world but doomed to disappear in the future. What is notable is the endless succession of polarities. There is a lucid analysis of each aspect of technological growth and industrialization, but the arguments stand in apparent isolation from one another, unreconciled and perhaps unreconcilable. Linking them all is only a negation of the present. It is a difficult set of positions to summarize, much less to capture in a single image. It is scarcely surprising that many Neo-Impressionist industrial scenes fail ultimately to cohere.[39]

38. Elisée Reclus, "The Evolution of Cities," *Contemporary Review,* LXVII (1895), 246. Reclus cited Scranton, Pittsburgh, and Buffalo for their appalling conditions. The uneasy attitude toward the city has strong echoes in socialist literature as well, beginning with Friedrich Engels' *The Condition of the Working Class in England* (London, 1846). A closer counterpart to the warring polarities of the anarchists on the topic is evident in the writings of the French Malonists and the British Fabians. See Walter Crane, "On the Influence of Modern Social and Economic Conditions on the Sense of Beauty," in *Ideals in Art* (London, 1905), 76–87, esp. 76–81.

39. See Reclus, "The Evolution of Cities," 253–64. Reclus returned to the themes of that essay in "La Cité du bon accord," *Almanach de la question sociale pour 1897* (Paris, 1897);

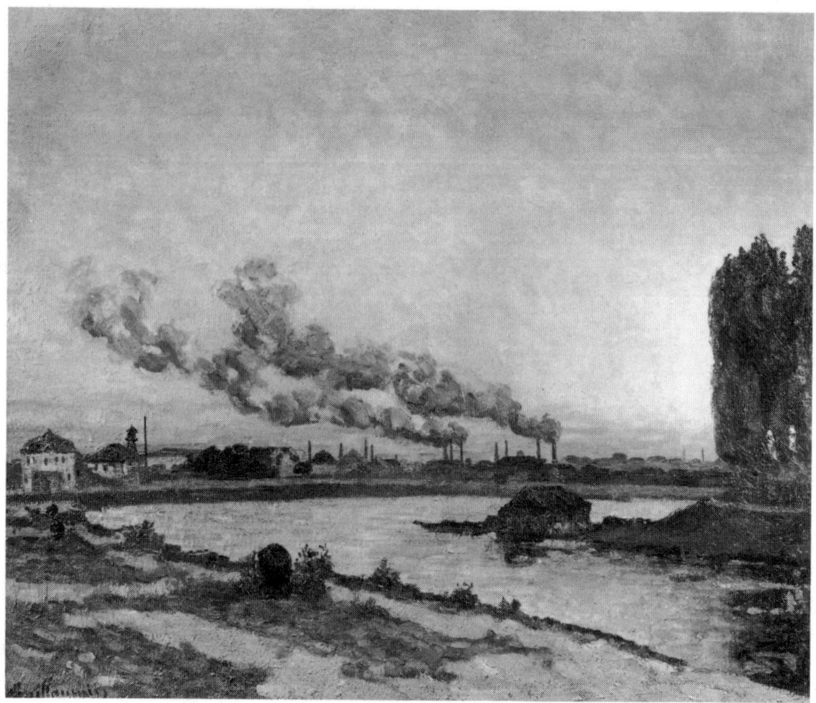

Figure 32   Armand Guillaumin, *Setting Sun at Ivry*
Oil on canvas, 1873. Musée d'Orsay, Paris. Giraudon/Art Resource, New York.

The Impressionists addressed the new industrial France not unlike the way they had rural France—in a set of images they edited to present an optimistic and harmonious whole: a beautified railroad bridge, a train set against a seemingly intact rural or suburban landscape, the steam escaping from the Gare Saint Lazare. The effect was hazy, distanced, and positive: the smoke of the factory blended with the clouds, the factory itself with the skyline. In Armand Guillaumin's *Setting Sun at Ivry,* of 1873 (Figure 32), a small and very distant factory and smokestack blend into a mundane landscape. The factory smoke was used for tonal effects, but the

excerpts are included in Max Nettlau's *Elisée Reclus: Anarchist und Gelehrter, 1830–1905* (Berlin, 1928), 296–98. See also Gary Dunbar, *Elisée Reclus, Historian of Nature* (Hamden, Conn., 1978), 118–20. The unresolved polarities in anarchocommunist theory are noted by Bob Galois in "Ideology and the Idea of Nature: The Case of Peter Kropotkin," *Antipode,* VIII (1976), 7.

inclusion of an object as vulgar as a factory prompted attacks from critics.[40]

The breakup of the Impressionist movement produced a fragmentation among those who claimed to be its successors. The "Impressionists and Synthetists" fled to Pont Aven, to what Francis Jourdain later scathingly termed the "return to solitude, to paradise lost, to the sanctity of innocence, to the virtues of ignorance."[41] Gauguin's search took him to the Caribbean, then to Tahiti, and finally to the Marquesas. Bernard, Charles Filiger, and the others took refuge in a make-believe Middle Ages.

Neo-Impressionists and the Urban World

By contrast, Neo-Impressionist artists showed an interest in French industrial imagery from the outset. Signac asserted that depictions of the industrial, urban world were a central preoccupation of Neo-Impressionist art: he offered as evidence the Neo fascination with "picturesque studies of the workers' blocks of Saint-Ouen and Montrouge, solid and dazzling; . . . the reproduction of the wide and curiously colored movements of a laborer next to a sandpile, of a smith in the incandescence of the forge."[42]

Seurat, Signac, and Angrand began to experiment with images of the industrial belt around Paris in the early 1880s. They focused on bleak industrial scenes of a sort that was anathema to the Impressionists. Yet works such as Seurat's *Suburb,* of 1881–1882 (Figure 33), and Signac's *Gas Tanks at Clichy,* of 1886 (Figure 34), are stamped by a persistent oddness, by a peculiar inner tension, only emphasized by the terms in which Signac was to describe them. "Picturesque" scenes? "Solid and dazzling"? In the novels of Zola, in the images by van Gogh, in newspaper and journalistic accounts, the industrial suburbs come across as anything but

40. See Robert L. Herbert's discussion of Monet's boating scenes on the Seine at Argenteuil in his "Industry in the Changing Landscape from Daubigny to Monet," in *French Cities in the Nineteenth Century,* ed. John M. Merriman (London, 1982), 154–55. See also Paul Hayes Tucker, *Monet at Argenteuil* (New Haven, 1982), 82. On the reception of *Setting Sun at Ivry,* see Roger Passeron, *Impressionist Prints* (London, 1974), 148. Richard Brettell argues that Guillaumin's industrial landscapes were less forceful than Pissarro's and largely came from travel imagery. See Bretell, *Pissarro and Pontoise,* 91–92.

41. Francis Jourdain, "Paul Signac, peintre et logicien," *La Pensée,* September–October, 1955, pp. 18–23.

42. Paul Signac, "Impressionnistes et Révolutionnaires," *La Révolte,* IV (June 13–19, 1891), 4.

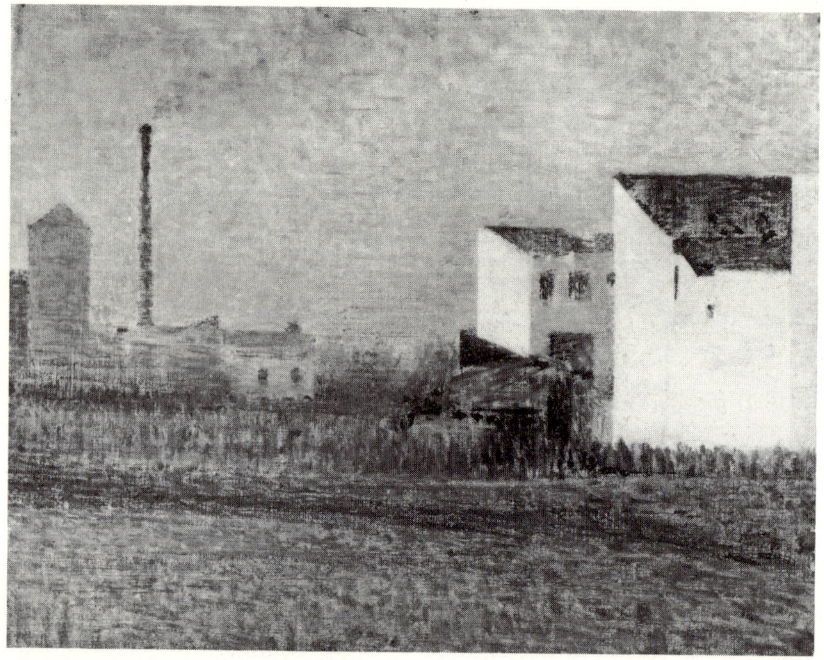

Figure 33   Georges Seurat, *Suburb*
La Banlieue, oil on canvas, 1881–82. Courtesy of Musée d'Art Moderne de Troyes.

picturesque. It is not a question of which rendering of the industrial suburb can retrospectively be recognized as more accurate. Rather, what demands notice is the manner in which the Neos chose to edit and arrange the scenes they presented.

Félix Fénéon, favorably reviewing Signac's works, commented on two contrasting qualities in these paintings. Fénéon saw that Signac was "beguiled" by surburban landscapes, which he described in grim terms: endless fences hung with work pants and other laundry, the desolation of scorched grass and peeling walls. In the same review, however, he remarked in passing on the way Signac "Marseillized the suburb," saturating it in the brilliant holiday tones of the Mediterranean.[43] Desolation and rich color jostle each other, unable to find a stable balance. For that reason, black-and-white reproductions of the paintings seem far grimmer and more depressing than the works themselves. Even Seurat's *Suburb*

43. For the assertion that Signac "emmarseillait les banlieues," see Félix Fénéon, "Les Impressionnistes en 1886," in his *Oeuvres plus que complètes,* ed. Joan Ungersma Halperin (Geneva, 1970), I, 37.

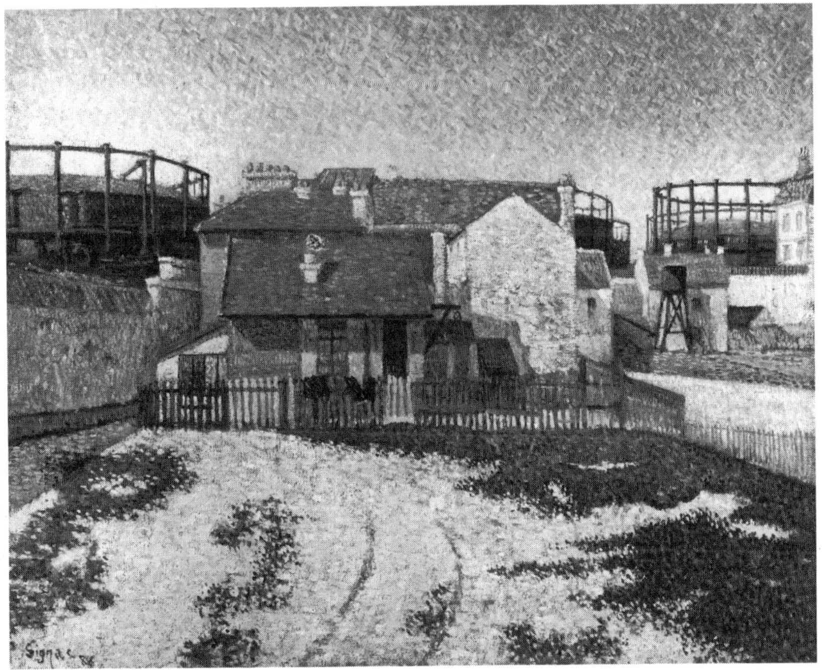

Figure 34   Paul Signac, *Gas Tanks at Clichy*
  Paul Signac 1863–1935 French, Gas Tanks at Clichy, 1886, oil on canvas, 65.0 x 81.0
  cm, Felton Bequest 1948, reproduced by permission of the National Gallery of Victoria, Melbourne.

seems curiously unfocused, the empty bleakness of the scene at war with the light palette of blue, white, and orange.

The industrial scenes of Seurat and Signac are empty, unpopulated, much like the paintings they did during the same period of resort towns, to which they also went as tourists. Richard Thomson ascribes the uneasy play between the bright and the grim to the experimental nature of the paintings.[44] But the same tension is evident in the works of Luce, a product of a Paris faubourg who followed Constantin Meunier to the industrial regions around Charleroi in the 1890s. Luce owned to his conflicting impressions: in a letter to Cross in 1895, he wrote, "It is [at once] so *terrible and so beautiful* that I doubt it can be rendered as I want."[45] The anarchist Georges Darien, in a review published in *La Plume,* called

44. Richard Thomson, *Seurat* (Oxford, 1985), 64.
45. Philippe Cazeau, *Maximilien Luce* (Paris, 1982), 87 ("Ce pays m'épouvante. . . . C'est tellement terrible et beau que je doute de rendre ce que je vois!").

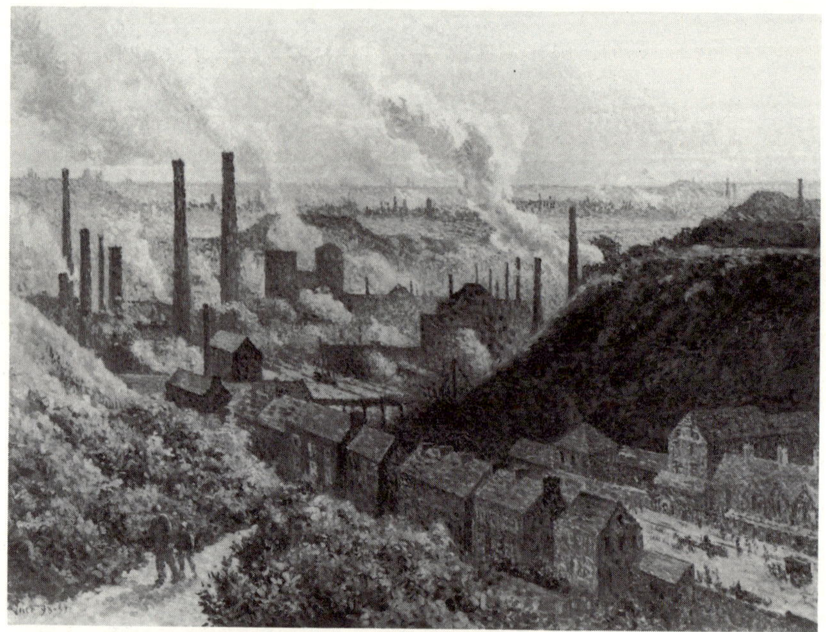

Figure 35   Maximilien Luce, *Factory Smokestacks, Couillet*
Oil on canvas, 1898–99. Courtesy of Walter F. Brown Collection, San Antonio, Texas.

Luce's artistic response a balance between a harsh critique of society and a hope for a better future. On the one hand was Luce's "violent, cruel, brutal painting," which evoked "the bleeding soul of the people, the life of multitudes anguished and inflamed by suffering and bitterness." On the other was his exhibition of "the calm of nature, the eternal sweetness of things." Darien added, "And it is poignant, this antithesis between the profound peace of certain canvases and the harsh brutality of certain others," an antithesis between the "soul of the plebeian, the soul of the infant, sweet and gay, and a wretched society besmeared with hatred."[46]

Darien was careful to locate the antithesis in the contrast between Luce's paintings. But the same antithesis can be found within individual canvases, such as his *Factory Smokestacks, Couillet,* of 1898–1899 (Figure 35). Industry and nature stand there in no rapport: a line of row houses forms a strong diagonal from lower right to upper left, the factories extend upward from the

46. Georges Darien, "Maximilien Luce," *La Plume,* LVII (1891), 300.

houses in the center, but both houses and factories are hemmed in by lush greenbelts at the upper right and the lower left. The zone of vegetation at the lower left is bisected by a pleasant path, with two strolling workers. The central factory and the diagonal of workers' housing dominate the painting, but these are offset by the lush greens of the surrounding foliage. Industrial desolation is counterpoised by greenery. Far from a pastoral, Luce's painting is not a stark scene of industrial desolation either. Above all, the various components of the painting are strikingly walled off and segregated from one another. The work fails to cohere; it is a jigsaw puzzle of autonomous zones.[47]

The lack of internal coherence is apparent as well in the manner in which the Neos began to diverge regarding industrial themes. Not long after Signac hailed the industrial landscape as a crucial and defining subject for the movement, it disappeared from his own work, which grew to prefer lush vacation resorts—Antibes and Saint Tropez. Other Neos went on painting the industrial world but with sharply differing attitudes and approaches. Camille Pissarro was captivated by the panorama of the industrial city, but he was far less engaged when the focus shifted to industry's nasty details. So long as industrialization and technology remained background motifs, Pissarro could welcome them into his art in conformity with the original Impressionist valorization of pure sensation. In a letter to Lucien in 1896, he described a view of Rouen as a series of brilliant contrasts, especially between the "always new and shining" Gare d'Orléans and the factory smokestacks. For Pissarro, the totality of the scene was "as beautiful as Venice." He added, "It is art; if I consult my sensations, I find that there is not only this motif, there are marvels on every side."[48]

Specific artifacts of the new industrial order evoked a rather different attitude, however. One of the most contested symbols of the French industrial era, the Eiffel Tower, was for middle-class progressives the epitome of scientific and educational progress. Zola, entranced, photographed it repeatedly at various stages of

47. The effort to contain the effects of industry so as to deny the intrusiveness of the industrial world into its surroundings dates back at least to the British experience of industrialization. Compare Luce's painting with *Arkwright's Cotton Mill,* produced by Joseph Wright of Derby, in 1785. Wright had the somewhat easier task of making a cotton mill look attractive; Luce had to strive for a similar effect while working with a smokestack factory.

48. Camille Pissarro to Lucien Pissarro, October 2, 1896, in Camille Pissarro's *Correspondance,* IV, 266–67.

completion. *Le Figaro* bubbled about the new tower in verse. For Louis Lockroy, "it summarized the industrial greatness and power of the present age." He added, "Its immense shaft, by burying itself in the clouds, had something symbolic about it; it seems the image of progress as we conceive of it today."[49]

The French far right was notably less enthusiastic. It attacked the tower as symbolizing the ascendancy of middle-class capital over religious faith. According to Edouard Drumont and Joris Karl Huysmans, Notre Dame was under religious attack by the new structure, a standard rising above "liturgical fetes of capital." A letter to *Le Temps* signed by forty-seven conservative artistic luminaries argued similarly that old Paris would be dwarfed by a "gigantic black factory chimney."[50]

Not atypically, both the Neos and the anarchists split down the middle over the tower. Lockroy's conception of the tower as a symbol of progress, an "unending spiral in which humanity gravitates in an eternal ascension," found an echo among anarchists. For Jourdain, as for Huysmans, the tower was the embodiment of a "new divinity"; for him, as for Zola, that new faith was a positive one—in science, the mechanism for the "apotheosis of the people of the whole world." Within the Neo-Impressionist circle, both Seurat and Louis Hayet seem to have shared in the celebration of the tower as incarnating scientific progress. Both painted small works on the subject; Seurat's small, unfinished oil (Figure 36), perhaps intended as a study for a never-executed larger work, suggested to Meyer Schapiro that Seurat was something of a procorporate technocrat. The mathematical ramifications of the tower must in any case have appealed to Seurat's love of precision and science.[51]

The anarchocommunist receptivity to science and technology, however, was scarcely unreserved. Although Kropotkin, Grave, and Reclus did not share fully in the delirious medievalism of their

49. Levin, *Republican Art and Ideology*, 41–45. See Debora L. Silverman, *Art Nouveau in Fin-de-Siècle France: Politics, Psychology, and Style* (Berkeley and Los Angeles, 1989), 2–5. *Le Figaro* wrote, "Gloire au Titan industriel / Qui fit cet escalier du ciel / La Tour énorme en s'embrasent / Nous donne l'oubli d'a présent" (Charles Braibant, *Histoire de la Tour Eiffel* [Paris, 1964], 137).

50. Joseph Harriss, *The Tallest Tower: Eiffel and the Belle Epoque* (Boston, 1975), 20–22. On Huysmans, see Braibant, *Histoire de la Tour Eiffel*, 194. See also Edouard Drumont, *La Fin d'un monde: Etude psychologique et social* (Paris, 1889), iv–v.

51. Levin, *Republican Art and Ideology*, 45; Braibant, *Histoire de la Tour Eiffel*, 140; Meyer Schapiro, "New Light on Seurat," *Art News*, LVII (April, 1958), 22–24, 44–45, 52.

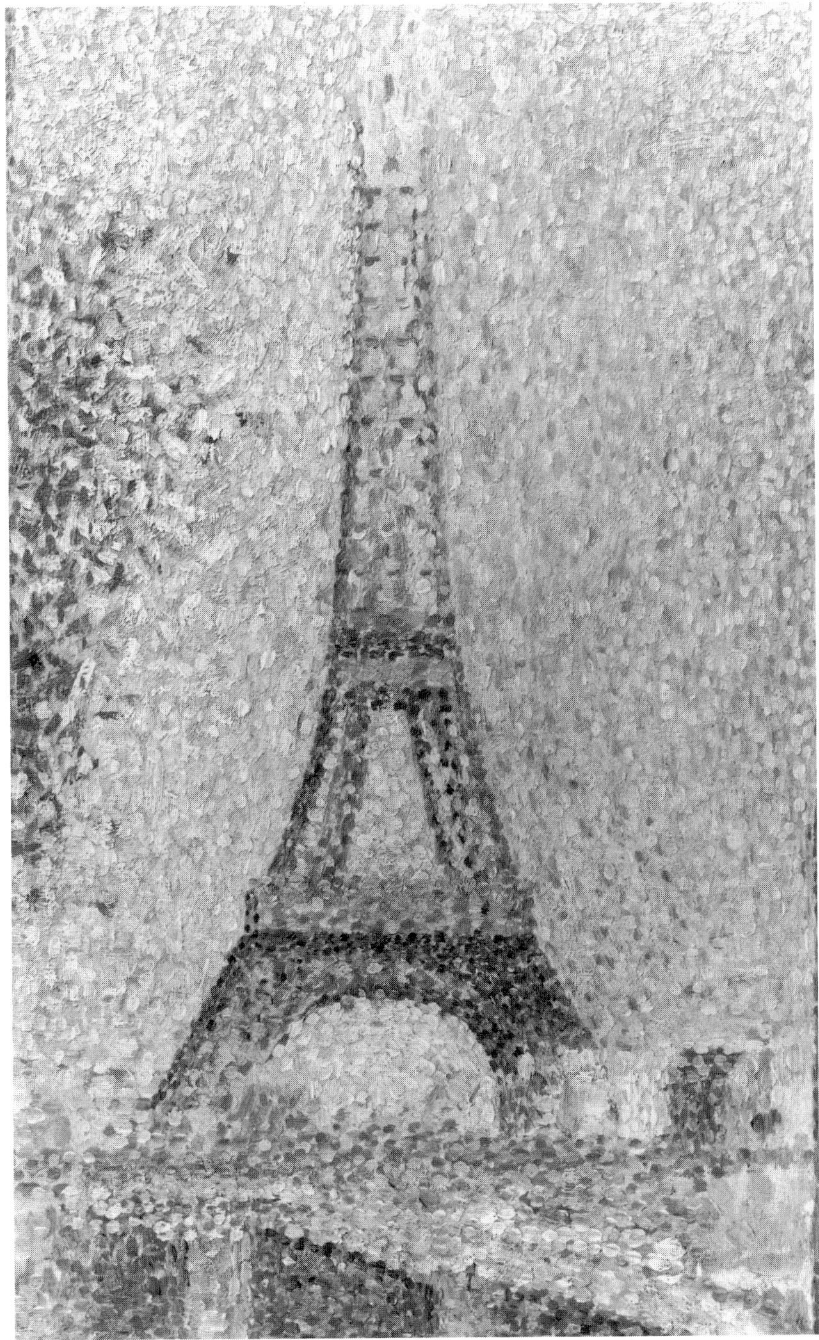

Figure 36   Georges Seurat, *Eiffel Tower*
Georges Pierre Seurat, French, 1859–91, *Eiffel Tower,* oil on panel, *ca.* 1889, 9 1/2 x 6″,
Fine Arts Museums of San Francisco, Museum purchase, William H. Noble Bequest
Fund.

European associates, they were conscious that technology would benefit humanity only in a nonexploitative society. The Eiffel Tower, on their view, was a monument to self-glorification and greed. The tower became an anarchist target even before it was completed: in 1886, the shadowy anarchist militant and bandit L. Schiroky-Ortiz denounced the structure for a host of failings, from ill-chosen terrain, to the vulgarity of the design, to the new taxes by which it was to be financed.[52]

As the 1889 World's Fair opened, anarchist attacks mounted. Although anarchist reviews took pains to praise the scientific and industrial exhibits, the tower did not always share in the approbation.[53] Mirbeau compared Paris to Babylon before its conquest by the Medes and Persians. *Le Père Peinard* disparaged the tower with its usual venom.[54]

In anarchist journals, the Eiffel Tower quickly became a symbol for the reigning system's contempt for the poor. A cartoon in *Le Père Peinard* (Figure 37) is entitled "July 14 of the Poor Buggers." It shows a poor family, on the brink of starvation, staring out in numbed anger at the fireworks display around the tower. A similar image, by the print artist Quinsac, appeared in the quasi-anarchist *Courrier français* in 1889; it is dedicated "to Jean Prolo, worker" (Figure 38). Again, a worker gazes from meager surroundings at the fireworks and searchlights of the tower and the fetes surrounding the fair. The legend reads, "He labors and . . . he despairs. It is not for you the lanterns burn."

Camille Pissarro was soon displaying a similar reaction. In a letter to Lucien, he censured a "hideous" painting by Hyacinthe Pozier as being so detestable that it could only be compared to Eiffel's new tower. "It is worthy," he repeated, "of the epoch of the Eiffel Tower." In the same letter, he attacked a painting by

52. L. Schiroky-Ortiz, "Chronique scientifique," *La Révolution cosmopolite*, I (September 4, 1886), 3. Concerning Ortiz, one of those convicted at the Procès des Trente, see Jean Maitron, *Le Mouvement anarchiste en France* (Paris, 1975), I, 253n7. See also Joan Ungersma Halperin, *Félix Fénéon: Aesthete and Anarchist in Fin-de-Siècle Paris* (New Haven, 1988), 286–91, *passim*.

53. For a favorable reaction to the scientific and industrial exhibits, see Lucien Weil, "Vive le machinisme!" *L'Attaque*, II (July 25–August 3, 1889), 3. See also "Le Foire de Champ-de-Mars," *Le Père Peinard*, I (April 28, 1889), 1–6.

54. For Mirbeau, the exposition as a whole was "le dernier élan d'une société moribonde . . . le suprème cri d'une civilisation qui agonise" (Reg Carr, *Anarchism in France: The Case of Octave Mirbeau* [Montreal, 1977], 29). See Fiona Fitzgerald, "The Prints of Lucien Pissarro from 1886 to 1896" (M.A. thesis, University of East Anglia, 1981), 3–5.

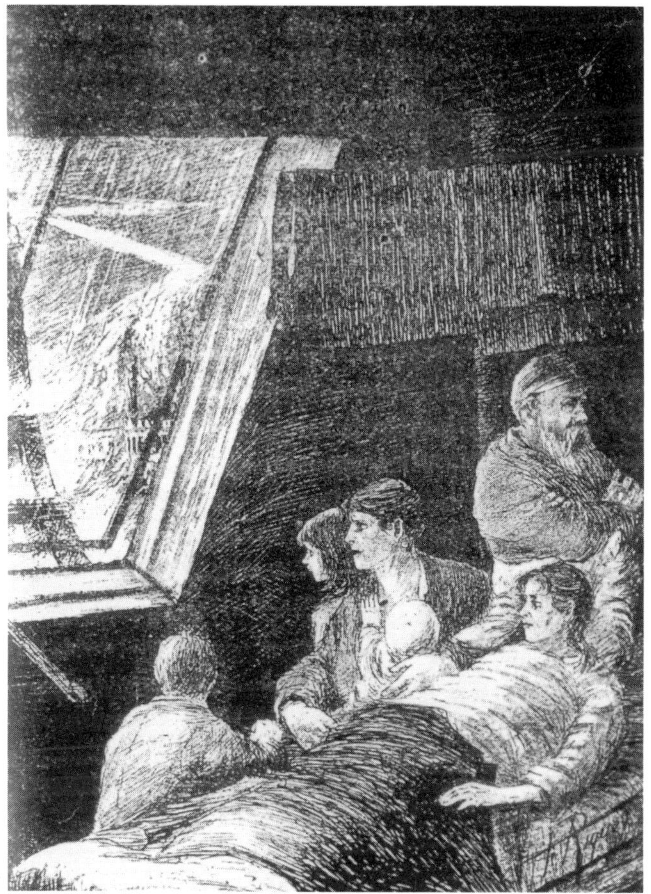

Figure 37   *July 14 of the Poor Buggers*
  In *Le Père Peinard,* 1889

Hayet of the Place de la Concorde, in which the tower is accorded
a prominent place.[55]

Pissarro's dissatisfaction with Hayet's painting was due at least
in part to differences in technique between the two artists. There
is no ambiguity, however, to the way Pissarro employed the Eiffel
Tower in his *Turpitudes sociales,* a dossier of pen-and-ink drawings

55. Camille Pissarro to Lucien Pissarro, September 9, 1889, in Camille Pissarro's *Correspondance,* II, 291–92.

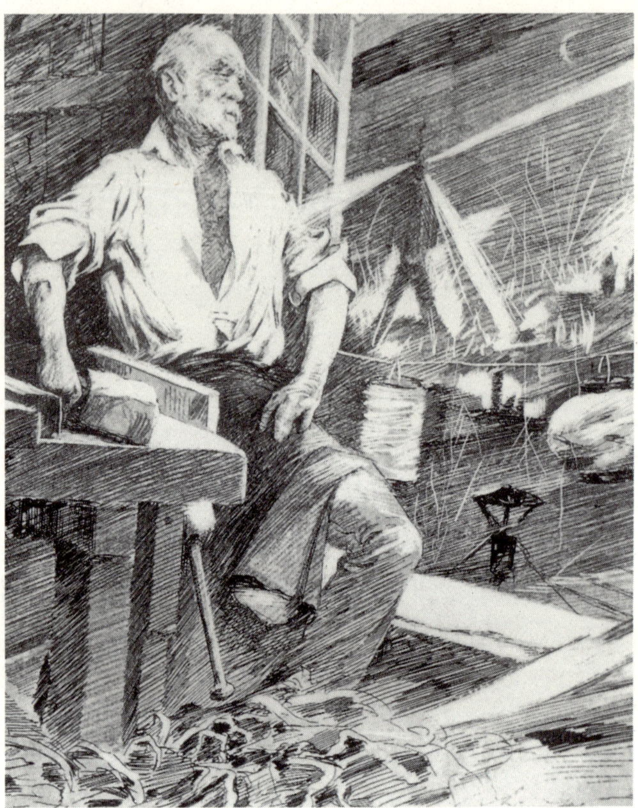

Figure 38   Paul François Quinsac, *To Jean Prolo, Worker*
In *Courrier français,* June 30, 1889

by which he meant to convert two of his nieces to anarchism. Pissarro counterposed stark images of poverty and exploitation to scenes of the lush but empty lives of the rich. The series—filled with extracts from anarchist journals—ends with images of the poor in revolt. *Turpitudes* features several images of the tower: the frontispiece shows the festive Paris of the Universal Exposition, with the tower clearly visible, from a high hilltop; on the summit, Father Time waits, scythe in hand, as the sun of anarchy dawns (Figure 4). In another drawing, the new tower is linked to capitalism and injustice: the image of the war between the "haves and have-nots" (Figure 39) is a typical caricature of a greedy capitalist, his wealth held tight to his chest, surrounded by a mob of the starving. The only two vertical objects in the panel, illuminated

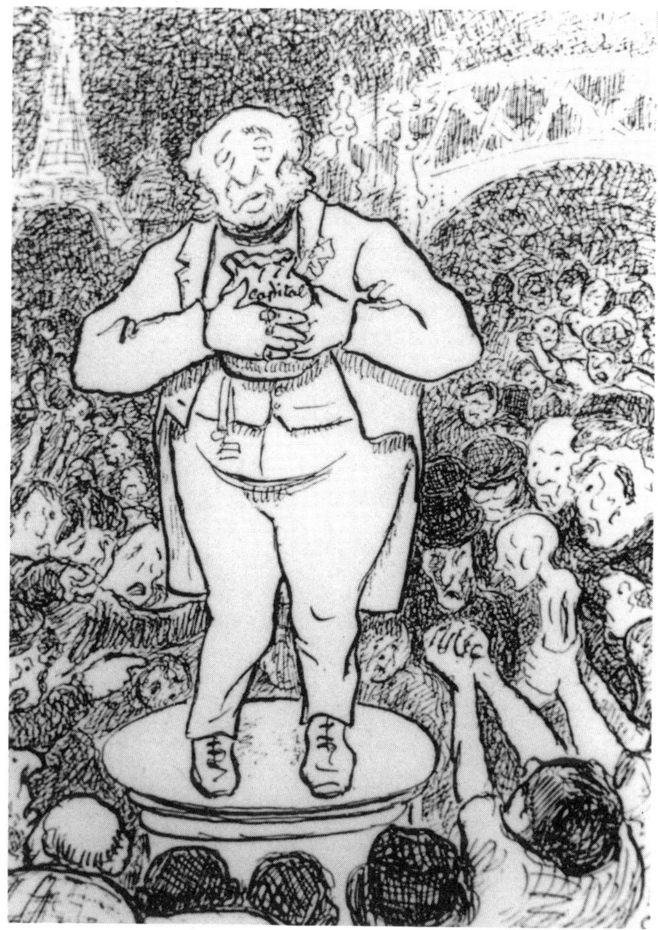

Figure 39   Camille Pissarro, *War Between the Haves and Have-Nots*
Pen-and-ink drawing, 1889. In *Turpitudes sociales.* Collection Skira.

equally to stand out clearly from the gloom, are the capitalist and
the tower, twin symbols of greed.[56]

   Turpitudes sociales also highlights another divergence within

56. Studies of *Turpitudes* remain relatively few. Especially useful is Richard Thomson's "Camille Pissarro, *Turpitudes sociales,* and the Universal Exhibition of 1889," *Arts Magazine,* LVI (April, 1982), 82–88. See also Ruth Forley, "Camille Pissarro's *Turpitudes sociales:* Documents of History" (M.A. thesis, Adelphi University, 1981), and John Hutton, "Camille Pissarro's *Turpitudes sociales* and Late Nineteenth-Century Anarchist Anti-Feminism," *History Workshop Journal,* XXIV (Autumn, 1987), 32–61.

Neo and, more generally, anarchocommunist circles—between contrasting views of the laborers who built and maintained the new industries and technologies. The industrial worker was the focus of a series of French novels and plays from the 1880s on, all combining fear of and fascination for the subject. The publication of Zola's *Germinal* in 1885 and Camille Lemonnier's *Happe-Chair* in 1886 introduced the theme; those works were followed by the dramatization of *Germinal* in 1888, the French adaptation of Gerhart Hauptmann's *The Weavers* in 1893, the opening of the play *L'Automne,* by the anarchist writers Paul Adam and Gabriel Mourey, in 1893, and the staging of Eugène Brieux' satirical play *Les Bienfaiteurs* in 1897. In 1898, two more plays on the subject were mounted by anarchist writers: Mirbeau's *Les Mauvais Bergers* and François de Curel's *Le Repas du lion.*

Germinal set the tone. Most of the works contrasted the horrible living and working conditions of those who had to earn their bread to the luxury in which the owners lived. The story lines had some fresh deprivation spark a strike or revolt or assassination, leading to military intervention and mass slaughter. Usually the conditions at the end were as bad as those at the beginning. The works are for the most part dominated by fears of bloody massacres: the present is miserable, but the future is a bloodbath.

Anarchist contributions to this genre differ from the norm only by making the employers a bit more stupid and arrogant, and laying out the resulting slaughter in more gruesome detail. Socialist critics found the anarchist plays troubling for their all-embracing gloom. Typically, *L'Automne* ends with the line "Here is the end of autumn; the evil days commence."[57]

Industrial workers were seldom heroes in anarchist writings. Instead, anarchism looked to the outcasts and the marginalized, discovering in tramps and vagabonds the incarnation of free indi-

---

57. Paul Adam and Gabriel Mourey, *L'Automne: Drame en trois actes* (Paris, 1893), 141–42. In the final scene a character "prophetically" notes, "The time will come when charity will no longer suffice. The people's hatred will rise like a miracle harvest and there will not be a sickle strong enough to cut it. Here is the astounding truth: the illusions of the world grow old, disappearing; the winter of humanity portends" (p. 141). For a response to Adam and Mourey, see Emile Portal, "Les Théâtres," *L'Ere nouvelle,* II (1894), 544. Portal says of the last line in *L'Automne,* "That which they take to be the autumn of civilization, these naïve pessimists or despicable epicures, is the spring of humanity, rejuvenated; it is the dawn of the red spring." For a review of Mirbeau's *Les Mauvais Bergers,* see Gaston Stiegler, "Chronique théâtrale," *Revue socialiste,* XXVII (1898), 99–102.

viduals, to be contrasted scornfully with the worker "drudge."[58] Whereas Marxist socialists saw the strength of the industrial working class in its ability to unite, even anarchocommunists often praised individuality above group action. In de Curel's *Le Repas du lion,* the hero is an entrepreneur capitalist who compares himself to the lion who brings down the hunt, whereas his workers are likened to jackals who steal the scraps. One worker finally guns the industrialist down, commenting, "The response of the jackal to the lion." The workers are as greedy and brutal as the employer is arrogant, but the employer at least has the merit of being a heroic individualist. Even Saint-Auban, Grave's close friend and collaborator, saluted de Curel's play in the most glowing terms.[59]

The Neo-Impressionist artists avoided imagery that was openly hostile to industrial workers. Of the circle, however, only Luce produced positive imagery of them. Emile Verhaeren was not alone in tracing that to Luce's roots in the faubourgs of Paris. In a review in 1899, he pointed out that "the art of Luce is Luce himself. A *faubourien,* loving Paris . . . and with the same soul as the people, ardent and revolutionary." Verhaeren went on to explain that "the worker has not appeared isolated to him. . . . He is . . . but an element [of] a group of figures in a totality."[60] For Luce, modern industrial labor was collective in nature. It was also inseparable from its geographies and workplaces, unthinkable if abstracted entirely from them. It is not an oversimplification to say that for Neos as different as Pissarro and Signac, the representation of *travail,* either urban or rural, functioned primarily as a symbol, whether of exploitation or of the joy of toil. For Luce, the symbol lay in the labor represented rather than in the representation of it.

58. On the anarchist image of the vagabond as a symbol of freedom, see Alain Pessin, *La Rêverie anarchiste* (Paris, 1982), 75–85. For a detailed listing of anarchist writings on the subject, see John Hutton, "'Les Prolos Vagabondent': Neo-Impressionism and the Anarchist Image of the *Trimardeur,*" *Art Bulletin,* LXXII (1990), 296–309.

59. See Saint-Auban, *L'Idée sociale,* 209–14. See also Alvan Sanborn, *Paris and the Social Revolution: A Study of the Revolutionary Elements in the Various Classes of Parisian Society* (Boston, 1905), 353–54. For a hostile socialist critique of the play from the period, see Georgi Plekhanov, "Art and Social Life," in *Writings on Aesthetics* (Moscow, 1981), 662–64, Vol. V of Plekhanov, *Selected Philosophical Works.*

60. Emile Verhaeren, "Exposition Maximilien Luce," *Revue blanche,* XX (1899), 309–10. In a section of *D'Eugène Delacroix au néo-impressionnisme* (1899; Paris, 1978) that is devoted to the diversity of the Neos as a group, Signac noted simply that Luce specialized in images of "the street, the people, labor" (p. 114).

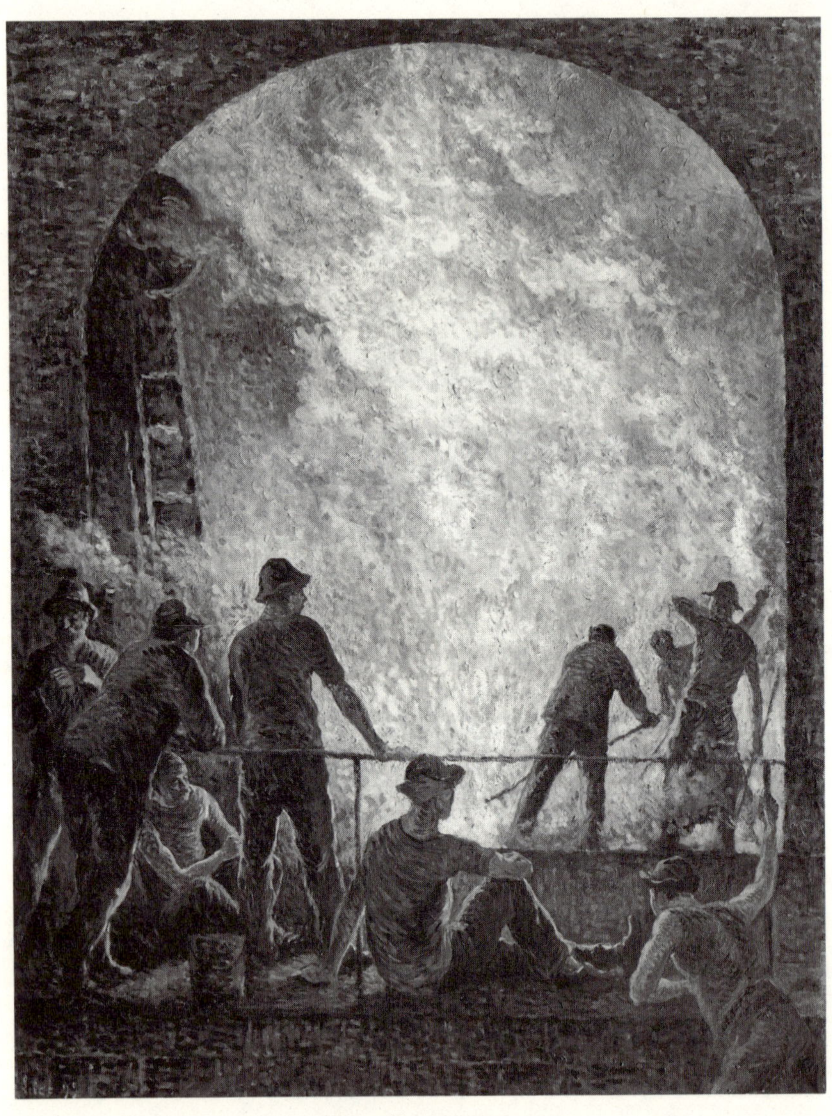

Figure 40   Maximilien Luce, *Steelworks*
L'Aciérie, oil on canvas, 1895. Courtesy of Musée du Petit Palais, Geneva.

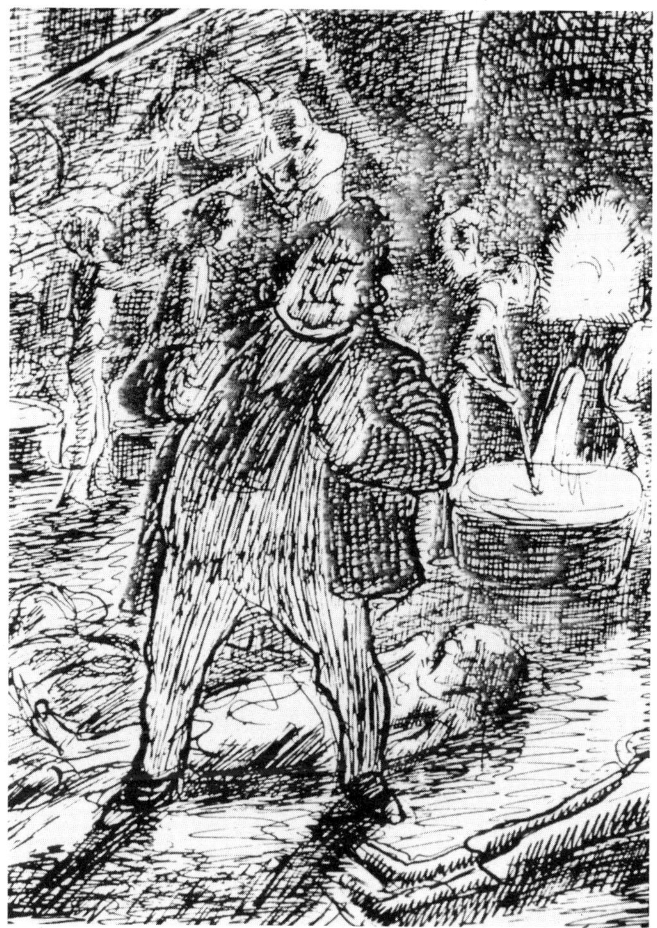

Figure 41   Camille Pissarro, *The Prison*
Pen-and-ink drawing, 1889. In *Turpitudes sociales*. Collection Skira.

His paintings sought to transfer the symbolic significance he found in the actuality to the canvas.

This distinction is apparent in a comparison of one of Luce's industrial scenes—say, his *Steelworks,* of 1895 (Figure 40)—with Signac's *Les Démolisseurs* (Figure 1) and Pissarro's *The Prison* from *Turpitudes sociales* (Figure 41). In Signac's print, the workers stand in darkness, with the sun of reason rising behind them. In Luce's *Steelworks,* there is a similar contrast between light and darkness, but the light is of the workers' own making; the light derives from the productive process, as the brilliant flames are tamed and controlled by the men themselves. The ironworkers are bathed in the deep hues of the foundry, their collective will and labor employing the heat and power to forge steel.

In Pissarro's *Turpitudes,* wage labor consistently appears solely in order to show oppression and exploitation. In *The Prison,* the bloated boss—Pissarro himself noted the deliberate resemblance to Louis Philippe—steps over the bodies of emaciated workers without noticing.[61] Similarly in his *The St. Honoré Prison* (Figure 42), which has seamstresses at work, a grim overseer watches every move of her employees; the cone of illumination highlights the surrounding gloom.

Pissarro pairs such scenes of exploitation in *Turpitudes* with final images of armed revolt. The inevitable rebellion clearly stamps the series as engaged in the cause of the *negation* of industrial, capitalist society. Both Luce's images of urban labor and Pissarro's of an idealized rural life offer some respect of redemption. By contrast, Pissarro's industrial workers starve, they are injured in accidents, they are thrown into prison or charnel-house hospitals, they rebel sometimes (if they are male), and they die. Urban labor is for Pissarro merely a cause for disaffection, one more reason to hate the modern world. Luce, on the other hand, seeks to depict industrial labor as part of a solution to exploitation and domination. In *Steelworks,* the overseer is pointedly absent, because he is ultimately irrelevant to the productive processes taking place. Luce's ironworkers are strong and confident, whereas the only workers in Pissarro's transfigured medieval dungeon factory not toiling frantically appear catatonic.

For Pissarro, factory labor is by its nature wholly negative. Luce's paintings of industrial labor are striking in that, increasingly, they lacked any critical edge at all; for Luce, the *beau* gradually won out over the *terrible*. The paintings cast their light on a new class in formation, and in a period when an awareness of that class provoked uneasiness, even panic, among the wealthy, the works' unabashed focus not just upon factories but upon those who worked within them could gain impact by being read as a defiant championing of the workers. But just how conjunctural such a reading must be is impressed on the viewer by Luce's later

61. See Forley, "Camille Pissarro's *Turpitudes sociales,*" 39–41.

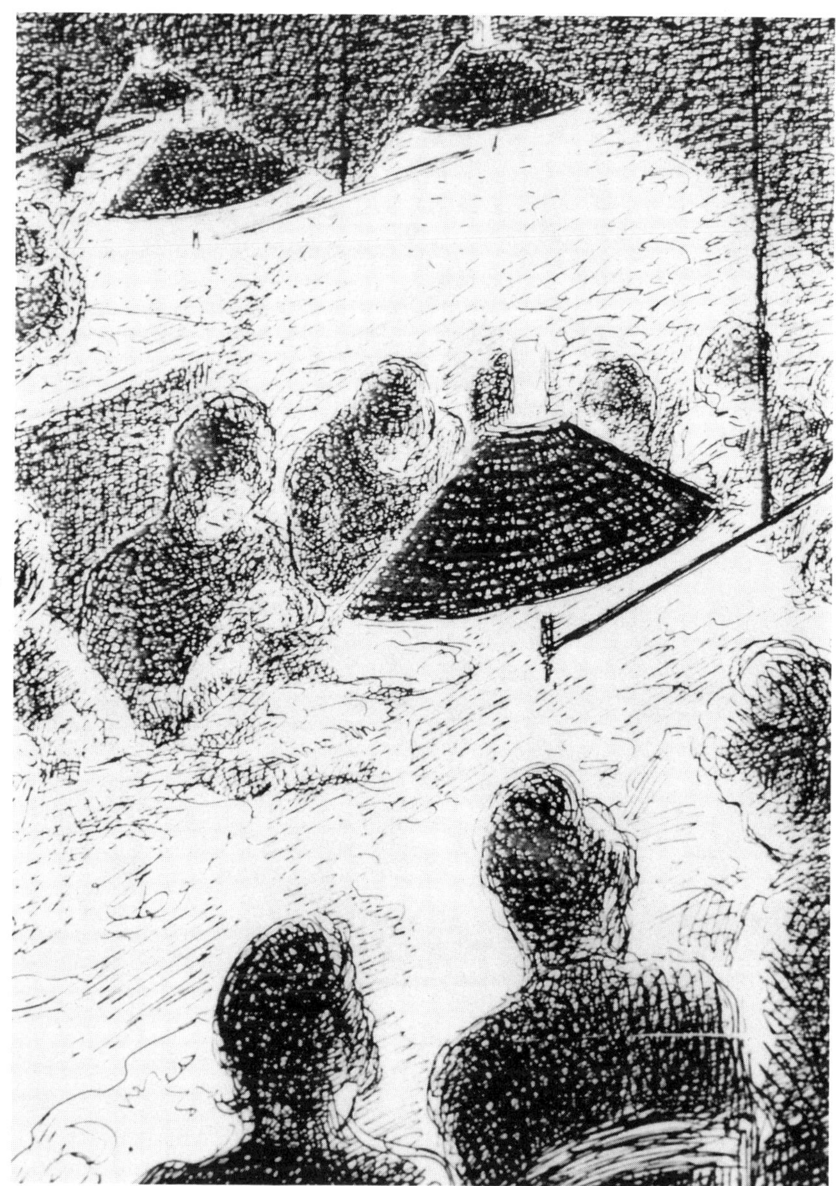

Figure 42   Camille Pissarro, *The St. Honoré Prison*
Pen–and–ink drawing, 1889. In *Turpitudes sociales*. Collection Skira.

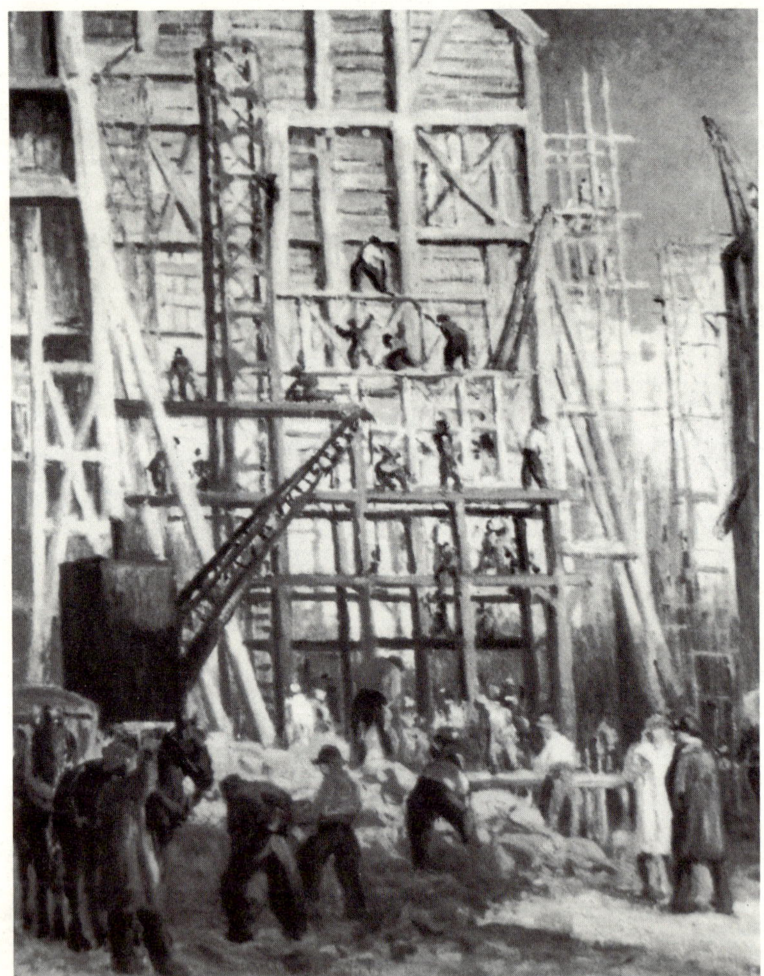

Figure 43   Maximilien Luce, *The Lumber Camp*
Le Chantier, oil on canvas, n.d. Musée d'Art et d'Histoire, Saint-Denis.

paintings of labor, like his undated *The Lumber Camp* (Figure 43) or his *The Masons,* of 1929. The bold reds, blacks, and violets have faded away in these, in favor of muted earth tones. Luce has turned from factory laborers to outdoor construction crews and craftworkers. Challenge is replaced by soothing reassurance; the workers are at their stations, contentedly going about their business.

Plaisirs de la Décadence: *Satire of Bourgeois Life*

Paul Signac, in his essay in 1891 for *La Révolte,* identified as a central motif of Neo-Impressionism its "synthetic representation of the pleasures of decadence: balls, *chahuts,* circuses . . ." That seems natural: the Neos lived in a society that was being shaped by the growth of a modern capitalist economy—by the new commercial mass entertainments, by the wealthy patrons they needed to buy their work, and especially by the dealers upon whom their livelihood depended. Their relationship to the new economic realities was neither purely antagonistic nor purely receptive. Alienated socially and politically from the dominant order, the Neos called for its abolition at the same time that their utter dependence upon both the market and rich buyers compelled them to soften their vehemence against it. Neo-Impressionist satirical imagery is the result of the forced cohabitation. Just as Luce's description of the new industrial world as "terrible and beautiful" captured the conflict within the anarchist image of that world, Signac's designation of the "pleasures of decadence" marked a sort of conceptual fault line in Neo-Impressionism, between an emphasis on decadence and one on pleasure.

Neo-Impressionist satirical imagery is most notable for its relative paucity after the death of Seurat. It had a fairly short-lived place in Signac's work; Camille Pissarro directed a caustic gaze toward the reigning society in *Turpitudes* but abandoned the theme thereafter; his son Lucien produced a few satirical scenes of bourgeois life in the 1890s. What is most striking about the course of Neo satirical imagery is how barbed, often corrosive critiques of middle-class life gradually yielded to carefully neutral images, and then to open celebrations of comfortable existence. This gradual dulling of Neo-Impressionism's satirical edge was both a vital phase in, and persuasive evidence of, the dissolution of the original Neo-Impressionist project.

Seurat and Social Satire

It was only in the work of Seurat—the aloof, the uncommitted—that there is a sustained critique of dominant society. Just as *Sunday Afternoon on the Isle of Grande Jatte* played with and subverted the themes it borrowed from contemporary artistic discourse, Seurat's later paintings—especially *The Chahut,* from

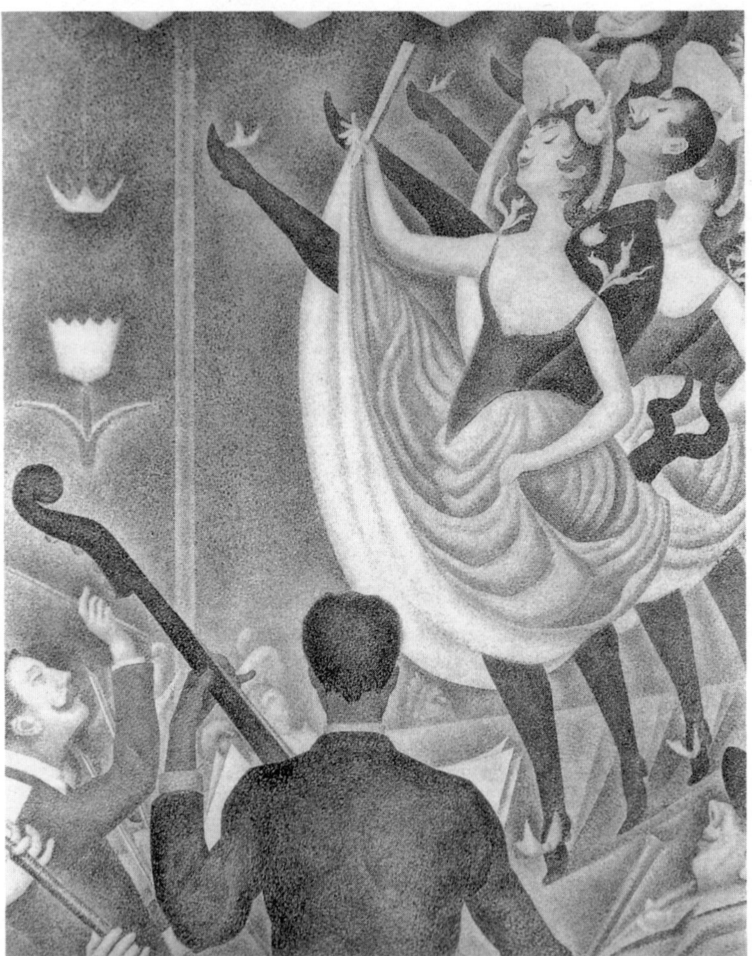

Figure 44   Georges Seurat, *The Chahut*
  Oil on canvas, 1889–90. Kröller-Müller Foundation, Otterlo.

1889–1890 (Figure 44), *The Sideshow,* from 1887–1888 (Figure 45), and the unfinished *The Circus,* from 1891 (Figure 46)—engage sourly with the mass, commercial pleasures of late-nineteenth-century France. These paintings center on marginalized and disreputable sectors of institutionalized, mercantile entertainment.
  The Sideshow is easily the most ominous of these works. Though the resemblance between this painting and Angrand's *An*

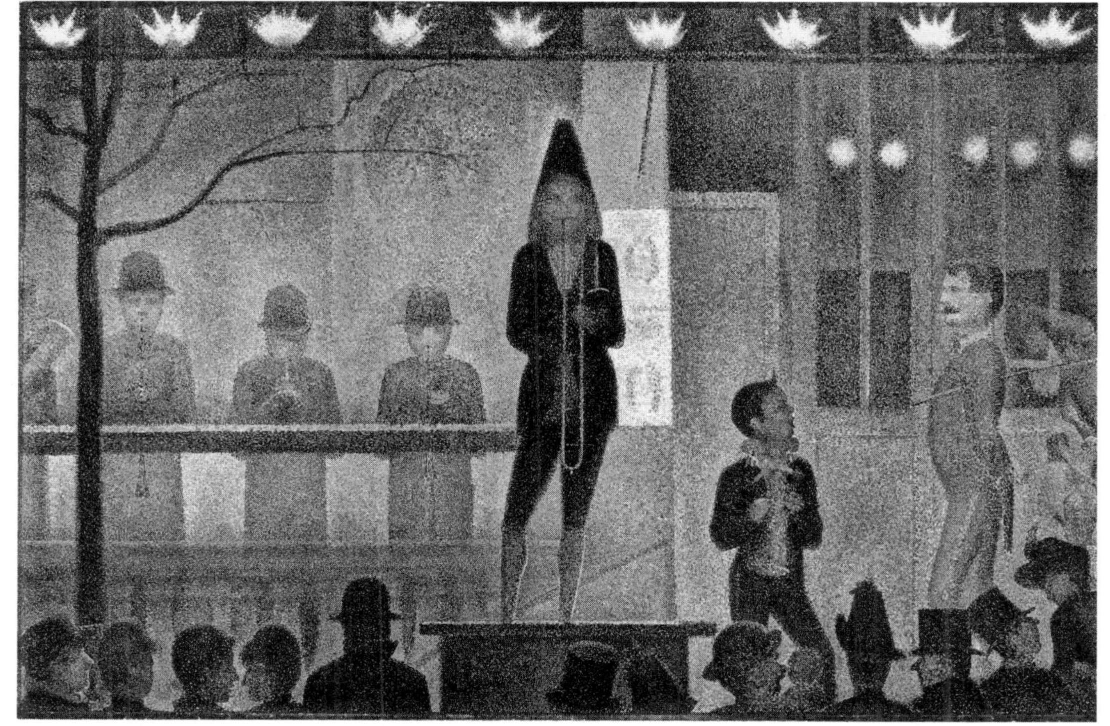

Figure 45   Georges Seurat, *The Sideshow*
Circus Sideshow, oil on canvas, 1887–88. The Metropolitan Museum of Art, Bequest of Stephen C. Clark, 1960 (61.101.17).

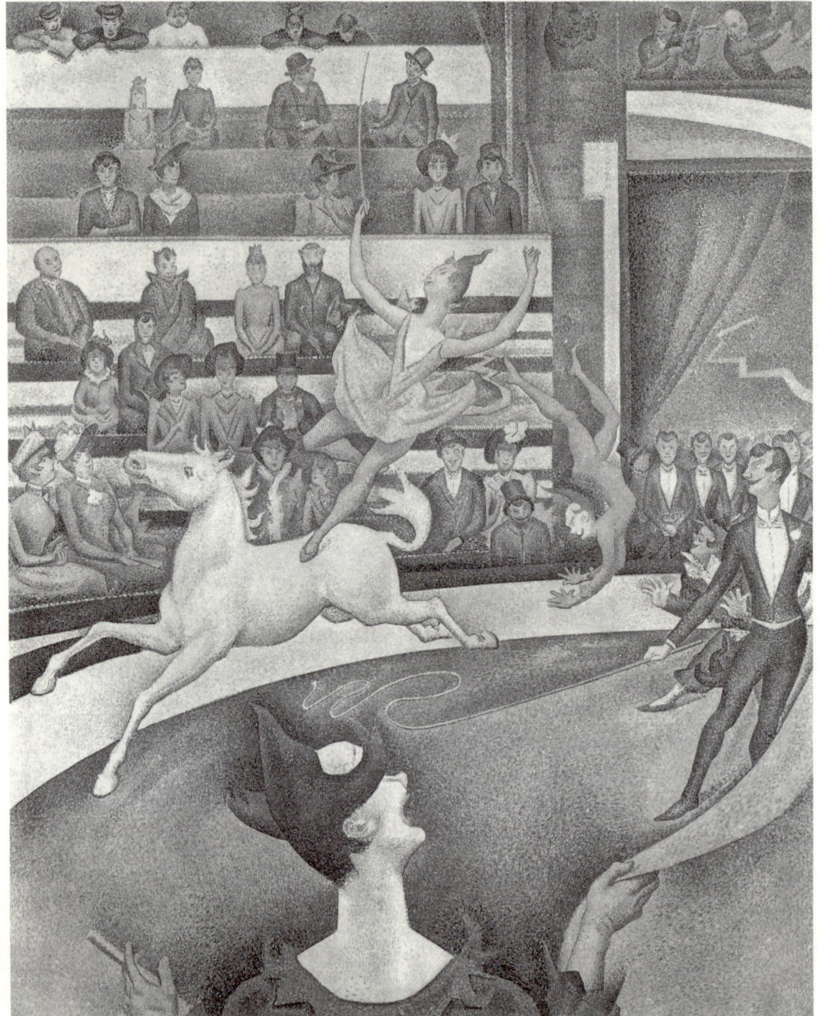

Figure 46   Georges Seurat, *The Circus*
Le Cirque, oil on canvas, 1891. Musée d'Orsay, Paris. Giraudon/Art Resource, New York.

Accident, of 1887 (Figure 47), has not eluded observers, they have made little more of it than a possible attempt by Seurat to outdo his colleague through a larger and more ambitious work.[62] In an

62. That resemblance is noted, for example, by Thomson in *Seurat,* 152. I am aware of no detailed study of the painting by Angrand; of the many studies of *The Sideshow,* the

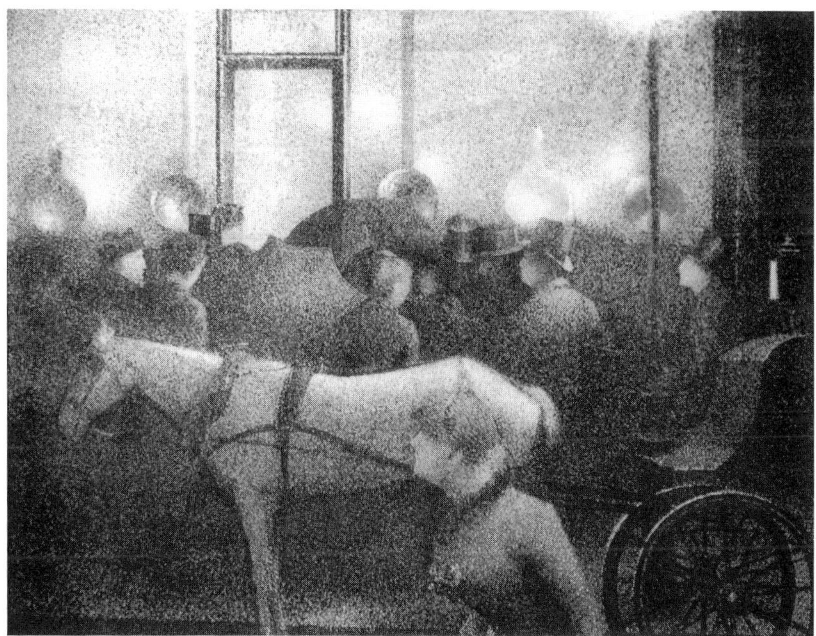

Figure 47   Charles Angrand, *An Accident*
Un Accident, oil on canvas, 1887. Josefowitz Collection.

artistic movement that had brilliant sunlight as a trademark, both paintings are nocturnal scenes, lit by harsh, artificial light—by the gaslights in *The Sideshow* and the globular lanterns in *An Accident.* In both paintings, the color scheme highlights dark reddish oranges and dull greens. There are structural parallels as well. In both, the viewer confronts a scene in which crucial data are screened off, inaccessible and unknowable. Particularly in Angrand, the implication is that something dreadful has taken place, but the viewer has no way of discovering cause, nature, duration, or extent. There is an oppressive stillness in both paintings; even the horse in the foreground of Angrand's stands stock-still as the coachman cranes his head to see—as we cannot—what has taken place.

Robert L. Herbert has interpreted *The Sideshow* as a modern morality tale in which varying classes seek a joyless distraction—a

most useful for the present study has been Robert L. Herbert's "*Parade de cirque* de Seurat et l'Esthétique scientifique de Charles Henry," *Revue de l'art,* L (1980), 9–23.

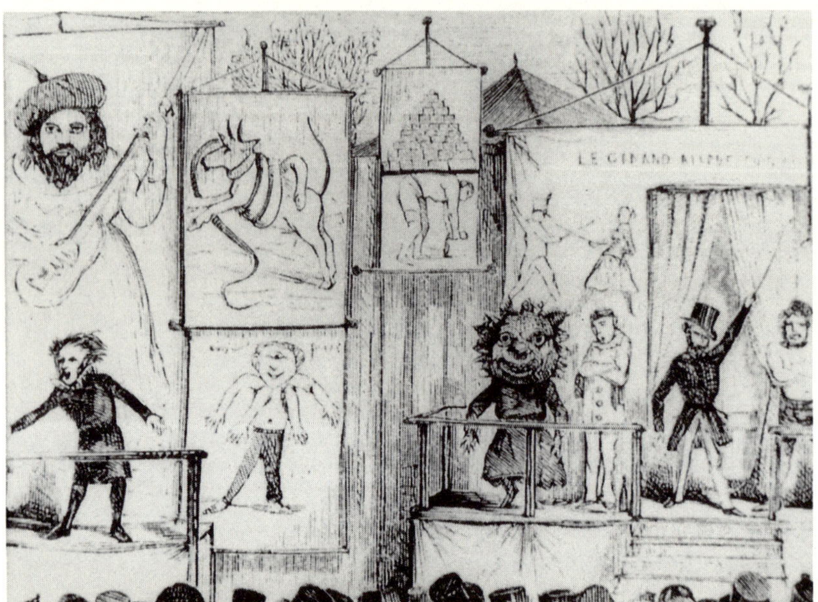

Figure 48   Edmond Texier, *The Traveling Carnival*
Engraving, 1852. In *Parisian Sights and French Principles* (New York, 1852), 101.

contemporary *vanitas* painting.[63] It is a plausible reading, but when the Seurat is paired with the Angrand, another facet of the Seurat becomes evident: the impression of something sinister and sad hidden at the heart of modern society. The carnivals of nineteenth-century Paris often featured the grotesque and the maimed. Edmond Texier's engraving *The Traveling Carnival,* from 1852 (Figure 48), features a four-armed man, a bearded woman, a man with enlarged breasts, a giant, an India-rubber man, and a man with the head of a beast. Texier's print is obviously a parody, but one with a foundation in a social reality, the intimation that beyond the ticket booth and curtained doorway were pleasures hidden away, unfit for the general eye. In *An Accident,* the unseen event takes on the aspect of a popular entertainment. Everyone crowds to see, while the huge lanterns impart a note of pseudogaiety, like the lights of a ghastly amusement park. A study of fin-de-siècle enter-tainment in France remarks, "Funeral processions, dog fights, collisions of wagons and omnibuses, a fallen horse being beaten by a

63. Robert L. Herbert, "*Parade de cirque* de Seurat," 18. See also Robert L. Herbert, "Seurat and Jules Cheret," *Art Bulletin,* XL (1958), 158.

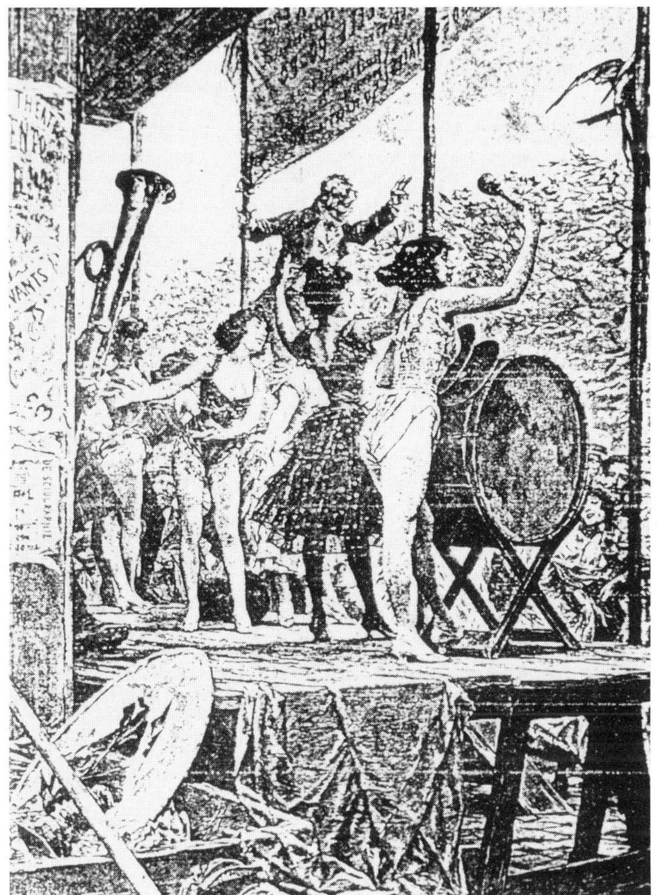

Figure 49   Frederik Kaemmerer, *The Parade*
  Oil on canvas, 1896. In *Catalogue illustré du Salon* (Paris, 1896).

furious master were special dramas that invariably drew audiences."[64] The sideshow and the accident shared a promise, however misleading, of the forbidden.

These paintings by Seurat and Angrand can be contrasted with Salon paintings on the same themes. Two works from the Salon of 1896 engage directly with the Neo-Impressionist works: Frederik Kaemmerer's *The Parade* (Figure 49) and Planels-Ricardo's *An*

64. Charles Rearick, *Pleasures of the Belle Epoque: Entertainment and Festivity in Turn-of-the-Century France* (New Haven, 1985), 172.

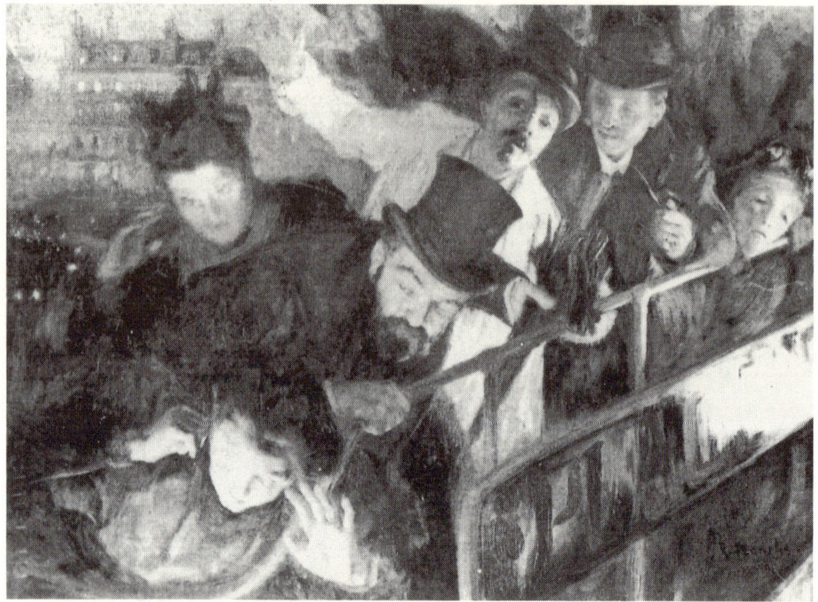

Figure 50   Planels-Ricardo, *An Accident*
  Oil on canvas, *ca.* 1896. In *Catalogue illustré du Salon.*

Accident (Figure 50). In Kaemmerer's rendering of a sideshow, smiling young women invite similarly smiling, conspicuously well dressed people into the carnival. The underlying shabbiness of the show is hinted at: the artist angles the stage so that we can see the end of the carpet spilling into discarded rubbish. But the emphasis remains the joyful, celebratory character of the event. In Planels-Ricardo's painting of what appears to be an omnibus accident, the event has taken place between—and below—the viewer and the customers. Neither of the paintings from the Salon of 1896 shields the viewer from the events. Nor do they combine themes of decadence and entertainment. The paintings by Kaemmerer and Planels-Ricardo are grounded solidly in surfaces and appearances; the impact is limited to painterly effects and the veristic recall of specific events, times, and places. The paintings by Seurat and Angrand are far more controlled and subdued in appearance; they hint at far more than they show. Their sustenance comes from underlying significances rather than literal recall.

Seurat's *The Chahut* (Figure 47) and the unfinished *The Circus*

(Figure 48) seem at first far more accessible than the shadowy, ambiguous *The Sideshow.* Both look forthrightly at the world of mass, mercantile entertainment. Not only Signac but also Gustave Kahn and Georges Lecomte singled out *The Chahut* for its graphic presentation of decadent pleasure. Kahn perceived the piglike face of the viewer at the lower right as the embodiment of "contemporary ignominy."[65]

Both *The Sideshow* and *The Circus* show a mix of social classes flocking to the new entertainments: both play with how the new forms of entertainment are at once "universal" and divided hierarchically by class. In both, there is a peculiar blend of whimsy and menace, especially in the repeated diabolic allusions: the repeated flame motifs, the cat eyes on the trombonist in *The Sideshow,* the serpent shapes reiterated throughout *The Circus.*[66]

Seurat's final paintings are marked by a consistent coolness and detachment. The irony is deadpan, presented with no explicit moralizing program appended. John House has concluded that Seurat's views did not "lead [him] to any overriding social or moral judgment." House discounts Signac's efforts to tie Seurat's satires to anarchist theory; their mood is "more detached and ironical, the message more equivocal." For House, the strength of Seurat's paintings lies precisely in their "multiple" vision, blending social satire with a profound aesthetic sense, carefully avoiding the slightest trace of polemic.[67]

House is surely correct to caution against Signac's and Kahn's attempts to read their own anarchism onto Seurat and his work. But attempts to square Seurat's paintings so neatly with a twentieth-century valorization of art that is uncommitted, detached, and "timeless" should also arouse skepticism. Seurat's paintings often address precisely those aspects of mass commercial entertainment which the anarchist and socialist left—and, to be fair, the far right—had attacked as expressions of a corrupt and decadent society. Though sometimes reviled by Third Republic politicians,

65. Gustave Kahn, "Seurat," *L'Art moderne,* XI (1891), 109–10.

66. The imagery of these works needs further study and critique. John House ("Meaning in Seurat's Figure Paintings," *Art History,* III (1980), 352) defends an analysis of *The Sideshow* similar to Herbert's. Both work to overturn the view William Innes Homer presents in *Seurat and the Science of Painting* (Cambridge, Mass., 1964), 219–23, according to which the painting is calm and tranquil. For a view contemporary with Seurat, see Albert Arnay, "Chronique artistique," *Floréal,* I (March, 1892), 84.

67. House, "Meaning in Seurat's Figure Painting," 354–55.

the new *café-concerts* and similar commercial amusements seem to have served as social safety valves, keeping the poor diverted and quiescent.[68] The image of a French society split by class but united in its love for the showy and the vulgar runs through Seurat's later paintings.

That various classes attended carnivals and circuses must not obscure the integral connection of the entertainments with the expansion of the market into every sphere of French society. When French socialists and anarchists complained that modern France was *un état bourgeois,* they scarcely meant that only capitalists lived in their country. Rather, they were lamenting the way the possessing classes had stamped their identity on every facet of modern life. In 1891, Bernard Lazare accused the French bourgeoisie of emulating every vice of the aristocracy it had overthrown a century before; the socialist Georges Diamandy believed that it had gone on to infect the rest of French society with its "mysticism, pornography, [and] depraved and senile prudishness."[69]

Whether or not Seurat fully aligned himself with the anarchist critique of modern, commercial entertainment, it is clear that his targets coincided almost perfectly with those of the anarchist left. It is difficult to ignore that though the dance of *The Chahut* was verging on the passé by the 1880s, French anarchists continued to impugn it as decadent; in at least one instance they seem to have blown up a *café-concert* in Lyon where it was performed.[70] It is to be expected that Kahn and Signac found in Seurat's paintings a confirmation of their vision of a corrupt capitalist France in decay.

What is unexpected is the failure of the anarchist militants of the Neo-Impressionist circle to extend and deepen what Seurat had begun. Instead, satirical imagery had a gradually decreasing presence in Neo-Impressionist art. Apart from Seurat and Signac, there are only a smattering of satirical paintings at all.

68. On this, see Richard Sennett, *The Fall of Public Man* (New York, 1974), 215: "When the café became a place of speech among peers at work, it threatened the social order; when the café became a place where alcoholism destroyed speech, it maintained social order."

69. Bernard Lazare, "Nouvelle Monarchie," *Entretiens politiques et littéraires,* III (1891), 160–64; Georges Diamandy, "Déclaration," *L'Ere nouvelle,* I (July 1, 1893), 10–11.

70. In March, 1882, the Lyon anarchist review *Le Droit social* denounced the Théâtre Bellecour as a pernicious social evil: "You can see there, especially after midnight, the fine flower of the bourgeoisie and of commerce." It concluded, "The first act of the social revolution must be to destroy these lairs." A few months later, the theater was bombed. It seems likely that anarchist sympathizers were involved, though the man the police charged was proved to be elsewhere. See Maitron, *Le Mouvement anarchiste en France,* I, 166–67 Thomson's account in *Seurat,* 207, is useful, but it misdates the event.

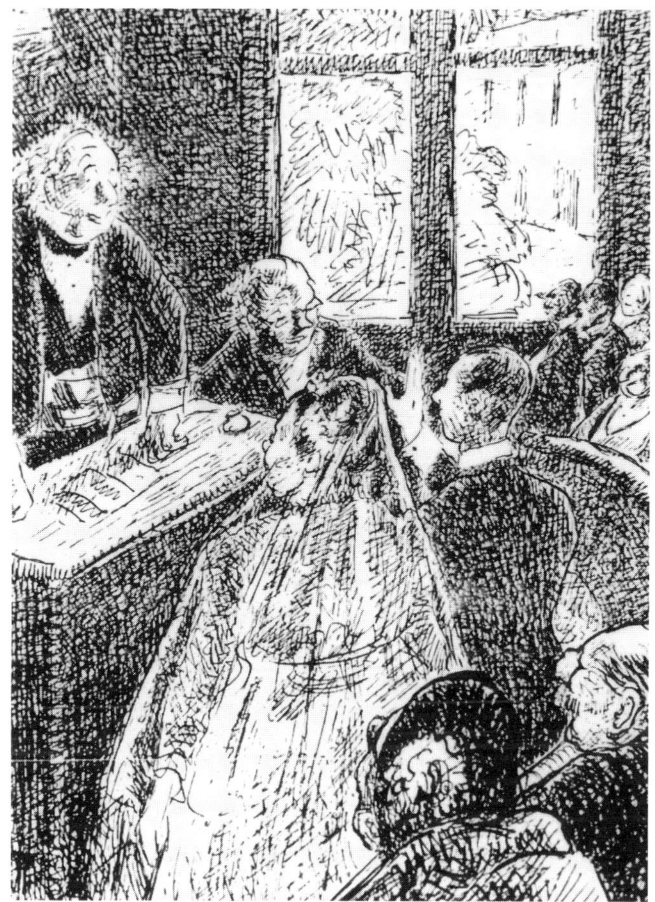

Figure 51   Camille Pissarro, *Marriage of Convenience*
Pen-and-ink drawing, 1889. In *Turpitudes sociales*. Collection Skira.

The most pointedly satirical images of bourgeois society appear
in Camille Pissarro's *Turpitudes sociales*. Though the drawings
there are primarily scenes of oppression and exploitation of the
urban poor, a few focus on bourgeois life, including *Marriage of
Convenience* (Figure 51) and *Virtue Rewarded—The Café des Princes*
(Figure 52). In *Marriage of Convenience,* an ill-matched couple wed
not for love but for the bride's large dowry. *Virtue Rewarded* is less
dependent upon the text: well-dressed men and women enjoy
themselves in a café while a poor woman, baby in arms, pleads for
food. Both images relate to the staple motif of anarchist writers

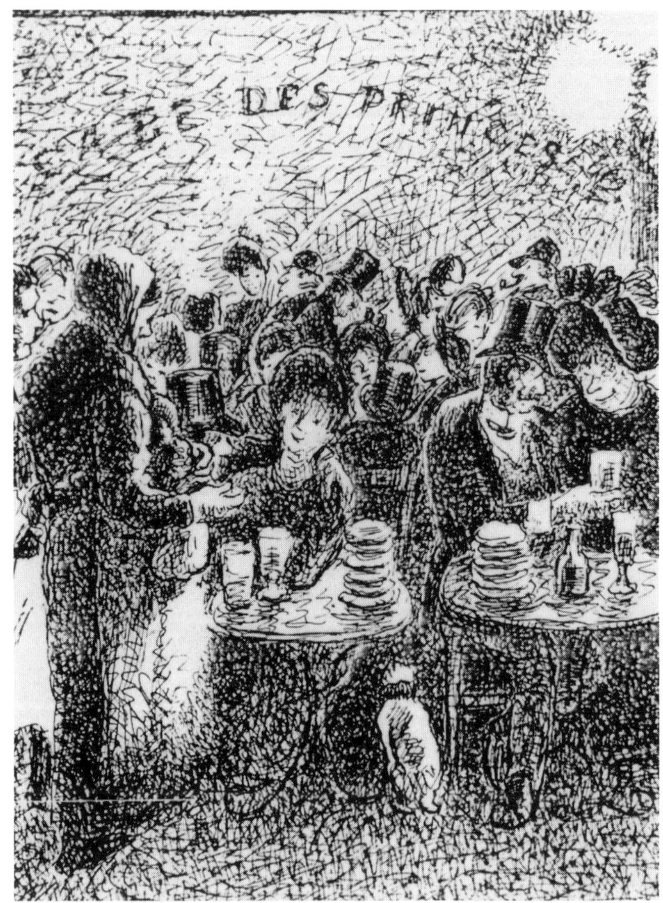

Figure 52   Camille Pissarro, *Virtue Rewarded—The Café des Princes*
Pen-and-ink drawing, 1889. In *Turpitudes sociales*. Collection Skira.

that bourgeois marriage was merely a legal form of prostitution.[71]
The cliché of middle-class writers that prostitutes had "invaded"
French social life was given a new twist by anarchist writers—

71. The misogynist strand in French anarchism built on Jean Jacques Rousseau's calls
for the complete domestication of women, in order to attack capitalist France for "destroy-
ing the natural order of the family." See Pierre Joseph Proudhon, *De la justice dans la revolution et de l'eglise* (Paris, 1858) and his posthumous *La Pornocratie; ou, Les Femmes dans les
temps modernes* (Paris, 1875). Hollis Clayson discusses thoroughly the propensity of middle-
class writers to see an invasion by prostitutes, in *Painted Love: Prostitution in French Art of
the Impressionist Era* (New Haven, 1991), esp. 1–16.

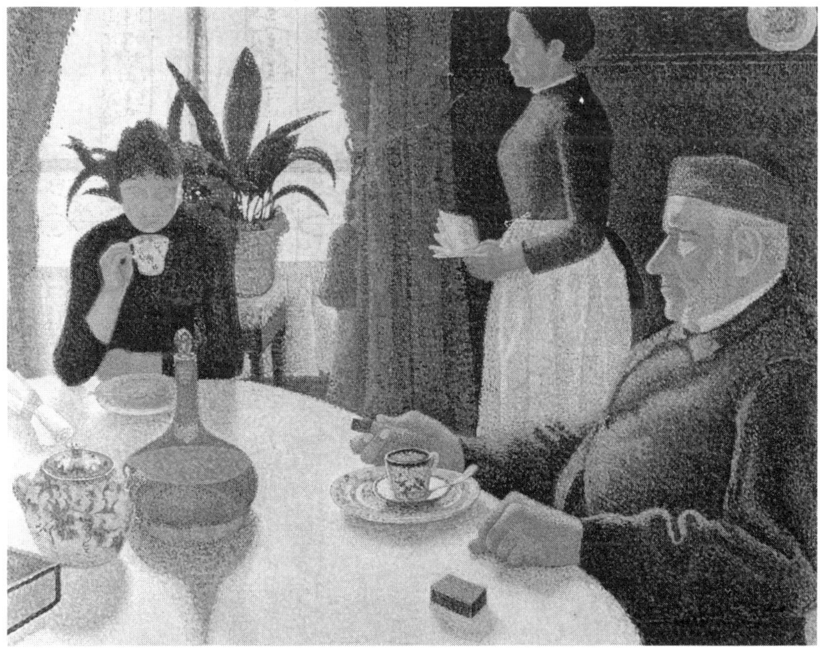

Figure 53   Paul Signac, *Breakfast*
Le Petit Déjeuner, oil on canvas, 1886–87. Kröller-Müller Foundation, Otterlo.

largely male—for whom bourgeois women were depraved both by upbringing and by class; they were held to be especially perni-cious role models for poor girls and women, luring them away from the "natural" virtues of home and family. Kropotkin, in his *Paroles d'un révolté,* of 1886, argued that bourgeois women were corrupt from early childhood and that bourgeois girls con-stituted a moral "gangrene" that infected young women of the proletariat.[72]

Satirical imagery like this appears in Pissarro's work only in *Turpitudes.* Signac, however, made several full-scale paintings lam-pooning both bourgeois life and bourgeois art, conspicuously *Breakfast,* of 1886–1887 (Figure 53), and *A Parisian Sunday,* of 1889 (Figure 54). These works bring together in an unlikely combina-tion scenes from paintings by the Impressionist painter Gustave

72. Peter Kropotkin, *Paroles d'un révolte* (Paris, 1885), 23. Emile Zola, who was no anarchist but a sometime admirer of Kropotkin, expressed more or less the same views in "L'Adultère dans la bourgeoisie," *Le Figaro,* February 28, 1881, p. 1.

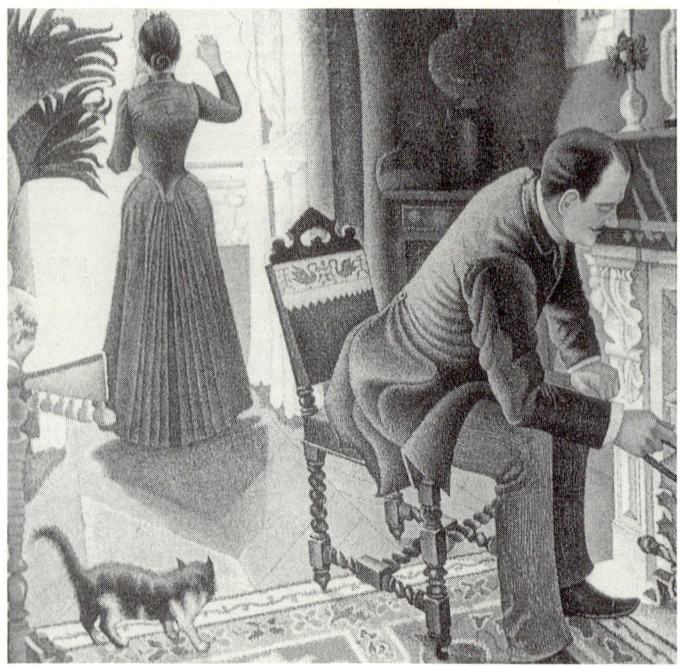

Figure 54   Paul Signac, *A Parisian Sunday*
   Oil on canvas, 1889. Private collection, Paris.

Caillebotte, and rigid, cartoonlike figures such as Seurat placed in his *Grande Jatte.* The works by Caillebotte corresponding to Signac's two paintings—*Luncheon,* of 1876 (Figure 55), and *Interior, Woman at the Window,* of 1880 (Figure 56)—are set in the family apartment on the Boulevard Haussmann; they typify the solid, stable middle-class world. Caillebotte, as an artist, seldom celebrated change and flux in the manner of Monet; his figures often admire the glittering world of Haussmannized Paris, but from the all too settled interiors or balconies of their comfortable homes.

In his *Breakfast,* Signac gives a mocking twist to Caillebotte's visions of bourgeois life. Caillebotte's heavily laden dinner table has been turned into one that is nearly bare; the man who had been finishing his meal in Caillebotte has become immobile, with the stub of a cigar in one hand, his ample waist stretching the too small jacket. The mother and son interact easily with the servant in the Caillebotte; in Signac, the three are as isolated as their models in the *Grande Jatte* and are reduced to two-dimensional caricatures. Kahn wrote in 1887 that Signac had carefully purged

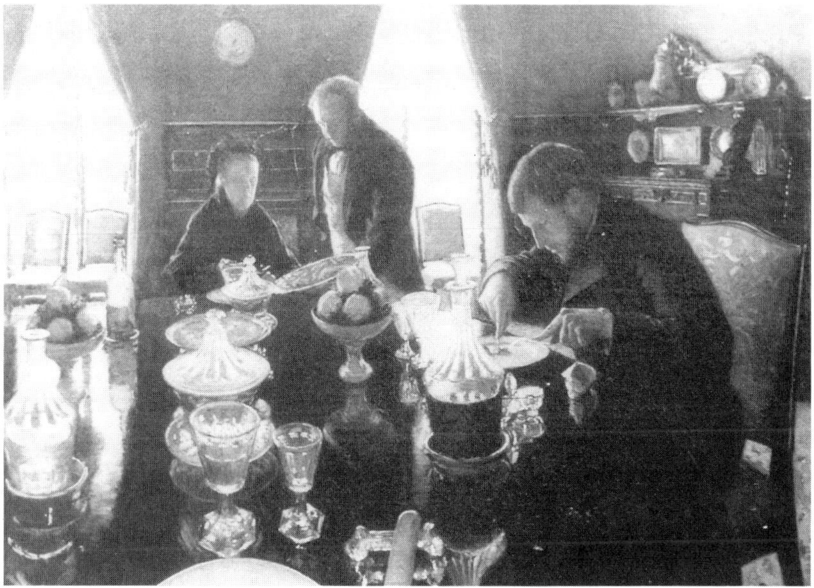

Figure 55   Gustave Caillebotte, *Luncheon*
Oil on canvas, 1876. Photographie Brame & Lorenceau.

his work of "every contortion, every joyful or suffering movement."[73]

The reworking and rethinking are more subtle and more complex in *A Parisian Sunday,* for Caillebotte's *Interior* is itself more nuanced than his *Luncheon.* The husband and wife are isolated from each other, neither speaking nor touching. Joris Karl Huysmans in 1880 wrote of the dominant boredom and tension between the woman and the man in Caillebotte's painting.[74] Signac, by removing the shop or boutique visible across the street in the Caillebotte, heightens the wistfulness of the woman gazing out into brilliant sunlight, turning her back on the domestic world and her stiff, stuffy husband.

Does this amount to a political or social critique of bourgeois life? Signac's painting is not a polemic; it shares the deadpan quality of Seurat's *Grande Jatte.* Signac was not the first of the Neos to take on Caillebotte, however, and his reworkings acquire a back-

73. *Signac: Musée du Louvre, décembre 1963—février 1964* (Paris, 1964), 19.
74. Joris Karl Huysmans, "L'Exposition des indépendants en 1880," in *L'Art moderne* (Paris, 1883), 94–95.

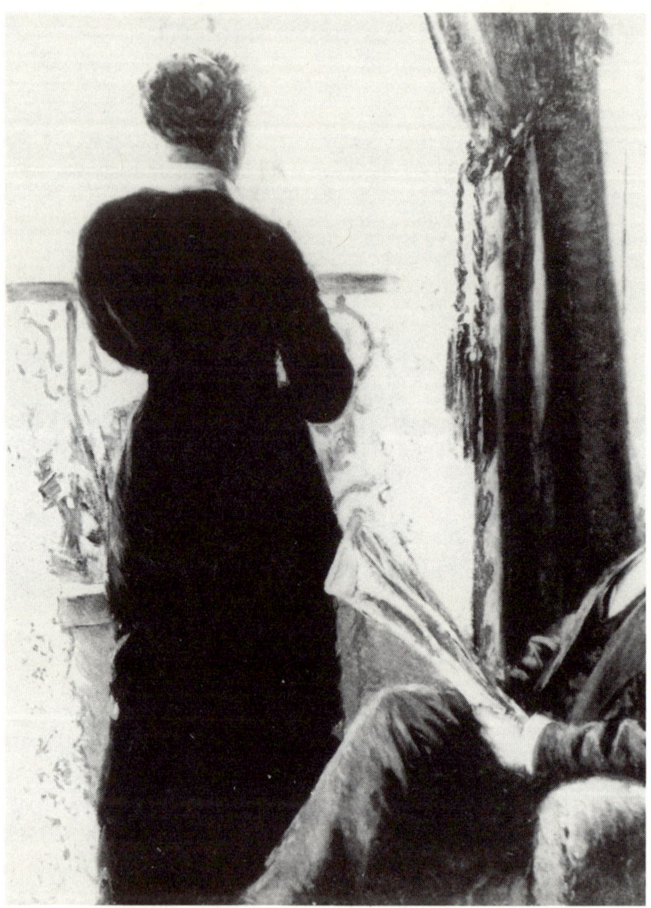

Figure 56   Gustave Caillebotte, *Interior, Woman at the Window*
Oil on canvas, 1880. Photographie Brame & Lorenceau.

drop in Lucien Pissarro's *During the July 14 Festival—Those Who Sulk* (Figure 57), printed in the Brussels journal *La Vie moderne* in 1888. Lucien's work is compositionally even closer to Caillebotte's original than Signac's; the younger Pissarro's innovation is to bring the husband onto center stage and transform the bearded, grave man of the Caillebotte into a vacant and pompous caricature of the bourgeois at home. The title adds to the mockery. The couple are abstaining not from festivities in general but from the commemoration of a revolutionary event, only one year before the event's centennial. Lucien Pissarro turns the depiction of an uncommuni-

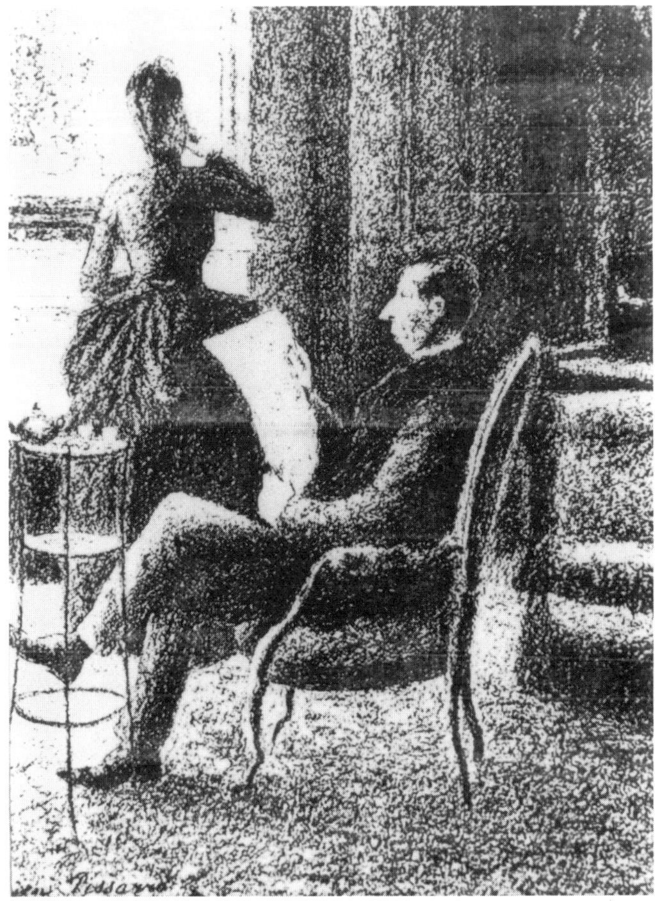

Figure 57   Lucien Pissarro, *During the July 14 Festival—Those Who Sulk*
  In *La Vie moderne,* July 22, 1888

cative man and woman into a symbol of the decidedly unrevolutionary, even antirevolutionary, bourgeoisie. There is also the oddly ambiguous gesture of the wife at the window. Is she sipping tea as she watches the fete? Or is her hand at her mouth in fear or anxiety?

Signac's paintings caricature bourgeois existence as stiff and empty. Indeed, he stripped his bourgeois figures of life and humanity with such success that some of the reviewers judged his paintings the creation of an incompetent. J. Leclerq wrote in the *Mercure de France* that Signac presented a boring world "without personality," an "interior scene without light . . . without style," filled with people lacking any vestige of character.[75] There is a certain irony here: confronted with an image of the sterility of bourgeois life, the reviewer can only view the painter as the problem. The critic does not fathom that Signac sees bourgeois existence as lacking in style, personality, and character. He assumes that Signac cannot express the fine qualities French domesticity embodies.

Signac's scenes of modern middle-class life are biting but aloof. His colleagues more often chose to celebrate bourgeois ways. Hayet and Lucien Pissarro sometimes returned to the *café-concerts* and performances captured by Seurat, but their small pen drawings and watercolors lack critical energy.

By the time Signac was mentioning the pleasures of decadent society as a motif of Neo-Impressionism, that range of experience had retreated to the margins of the movement's attention. When the pleasures of decadence appeared in the Neos' works, it was almost always to adorn anarchist publications and such quasi-radical reviews as the *Courrier français*. Luce, the most openly didactic of the group, produced very few images of the bourgeoisie—a part of the population he seemed to feel too little in common with even to ridicule. The bourgeois and the politician appear in his polemical works almost entirely as solitary symbols of the oppressor. Lucien Pissarro and his brother Georges Henri ("Manzana") continued to produce satirical scenes of bourgeois life, but without teeth. More interesting are Manzana Pissarro's later celebrations of the world of high fashion, filled with juxtaposed women and jungle animals, suggestive of Ernst Kirchner on Valium.

The decay of Neo-Impressionist satirical imagery into pro forma cartoons of dumpy bourgeois and opulent scenes of upper-class luxury is related to the peace most of the Neos made with the bourgeois system. The tension between the Neos' alienation from bourgeois society and their dependence upon the propertied classes for their livelihood could not be sustained—especially in the face of a new, more militant socialist art.

75. *Signac: Musée du Louvre*, 34. See on p. 35 the comments of Antoine de La Rochefoucauld, who, drawing on Charles Henry's theories, interprets the painting as a study of intense sadness.

6

The Turn to Activist Art:
"To Crowds Still in Bondage"

The Neos arose in protest against not only the injustice but what might be termed the incoherence of modern existence. Though they offered a solution quite distinct from that of the conservative Catholic Pont Aven painters, both groups desired to find solid ground—whether political or theological—on which to rebuild an integrated society that accorded art an honored place. By 1900, their radical project was being superseded by a qualitatively different one, however. With the rise of unified socialist and syndicalist movements, the goal of restoring harmony and justice gave way to that of the conquest of power. Instead of encouraging amelioration, the new language spoke of combat and struggle. *Art social* had sought to give hope by capturing the image of a better future; the new movements called on artists to become active militants.

The belated growth of French industry in the latter half of the nineteenth century meant that a sizable industrial working class was forming, however small it might seem by British or German standards. By 1902, France had nearly 3.3 million industrial workers, of which somewhat less than 20 percent were members of labor unions.[1] The establishment of larger and more centralized industries, even the sheer growth of the industrial work force, led gradually to a drastic reordering and restructuring of the French socialist movement. Among the union, the socialist-led Fédération Nationale des Syndicats (FNS), founded in 1886, and the anarchist-oriented Fédération des Bourses du Travail (FBT), constituted in 1892, gradually moved closer together, consolidating in 1900 as the Confédération Générale du Travail (CGT). The leadership of the CGT was at first dominated by anarchists, includ-

---

1. Edouard Dolléans, *Histoire du mouvement ouvrier* (Paris, 1946–47), II, 31.

ing Fernand Pelloutier and Victor Griffuelhes, who served as secretary-general. The CGT paper, *La Voix du peuple,* was edited by Emile Pouget, the former publisher of the "worker anarchist" paper *Le Père Peinard.* At the time of its founding, the CGT had nearly 500,000 members.[2]

The path to a unified socialist movement was more protracted: as late as 1896 there were still six mutually hostile socialist parties or federations in France. Unity had almost been achieved in 1900, when controversy over the participation of the Independent Socialist Alexandre Millerand in a coalition government split the movement into two rival factions. An ultimatum from the Socialist International led to the formation of a unity commission in 1904; in 1905, the inaugural congress of the new Parti Socialiste, Section Française de l'Internationale Ouvrière (SFIO) took place.[3]

The CGT and the SFIO each found themselves at the convergence of a number of competing political currents, but in varying degrees they both rejected the notion of the anarchocommunists that the golden age would arrive through the natural evolution of society. Both maintained that socialism would become a reality only through concerted human action. To be sure, the voluntarist theme was never altogether dominant: there was a continued insistence that socialism and communism were the outcome of an evolutionary process. But activism received an emphasis beyond anything in the thinking of Kropotkin, Grave, and Reclus. Both organizations stressed that there was a pressing need to organize and mobilize the workers to take power. The unifying resolution that created the SFIO stated, "The Socialist party is founded on the following principles: —international agreement and organization of the workers; —political and economic organization of the proletariat in a class party for the conquest of power and the socialization of the means of production and exchange, that is to say, the transformation of capitalist society into a collectivist or communist society."[4] Gustave Hervé, standing on the far left of the SFIO, was more emphatic: "The Socialist party is the mouthpiece, the standard-bearer of the rebels; it is above all an organization of

2. Georges Lefranc, *Le Mouvement syndical sous la troisième république* (Paris, 1967), 64–74.

3. Madeleine Rébérioux, "Le Socialisme français du 1871 à 1914," in *Histoire générale du socialisme,* ed. Jacques Droz (Paris, 1974), II, 191–95; Georges Lefranc, *Le Mouvement socialiste sous la troisième république* (Paris, 1963), 99–133; Aaron Noland, *The Founding of the French Socialist Party, 1893–1905* (Cambridge, Mass., 1956), 86–140.

4. Lefranc, *Le Mouvement socialiste,* 123.

propaganda, agitation, and intransigent opposition in every country." That theme was strongest in the pronouncements of the syndicalist leaders of the CGT: Griffuelhes wrote, "Against all the forces of the State, against the corruptions of the politicians, against capitalist exploitation, syndicalism calls the workers to struggle." Syndicalism was to reveal itself as the "power capable of regenerating the world. It is today the great instrument of combat; tomorrow it will be the great renovator."[5] Both socialists and the syndicalists of the CGT saw change as coming out of the joint action of evolution and conscious effort; further, far more than the anarchocommunists, they saw it as springing from a single class. The socialist leader Jean Jaurès wrote that "the universal proletariat holds, in itself, the dual revolutionary force of nature: the force of eruption and the force of erosion."[6]

The revolutionary syndicalists of the CGT, though still viewing themselves as part of the anarchist tradition, expressed little more than contempt for the anarchocommunist views that had dominated their movement. The young union leader Pierre Monatte, defending the syndicalists at the International Anarchist Congress in Amsterdam in August, 1907, asserted flatly that both the old socialist and the anarchist movements had allowed the idea of revolution to be gutted and all but destroyed. For the "scientific socialist" Jules Guesde and his followers, Monatte maintained, *revolution* meant only winning elections. As for the anarchists, "their revolutionism was only a superb way of taking refuge in an ivory tower of philosophical speculation." Syndicalism was necessary to redress the insufficiency of the older movements. For the first time since the day of the *attentats,* said Monatte, the French bourgeoisie was afraid. He concluded on a triumphalist note: "Syndicalism does not merely promise the workers a terrestrial paradise. It demands that they conquer it, in the assurance that their action will not be in vain. It is a school of voluntarism, of energy, of fertile thought. It opens the possibility to anarchism, which has for too long retreated into itself, to new perspectives and new hopes."[7]

<hr>

5. Gustave Hervé, *Vers la révolution* (Paris, 1908), 24; Victor Griffuelhes, *Le Syndicalisme révolutionnaire* (Paris, 1910), quoted by LeFranc in *Le Mouvement syndical,* 84.

6. Jean Jaurès, "La Paix et le Socialisme," *L'Humanité,* July 9, 1905, p. 2.

7. Monatte's remarks are reproduced in *Congrès anarchiste tenu à Amsterdam, août 1907* (Paris, 1908), 62–71. For the remarks here, see p. 69. For a summary in English, with reply by the veteran anarchocommunist Enrico Malatesta, see Emma Goldman, "The International Anarchist Congress," *Mother Earth,* II (1907), 307–19. For a similar argument, see

The new hopes, however, did not elate Grave and his associates. Though Grave opened his reviews to syndicalists from time to time—as well as to harsh polemics against them—a gulf developed between the old anarchists and the new. Grave had previously called on anarchists to join with the workers' movement, to give it a revolutionary perspective. But once the workers began to flex their might, he and his associates backed away, as if terrified by what they had helped bring forth.[8] The anarchocommunists accused syndicalism of letting itself be just a new front for Marxist ideas. Anarchocommunists, Grave reminded his readers, did not believe in social classes but collaborated in a movement for the oppressed that was open to "rebels" of whatever background. Grave wrote that syndicalism would inevitably bog down in day-to-day—that is, reformist—activities instead of educating the public for a total social transformation. Furthermore, he reasoned, by presenting labor unions as the nucleus of a new social order, the syndicalists were involved in a covert rehabilitation of the state.[9]

Increasingly, however, Grave was speaking to himself. While in Spain the anarchist movement integrated itself with the new syndicalism, in France the anarchocommunists retreated to publishing papers and pamphlets and holding occasional lectures. In 1914, what was left of the movement tore itself in two over the First World War: Kropotkin, Grave, and a majority of his colleagues—

---

the syndicalist Amédée Dunois' "L'Anarchisme ouvrière," *L'Action directe,* I (January 29, 1908), 1–2. Dunois asserted that anarchism had degenerated into intellectual abstractions and was no longer a revolutionary theory expressing "the needs, the aspirations, the desires of an enslaved class" but reflected merely a "philosophical conception of human existence." He concluded that, "too preoccupied . . . to comprehend the world in the spirit of transforming it by action," anarchism had become just a "school for 'thinkers' and the 'learned,' the best-known of the bourgeoisie."

8. See Jean Grave, "Les Unions ouvrières," *La Révolte,* V (January 16–22, 1891), 1; Jean Grave, "Les Groupements ouvriers," *La Révolte,* V (March 5–11, 1891), 1; and Jean Grave, "Au sujet des syndicats," *La Révolte,* V (July 9–15, 1892), 1–2. On the manner in which traditional anarchism cut itself off from mass movements in this era in favor of a suicidal quest for doctrinal purity, see Daniel Guérin, *L'Anarchisme: De la doctrine à l'action* (Paris, 1965).

9. Cf. M. Pierrot, "Anarchistes et Syndicalistes," *Les Temps nouveaux,* XII (April 13, 1907), 1–2; and Enrico Malatesta, "Anarchisme et Syndicalisme," *Les Temps nouveaux,* XIII (December 7, 1907). Grave's arguments are in *Réformes, Révolution* (Paris, 1910), 223–36. On the syndicalist idea of unions as the *cellules* of the new order, see "Déclaration," *L'Avant-garde,* I (April 23, 1905), 1. For a detailed refutation of anarchist attacks on syndicalism, see Edouard Berth, "Anarchisme individualiste, Marxisme orthodoxe et Syndicalisme révolutionnaire," *Le Mouvement socialiste,* No. 154 (May 1, 1905), 5–35.

including Maximilien Luce, though not Paul Signac—decided to forsake their prior antiwar resolutions and support the Allied cause against Germany and the Central Powers.[10] Grave's fortunes went into a permanent slide: in 1925, when he sought a publisher for his memoirs, even the Bibliothèque Charpentier, a major publisher of anarchist texts twenty-five years before, rejected the work on the grounds that the events and persons described in it were for the most part "totally forgotten today."[11]

New Ideas on the Arts

There was no single, unifying taste or aesthetic that bound together the leaders of the new socialist and syndicalist movements. Nonetheless, the movements had major impacts on the idea of what it meant to be a socialist artist, as well as on what it entailed to make socialist art. In a speech in 1900, Jaurès called typically for a return to activist notions of art: workers, he believed, stood at the end of a long period of bourgeois rule, on the eve of their own rise to power. The burgeoning power of the working class inevitably meant the first stirrings of proletarian culture, and he called on artists to become an active ingredient in the struggle.[12]

The leadership of both the SFIO and the CGT rejected the premise of anarchocommunism that a "social art" would develop as part of the evolution of humanity, in accordance with the inexorable laws of science. Indeed, for many of the syndicalists in particular, the whole idea of "science" as proposed by Kropotkin, Grave, and Reclus was preposterous, an excuse for passivity. The syndicalist theoretician Edouard Berth deplored what he called the "Religion of Science," which had, he asserted, dominated both anarchocommunism and Guesde's "orthodox Marxism": he called it "formal, abstract, systematic, dogmatic, a sort of metaphysical cosmology, quite removed from reality," and thought it was

10. Letters by Signac and Luce on the war—both undated—are in the Jean Grave Archives of the Institut Français d'Histoire Sociale, in Paris. Signac wrote that he could not understand Grave's new distinction between "good and bad war: you have taught me that war is bad, always odious." Luce expressed a reluctant support of what he saw as a defensive war against the "Knouto-Germanic Empire." He added, "I am not a nationalist. Every nation in wartime is returned to the state of savagery, but with the Germans this is done methodically, regularly."

11. Eugène Fasquelle to Jean Grave, February 17, 1925, in Jean Grave Archives.

12. Jean Jaurès, "L'Art et le Socialisme," *Le Mouvement socialiste,* III (1900), 590.

marked by an attempt to reduce a "diverse and prodigiously complex reality to the unity of abstract and simple formulas." Exponents of that view of "Science," Berth argued, felt absolved of doing anything concrete to change the world: "Science" would do it for them. "Who will resist it?" he asked sarcastically. "Who will deny the brilliant, imperious, one and universal Truth of Science?"[13] To the syndicalists, there was no science with a capital *s,* only individual sciences, which had to be consciously employed to achieve any result whatever. Evolution and the laws of social development created opportunities; they mandated nothing.

Consequently, the new socialist and syndicalist movements tended to evaluate the state of the arts rather differently from the anarchocommunists: they were unmoved by the notion that an irresistible drive toward socialism had generated a new, social art. Where anarchist—and panicked conservative—critics had seen a flood of (unconsciously) anarchist and socialist art and literature, socialist and syndicalist reviews saw merely the bourgeois influence dominant everywhere. Henry Bauer wrote in the prosyndicalist *Le Mouvement socialiste* that painting in France was imbued with the spirit of a bourgeoisie in decay—"the same deceits, the same sophistications of taste, the supremacy of charm, which is the bourgeois form of ugliness."[14] The American anarchocommunist Emma Goldman saw European theater as the "dynamite which undermines superstition, shakes the social pillars, and prepares men and women for the reconstruction"; a reviewer in *Le Mouvement socialiste* argued on the contrary that the vast preponderance of modern plays and novels were altogether false.[15]

The most comprehensive attack on the relationship between anarchism and the arts came from Georges Sorel. In a letter to Daniel Halévy in 1907 that is included as a preface to Sorel's *Réflexions sur la violence,* he argued that the art and literature of the day were a mere "*residue* left to us by an aristocratic society, a residue, moreover, that has been strongly corrupted by the bourgeoisie." Nonetheless, the anarchists of the prior generation had idolized that art

13. Berth, "Anarchisme individualiste," 15–16. For a parallel attack on anarchocommunism for its passivity and complacency, see Dunois, "L'Anarchisme ouvrière," 2.

14. Henry Bauer, "Critique littéraire et artistique: Notes et Protestations," *Le Mouvement socialiste,* I (1899), 41. To be sure, Bauer's alternative to such art echoed the formulations of the proponents of *art social:* he called on artists to depict "reality and truth, which will animate the dreams of the new world."

15. Emma Goldman, *The Social Significance of the Modern Drama* (Boston, 1914), 8; Lionel Landray, "Chronique littéraire," *Le Mouvement socialiste,* I (1899), 167–68.

and its artists. In return, artists and writers had become enthusiastic supporters of the anarchists—a "sympathy that has astonished people who are ignorant of what a force vanity is in the world of aesthetics." Sorel maintained that both the art and the anarchism that nurtured it were "intellectually wholly bourgeois." The socialists of the past had accused the anarchists of being mired in passivity, "servile pupils of the accursed past." The anarchists' retort had been that the socialists were mere reformers in socialist garb. Only syndicalism opened the way for the genuinely revolutionary, Sorel thought. It could inspire a new art capable of leading people "to comprehend what will be the qualities of the worker of the future." [16]

Socialist and syndicalist theorists were persuaded that bourgeois domination of the arts was inevitable in a capitalist society, especially without the counterforce of a strong workers' movement. "Art has not penetrated labor more deeply," Jaurès argued, "because democracy itself has penetrated no farther; democracy is arrested at the surface of the political order." [17] The Belgian socialist Emile Vandervelde understood that artists had to address that section of *la classe riche* interested in the arts because only the wealthy could purchase, or subsidize, the arts—publish and buy books, go to the theater, form committees to finance concerts and museums, exert influence on government ministers and local magistrates to commission paintings and sculptures. "And, naturally, [the bourgeoisie] tends to impose its taste on the art workers who depend upon it." Artists were thus trapped within the cage of bourgeois demands and interests: those who were poor needed to please bourgeois patrons, while those who were independently wealthy were the products of their own bourgeois backgrounds and affiliations—"their bourgeois fortune, bourgeois education, bourgeois relations, who provide them with their taste, the habits of the spirit, the prejudices of the class." The subjection of the manual laborer, he concluded, meant inevitably the subjection also of the proletarian artist and intellectual. [18]

Neither socialist nor syndicalist writers denied that artists could

---

16. Georges Sorel, *Reflections on Violence,* trans. T. E. Hulme (1907; rpr. New York, 1961), 54, 55. See also the discussion of Sorel's views on culture by Larry Portis in *Georges Sorel* (London, 1980), 88–107.

17. Jaurès, "L'Art et le Socialisme," 524.

18. Emile Vandervelde, "L'Art en régime bourgeois," in *Essais socialistes* (Paris, 1906), 201–206. See also Emile Vandervelde, "A quoi servent les intellectuels?" *Le Socialiste,* n.s., XXIII (March 3–10, 1907), 1–2.

rebel against the constraints upon them; they called on them to do precisely that. Rejected was the idea that it was possible to step at will out of the existing nexus of class relations so as to harmonize with "social evolution" in a manner that would automatically generate a social art. Jaurès asserted that the first, tentative examples of socialist art would be, necessarily, as halting and sometimes as bizarre as the first formulations of socialist thought by the Saint-Simonians or Charles Fourier.[19]

Vandervelde argued that point in greater detail. He observed that, in a period in which socialism was emerging as a real social and political force for the first time, some artists "seeking support in the soul of the awakening plebeians, proclaim with Wagner the united triumph of art and revolution." But he warned, "Whatever the beauty, even the sublimity of their works, as yet they are and can only be forerunners. In order that a new art may flourish, wide and great as humanity itself, humanity will have to know peace after struggle, leisure after work, communion of minds and hearts after the antagonisms which rend them today." He continued,

> Periods of transition, of criticism, of revolution like ours can only produce stormy and incomplete works. What was, is no more. What will be, is not yet. Action mars the seer's vision. Those who are laying the foundations of new societies have hardly time to think of other things and, too often, *the artists who speak to crowds still in bondage wait in vain for an answering echo.* But when the emancipated proletariat shall live a truly human life, when all the workers shall have culture sufficient to be open to the sensations of art, when all shall have, after their day's work is done, those hours of leisure . . . then and only then aesthetic pleasure shall cease to be a luxurious enjoyment, and become a need common to all members of the community; then and only then will great works of art be born in perfect beauty from the prolific co-operation of the individual creator, sure of being understood, and society, palpitating, sure of understanding him.[20]

Much of this echoes Paul Signac or Charles Albert; yet there is an important new note as well. The socialists of the early twentieth century demanded not only basic reforms such as the eight-hour day—as crucial first steps toward the liberation of the worker and

19. Jaurès, "L'Art et le Socialisme," 524.
20. Emile Vandervelde, *Collectivism and Industrial Evolution* (London, 1907), 241. For a more optimistic critique of "artists in revolt," see, however, Austin Lewis, "The Revolt of the Artist," *International Socialist Review,* III (1903), 720–24.

the provision of time and energy to fight but also as attainable goals that, once won, would lead to new victories. They demanded also initial steps, however small, toward an art for the workers. If, as Jaurès had maintained, workers had been "disinherited" of the riches of art, concrete steps had to be taken to return to the plebeian majority its birthright.[21]

For the most part, socialists and syndicalists alike were careful not to restrict their vision of art to what had utility in direct agitation. But the syndicalists especially did emphasize how art could be a vital tool in the fight for a better society. Pelloutier delivered a lecture to the anarchist Groupe de l'Art Social in 1896 that helped delineate the ways the old gradualist and automatic concepts of *art social* were being replaced by a more activist and militant view. For Pelloutier, art could be a lever with which to pry open the bars of bourgeois ideology confining the workers. Signac and Reclus had hailed artistic revolts, whether openly political or purely aesthetic, as "rebel art" inherently in league with the libertarian cause. Pelloutier sought to enlist artists in more specific social action; he wished to see painters expose the conditions under which the people lived and worked, to make clear the nature of their chains.[22] Extending—and oversimplifying—his views, a writer in the CGT's newspaper *La Voix du peuple* stressed that the struggle of the workers had to avail itself of the arts: "With a return to propaganda by art," the author concluded, "I estimate that the intellectual transformation of the proletariat will march in step with its economic transformation. . . . A purely revolutionary view of art, in all its forms, will see it in the first place as a weapon of combat."[23]

The wording here closely parallels that of Peter Kropotkin and

21. Jaurès, "L'Art et le Socialisme," 582; Vandervelde, "L'Art en régime bourgeois," 200–201. For a condensation of Vandervelde's views, see his "Art Under Capitalism," *Socialist Review,* IV (September, 1909), 9–17.

22. Fernand Pelloutier, *L'Art et la Révolte* (Paris, 1896), 5–6, 27. The implications of Pelloutier's theory of culture are examined by Alan B. Spitzer in "Anarchy and Culture: Fernand Pelloutier and the Dilemma of Revolutionary Syndicalism," *International Review of Social History,* VIII (1963), 379–88, and by Anthony S. Baker in "Fernand Pelloutier and the Making of Revolutionary Syndicalism," in *Essays on Modern European Revolutionary History,* ed. Bede K. Lackner and Kenneth Roy Philip (Austin, Tex., 1977), esp. 47–51. Spitzer in particular sees Pelloutier's views as sincere but manipulative and elitist. Pelloutier's conception of bourgeois ideology and culture as a chain on the working class closely resembles that of Sorel. See Georges Sorel, *Les Illusions du progrès* (Paris, 1908).

23. Doublier [pseud.], "L'Art et la Révolte," *La Voix du peuple,* VI (August 15–21, 1906), 2.

Jean Grave—no doubt deliberately. Between the Kropotkin of *Paroles d'un révolté,* in 1886, and the Pelloutier of *L'Art et la Révolte,* in 1896, however, French society had changed—not especially in the degree of industrialization, which had not altered radically in a decade, but much more in the manner in which the working poor of France had begun self-organization and mobilization. Kropotkin had looked back at a France that was already slipping away, a France of peasants, freeholders, and skilled artisans working in small shops. By 1896, these still played a large role numerically, but the millions of industrial workers had become a social and political concentration that had a very different notion of the world and the way to change it.

Kropotkin and Grave had visualized their movement as one of gradual enlightenment and individual conversion, the accretion of one new adherent at a time. Even "communism" was a matter of individual decisions to live in accordance with anarchist ideals. Camille Pissarro's description of himself as a worker without overalls was at best metaphorical: he and his fellow Neo-Impressionists sold their art to dealers, who sold it to those with the money and taste to buy it. Even the short-lived Neo boutique only eliminated the dealer as an unnecessary intermediary, to give the painter full profit for each sale. The buyers remained the same as before, as did the artists' relation to them. True to Vandervelde's thesis, each artist was still enmeshed by the demands of a bourgeois public and its tastes.

Pelloutier's call of 1896, on the other hand, derived its potential from a new union movement of hundreds of thousands of members working together in mines and factories across the country. The utopian element was still present in syndicalism, in the idea that the local syndicates formed the *cellules* of the society of the future. But that is a qualitatively different utopianism, a collective one, emphasizing not the decision of an individual to embrace an ideal but the importance of collective labor and the actions of workers as a class to change society. The difference opened—as did the birth of a mass socialist party—the possibility of a new source of arts patronage, as well as a new audience: the workers in their union halls and local party organizations. Vandervelde maintained in his essay in 1906 that artists would remain bound to the middle classes until a new source of support, a new home for art, could liberate them and intellectuals alike from their dependence.[24]

24. Vandervelde, "L'Art en régime bourgeois," 206.

Education and Culture: The Bourse du Travail *and*
Maison du Peuple

Both socialists and syndicalists expected socialism to arise from institutions that had been created in this period. The syndicalists wanted the local *bourse du travail* to become the center not only of union activity and job hunting but of an entire range of activities of improvement for workers and their families. Pelloutier called for each *bourse du travail* to conduct classes for workers and their families, to set up libraries, and to include *musées du travail* to acquaint workers with the accomplishments of their class. At the same time, the socialists across Europe were beginning to create a virtual society within a society: a vast network of sports clubs, book clubs, theaters, choral groups, hiking clubs, schools, and social centers, all linked to the party. Cultural activities centered on local halls—the German and Austrian *Volkshäuser,* the Italian *casas del popolo,* the Belgian (and later French) *maisons du peuple*—where workers could hear lectures, see art, take classes, hold discussions, or read in workers' libraries.[25]

As these local institutions began to open, suggestions multiplied concerning their relation to art and artists. In 1907, a writer related in Jean Grave's *Les Temps nouveaux* that he had been asked by the secretary of his local *bourse du travail* to decorate the hall in a manner appropriate to its purpose. He lamented his inability to obtain quality reproduction of the works of artists "who, in some degree and in diverse ways, revolt against social tyrannies"—a group in which he included Constantin Meunier, Jules Adler, Théophile Steinlen, Camille Pissarro, Félix Vallotton, Francis Jourdain, Jean Raffaëlli, and the satirists Jules Félix Grandjouan and Hermann-Paul. More important, he called upon the syndicalist CGT and artists to see each other as allies. He exhorted artists to see the *bourses* and *syndicats ouvriers* as presenting new fields in which to practice: walls to cover and fill, new audiences to win for

25. On the *maisons,* see *Architecture pour le peuple: Maisons du peuple* (Brussels, 1984), a study of the buildings in which the *maisons* were housed. See also Franco Borsi, *La Maison du peuple: Sindacalismo come arte* (Bari, 1978), and Sura Levine, "'A Palace for the People': Victor Horta's *Maison du Peuple* in Brussels," a paper delivered at the annual conference of the Society of Architectural Historians in San Francisco, April, 1987. On the scope of the *section d'art et d'enseignement* of the Brussels *maison,* see the first (and apparently only) *Annuaire de la section d'art et d'enseignement* (Brussels, 1893). On the *bourses du travail,* see Fernand Pelloutier, *Histoire des bourses du travail* (Paris, 1902), esp. 111–26; and Charles Frecy, *Les Bourses du travail et la Confédération générale du travail* (Paris, 1910), 114–41.

art. As for the syndicalists, he wrote, "The CGT has launched a campaign for the conquest of leisure time. Why does it not today launch a complementary campaign for less ugliness in the street, even for more beauty in life? . . . Would that not be the logical corollary of the proletarian muster, in march toward the City of Harmony?" The syndicalist movement, the writer concluded, had to recognize at last that "beauty is a force. It is a revolutionary force." Anything that lessened the misery and despair of working-class life helped to the same extent to free the workers for new struggles and gave them hope of a better life, for art "constitutes an eloquent protest against the ugliness and misery of contemporary society."[26]

The socialists initiated the most far-reaching attempt to create centers of popular culture and education, in the *maisons du peuple.* The Belgian Workers' party's *maison* in Brussels constituted a model for the centers. In 1892, the Brussels *maison* established a *section d'art,* assisted by artists and intellectuals, including the poet Emile Verhaeren and the novelist and critic Camille Lemonnier. The *section d'art* embarked on an ambitious program of lectures, concerts, and tours of museums and art galleries. Among the early programs were a presentation of songs by the Renaissance poet Hans Sachs; concerts of the music of Tchaikovsky, Rimski-Korsakov, Glazunov, Wagner, Berlioz, Liszt, Beethoven, and Bach; a discussion of the works of Ibsen; a talk on "education in the socialist commune"; and sessions on the novelists Lemonnier, Zola, and Léon Cladel. Visits to exhibitions of contemporary art were organized on museums' free days, with explanatory talks by artists.[27]

The new educational centers set up by the socialists sought to bring a familiarity with art, music, and literature to the workers. At the Université Nouvelle, founded by the Belgian socialists in

26. Aristide Pratelle, "Vulgarisons la beauté," *Les Temps nouveaux,* XII (February 9, 1907), 2, (February 16, 1907), 2.

27. Jules Destrée and Emile Vandervelde, *Le Socialisme en Belgique* (Paris, 1898), 218, 236–40. See also Jules Destrée, "Préoccupations intellectuelles, esthétiques et morales du Parti Socialiste Belge," *Revue socialiste,* XXVI (1897), 307–29, esp. 319–22. Vandervelde noted some of the limitations of the *maisons* in his *Essais socialistes,* 198–200. Those are discussed by Eugenia W. Herbert in *The Artist and Social Reform: France and Belgium, 1885–1898* (New Haven, 1961), esp. 31–34. For a later assessment than Vandervelde's, see Henri de Man, "L'Oeuvre d'éducation ouvrière du Parti Socialiste Belge," *Le Mouvement socialiste,* XIV (1912), 356–69.

1894, the curriculum included courses on the "permanent features in the evolution of art," classical literature, the literature of the French and other contemporary peoples, "cosmopolitan features in literature," the industrial arts, the history of sculpture and architecture, and the history of music. Courses were taught by artists and intellectuals, including Jules Destrée, Joris Karl Huysmans, Edmond Picard, Elisée Reclus, Emile Verhaeren, and Henry van de Velde.[28]

For socialists, the *maisons du peuple* were more than places to give concerts and lectures. They were proof of the growing impact of the working class. Berth wrote that they encouraged within the proletariat love for the "high and pure emotions of art," set the basis for "a real aspiration toward beauty, a real concern not solely for material bread, but also for a superior life."[29] He was convinced that the Belgian *maison du peuple* flourished while the tiny Parisian *maison* remained rudimentary precisely because the Belgian party had begun to amass the wealth and influence to support the arts on its own, rather than having to rely on the art generated by the bourgeoisie. The cooperative in particular—an organizational constituent of the Belgian Parti Ouvrier though not of the French SFIO, which distrusted autonomous bodies within the party—provided support and the "wealth that is everywhere necessary for the development of art."[30]

The socialist *maisons du peuple* were successful enough to spark imitations from the Catholic parties: the Christian Democrats of Lille, for example, created their own *maison des ouvriers* to keep the workers away from socialist influence. The socialist centers played a far greater role in working-class life, however. In a play published by the socialist journal *L'Humanité*, the *maisons* were presented as the new cathedrals. Just as cathedrals were at the center of civic, social, educational, and artistic life in the Middle Ages, the "new cathedrals" were to become the centers of workers' lives

28. Odon Por, "The New University of Brussels," *International Socialist Review*, VII (1906), 214–15.

29. Edouard Berth, *Dialogues socialistes* (Paris, 1901), 188–89.

30. *Ibid.*, 189. Berth terms the *maisons* an "education in beauty and social justice" (p. 211). The campaign to replace the tiny Paris *maison*, founded in 1892, with a larger structure is discussed in "A la maison du peuple de Paris," *Revue socialiste*, XXII (1895), 610–12. The social and economic roots of the *maisons* in Brussels are examined by Frederic C. Howe in "Conquering a Nation with Bread," *Outlook*, XCIV (1910), 682–89. See also Marcel Liebman, *Les Socialistes belges, 1885–1914* (Brussels, 1979), 187–94.

in the society of the future.[31] An article by the Belgian socialist Henri de Man in 1912 asserted that tentatively, step by step, the *maisons* were becoming the center of a "system of artistic education truly suited to the tastes and the aspirations of the working class."[32]

The art commissioned and displayed in a local *bourse du travail* or *maison du pueple* did not simply introduce workers to the idea of art; it also, to a large degree, focused on the workers themselves. Observers in this period frequently noted a newfound fascination of European workers with themselves—with their appearance, their goals, their lives.[33] In Marx's terms, the working class—or at least that aroused portion of the workers participating in the growing socialist and labor movements—was in transition from being a class in itself to becoming a class for itself. The German Käthe Kollwitz, like more than a few other artists, fell under the spell of that change: looking back on the period, she remembered that by the 1890s, "middle class people held no appeal for me at all. Bourgeois life as a whole seemed to me pedantic. The proletariat, on the other hand, had a greatness of manner, a breadth in their lives."[34]

Characteristics of Socialist Art

There was no single yardstick applied in generating and evaluating socialist or syndicalist art. "Realists" such as Steinlen and Adler played a role in the new socialist art, but so did the Belgian Symbolist Fernand Khnopff. Both the socialist Jaurès and the syndicalist Berth praised the work of Pierre Puvis de Chavannes in the strongest terms.

31. Maurice Ponthière, *La Maison du peuple* (Reims, 1906), 9; Maurice Bouchor, *La Maison du peuple: Scène dramatique* (Paris, 1910), esp. 39–40, 51–52. The idea of the *maisons* as proletarian cathedrals proved a long-lasting one. See Paul Signac, "Messages aux artistes," *Commune,* II (1934), 1037.

32. Henri de Man, "L'Oeuvre d'éducation," 365. The same tone pervades "Le Progrès social," *L'Humanité,* July 22, 1905, p. 4. There a *maison du peuple* in Montmartre focuses a discussion of the role of education and culture in organizing workers.

33. Maurice Robin, *L'Art et le Peuple* (Paris, 1910), 25–26; Gustave Geffroy, *Musée du soir aux quartiers ouvriers* (Paris, 1895), 7–11.

34. *The Diaries and Letters of Käthe Kollwitz,* trans. Richard Winston and Clara Winston, ed. Hans Kollwitz (Chicago, 1955), 43. See also Martha Kearns, *Käthe Kollwitz: Woman and Artist* (Old Westbury, N.Y., 1976), 79–108.

If there were no hard and fast guidelines for the art favored by the mass socialist and labor movements, the writers and militants of both movements ever reiterated that something identifiable as socialist art was beginning to appear out of the strengthening socialist forces. Berth wrote, "It is the new social forces that increase. Socialism swells like a great tide that appalls some and delights others; no more the *atonie,* the desolate and doleful sky; rather, on the horizon, a light is born and the dawn seems to hover in the sky." He added, "And art—already it is renewed."[35]

The Belgian sculptor Constantin Meunier was frequently singled out as the first artist to capture successfully the spirit of the industrial worker. Lemonnier declared that the art of Meunier marked a historic moment in the history of the working class, even a conceptual revolution in contemporary representation. According to Lemonnier, Meunier's statues and paintings marked the date when the "worker received the baptism of art," when the "militias of the faceless and the nameless" took their place in the "fatherland of the spirit."[36]

What is new in Meunier's image of the worker? A comparison of a typical Meunier bronze, his *The Puddler,* of 1884 (Figure 58), with a later image by the premier leftist sculptor of the previous generation, the maquette Jules Dalou made for a never-finished monument to the working class around 1900 (Figure 59), can help answer the question. After Dalou returned to Paris in 1879 from the refuge abroad that he had taken after the defeat of the Commune, he attempted to combine traditional republican iconography with some of the new icons of the socialist movement, most

35. Berth, *Dialogues socialistes,* 214. For attempts to define a relationship between socialist movements and visual imagery, see Jean Lambart, "Les Formes de l'art et le socialisme," *Revue socialiste,* I (1885), 329–39; Justin Alavaill, "Symbolisme socialiste," in *Almanach de la question sociale pour 1897* (Paris, 1897), 103–107; Camille Mauclair, "L'Oeuvre social de l'art moderne: Les Beaux-Arts," *Revue socialiste,* XXXIV (1901), 421–35; and Marius-Ary Leblond, "L'Idéal artistique du socialisme et son élaboration au XIXᵉ siècle," *Revue socialiste,* XXXVII (1902), 66–81, 181–202.

36. Camille Lemonnier, *Constantin Meunier, sculpteur et peintre* (Paris, 1904), 82–83. For other assessments from the left, see Camille Lemonnier, "Constantin Meunier," *Le Coq rouge,* II (1896–97), 337–42; Charles Albert, "Constantin Meunier," *La Sociale,* II (March 1–8, 1896), 2–3; Camille Lemonnier, "Le Monument au travail," *L'Art moderne,* XV (1905), 49–51; John Spargo, "Constantin Meunier, Painter and Sculptor of Toil," *Comrade,* II (1902), 246–48; Emile Vandervelde, "Constantin Meunier," *Die neue Gesellschaft,* I (April 12, 1905), 19–20; and Marius Renard, *La Glorification du travail: Constantin Meunier* (Hornu, 1904). I am indebted to Sura Levine for several of these sources.

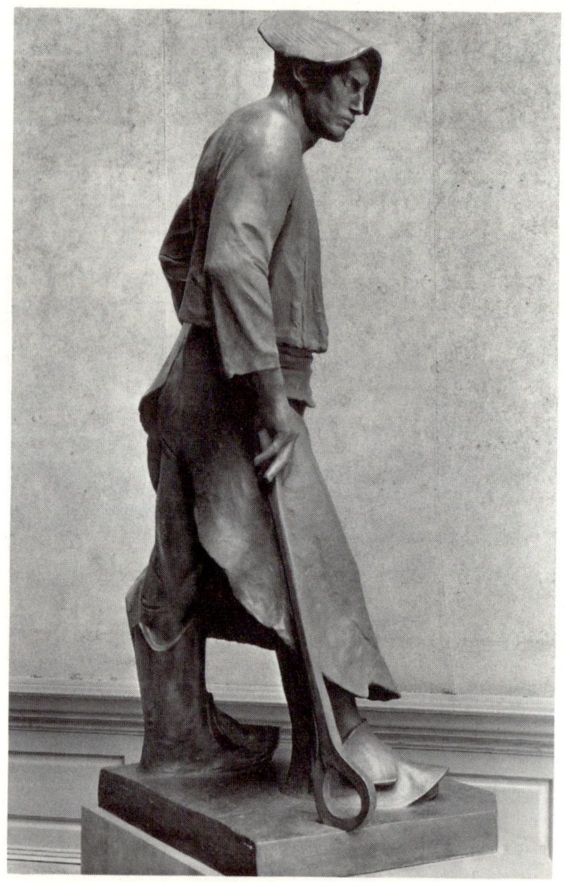

Figure 58   Constantin Meunier, *The Puddler*
Constantin Emile Meunier, Belgian, 1831–1905, The Hammerman, bronze, 1884, ht.: 194.3 cm, Robert Waller Fund, 1920.30. side view, photograph © 1994, The Art Institute of Chicago, All Rights Reserved.

notably that of the solitary worker. The abortive monument to the workers was his clearest attempt to identify with the new socialist movement through his art.[37] He captured a worker—as did

37. See John M. Hunisak, "Rodin, Dalou, and the Monument to Labor," in *Art the Ape of Nature: Studies in Honor of H. W. Janson,* ed. Moshe Barasch and Lucy Freeman Sandler (Englewood Cliffs, N.J., 1981), 689–705. See also Anthony Blunt, "Dalou and His Workers' Monument," *Left Review,* II (1936), 693–98; and Marie Bouchhard, "'Un Monument au Travail': The Projects of Meunier, Dalou, Rodin, and Bouchard," *Oxford Art*

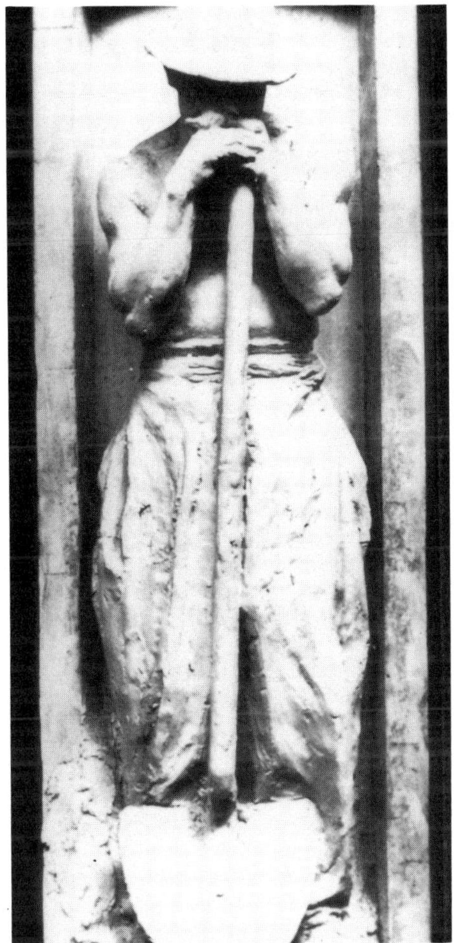

Figure 59   Jules Dalou, maquette for a monument to the working class
Plaster, *ca.* 1900. Petit Palais, Paris.

Meunier—in a moment of rest. Yet the feel of the two is altogether different. Dalou simply provided us with one of Courbet's stone-breakers standing erect: the head is tilted down, the face masked

Journal, IV (November, 1981), 28–35. An excellent, still-unpublished discussion is Sura Levine's "Contested Spaces: Siting Constantin Meunier's *Monument to Labor,*" delivered to the Seventeenth Annual Colloquium on Nineteenth-Century French Studies, in New Orleans, October 1991.

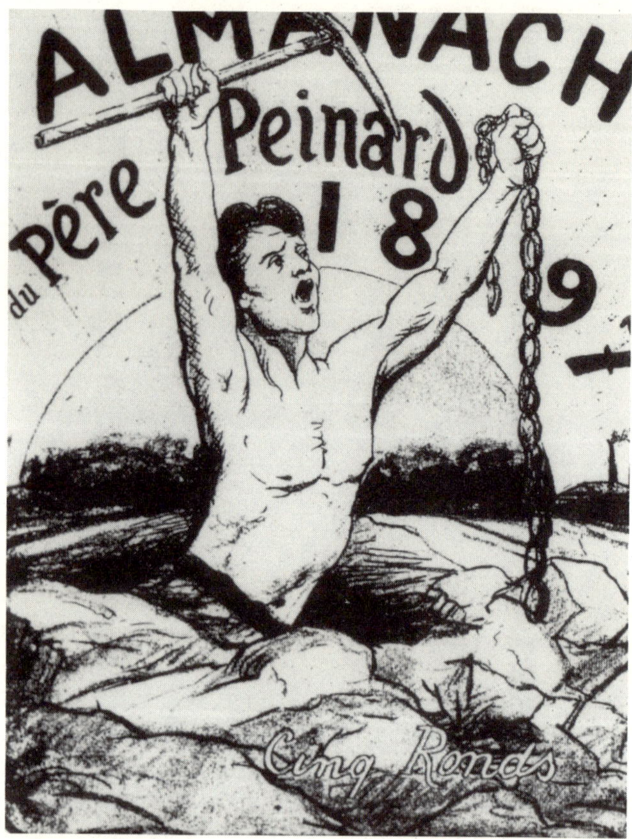

Figure 60   Cover illustration for *Almanach du Père Peinard*, 1897

by the brim of the hat. The emphasis is on the toil of the worker; the sense is of a man worn down, exhausted. By contrast, in Meunier's work the focus is on quiet strength and self-confidence. Lemonnier said of the Meunier that its creator depicted an "invincible titan who yields to a momentary lassitude but who is spared moral anguish."[38]

The motif of the titan was by no means unique to Meunier. In the art of both the syndicalist and the socialist movement, there recurred the male worker, usually seminude, standing erect, often breaking the chains that had bound him. The figure appeared on the cover of the 1897 *Almanach du Père Peinard* (Figure 60) as well

38. Lemonnier, *Constantin Meunier*, 107.

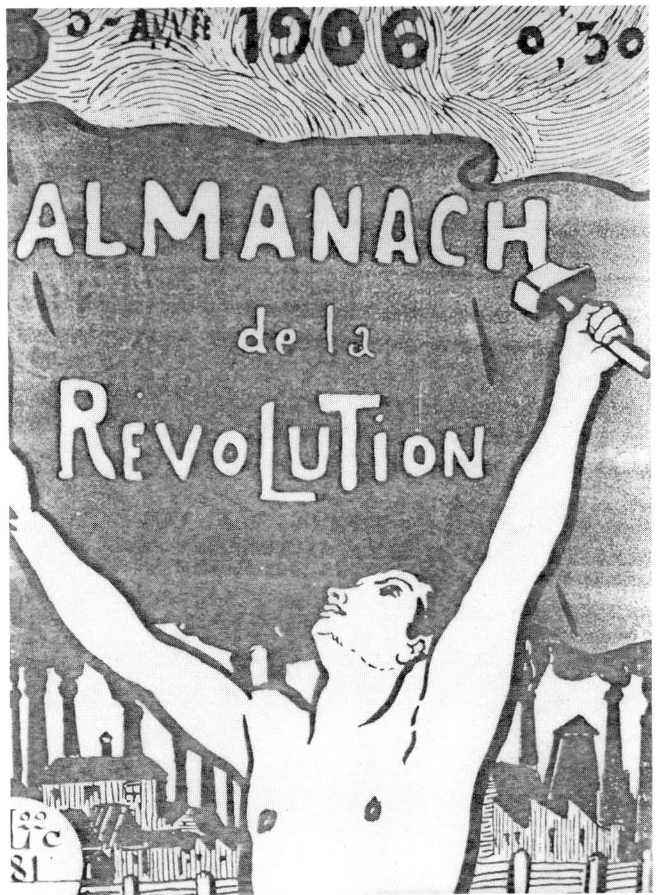

Figure 61   Cover illustration for *Almanach de la révolution,* 1906

as on the cover of the 1906 *Almanach de la révolution* (Figure 61); an analogous image was produced for the Italian socialist newspaper *Avanti!* The worker holds up a severed chain and a pick in the first picture, a hammer and a revolutionary banner in the second. In the third, he holds aloft only the manacles and the broken chain.

The triumphant, liberated titan has deep roots in the art of European revolutionary movements. It has a direct lineage, for example, from an etching from the French revolution, Jacques Louis Pérée's *Regenerated Man,* of 1795 (Figure 62). In that earlier depiction, the "new man" of the revolutionary world holds the Declaration of the Rights of Man in one hand and an ax in the other;

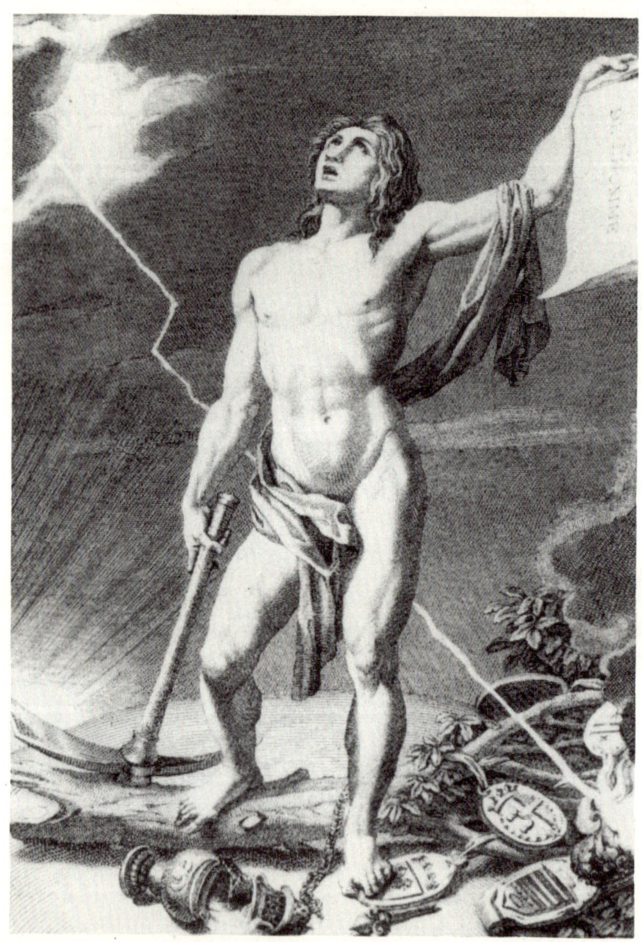

Figure 62   Jacques Louis Pérée, *Regenerated Man*
L'Homme régénéré, etching, 1795. Bibliothèque Nationale, Paris.

around him, shattered, like the tokens of the old royalist regime. Even God lends a hand as lightning strikes a fallen crown.

In the late nineteenth century, the figure of the worker as risen titan reflected a conscious attempt to provide the new and still scattered workers' movement with an emphatic sense of unity, and power. In Victor Hugo's "Le Satyre," the worker becomes Atlas, bearing the weight of the entire globe. In Upton Sinclair's *The Jungle,* of 1905, which was published in a popular French two-part edition in 1905–1906, the identical image occurs. A speaker tells an enthusiastic crowd of workers, "The voice of Labor, despised and outraged; a mighty giant, lying prostrate—mountainous and colossal, but blinded, bound and ignorant of his strength. And now a dream of resistance haunts him, hope battling with fear; until suddenly he stirs, and a fetter snaps—and a thrill shoots through him, to the farthest end of his huge body, and in a flash the dream becomes act! He starts, he lifts himself, and the bonds are shattered, the burdens roll off him; he rises—towering and gigantic; he springs to his feet, he shouts in newborn exultation."[39]

Nothing remains here of the idea that social art is supposed to embody calm, that it should soothe the viewer and capture the tranquillity of the golden age. As Monatte said of syndicalism, this art does not promise an earthly paradise: its goal is to stir its viewers to action, to rouse them to conquer.

It is also an art that is profoundly conservative in its sense of gender roles: action remains exclusively a male prerogative. The images of women are, by contrast, highly abstract and allegorical, as the cover of the issue of *L'Assiette au beurre* for May Day, 1906, illustrates (Figure 63). It is not difficult to imagine a male worker identifying with the figure of the emancipated titan. It is an image of empowerment, promising strength and freedom to a worker who has had neither. It is impossible, on the other hand, to imagine a woman identifying with the nude figure representing "eight hours of leisure." The nude males with their picks and broken chains radiate strength; by contrast, the allegorical figure of "eight hours of labor" on the front of *L'Assiette au beurre* seems preposterous. Unlike Meunier's occasional images of women miners, the figure in the May Day illustration, with her pickax, scarf, and daisy chain, is lifeless and clichéd.[40]

39. Upton Sinclair, *The Jungle* (Cambridge, Mass., 1946), 304. The two parts of the French edition appeared as *La Jungle* (Paris, 1905) and *Le Fin de la Jungle* (Paris, 1906). The worker as titan breaking free of his chains had a presence in German working-class art as well. A cover of *Der Wahre Jacob* from 1902 shows a confident, smiling worker surrounded by bourgeois pygmies who are trying to tie him down; the same journal in 1915 depicted the proletariat as Prometheus chained to a rock. The images are reproduced in *Proletariat: Culture and Lifestyle in the Nineteenth Century,* ed. Dietrich Muhlberg, trans. Katherine Vanovitch (Leipzig, 1988), 13, 248. Vandervelde made use of Victor Hugo's image of the worker as satyr, despised when weak and dirty but steadily growing in power. See Vandervelde, *Collectivism and Industrial Evolution,* 245.

40. For an important attempt to compare and contrast socialist images of men and women, see Eric Hobsbawm, "Man and Woman in Socialist Iconography," *History Workshop Journal,* VI (1978). Hobsbawm seems unaware of the tradition in European art of the triumphal male nude as a revolutionary symbol (see, for example, pp. 129–30), and his

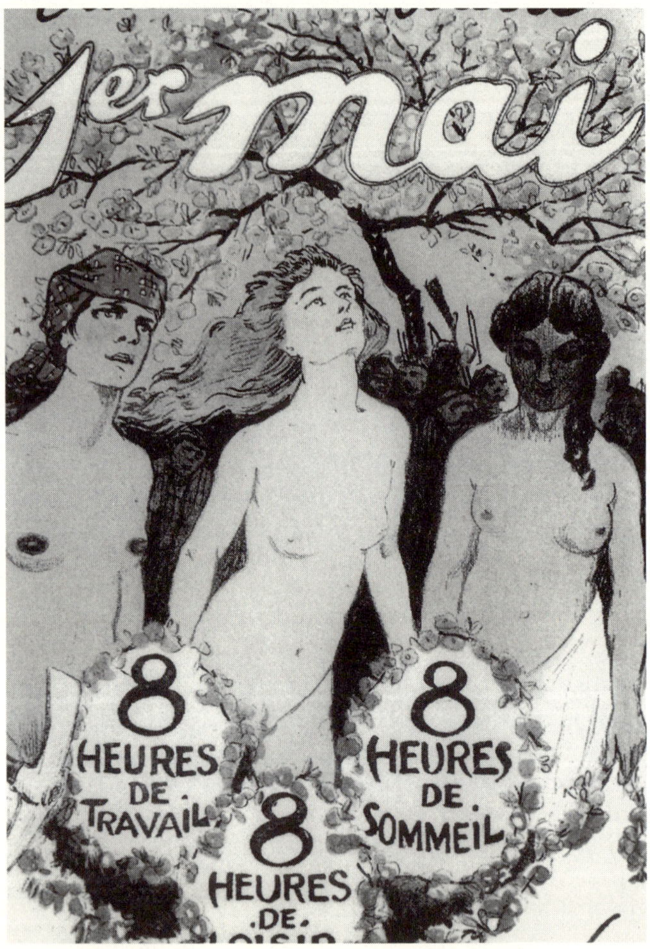

Figure 63   Grandjouan, cover illustration for *L'Assiette au beurre*, April 28, 1906

Much the same can be said of Steinlen's *March 18,* a color lithograph from the cover of *Le Chambard socialiste,* of March 17, 1894 (Figure 64). That commemoration of the Commune carefully distinguishes between the male figures in the foreground: a peasant, a manual laborer, an artisan, even an artist marching, rather improbably, with his palette and mallstick. All the men are recogniz-

____

discussion of the iconography of women is often questionable. See also the rebuttals that ran in the journal from Autumn, 1979, until Autumn, 1982.

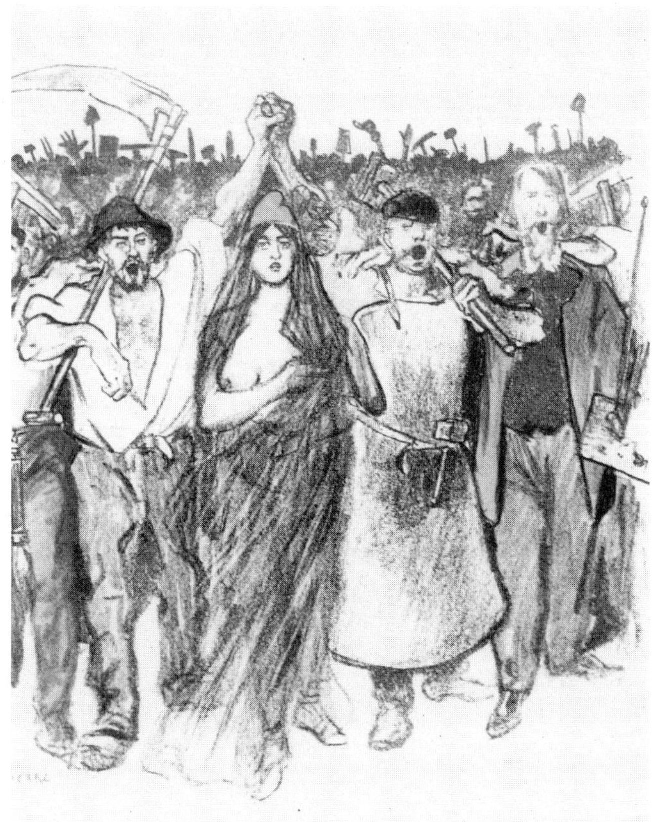

Figure 64   Théophile Steinlen, *March 18*
  Colored lithograph, 1894. Cover illustration for *Le Chambard socialiste,* March 17, 1894.

able social types; the only woman in the picture, however, is purely allegorical: Marianne, the incarnation of the spirit of the republic. Only in a relatively small number of prints and paintings—Steinlen's paintings of Louise Michel on the barricades, certain agitational posters by Steinlen and Adler—do there appear living women marching alongside living men as part of a unified struggle.

Neo-Impressionism and the New Socialist Art

For all the literary references in anarchist writings to calm and harmony, anarchist editors and militants often reproached Neo-

Impressionist painting for being cold and unfeeling. In practice, Neo-Impressionist art—usually prints—that was deliberately aimed at anarchist audiences tended to fall back upon traditional republican iconography. There were major differences: art in Pouget's *Le Père Peinard* was directly agitational and didactic, marked by a biting wit; its "worker anarchism" was part of the current that flowed into syndicalism. Grave's *La Révolte,* and later, *Les Temps nouveaux,* were calmer, self-consciously "elevated" in tone. Both Pouget and Grave saw their mission as educational, however, and that required an art understood by a broad audience.[41]

The educational mission they envisioned paralleled the Neo-Impressionist pursuit—at least as Signac described it—of a scientific art toward which the workers could be educated. In practice, though, the demands of anarchist journals—art on specific themes, sometimes to illustrate specific essays or build support for certain causes—generated irritation among, and friction with, the Neos.

Of the Neo-Impressionists, only Luce was able to move with ease between the world of the avant-garde and the world of anarchist journals: between 1895 and 1914, he contributed more than forty illustrations to *Les Temps nouveaux* and perhaps another hundred to *Le Père Peinard.*[42] One study of anarchist art in Grave's journals credits Luce with being the only Neo-Impressionist to align himself fully with the requirements of the movement.[43] Luce's anarchist prints share with his Neo-Impressionist work.

41. On Pouget and his journals, see Christian de Goustine, *Pouget: Les Matins noirs du syndicalisme* (Paris, 1972), 29–45; Félix Dubois, *Le Péril anarchiste* (Paris, 1894), 116–23; Charles Flor [Flor O'Squarr], *Les Coulisses de l'anarchie* (Paris, 1892), 74–81; Alvan Sanborn, *Paris and the Social Revolution: A Study of the Revolutionary Elements in the Various Classes of Parisian Society* (Boston, 1905), 67–70; and Jean Maitron, *Histoire du mouvement anarchiste en France* (Paris, 1955), 139–42. On Grave and his journals, see Louis Patsouras, *Jean Grave and French Anarchism* (Dubuque, Iowa, 1978), esp. 22–27; Dubois, *Le Péril anarchiste,* 105–16; O'Squarr, *Les Coulisses,* 67–73; Sanborn, *Paris and the Social Revolution,* 62–65; and E. V. Zenker, *Anarchism: A Criticism and a History of the Anarchist Theory* (London, 1898), 164–68. The audience for the anarchist reviews is studied by Jeanne Lambert and Joelle Saiac in "Les Almanachs socialistes et anarchistes, 1891–1914" (Dissertation, University of Paris, 1973), I, 13–16, 40–51.

42. Aline Dardel, "Catalogues des dessins et publications illustrées du journal anarchiste *Les Temps nouveaux,* 1895–1914" (Dissertation, University of Paris IV, n.d.), I, 34. The count for *Le Père Peinard* is from Max Nettlau's *Geschichte der Anarchie* (Vaduz, 1981), IV, 260.

43. Dardel, "Catalogues," I, 38. See also Aline Dardel, "Illustrateurs et Satiristes, V: La Révolte, ou le drapeau noir—Luce, Camille et Lucien Pissarro," *Gazette de l'Hôtel Drouot,* December 11, 1981, p. 50.

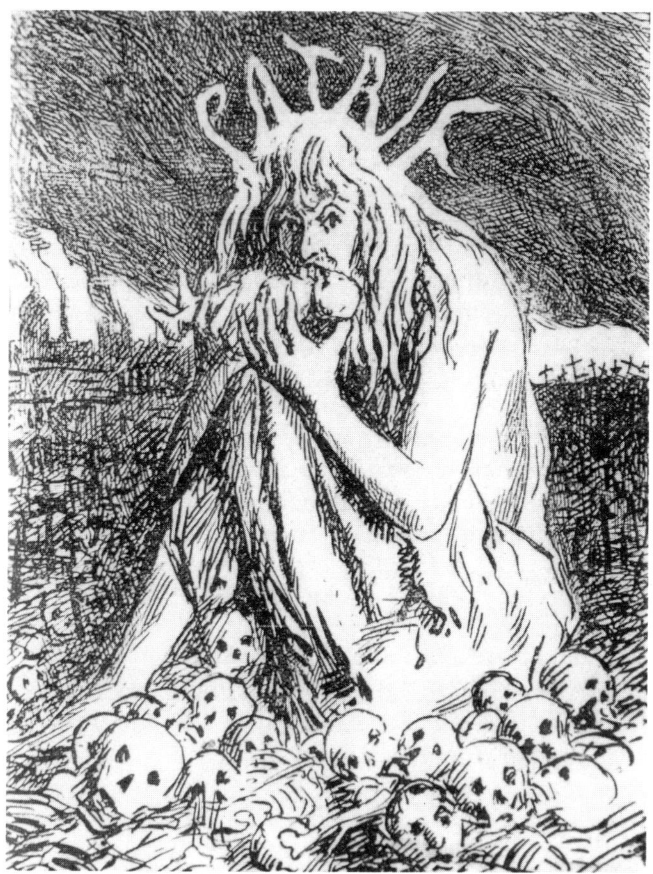

Figure 65 Maximilien Luce, *Patrie*
In *Almanach du Père Peinard,* 1894

Images such as his *Patrie* (Figure 65), printed in *Le Père Peinard* in 1891 and again in the *Almanach du Père Peinard* in 1894, combine a powerful graphic iconography with the clear text of a plainspoken legend. The image carries the words "The abominable ghoul is never satisfied! Rough bitch, Madame Patrie: she devours her children!" Patrie herself, gnawing on an infant, derives from a tradition as least as old as Goya's Saturn, though the particular misogyny of the fin de siècle is the force transmuting a *patrie* into a woman.

Of the others in the circle, only Lucien Pissarro was a prolific illustrator, for journals ranging from the avowedly anarchist *Le*

Père Peinard, and the *Torch,* of Britain, to the quasi-radical *Courrier français* and *La Vie moderne.*[44] Much like Luce, Lucien Pissarro adapted his imagery to the periodicals for which he was illustrating. The vital difference between the two is that Luce moved toward an open social message, whereas Lucien Pissarro gradually emptied his art of any overt message.

The consequence is that these two Neos felt different hindrances in their work for anarchist presses. Lucien Pissarro grumbled that the editors for whom he worked imposed unacceptable demands regarding form and content. Luce, by contrast, wrote Grave begging for suggestions: "Inspire me, give me a suggestion. . . . I am searching, but I am not imaginative enough."[45]

Lucien Pissarro's complaints about editorial interference were echoed even more strongly by his associates. By the early 1900s—at precisely the moment a new, more activist art was rising—most of the group were voicing a marked reluctance to produce new designs for the anarchist cause. In an undated letter to Grave, Signac answered a request for new art, "Frankly, I don't much believe in the utility of the image." He suggested that Grave turn to specialists in agitational art—specifically mentioning Steinlen and Hermann Paul—because other artists were bored with the repetitive subject matter.[46] Henri Edmond Cross became even more dismissive. In a letter to Charles Angrand in 1903 he wrote that he had just mailed off a drawing to Grave: "Let's forget about it. It is more literary than plastic." In 1906, he wrote to Grave directly, "The genre of drawings demanded by *Les Temps nouveaux* is no longer much my business, in the sense that my thoughts—from the plastic point of view—are in a direction wholly different." He was no longer willing to accept the constraints and effort required for such work.[47]

Accordingly, only Luce made the transition to the newer, more activist art of the fin-de-siècle socialist and syndicalist movements. Pouget jettisoned *Le Père Peinard* when he became editor of the

<hr>

44. Janine Bailly-Herzberg and Aline Dardel, "Lucien Pissarro et les Illustrations françaises," *Nouvelles de l'estampe,* No. 54 (November–December, 1980), 8–16.

45. Maximilien Luce to Jean Grave, n.d., in Jean Grave Archives. Lucien Pissarro wrote, "I am at the moment overwhelmed with making cartoons for the anarchist press, so that I'm a bit bored. . . . Zo d'Axa is the most boring of all; he gives you subjects to do, and he even gives you the compositional details" (Lucien Pissarro to Camille Pissarro, December, 1894, in Pissarro Archives, Ashmolean Museum, Oxford University).

46. Paul Signac to Jean Grave, n.d., in Jean Grave Archives.

47. Henri Edmond Cross to Charles Angrand, March 2, 1903, in *H. E. Cross,* by Isabelle Compin (Paris, 1964), 53.

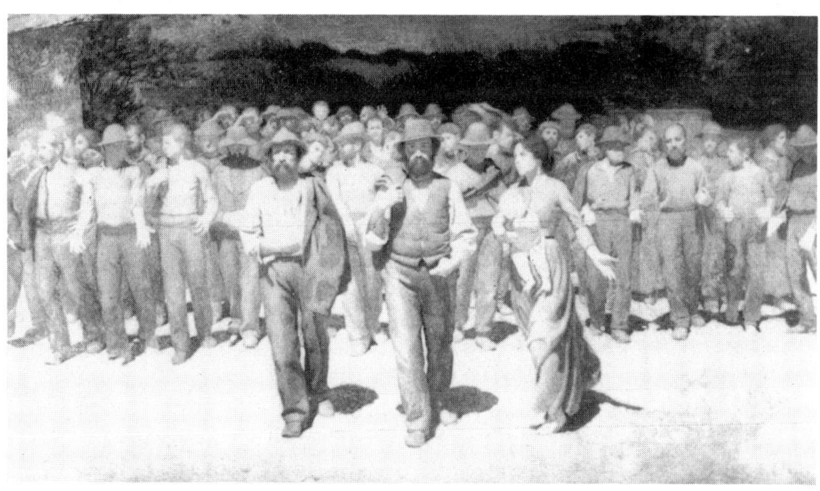

Figure 66   Giuseppe Pellizza da Volpedo, *The Fourth Estate*
Il quarto stato, oil on canvas, 1899–1901. Courtesy of Galleria d'Arte Moderna, Milan.

CGT's *La Voix du peuple,* and Luce followed him, contributing to his new newspaper and to *La Guerre sociale,* the organ of Gustave Hervé's ultraradical wing of the SFIO.

The other Neos seem never to have contemplated such an upheaval in their principles. It would have meant a practical repudiation of the whole concept of high (or "true") art to which they had always adhered. Just as the anarchocommunists recoiled from syndicalism, from the day-to-day battles that might bring a bettering of the workers' lot in the near term, the Neo-Impressionists continued to take solace from the idea that only the people of the distant emancipated future could hope to comprehend their work.[48] They conformed to the institutional framework of French painting—not the discarded model of the Academy but that of the patron and private dealer.

The course from which the Neo-Impressionists shut themselves off can be fairly clearly discerned in the work of their Italian cousins, the Divisionists. In 1901, Giuseppe Pellizza da Volpedo completed for a union hall his *The Fourth Estate* (Figure 66), which was a response to the massacre of the Bava Beccaris workers in Milan in November, 1898. In Pellizza's words, the painting depicts a "crowd of people, workers of the soil, who are intelligent, strong,

48. See, for example, Signac's speech, *ca.* 1902, quoted by Robert L. Herbert in "Les Artistes et l'Anarchisme," *Le Mouvement social,* XXXVI (July–September, 1961), 9.

robust, united," advancing "like a torrent, overthrowing every obstacle in its path," as part of its unstoppable drive for justice. Pellizza's aim was for the painting to show that "the true force lies in the intelligent and good workers who, with the tenacity of their ideals, oblige other men to follow them or to clear the way because retrograde power cannot stop them."[49]

The image of the massed poor and workers sweeping to victory captured the imagination of artists across Europe. But it is utterly at odds with the art of the French and Belgian Neos in its activism and sense of insurgent power. By this time, Neo art was focusing on amelioration and harmony, attempting to smooth over precisely the ruptures Pellizza's art sought to widen.

Grave did not intentionally shackle the Neo-Impressionist artists in commissioning illustrative work for his journals and, more generally, his press. He repeatedly assured the artists he drew upon that he supported the "most complete liberty of choice in subject and execution."[50] Nor did the other important socialist and syndicalist leaders seek to impose a straitjacket on the arts; Socialist Realism was not yet even a blur on the horizon. At stake was rather a concept of what—and whom—art was to be for. The problems the Neos felt with Grave or Pouget prefigured in miniature those which resulted as mass socialist and syndicalist movements became the center of patronage, with new needs and pressures.

The Neo-Impressionists continued to donate art from their studios for auctions and other fund raising in behalf of the anarchist cause.[51] Some of the group gradually concluded that their political art was not politically effective. Others—such as Cross—came to reject the possibility of an art derived from outside the artist's personal vision. In their judgment, Grave's pressure for an art he could put to use disqualified itself as unacceptable in principle.

49. Sandra Berresford, "Divisionism: Its Origins, Its Aims, and Its Relations to French Post-Impressionist Painting," in the Royal Academy's *Post-Impressionism* (London, 1978), 245–46.

50. The full letter is reproduced in *Artists, Writers, Politics: Camille Pissarro and His Friends,* comp. Anne Thorold (Oxford, 1980), 60.

51. See, for example, the lists of contributors—and contributions—to an anarchist fund raiser, in *Les Temps nouveaux,* IV (April 15–21, 1899), 4, (April 22–28, 1899), 4. Among the works donated for sale were a gouache by Camille Pissarro, a watercolor by Cross, a "tableau" by Luce, a watercolor by Signac, a watercolor by van Rysselberghe, "Japanese embroidery" from Madame Signac, a drawing by Angrand, three "painted studies" by Ludovic-Rodo Pissarro, and a "tableau" by Manzana Pissarro. Félix Vallotton, Edouard Vuillard, and Albert André also donated works of art.

7

The Moment of Neo-Impressionism

The nineteenth century has in many ways satisfied and has in even more ways deceived the optimist. . . . It has compelled him to transfer most of his hopes to the twentieth century. . . . And now that century has come! What has it brought with it at the outset? In France—the poisonous foam of racial hatred; . . . in South Africa—the agony of a tiny people which is being murdered by a colossus. . . . Hatred and murder, famine and blood. . . . It seems as if this new century . . . were bent at the very moment of its appearance to drive the optimist into absolute pessimism. . . . Death to Utopia! Death to faith! Death to love! Death to hope! thunders the twentieth century. . . . Surrender, you pathetic dreamer. Here I am, your long-awaited twentieth century, your "future."

—No, replies the unhumbled optimist: You—you are only the *present.*

—Leon Trotsky (1902)

In 1921, Jean Grave began publication of a new journal in an effort to rebuild the shattered anarchocommunist movement. His attempt was a protracted failure: beginning with some two hundred to three hundred subscribers, he struggled on until advanced age and mounting debts forced him to cease publication in 1936.

Grave's movement in the 1880s and 1890s had claimed—had sought—to move in harmony with history, but his postwar effort was self-consciously nostalgic. The very name of his review—*Publications de "La Révolte" et "Temps nouveaux"*—was a calculated invocation of the past. To strengthen the connection with the past, Grave from 1924 until 1931 reprinted as cover illustrations works Luce, Signac, Steinlen, and their colleagues had submitted in the 1890s.[1] In 1925, these included a watercolor by Paul Signac entitled *The Destruction of the State;* his undistinguished picture was meant to communicate the anarchocommunist precept that the state would crumble by itself as mutual aid and human solidarity reblossomed.

If Signac was aware of the republication of the old anarchist

---

1. Louis Patsouras, *Jean Grave and French Anarchism* (Dubuque, Iowa, 1978), 97–100.

image, he must have felt embarrassment. He had become a supporter of the French Communist party, and Grave's new review
was venomously anti-Soviet.[2] The notion of the self-destruction
of the state was a relic by 1925: the state had proved with a ven-
geance that it could survive. All that had fallen apart was the
anarchist-communist movement. An image that would have reso-
nated strongly in the 1890s in its attunement with the rejection of
capitalism and the bourgeois state by a wide stratum of intellectuals was by 1925 little more than a historical curiosity.

It is difficult to evaluate the icons and catchphrases of movements that have died. Certainly, the major premises of anarchocommunism proved incorrect. The Third Republic did not fall
until 1940, and when it did, the few followers of Grave who remained might well have wished it back. Industrialization in France
did not lead to decentralization and rural communes but to the
same industrial belts and conurbations as elsewhere.

Alongside the erroneous predictions of the theoreticians of anarchocommunism, the failures of Neo-Impressionism appear at
worst minor. Art did not, as Signac predicted it would, deliver a
blow of the pick to the social edifice. But then, if a generation of
strikes and two world wars failed, as well, to deliver that blow, it
scarcely seems fair to blame painting for falling short.

Nor was anarchocommunism all that left behind disappointed
expectations in this era. Georges Clemenceau and his Radical party
came to office in 1906 promising to incorporate workers into the
life of France and wound up putting a number of them in the ceme-
tery instead. The triumphalism of the syndicalists and the SFIO
died a hard death—for the syndicalists in the bloody, disastrous
general strike of 1906 and the railroad strike of 1910, for the socialists in the trenches of the First World War. As for the Catholic
Revivalists, including a number of the Pont Aven painters, some
had the misfortune to see their beliefs put into practice at Vichy in
the 1940s.

It is perhaps characteristic of the present time and culture that
such disasters seem somehow neither surprising nor even necessarily very interesting. Modern studies assert that the majority of
French workers never really supported revolutionary syndicalism,
that the SFIO never intended revolution, and that the anarchist
intellectuals of the 1890s were for the most part riding a sort of fad.

The history of Neo-Impressionism from the mid-1890s is one
of secession, schism, and gradual accommodation to the estab-

2. *Ibid.*, 97.

lished order, in art as well as society. As the anarchocommunist vision faded, the boast of Neo-Impressionism to embody a global artisticopolitical theory came to seem either ridiculous or irrelevant.

The first to secede—Louis Hayet, Hippolyte Petitjean, and Camille Pissarro—all did so in the name of anarchism itself, though Hayet's departure was assisted by a growing paranoia that in time led to his estrangement from even his closest friends.[3] Pissarro's break has been dated as early as 1891, on the basis of his statement to Lucien that pointillism died with Seurat.[4] The break is more properly seen as having taken place over several years and as having been marked by considerable hesitation and self-doubt on Pissarro's part. In 1892, his friend Octave Mirbeau was still discussing Pissarro's work entirely by reference to the scientific ideas of Ernest Chevreul and Charles Henry.[5] In 1893, Pissarro was invited to participate in the Neos' new boutique. By that point, the artist had clearly rejected the theoretical basis for the movement, with all its constraints. "As for me," he wrote his son, "my nest is made. I remain with the old. Signac wanted me to decide for him, but I decline."[6]

Pissarro's most explicit distancing of himself from Neo-Impressionism came in a letter to Henry van de Velde in 1896. Van de Velde had included Pissarro among the ranks of the Neos; Pissarro responded that he could no longer accept that classification. He no longer believed that Neo-Impressionism's methods could capture fugitive sensations, nor did he think they could do justice to life and movement. He added, "I can't find harmony or modern life [in Neo-Impressionism]. . . . The great task of Signac is obviously a laudable and courageous endeavor, but I am not convinced—on the contrary."[7]

3. See Jean Sutter, "Louis Hayet, 1864–1940," in *The Neo-Impressionists,* ed. Jean Sutter, trans. Chantal Deliss (Greenwich, Conn., 1970), 112.

4. See Fiona Fitzgerald, "The Prints of Lucien Pissarro from 1886 to 1896" (M.A. thesis, University of East Anglia, 1981), 15. Actually, Lucien—not Camille—stated that pointillism died with Seurat (Lucien Pissarro to Camille Pissarro, March, 1891, in Camille Pissarro's *Lettres à son fils Lucien,* ed. John Rewald [Paris, 1947], 194). His father agreed but insisted that Seurat's work had continuing ramifications in the world of art (Camille Pissarro to Lucien Pissarro, April 1, 1891, in Camille Pissarro's *Lettres a son fils Lucien,* 195).

5. Octave Mirbeau, "Camille Pissarro," in *Des Artistes: Peintres et Sculpteurs* (Paris, 1922–24), I, 148.

6. Camille Pissarro to Lucien Pissarro, December 10, 1893, in Camille Pissarro's *Correspondance,* ed. Janine Bailly-Herzberg (Paris, 1980–), III, 407.

7. Camille Pissarro to Henry van de Velde, March 27, 1896, in *Artists, Writers, Politics: Camille Pissarro and His Friends,* comp. Anne Thorold (Oxford, 1980), 28.

Pissarro's separation from Neo-Impressionism—which paralleled Petitjean's—was that of an anarchist militant of long standing acting on doubts and arguments that echoed Paterne Berrichon's and other anarchist writers'.[8] The perennial tension in anarcho-communist theory between scientific law and individual freedom broke apart, and Pissarro and Petitjean came down squarely on the side of the individual as creator. It was one thing to assert, with Peter Kropotkin and Jean Grave, that human freedom existed within and depended upon a predetermined matrix of physical and moral laws. For Pissarro, it was quite another to extend those laws so that they prescribed a mode of painting. He never abandoned the goal of a synthesis of the ideal and the real, but he despaired of Neo-Impressionism's bestowing the means to discover that synthesis.

Signac, by contrast, stood firm. His *D'Eugène Delacroix au néo-impressionnisme* is neither a historical survey nor a systematic statement of Neo-Impressionist theory; it is a tract, a passionate pronouncement about the necessity of an art rooted in science and about the necessity of the historical evolution of nineteenth-century art. In 1894, Signac wrote to Pissarro that the Neo-Impressionist synthesis had proved more difficult to achieve than he had anticipated; he thought, however, that the struggle to attain the synthesis remained the only possible method for trying to render clearly and rigorously "harmony, light, coloration."[9]

Signac became the defender of the faith—and the judge of the shortcomings of his colleagues. By the mid-1890s, Maximilien Luce, Henri Edmond Cross, Charles Angrand, and Théo van Rysselberghe were all endeavoring somehow to meld Neo-Impressionism with more traditional drawing and color. Even their lukewarm Neo-Impressionism was too much for Pissarro, whose letters were filled with sarcastic asides on his former allies.[10] Signac considered the trend disturbing indeed. In a journal entry of March 15, 1899, he took both van Rysselberghe and Luce to task in terms that make his apprehensions quite clear. He deemed van Rysselberghe's portraits utterly bourgeois in character, remi-

8. On Petitjean's separation from the movement, see Hippolyte Petitjean to Lucien Pissarro, September 1, 1893, in *Artists, Writers, Politics,* comp. Thorold, 19.

9. Paul Signac to Camille Pissarro, January 25, 1894, in Camille Pissarro's *Lettres à son fils Lucien,* 330–31.

10. See Camille Pissarro to Lucien Pissarro, January 14, 1895 (attacking van Rysselberghe), October 23, 1895 (referring to Angrand), April 25, 1896 (referring to Signac, Cross, and Luce), in Camille Pissarro's *Correspondance,* IV, 16–17, 106, 194–95.

niscent of the paintings of Henri Gervex, and he deplored how for van Rysselberghe divisionist technique had become merely a means of heightening areas of color. About Luce, Signac wrote, "He is a vulgar stand-in for Sisley and Guillaumin."[11] The comparisons are telling. Gervex was despised in avant-garde circles for a willingness to adulterate new ideas in producing fashionable, and profitable, works extolling the beautiful life. Signac called van Rysselberghe's works "bourgeois, Ecole," and in effect accused him of collaborating with the enemy. Luce he saw as a backslider, returning to the discarded ways of the "Romantic Impressionists." Pissarro was attacking the movement he had been part of from without; Signac worried that his associates were eroding it from within.

The unraveling of the Neo-Impressionist project was in large part a crisis of signification. Neo-Impressionism had promised the possibility of total control to artists who felt they had none—of content indissolubly linked to form and color, so that every tone, every hue, every gesture contributed to the work's meaning. Neo-Impressionist painting was to be harmonious as no other painting could be: it was to be scientifically designed so that meaning saturated not just the overt subject, the painted figures, but even the lines and colors—each subliminally reinforcing the idea, the message impressed upon the subject by the artist.[12] It was a project emanating from both artistic and political theory. Kropotkin's scientific anarchism explained everything; it left no room for error, embracing the totality of painting from its aesthetics to its ethics.

Yet in practice the linkage seemed elusive at best—to the public, the critics, even to the painters. Neo-Impressionism was praised for its luminosity; individual Neos were commended for their subjects, for their love of the workers or the land. But the awareness of any integration between the techniques of Neo-Impressionism and the content of particular paintings usually required a prior knowledge of Neo-Impressionist theory.

An examination of anarchist illustrations and especially of anarchist criticism of art of the time reveals little insistence by the anarchist press and anarchist writers upon simplistic propaganda

11. John Rewald, ed., "Extraits du journal inédit de Paul Signac," *Gazette des beaux-arts,* 6th ser., XLII (1953), 46. The entry is for March 15, 1899. Oddly, Signac was much more sympathetic to the work of his former colleague Petitjean. See his entry for April 26, 1895, in "Extraits du journal inédit," *ibid.,* XXXVI (1949), 118.

12. See Paul Signac, *D'Eugène Delacroix au néo-impressionnisme* (1899; Paris, 1978), 65–66.

images. Anarchist critics of the arts reacted favorably to work far removed from any explicit political statement, such as Claude Monet's and Pierre Puvis de Chavannes'. What they found problematic in Neo-Impressionism was its claim to be a "scientific art." Accustomed to analogous claims in literature—from the Naturalists to René Ghil's "scientific poetry"—they were disposed to see Neo-Impressionist art as uninvolved, as cold and aloof.

Artists broke with Signac's codification of Neo-Impressionist theory by moving in different directions. Cross and his friend van Rysselberghe argued, along with Pissarro, that they were simply reasserting the "plastic values" of their art. "Plastic values," however, are neutral; even setting aside questions of signification, any subject should theoretically be capable of yielding—whatever the artistic theory—a suitable painting. But for Cross *plastic values* always meant apoliticism in art.[13]

Cries for the supremacy of "plastic values" may seem a plea for art for art's sake, for a free art untrammeled by politics.[14] But the portraits and landscapes of Cross and van Rysselberghe are no more "pure" as art than Luce's pictures of workers or industrial quarters. A dancing nymph is no less literary or programmatic than a worker, or than Pissarro's bustling peasant markets. A wealthy young woman admiring herself in a mirror is as constraining an artistic device as a stevedore or a seamstress. Luce's decision to move to a looser style and to adopt a self-consciously socialist emphasis in his work is obviously political, but so is the choice of painting glamorous portraits of the French and Belgian leisure class.

For all the artists of the movement except Signac, Neo-Impressionism devolved from a global system into a mannerism. For Luce, the continuing emphasis was on a choppy brushstroke and a preference for relatively pure color, for van Rysselberghe on the use of the point as a means of bringing out certain features. Luce at one extreme and van Rysselberghe at the other conventionalized their art to make it more acceptable. Both aimed at a market. Luce's was much larger, but van Rysselberghe's was a good deal wealthier. Characteristically, art history has been kinder to van Rysselberghe—and Cross—than to Luce; the art market has not

13. See, for example, the letters by Cross that Isabelle Compin included in *H. E. Cross* (Paris, 1964), 53.

14. Donald Drew Egbert makes this argument in *Social Radicalism and the Arts—Western Europe: A Cultural History from the French Revolution to 1968* (New York, 1970), 248–49.

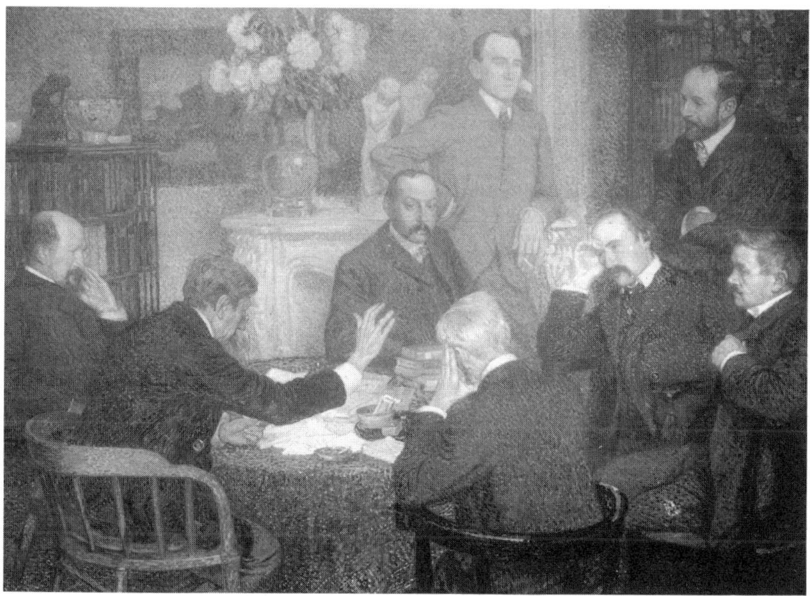

Figure 67   Théo van Rysselberghe, *The Lecture*
Oil on canvas, 1903. Museum of Fine Arts, Ghent, Belgium.

changed that much in the intervening century, and if Luce's faith in the workers seems naïve in our era, the wealthy still like to admire themselves on canvas.

Thus the former allies drifted apart. Angrand, after the death of his father, in 1896, returned to his family village of Saint Laurent, in Normandy, devoting himself to endless charcoal sketches on the joys of motherhood. Cross, bothered by severe rheumatism, applied his later art to the beauties of Venice, which he visited in 1903, the coasts of southern France, and dancing nymphs. Van Rysselberghe never formally broke with Neo–Impressionism, but its influence became more and more vestigial in his work. Luce, identifying himself with the leadership of the CGT, became both more didactic and more eclectic in his work, quoting from artists ranging from Ernest Meissonier to Honoré Daumier.

Though most of the Neos never formally renounced their earlier political beliefs, their anarchism gradually became little more than a reflexive defense of individual creativity and a nostalgic memory. Van Rysselberghe's painting *The Lecture,* of 1903 (Figure 67), shows how attenuated the impulses of anarchism could become: prominent among the assembled artists and intellectuals—

including Félix Fénéon, André Gide, Maurice Maeterlinck, Henry van de Velde, and Emile Verhaeren— is Félix Le Dantec. Le Dantec represented the antithesis of the humanitarian anarchism of Grave and Kropotkin; he was a dogmatic social Darwinist who viewed life as a war to the knife of one against all. Only seven years before, van Rysselberghe had movingly portrayed the plight of homeless vagabonds, as symbols of the oppressions of the dominant system. Le Dantec was not personally responsible for the millions driven from their land, many to starve, but he promoted an ideological basis for defending misery and starvation as necessary and even beneficial to society. In van Rysselberghe's painting, Le Dantec sits calmly, a bit bored, as Verhaeren dramatically recounts some point. There is no tension or bitterness in the group between men who had been on opposite sides of the barricade scant years before. For most of them, the war was over.

Signac held on—to his militancy, and to the system he helped invent and dogmatize. He did so, however, at the cost of a theoretical split personality. Confronted with artistic colleagues who argued that plastic values took precedence over subject, and his communist friends, who called for a proletarian art, dedicated to revolution, Signac agreed with both, depending upon his audience. Writing in *L'Encyclopédie française* on the "subject in painting," he submitted that "true painting" required "new values, freed from the constraints and the servitude of external nature"— and even the subject itself. In *Commune,* the organ of the Communist-led Association of Revolutionary Artists and Writers, of which he was a founding member, he wrote that salvation of artist and country required the proletariat, "the strongest, the purest, the most noble element of our country," whose spirit must infuse each work of art.[15] To both audiences, Signac offered his scenes of radiantly lit seaports and riverbanks as examples. It was for others to resolve the contradictions in his work, as it was for him to do so in his life.

Neo-Impressionism and Its Legacy

In art history, the collapse of the Neo-Impressionist movement has not so much been analyzed as taken for granted. The failure of

15. Paul Signac, "Le Sujet en peinture," *L'Encyclopédie française* (Paris, 1935), Vol. XVI, Chap. II, 3 (*les besoins individuels et la peinture,* ref. 16.84, p. 10); Paul Signac, "Message aux artistes," *Commune,* II (1934), 1036.

Neo-Impressionism to revolutionize society through art does not demand examination, it is supposed, because any such task is destined to failure from the outset. It is not that conditions in the present justify either utter cynicism about the attempt or applause for the status quo; on the contrary, it can be argued that the need for a thoroughgoing social transformation is more compelling than ever. But the path to social change that the radical intelligentsia of the fin de siècle tried to clear has been anticipated and blocked. As Bertolt Brecht has pointed out, "Methods wear out, stimuli fail. New problems loom up and demand new techniques. Reality alters; to represent it, the means of representation must alter, too. Nothing arises from nothing; the new springs from the old, but that is just what makes it new." He added, "The oppressors do not always appear in the same mask. The masks cannot always be stripped off in the same way. There are so many tricks for dodging the mirror that is held out. . . . Yes, it takes ingenuity to change the hunter into the quarry. What was popular yesterday is no longer so today, for the people of yesterday were not the people as it is today."[16]

What especially matters is not the pseudoscientific aspect of Neo-Impressionist theory—or, rather, that must be seen in relationship to the social nexus within which that theory was born. In a period during which the Academy was shattered, during which artists had to confront the shifting demands of a newly powerful market, and during which political, economic, and social crises all but tore France apart, Neo-Impressionism seemed to offer a way out—the promise of solid ground.

Lucien Goldmann has advanced the concept of the "tragic man"—the product of a deep and ongoing rupture between humanity and its "social and spiritual world." There are moments, he argues, when the rupture seems so deep and total that many of the best and most compassionate thinkers of the day seek to deny it altogether. The tragic mind, "torn between 'Yes' and 'No,' will always scorn those who choose an intermediary position, and will remain instead on the only level [it] recognizes to be adequate: that of saying both 'Yes' *and* 'No,' of attempting to realize a synthesis." This synthesis is not the golden mean, an imagined steady solution midway between acceptance and rejection of the world as it is.

---

16. Bertolt Brecht, "The Popular and the Realistic," in *Brecht on Theatre,* ed. John Willett (New York, 1964), 110. Though apparently written between 1937 and 1938, the essay was first published in 1958.

Rather, the demand is for a *reconciliation* of polarities, in which realism is forcibly fused with the ideal. At times a clear and unambiguous synthesis is proclaimed, but the synthetic fusion is always apparent, rather than real. Eventually it collapses, and, as before, there are only the stark alternatives.[17]

The tragic mind of Goldmann's postulation was at work no less in the era of the Neo-Impressionists than in the seventeenth century of the Jansenists about which he wrote. The goal of a synthesis of the real and the ideal on some "ideally real" plane, the attempt to appraise existing society and depict the utopian alternative to it, the endeavor to render a subjective ideal objective and "scientific" (while insisting that the entire process is a reflection of an evolving universal reality)—all that is evident in the effort to tie Neo-Impressionism at some level to virtually every strand of social and aesthetic thought. Neo-Impressionism sought to function and even thrive within a social environment it found unacceptable but which it hoped to transform. As that goal proved elusive, the artists affiliated with the movement began to pull away in their own directions.

In the course of Neo-Impressionism's dissolution, its precepts in whole or, more often, in part won adherence by others, who gutted them, however, of their ideological and theoretical substance and converted them into merely stylistic mannerisms. By virtue of that, Neo-Impressionism has transmitted a formal heritage, by way of the Fauves and the Cubists.

Does Neo-Impressionism offer any heritage beyond that—in its attempt to forge an art operating in tandem with human liberation, as an interactive component of the very process of emancipation? The effort to produce such a social art is important in and of itself and is continuous with other efforts by artists to ground their art in the social struggles of their day. If Henri Matisse saw his art as a comfort to weary business leaders, his friend Maurice de Vlaminck viewed his as a legal alternative to blowing them up. Others, from Pablo Picasso to Fernand Léger, from Piet Mondrian to George Grosz, from the Mexican Muralists to the Russian Futurists to the artists of Cuba and Nicaragua—have tried to develop an art that would inspire and mobilize. Neo-Impressionism forms a primal link in that chain, in its attempt to break out from

17. Lucien Goldmann, *The Hidden God,* trans. Philip Thody (London, 1964), 41–58. See Robert Sayre, "Lucien Goldmann and the Sociology of Culture," *Praxis,* I (Winter, 1976), 129–48.

a literal realism to strike at the core of human problems and social relations.

"They tried" is not much of an epitaph for a movement. But it is necessary as well to count as part of the heritage of the Neos the art they left behind—works that can in many instances still move us, still evoke some of the spirit, whether tranquillity or outrage, that moved them to act in the way they understood best, through their art. At least some of the Neo-Impressionists also demonstrate the possibility of refusing to yield, of holding firm to one's beliefs and art in the face of savage attack. There were retreats and compromises by the Neos—van Rysselberghe's decline back to comfortable Salon portraits and Lucien Pissarro's endless fairy-tale illustrations and scenes of the Acton Railroad—but others continued to fight as best they knew how. Luce continued in his faith in the workers of his day, and Signac doggedly refused any trade in his artistic or political integrity.

In 1891, Signac predicted that a blow of the pick was about to smash the social edifice; in 1933, he still waited. In a pamphlet that year, he saluted the young artists who fought on for socialism and reminded them that he had fought for the same goals from his own youth, "in the times of Emile Henry and Vaillant." [18] If the names he invoked—Henry, Auguste Vaillant, Elisée Reclus—were obscure to young militants of the 1930s, their spirit was not. In the same year, he wrote in a short note in *Commune,* "Tout mon coeur va à la Révolution." [19] In the late twentieth century, amid the disintegration of the hopes of another generation of young rebels and the drums of the latest wars, the very maintenance of hope—and the continued fight to give reason to such hope through art, however painfully and partially—retains its vital importance.

Neo-Impressionism—like its parent political movement—often seems naïve in retrospect, an effort to guarantee that social and aesthetic upheavals would take care of themselves. Its relationship to the poor whom it depicted so often was not organic but philanthropic—for, not of, the poor. The relationship proved fragile; the strands of Neo-Impressionist thought failed over time to cohere, and the movement foundered.

18. "Nonetheless, I would have so much to say. For it is very hard at my age to see everything one has worked for or fought for all one's life fall apart. I refer to my youth when I stood with Reclus, in the time of Emile Henry and Vaillant" ("Signac," in *Ceux qui ont choisi: Contre le fascisme en Allemagne, contre l'impérialisme en France* [Paris, n.d. (1933?)], 23).

19. Paul Signac, "Note," *Commune,* I (1933), 95.

What the Neos leave behind is not their theories, which have been superseded, but their aspirations, which remain unfulfilled. It is worthwhile looking again at Signac's lithograph *Les Démolisseurs* (Figure 1). As an image, it has outlived the frailties and errors of the Neos. It can still speak to us. The edifice at which the workers hack away still stands; it has proved far more resilient than Signac predicted. The workers still stand in darkness. But behind them, the sun rises. It always rises.

Appendix
Impressionists and Revolutionaries,
by "an Impressionist Comrade"

A few weeks ago, at the Exhibition of Independent Artists, you could hear before the canvases of the Impressionist painters exclamations by characters whose incurable vulgarity the great ironist Forain depicted so well; and as though to make up for it, on Sunday, some intrigued proletarians showed their interest.

The jeering ill will of the first group and the sympathetic reserve of the second can be explained by the revolutionary tendency of the Impressionist painters. Technically, they are innovators: they replace with a logical and scientific arrangement of tones and colors the outmoded methods—the meticulous mixtures on the palette, the glazings too long honored, and the heavy impastos that are most often the sign of a false impetuosity. Morally, they give an all too rare example to our pleasure-seeking epoch: faithful to their artistic ideal, convinced of the superiority of their way of painting, they remain poor while they could, like so many others, receive in exchange for a few concessions the praises of the hackneyed and powerful critics whose stale prose translates into beautiful gold coins, honors, and decorations for the artist.

For these reasons alone the Impressionist artists, banished from art as revolutionaries are from current society, would deserve a sympathetic salute from everyone who applauds the collapse of all prejudices and routines. But they are entitled to this honor for a more important reason: their works, resulting from a purely aesthetic emotion produced by the picturesque quality of things and beings, have the same social, unconscious dimension that has already marked contemporary literature. Novels by Flaubert, the Goncourt brothers, Zola, and their emulators, written with a purely literary aim in mind, according to lived experience, have served the revolutionary cause much more potently than all the novels in which political preoccupations take precedence over the literary aspect.

Two examples: *Germinal,* whose influence on contemporary

Translated by Alan Astro from *La Révolte,* IV (June 13–19, 1891). Paul Signac is the "Impressionist Comrade."

minds has been undeniable and which has in several circumstances furthered proletarian demands (remember the Basly election and, when strikes followed, the subscriptions to which individuals contributed who until then had been indifferent to the social moment); and *The Sentimental Education,* in which the aristocratic and skeptical Flaubert, seized by the truth, bears eloquent witness to the ignominious and bloodthirsty cruelty of the victors in the June, 1848, insurrection.

From the revolutionary point of view, one can hardly deny that these works are superior to the moralistic novels of George Sand and Eugène Sue or to the vast joke [*fumisterie*] entitled *Les Misérables,* a novel read by all bourgeois which could only strengthen their acceptance of the principles of which Jean Valjean is the apostle:

1. Hasten to make a fortune.
2. Speculate on the work of others.
3. Establish institutions, nurseries, homes for the aged when you definitely have far too much and can no longer enjoy it (the Boucicault, Chachard, Pruvot & Co. system).

In the same book are found the meager escapades of petty youth convinced that the Revolution of 1789 took place to allow their daddies to buy national properties. Come the insurrection, and they will not swell the ranks of rebels but will instead put up useless barricades just for the fun of it.

Setting aside literary writings, if we return to artistic testimony, we note something analogous. Millet, remaining a peasant, completely taken up with his art, produced a work with a far more pronounced social dimension than some canvas with philosophical pretensions by the thinker and painter Courbet—to take as an example an artist of comparable tendency.

At this moment, at the National Exhibition of Fine Arts, there is on display a small watercolor by Meissonnier, *The Barricade,* which is a terrible accusation against the social state established one hundred years ago by the bourgeoisie. The riot is quelled; in a desolate street bodies lie mutilated amid paving stones and broken barrels; faces are contracted in supreme agony; the blouse of the rebel grazes the red pants of the soldier of the line. Your heart is rent before this scene summarily shown by a few pen strokes heightened by a bit of color, for you feel something has been seen and rendered in complete sincerity by an artist who was simply attracted to the strangeness of the scene and the effect of its colorations. For Meissonier was a bourgeois who carried his hatred of the socialists to the point of banning Courbet from the official Salon after the Commune took place, because the Ornans painter had participated in the insurrection of March 18.

It would thus be a mistake—committed all too often by the best-intentioned revolutionaries, like Proudhon—to make it a standard demand that works of art have a precise socialist thrust, for that thrust will appear more strongly and eloquently in the pure aesthetes, revolutionaries by temperament, who leave the beaten path to paint what they see, as they feel it, and who very often unconsciously deal a solid blow of the pick to the old social edifice that, worm-eaten, cracks and crumbles like an old, deconsecrated cathedral.

You could easily notice this in the works that the Impressionist painters sent to the Exhibition of Independents. By their new technique, diametrically opposed to the hallowed rules, they showed the vanity of inalterable practices. By their picturesque studies of the workers' blocks of Saint-Ouen and Montrouge, solid and dazzling, by the reproduction of the broad and curiously colored movements of a laborer next to a sandpile, of a smith in the incandescence of a forge, or better yet, by the synthetic representation of decadent pleasures—balls, *chahuts,* circuses (as in the case of Seurat, who had such a vivid awareness of the debasement of the epoch in transition)—they brought their testimony to the great social proceeding under way between workers and capital.

Now, it is incontestable that the reproduction of such subjects prompts a more sincere feeling for justice and more far-ranging reflection than a melodramatic composition representing an "unhappy family," where the father has an Italian-style beard, the mother a virginal face, and the children cherubic hair, in the midst of tawdry finery and comic-opera props; or than the vast decorations made for city and town halls, many of which can be seen at the Salon of the Champ de Mars, in which the artists paint, besides episodes from the war and the siege, the hard labors taking place at work sites and in factories. Such commissioned scenes, painted by those who care not at all for the republic and the people, leave the viewer unmoved, for there emanates from them neither art nor conviction. The proof: for ten years, patriotic groups have been depicted by a sculptor who during the war boasted of his receipt of the Rome Prize, so as not to have to go to the enemy.

For these reasons, only artists gripped by pure art, and in particular the Impressionist painters, whose technique is the negation of old artistic routines, deserve the entire accord of those who applaud the collapse of outmoded prejudices.

I exclude the Symbolist-Impressionists, who, confining themselves to retrograde subjects, fall back into the old vagaries and forget that art consists much more in searching into the future than in disinterring the legends of the past, no matter how golden they may be.

Sooner or later, true artists will be found on the side of the rebels, united with them in one and the same idea of justice.

Selected Bibliography

Sources from the Period

"A la maison du peuple de Paris." *Revue socialiste,* XXII (1895), 610–12.

Adam, Paul. *Critique des moeurs.* Paris, 1893.

———. "Critique du socialisme et de l'anarchie." *Revue blanche,* XIX (1893), 370–76.

———. "Les Peintres impressionnistes." *Revue contemporaine,* IV (1886), 541–51.

Ajalbert, Jean. "Le Salon des impressionnistes." *Revue moderne,* XXX (1886), 385–93.

Alavaill, Justin. "Symbolisme socialiste." In *Almanach de la question sociale pour 1897,* 103–107. Paris, 1897.

Albert, Charles. "A M. Emile Zola." *Les Temps nouveaux,* III (January 29–February 4, 1896), 1–2.

———. "A Propos de Rodin." *Les Temps nouveaux,* IV (June 11–17, 1898), 2.

———. "L'Art et la Société." *L'Art socidl,* n.s., VI (1896), 161–73.

———. "Art et Société." *Les Temps nouveaux,* I (November 23–29, 1895), 1–2.

———. "Entreprendre une définition de l'art." *Les Temps nouveaux,* X (September 17–23, 1904), 4–5, (October 1–7, 1904), 2–3.

———. *Qu'est-ce que l'art?* Paris, 1909.

———. "La 21° Exposition des Artistes Indépendants." *Les Temps nouveaux,* X (April 8–14, 1905), 6–7.

Antoine, Jules. "Dubois-Pillet." *La Plume,* LVII (1891), 299.

"L'Art." *L'Idée,* 2nd ser., I (September 15, 1894), 47.

"L'Art communiste." *La Révolte,* VII (December 25–31, 1893), 1–2.

"L'Art et le Socialisme." *L'Art moderne,* XI (1891), 275–77.

"L'Art social." *L'Art social,* I (1891), 1.

Atôme [pseud.]. "La Révolution dans les Beaux-Arts." *Le Libertaire,* 3rd ser., VII (June 29–July 6, 1901), 4–5.

"Aux artistes." *La Révolte,* VII (December 9–16, 1893), 1–2.

Baffier, Jean. "L'Art c'est la vie." *L'Enclos,* III (June, 1895), 33–36.

Baju, Anatole. *L'Anarchie littéraire.* Paris, 1904.

Barrucand, Victor. *Avec le feu: Roman.* Paris, 1900.

Bataille, Albert. *Causes criminelles et mondaines de 1894: Les Procès anarchistes.* Paris, 1895.

Batilliat, Marcel. "Le Naturalisme et l'Art social." *L'Art social,* II (1892), 84–86.

Bazalgette, Léon. "Naturalisme et Naturisme: Emile Zola devant l'esprit nouveau." *L'Humanité nouvelle,* III, 77–82, 327–36.

Beaume, Georges. "L'Art social." *Revue socialiste,* XIV (1891), 730–32.

Bérenger, Henry. "L'Art, la Science et la Démocratie." *Essais d'art libre,* I (February, 1892), 1–10.

Bernier, Robert. "Le Socialisme et l'Art." *Revue socialiste,* XIII (1891), 599–604.

Berrichon, Paterne. "Sur la peinture." *Le Libertaire,* II (December 28, 1895–January 4, 1896), 4, (January 4–11, 1896), 4.

Berth, Edouard. "Anarchisme individualiste, Marxisme orthodoxe et Syndicalisme révolutionnaire." *Le Mouvement socialiste,* No. 154 (May 1, 1905), 5–35.

———. *Dialogues socialistes.* Paris, 1901.

Bouchor, Maurice. *La Maison du peuple: Scène dramatique.* Paris, 1910.

———. "La Muse et l'Ouvrier: Dialogue." *Revue socialiste,* XXX (1899), 515–26.

Brieu, Jacques. "L'Art intégral." *La Plume,* C (1893), 263–64.

C.B. [pseud.]. "Art et Socialisme." *Le Socialiste,* April 10, 1886, p. 2.

C.B. [pseud.]. "Socialisme et Art." *Le Socialiste,* December 4, 1886, p. 2.

Calmeilles, Charles. *Quelques Considérations sur l'anarchie: Ses causes, ses effets, le remède.* Tours, 1895.

Cammaerts, E. "A propos de l'art et la révolution de Richard Wagner." *L'Humanité nouvelle,* IV (January, 1899), 43–50.

Caraguel, Joseph. "Les Groupes révolutionnaires." *Revue indépendante,* II (1884), 1–15.

Catonné, Amédée. "L'Art et l'Etat." *Les Temps nouveaux,* X (January 21–27, 1905), 1–2.

———. "Aux Indépendants." *Les Temps nouveaux,* X (April 15–20, 1905), 6–7.

Chevrier, G. "Banqueroute." *Revue indépendante,* II (1884), 91–98.

Christophe, Jules. "Georges Seurat." *La Plume,* LVII (1891), 292.

Cipriani, Amilcare. "Démolissons!" *Le Plébéian,* II (September 1–15, 1895), 2–3.

"Club de l'art social." *Annales artistiques et littéraires,* II (1889), 320, 384.

"Club de l'art social: Statutes." *Annales artistiques et littéraires,* II (1889), 288.

Coustourier, Edmond. "L'Art dans la société future." *Entretiens politiques et littéraires,* V (1892), 212–18.

———. "Notes d'art." *Entretiens politiques et littéraires,* VI (1893), 75–77, 331–33.

Crane, Walter. "L'Art et les Artistes." *La Plume,* IX (1893), 212–13.

———. "Le Socialisme et les Artistes." *La Révolte,* V (1892), Literary Supplement, 1–2.

Crépin, Georges. "L'Art et le Socialisme." *Le Socialiste,* January 27, 1894, p. 2.

Darien, Georges. "Maximilien Luce." *La Plume,* VII (1891), 299–300.

Darzens, Rodolphe. "Chronique artistique: Exposition des Impressionnistes." *La Pléiade,* I (1886), 85–91.

"De l'art." *L'Enclos,* II (December, 1896), 35–36.

Delon, A. "Pessimisme et Socialisme." *Revue socialiste,* XII (1890), 677–91.

Delville, Jean. "Art et Socialisme." *La Jeune Belgique,* n.s., I (1896), 339–41.

Demolder, Eugène. "Constantin Meunier." *La Société nouvelle,* V (1889), 47–55.

Denauroy, Jean. "Exposition Claude Monet." *Les Temps nouveaux,* X (May 21–27, 1904), 6.

————. "Exposition Maximilien Luce et Notes sur le paysage." *Les Temps nouveaux*, XII (March 2, 1907), 6–7.

Deshhairs, Léon. "Chronique artistique: Puvis de Chavannes." *Le Mouvement socialiste*, II (1899), 178.

Destrée, Jules. *Art et Socialisme*. Brussels, 1896.

————. "Chronique artistique: L'Exposition des XX." *La Jeune Belgique*, VI (1887), 130–34.

Dhure, Pierre. "Art." *Journal du peuple*, February 26, 1899, p. 3, March 23, 1899, pp. 2–3, April 7, 1899, p. 2, April 23, 1899, p. 2.

Diamandy, Georges. "Déclaration." *L'Ere nouvelle*, I (July 1, 1893), 1–11.

Doublier [pseud.]. "L'Art et la Révolte." *La Voix du peuple*, VI (August 15–21, 1906), 2.

Drumont, Edouard. *De l'or, de la boue, du sang: Du Panama à l'anarchie*. Paris, 1895.

————. *La Fin d'un monde: Etude psychologique et sociale*. Paris, 1889.

Dubois, Félix. *Le Péril anarchiste*. Paris, 1894.

Dunois, Amédée. "L'Anarchisme ouvrière." *L'Action directe*, I (January 29, 1908), 1–2.

Ehrly, Charles Jacques. "La Nature et la Vie dans la peinture." *Le Libertaire*, VII (February 3–9, 1901), 13–14.

F. Fagus, "Louis Hayet." *Revue blanche*, XXIX (1903), 619.

Faure, Sebastien. *Almanach anarchiste pour 1892*. Paris, 1892.

————. *"Mon Communisme": Le Bonheur universel*. Paris, 1921.

Fénéon, Félix. *Oeuvres plus que complètes*. Edited by Joan Halperin. 2 vols. Geneva, 1970.

Fèvre, Henry. *Etude sur le Salon de 1886 et sur l'Exposition des Impressionistes*. Paris, 1886.

Fierens-Gevaert, Hippolyte. *La Tristesse contemporaine: Essai sur les grands courants moreaux et intellectuels*. Paris, 1899.

Flaustier, P. "Le Symbolisme pseudo-libertaire." *Le Plébéian*, II (September 1–15, 1895), 1–2.

————. "Travestissement symbolique." *Le Plébéian*, II (October 6–20, 1895), 3.

Flor, Charles [Flor O'Squarr]. *Les Coulisses de l'anarchie*. Paris, 1892.

Fournière, Eugène. "Les Fêtes du peuple." *L'Humanité*, July 10, 1905, pp. 1–2.

Freddis [pseud.]. "Notes sur l'art." *Revue socialiste*, XV (1892), 457–59.

Gamp, T. "Why We Are Anarchists." *Torch*, n.s., V (October 31, 1894), 1–2.

Garraud, R. *L'Anarchie et la Répression*. Paris, 1895.

Geffroy, Gustave. "Chronique: Pointillé-Cloisonnisme." *La Justice*, April 11, 1888, p. 1.

————. "Chronique d'art: Indépendants." *Revue d'aujourd'hui*, I (1890), 267–70.

————. *Musée du soir aux quartiers ouvriers*. Paris, 1895.

Gérault-Richard, Alfred Léon. "Individualistes." *Le Chambard socialiste*, II (August 11, 1894), 2.

Germain, Alphonse. "Aux intellectuels." *Entretiens politiques et littéraires*, II (1891), 40–44.

————. "Théorie chromo-luminariste: Exposé et Critique." *La Plume,* LVII (1891), 285–87.

Gervaise [pseud.]. "Le Salon de 1889." *L'Attaque,* II (May 11–18, 1889), 1–2.

————. "Tentative de théâtre social." *Le Socialiste,* February 8, 1894, p. 4.

Ghil, René. "L'Art humain." In *Almanach de la question sociale pour 1897,* 92–94. Paris, 1897.

————. "L'Organisme-Humanité." *L'Enclos,* I (April, 1895), 6–10.

Gilkin, Ivan. "L'Art social." *La Jeune Belgique,* n.s., I (1896), 67–69.

Girard, André. "L'Art de masses." *Le Libertaire,* II (February 15–22, 1896), 2.

————. "L'Art du peuple." *Les Temps nouveaux,* IV (July 2–8, 1898), 1.

————. "Art nouveau." *Les Temps nouveaux,* I (May 11–17, 1895), 2.

————. "Art officiel." *Les Temps nouveaux,* III (February 12–18, 1898), 1–2.

————. "Le Droit à la beauté." *Les Temps nouveaux,* V (May 27–June 2, 1899), 2.

Giraud, Albert. "Etudes d'esthétique: I. L'Art social." *La Jeune Belgique,* II (1882–83), 369–79.

Goldberg, Mécislas. "Idéalisme social." *Mercure de France,* XVI (1895), 364–69.

Gourmont, Remy de. "Pour l'individualisme (contre le communisme et le collectivisme)." *L'Action,* I (1896), 1.

Grave, Jean. "L'Art dans la société bourgeoise: L'Oeuvre par M. Emile Zola." *La Révolte,* VIII (June 19–25, 1886), 4, (July 17–23, 1886), 3–4, (August 21–27, 1886), 3–4.

————. *L'Individu et la Société.* Paris, 1897.

————. *Malfaiteurs! Roman.* Paris, 1903.

————. *Moribund Society and Anarchy.* Translated by Voltairine de Cleyre. San Francisco, 1899.

————. *Le Mouvement libertaire sous la troisième république.* Paris, 1930.

————. *Réformes, Révolution.* Paris, 1910.

————. *La Société future.* Paris, 1895.

————. *Terre libre: Les Pionniers.* Paris, 1908.

————. "La Thèse dans l'art." *Les Temps nouveaux,* V (November 18–24, 1899), 1–2.

Griffuelhes, Victor. "Le Syndicalisme révolutionnaire." *Le Mouvement socialiste,* VI (1905), 1–17.

Guebhard, Caroline Remy [Séverine]. *Notes d'une frondeuse: De la boulange au Panama.* Paris, 1894.

————. *Pages rouges.* Paris, 1893.

Guesde, Jules. *Contre les lois scélérates.* Lille, 1894.

Hamon, Augustin. "The March of Socialism in France." *Free Review,* IV (1895), 385–96.

————. *Psychologie de l'anarchiste socialiste.* Paris, 1895.

Hamon, Augustin, and Georges Bachot. *L'Agonie d'une société: Histoire d'aujourd'hui.* Paris, 1889.

Harrison, Frederic. "A Breakfast Party in Paris." *Nineteenth Century,* XXVI (1889), 173–85.

Henry, Charles. "Cercle chromatique et Sensation de couleur." *Revue indépendante*, 3rd ser., V (1888), 73–90.

———. "L'Esthétique des formes." *Revue blanche*, VII (1894), 118–29, 308–22, 511–25, VIII (1895), 117–20.

———. "Harmonie de couleurs." *Revue indépendante*, 3rd ser., VII (1888), 458–78.

Hervé, Gustave. *Vers la révolution.* Paris, 1908.

Howe, Frederic C. "Conquering a Nation with Bread." *Outlook*, XCIV (1910), 682–89.

Huret, Jules. *Enquête sur l'évolution littéraire.* Paris, 1891.

Hurlbert, William Henry. "A Republic in Extremis." *Fortnightly Review*, n.s., XLVI (1889), 633–49.

Huysmans, Joris Karl. *Oeuvres complètes.* 18 vols. Paris, 1928–34.

Jaurès, Jean. "L'Art et le Socialisme." *Le Mouvement socialiste*, III (1900), 513–25, 582–90.

Jourdain, Francis. "L'Art officiel." *La Révolte*, VI (1893), Literary Supplement, 77-78.

———. "Ce que présent les artistes." *La Révolte*, VI (1893), Literary Supplement, 74.

———. "Les Salons de 1899." *Journal du peuple*, May 1, 1899, p. 2.

Kahn, Gustave. "Au temps du pointillisme." *Mercure de France*, CLXXI (1924), 5–23.

———. "Paul Signac." *Mercure de France*, No. 263 (1935), 168–72.

———. "Seurat." *L'Art moderne*, XI (1891), 107–110.

———. *Symbolistes et Décadents.* Paris, 1902.

———. "La Vie artistique." *La Vie moderne*, IX (1887), 229–31.

Kahn, Gustave, and Félix Fénéon. "Le Courrier social." *La Vogue*, I (April 4, 1886), 27–28.

Kropotkin[e], Peter [Pierre]. *Fields, Factories, and Workshops.* 1899; London, 1974.

———. *Memoirs of a Revolutionist.* 1899; rpr. New York, 1971.

———. *Modern Science and Anarchism.* London, 1912.

———. *Mutual Aid: A Factor of Evolution.* 1902; rpr. Boston, 1914.

———. *Paroles d'un révolté.* Paris, 1885.

———. *Revolutionary Pamphlets.* Edited by Roger N. Baldwin, New York, 1927.

———. *Selected Writings on Anarchism and Revolution.* Edited by Martin A. Miller. Cambridge, Mass., 1970.

———. *Les Temps nouveaux: Conférence faite à Londres.* Paris, 1894.

Lambart, Jean. "Les Formes de l'art et le Socialisme." *Revue socialiste*, I (1885), 329–39.

La Salle, Gabriel de. *Les Révoltes: Luttes stériles.* Paris, 1892.

Lazare, Bernard. "Ce que nous pensons." *L'Action*, I (1896), 1.

———. "L'Ecrivain et l'Art social." *L'Art social*, n.s., I (1896), 7–14.

———. *Figures contemporains, ceux d'aujourd'hui, ceux de demain.* Paris, 1895.

———. "Nouvelle Monarchie." *Entretiens politiques et littéraires*, III (1891), 160–64.

Lebey, André. "Mouvement artistique: L'Art et le Socialisme." *Revue socialiste,* LVI (1912), 460–76, 545–62.

Leblond, Marius-Ary. "L'Anarchiste dans le roman français." *Revue socialiste,* XXXVIII (1903), 185–213.

————. "L'Idéal artistique du socialisme et son élaboration au XIXe siècle." *Revue socialiste,* XXXVII (1902), 66–81, 181–202.

Lemonnier, Camille. "Constantin Meunier." *Le Coq rouge,* II (1896–97), 337–42.

————. *La Fin des bourgeois.* Paris, 1892.

————. *Happe-Chair.* Paris, 1886.

————. *Les Peintres de la vie.* Paris, 1888.

Lombroso, Cesare. *Les Anarchistes.* Translated by M. Hamel and A. Marie. Paris, 1898.

Lorulot, André. *Une Révolution: Est-elle possible?* Paris, 1910.

Louis, Paul. "The Present State of French Socialism." *New Review,* I (1913), 101–106.

"Les Machines." *La Lutte sociale* (Lyon), I (September 18, 1886), 2.

Mackay, John Henry. *The Anarchists: A Picture of Civilization at the Close of the Nineteenth Century.* Boston, 1891.

Malato, Charles. *L'Homme nouveau.* Paris, 1898.

————. *Philosophie de l'anarchie, 1888–1897.* 3rd ed. Paris, 1897.

————. "Some Anarchist Portraits." *Fortnightly Review,* n.s., LXII (1894), 315–33.

Mallarmé, Stéphane. *Oeuvres complètes.* 2 vols. Paris, 1945.

Malon, Benoît. "Socialisme réformiste." *Revue socialiste,* II (1885), 881–906.

————. "L'Utopie dans l'histoire." *Revue socialiste,* XVIII (1893), 129–57.

Marki, Charles. "Art social." *Mercure de France,* VII (1893), 370–73.

Martí, José. "A New Exhibition of Impressionist Painters." In *On Art and Literature by José Martí: Critical Writings,* translated by Elinor Randall, edited by Philip S. Foner, 118–24. New York, 1982.

Martinet, Octave. "Evolution et Révolution." *L'Enclos,* II (May, 1895), 17–20.

Massard, Emile. "L'Art et le Socialisme." *L'Attaque,* I (June 20–27, 1888), 2.

Mauclair, Camille. "Les Impressionistes." *Annales artistiques et littéraires,* I (1889), 265–68.

————. "L'Oeuvre sociale de l'art moderne: Les Beaux-Arts." *Revue socialiste,* XXXIV (1901), 421–35.

Maussa [pseud.]. "Le Théâtre socialiste." *Le Socialiste,* December 1, 1895, p. 3.

Mazade, Charles de. "Chronique de la quinzaine." *Revue des deux mondes,* XCI (1889), 226–36.

Mazel, Henri. "L'Anarchisme." *Essais d'art libre,* I (1892), 198–207.

Mirbeau, Octave. "L'Art bourgeois." *La Révolte,* VI (1893), Literary Supplement, 43.

————. "Camille Pissarro." *L'Art dans les deux mondes,* VIII (January 10, 1891), 83–84.

————. *Des artistes: Peintres et Sculpteurs.* 2 vols. 1922–24; Paris, 1986.

————. *Les Mauvais Bergers: Pièce en cinq actes.* Paris, 1898.

Mockel, Albert. "L'Art social: Les Symbolistes." *La Wallonie,* I (1886), 142–49.

Monatte, Pierre. "Syndicalisme et Anarchisme." In *Congrès anarchiste tenu à Amsterdam, août, 1907,* 62–71. Paris, 1908.

Mordod, Gabriel. "The Political Situation in France." *Contemporary Review,* XLVII (1895), 592–608.

Mornas, Antoine. "L'Anarchie et les Artistes." *Les Temps nouveaux,* I (March 14–20, 1896), 2–3.

Mourey, Gabriel. *Passé de Detroit: La Vie et l'Art à Londres.* Paris, 1895.

Museux, Ernest. "Mission." *L'Art social,* I (1891), 26–28.

Natanson, Thadée. "Primitif d'aujourd'hui: Georges Seurat." *Revue blanche,* XXI (1900), 609–14.

"Les Néo-Impressionnistes." *L'Escarmouche,* II (January 7, 1894).

Nettlau, Max. *Bibliographie de l'anarchie.* Brussels, 1897.

Nordau, Max. *Entartung.* 2 vols. Berlin, 1892–93.

Olin, Pierre. "Les XX." *Mercure de France,* IV (1892), 341–45.

"Opinions d'artiste." *L'Escarmouche,* I (November 19, 1893).

Péladan, Joséphin. *L'Art idéaliste et mystique: Doctrine de l'ordre.* 10th ed. Paris, 1894.

————. *Le Décadence esthétique.* Paris, 1888.

————. "Etudes esthétiques de décadence: Gustave Courbet." *L'Artiste,* LIV (1884), 406–12.

Pelloutier, Fernand. *L'Art et la Révolte.* Paris, 1896.

————. *Histoire des bourses du travail.* Paris, 1902.

Pert, Camille. *En anarchie: Roman.* Paris, 1901.

Picard, Edmond. "L'Art et la Révolution." *La Société nouvelle,* II (1886), 208–31.

————. "Un Nouveau Moyen-Age." *L'Art moderne,* X (1890), 9–11.

————. "La Socialisation de l'art." *L'Art moderne,* XV (1895), 98–100, 109, 116.

Pissarro, Camille. *Correspondance.* Edited by Janine Bailly-Herzberg. 5 vols. projected. Paris, 1980–.

————. *Lettres à son fils Lucien.* Edited by John Rewald. Paris, 1947.

————. *Turpitudes sociales.* Geneva, 1972.

Pissarro, Lucien. "Art et Société." *Les Temps nouveaux,* I (December 7–13, 1895), 1–2.

Plekhanoff[nov], Georges[gi]. *Anarchisme et Socialisme.* Paris, 1897.

————. *Writings on Aesthetics.* Moscow, 1981. Vol. V of Plekhanov, *Selected Philosophical Works.* 5 vols.

Poey, André. *L'Anarchie mondiale: Sa psychologie morbide.* 2nd ed. Paris, 1912.

Ponthière, Maurice. *La Maison du peuple.* Reims, 1906.

Por, Odon. "The New University of Brussels." *International Socialist Review,* VII (1906), 209–20.

Portal, Emile. "De la responsabilité sociale des écrivains." *L'Art social,* III (1894), 7–10.

Pouget, Emile, and Francis de Pressensé. *Les Lois scélérates de 1893–1894.* Paris, 1899.

Pratelle, Aristide. *Les Résolutions: Poésies sociales*. Paris, 1902.

————. "Vulgarisons la beauté." *Les Temps nouveaux*, XII (February 9, 1907), 2, (February 16, 1907), 2–3.

Un Prolétaire. "L'Exploitation universelle en 1878." *L'Egalité*, May 12, 1878, pp. 1–2, June 2, 1878, pp. 4–5.

Proudhon, Pierre Joseph. *Du principe de l'art et de sa destination sociale*. Paris, 1865.

"Question d'art." *La Révolte*, IV (July 10–17, 1891), 2.

Quillard, Pierre. "L'Anarchie par la littérature." *Entretiens politiques et littéraires*, IV (1892), 149–51.

Reclus, Elisée. "Anarchy: By an Anarchist." *Contemporary Review*, XLV (1884), 627–41.

————. "L'Art et le Peuple." In *Almanach de la révolution pour 1904*, 21–25. Paris, 1904.

————. "Aux compagnons rédacteurs des *Entretiens*." *Entretiens politiques et littéraires*, IV (1892), 3–6.

————. *L'Evolution, la Révolution et l'Idéal anarchique*. Paris, 1898.

————. "The Evolution of Cities." *Contemporary Review*, LXVII (1895), 246–64.

————. "Pourquoi nous sommes anarchistes!" *La Société nouvelle*, V (1889), 153–55.

————. "The Progress of Mankind." *Contemporary Review*, LXX (1896), 761–83.

"Un Réferendum: Artistique et social." *L'Ermitage*, VII (July, 1893), 1–24.

Renard, Georges. *Paroles d'avenir*. Paris, 1904.

"Réponse à quelques objections." *L'Etendard révolutionnaire*, I (October 8, 1882), 3.

"Réponse d'une artiste." *La Révolte*, VII (December 30, 1893–January 5, 1894), 1–2.

Retté, Adolphe. "L'Art et l'Anarchie." *La Plume*, XCI (1893), 1–2.

————. *Promenades subversives*. Paris, 1896.

————. *Réflexions sur l'anarchie*. Paris, 1894.

————. *Le Règne de la bête*. Paris, 1908.

Robin, Maurice. *L'Art et le Peuple*. Paris, 1910.

Rochel, Clement. "L'Art et la Vie," *L'Art social*, III (1893), 73–79.

Rosny, J. H. *Les Ames perdues*. Paris, 1899.

————. "Anarchy in Paris." *Harper's Weekly*, XXXIX (1895), 967–69.

————. *Le Bilatéral: Moeurs révolutionnaires parisiennes*. Paris, 1887.

Rossetti, Olivia, and Helen Rossetti [Isabel Meredith]. *A Girl Among the Anarchists*. London, 1903.

Saint-Auban, Emile de. *L'Idée sociale au théâtre*. Paris, 1901.

Sanborn, Alvan F. *Paris and the Social Revolution: A Study of the Revolutionary Elements in the Various Classes of Parisian Society*. Boston, 1905.

Saunier, C. "Louis Hayet." *Revue blanche*, XXVII (1902), 621.

Sautarel, Jacques. "L'Ouvrier d'art." *Le Libertaire*, 3rd ser., VII (June 29–July 6, 1901), 6–7.

Schaack, Michael J. *Anarchy and Anarchists: A History of the Red Terror and the Social Revolution in America and Europe*. Chicago, 1889.

Signac, Paul. *D'Eugène Delacroix au néo-impressionnisme.* 1899; Paris, 1978.

———. "Extraits du journal inédit de Paul Signac." Edited by John Rewald. *Gazette des beaux-arts,* 6th ser., XXXVI (1949), 97–128, XXXIX (1952), 265–84, XLII (1953), 27–57.

———. "Fragments du journal." *Arts de France,* XI (1947), 97–102, XVII–XVIII (1949), 75–82.

——— [Un Impressioniste Camarade]. "Impressionistes et Révolutionnaires." *La Révolte,* IV (June 13–19, 1891), 3–4.

——— [Néo]. "A minuit: IVᵉ Exposition des artistes indépendantes." *Le Cri du peuple,* 2nd ser., V (March 29, 1888), 3.

——— [Néo]. "A minuit: Les XX." *Le Cri du peuple,* 2nd ser., V (February 9, 1888), 3.

Sorel, Georges. "Contributions psycho-physiques à l'esthétique." *Revue philosophique,* XXIX (1890), 561–79.

———. "Esthétique et Psychophysique." *Revue philosophique,* XXIX (1890), 182–84.

———. *Reflections on Violence.* Translated by T. E. Hulme. 1907; rpr. New York, 1961.

Souvraz, Laurentine. "A tous: Les Beautés de la nature." *Le Libertaire,* II (March 7–14, 1896), 2.

"Statutes de la Théâtre d'Art Social." *L'Art social,* II (February, 1892), back cover.

Stiegler, Gaston. "Chronique théâtralé." *Revue socialiste,* XXVII (1898), 99–102.

Sulzberger, Max. "La Démocratie et l'Art." *La Société nouvelle,* IV (1888), 256–64.

———. *Le Réalisme en France et en Belgique: Courbet et de Groux.* Brussels, 1874.

Tabarant, Adolphe. "Chronique: A la maison du peuple." *La Petite République,* July 9, 1894, p. 1.

———. "Le Club de l'art social." *Revue socialiste,* II (1890), 101–106.

———. "Impressions quotidiennes." *La Petite République,* December 16, 1894, p. 1.

"Théâtre social." *Revue socialiste,* XXXI (1895), 500–502.

Thébault, Eugène. "L'Art social." *L'Art social,* II (1892), 179–81.

"The Trial of the Thirty." *Freedom,* VIII (October, 1894), 1.

"The Trial of the Thirty." *Spectator,* LXXIII (August 18, 1894), 200–201.

van de Velde, Henry. "Georges Seurat." *La Wallonie,* V (1890), 167–71.

Vandervelde, Emile. "A quoi servent les intellectuels?" *Le Socialiste,* n.s., XXIII (March 3–10, 1907), 1–2.

———. "Art Under Capitalism." *Socialist Review,* IV (September, 1909), 9–17.

———. "Constantin Meunier." *Die neue Gesellschaft,* I (April 12, 1905), 19–20.

———. *Essais socialistes.* Paris, 1906.

van Gogh, Vincent. *The Letters of Vincent van Gogh.* Edited by Mark Roskill. New York, 1982.

Vanzype, Gustave. "Constantin Meunier." *L'Art et les Artistes,* I (June, 1905), 120–23.

Veidaux, André. "L'Art individualiste." *L'Art social,* II (1892), 100–101.

———. "Le Néant de l'art bourgeois." *Revue libertaire,* II (1894), 45–47, 67–69.

Verhaeren, Emile. "Chronique artistique: L'Exposition Meunier au cercle artistique." *La Jeune Belgique,* III (1883–84), 111–13.

———. "Exposition Maximilien Luce." *Revue blanche,* XX (1899), 309–11.

———. "Henri-Edmond Cross." *Nouvelle Revue française,* IV (July, 1910), 44.

———. "Le Salon des XX à Bruxelles." *La Vie moderne,* IX (1887), 135–39.

———. *Les Villes tentaculaires.* Brussels, 1895.

Verland, Ernest. "Chronique artistique: Le Salon des XX." *La Jeune Belgique,* XI (1892), 188–94.

Vertpré, R. "De l'évolution de l'art." *Le Libertaire,* 3rd ser., VII (February 9–16, 1901), 3.

Villatte, Louis. "L'Art social." *Le Décadent,* III (September 1–30, 1888), 8–11.

Vizatelly, Ernest Alfred. *The Anarchists.* New York, 1911.

Waller, Max. "Chronique artistique: L'Exposition des XX." *La Jeune Belgique,* IV (1884–85), 222–29.

Weil, Lucien. "Vive la banqueroute!" *L'Attaque,* II (June 15–22, 1889), 1.

———. "Vive le machinisme!" *L'Attaque,* II (July 25–August 3, 1889), 3.

Wilde, Oscar. *The Soul of Man Under Socialism.* Chicago, 1984.

Zenker, E. V. *Anarchism: A Criticism and a History of the Anarchist Theory.* London: 1898.

Zisly, Henry. "La Littérature libertaire." *Le Plébéian,* II (October 6–20, 1895), 3.

Modern and Secondary Sources

Angrand, Pierre. *Naissance des artistes indépendants, 1884.* Paris, 1965.

Arbeit und Alltag: Soziale Wirklichkeit in der belgischen Kunst, 1830–1914. West Berlin, 1979.

Architecture pour le peuple: Maisons du peuple. Brussels, 1984.

Argüelles, José A. *Charles Henry and the Formation of a Psychophysical Aesthetic.* Chicago, 1972.

Arte e socialità in Italia dal realismo al simbolismo. Milan, 1979.

Aubrey, Pierre. "The Anarchism of the Literati of the Symbolist Period." *French Review,* XLII (October, 1968), 39–47.

Bailly-Herzberg, Janine, and Aline Dardel. "Lucien Pissarro et les Illustrations françaises." *Nouvelles de l'estampe,* No. 54 (November–December, 1980), 8–16.

Baker, Anthony S. "Fernand Pelloutier and the Making of Revolutionary Syndicalism." In *Essays on Modern European Revolutionary History,* edited by Bede K. Lackner and Kenneth Roy Philip, 39–69. Austin, Tex., 1977.

Barrows, Susanna. *Distorting Mirrors: Visions of the Crowd in Late Nineteenth-Century France.* New Haven, 1981.

Bazalgette, Lily. *Albert Dubois-Pillet: Sa vie, son oeuvre, 1846–1890.* Paris, 1976.

Bellioli, Andrea P., ed. *A Day in the Country: Impressionism and the French Landscape.* Los Angeles, 1984.

Benjamin, Walter. *Charles Baudelaire: A Lyric Poet in the Era of High Capitalism.* Translated by Harry Zohn. London, 1983.

Bernstein, Samuel. *The Beginnings of Marxian Socialism in France.* Rev. ed. New York, 1965.

Billy, André. *L'Epoque 1900: 1885–1905.* Paris, 1951.

Block, Jane. *Les XX and the Belgian Avant-Garde, 1868–1894.* Ann Arbor, Mich., 1984.

Boime, Albert. *The Academy and French Painting in the Nineteenth Century.* London, 1971.

Bouchard, Marie. "'Un Monument au Travail': The Projects of Meunier, Dalou, Rodin, and Bouchard." *Oxford Art Journal,* IV (November, 1981), 28–35.

Breitbart, Myrna. "Impressions of an Anarchist Landscape." *Antipode,* VII (1975), 44–49.

Brettell, Richard. *Pissarro and Pontoise: The Painter in a Landscape.* New Haven, 1990.

Brooklyn Museum. *Belgian Art, 1880–1914.* New York, 1980

Cachin, Françoise. "The Neo-Impressionist Avant-Garde." *Art News Annual,* XXXIV (1968), 54–65.

———. *Paul Signac.* Translated by Michael Bullock. Greenwich, Conn., 1971.

Caran, Françoise. *An Economic History of Modern France.* Translated by Barbara Bray. London, 1979.

Carr, Reg. *Anarchism in France: The Case of Octave Mirbeau.* Montreal, 1977.

Case, Frederick Ivor. *La Cité idéale dans "Travail" d'Emile Zola.* Toronto, 1974.

Cazeau, Philippe. *Maximilien Luce.* Paris, 1982.

Chasée, Charles. *The Nabis and Their Period.* Translated by Michael Bullock. New York, 1969.

Clark, T. J. *The Painting of Modern Life: Paris in the Art of Manet and His Followers.* New York, 1984.

Clayson, Hollis. "The Family and the Father: The *Grande Jatte* and Its Absences." *Museum Studies,* XIV (1989), 155–64.

———. *Painted Love: Prostitution in French Art of the Impressionist Era.* New Haven, 1991.

Cole, G. D. H. *A History of Socialist Thought.* 4 vols. London, 1953–58.

Compin, Isabelle. *H. E. Cross.* Paris, 1964.

Coustourier, Lucie. *Henri-Edmond Cross.* Paris, 1932.

———. *Paul Signac.* Paris, 1922.

Crow, Thomas. "Modernism and Mass Culture in the Visual Arts." In *Modernism and Modernity: The Vancouver Conference Papers,* 215–64. Halifax, N.S., 1983.

Dardel, Aline. "Catalogues des dessins et publications illustrées du journal anarchiste *Les Temps nouveaux,* 1895–1914." 2 vols. Dissertation, University of Paris IV, 1980.

———. "L'Etude des dessins dans les journeaux anarchistes de 1895 à 1914." Thesis, University of Paris, n.d.

———. "Illustrateurs et Satiristes, V: La Révolte, ou le drapeau noir—Luce, Camille et Lucien Pissarro." *Gazette de l'Hôtel Drouot,* December 11, 1981, pp. 50–51.

———. "Illustrateurs et Satiristes, VI: La Révolte, ou le drapeau noir—

Naudin, Bradbury, Delannoy, Grandjouan." *Gazette de l'Hôtel Drouot,* December 18, 1981, pp. 28–29.

Daudet, Léon. *Le Stupide XIXᵉ Siècle.* Paris, 1922.

Dolléans, Edouard. *Histoire du mouvement ouvrier.* 2 vols. Paris, 1946–47.

Droz, Jacques, ed. *Histoire générale du socialisme.* 4 vols. Paris, 1974.

Duby, Georges, and Armand Wallon, eds. *Histoire de la France rurale.* 4 vols. Paris, 1975–76.

Dunbar, Gary. "Elisée Reclus, Geographer and Anarchist." *Antipode,* X–XI (1979), 16–21.

———. *Elisée Reclus, Historian of Nature.* Hamden, Conn., 1978.

Duncan, Carol. "Virility and Domination in Early Twentieth-Century Vanguard Painting." In *Feminism and Art History: Questioning the Litany,* edited by Norma Broude and Mary D. Garrard, 293–313. New York, 1982.

Durand, Xavier. "L'Art social au théâtre: Deux Expériences, 1893, 1897." *Le Mouvement social,* XCI (April–June, 1975), 13–33.

Egbert, Donald Drew. "The Idea of 'Avant-Garde' in Art and Politics." *American Historical Review,* LXXIII (1967), 339–66.

———. *Social Radicalism and the Arts—Western Europe: A Cultural History from the French Revolution to 1968.* New York, 1970.

Eisenman, Stephen F. "Seeing Seurat Politically." *Museum Studies,* XIV (1989), 211–21.

Elwitt, Sanford. "Social Reform and Social Order in Late Nineteenth-Century France: The *Musée Social* and Its Friends." *French Historical Studies,* XI (1980), 431–51.

Finley, Nancy A. "Fourierist Art Criticism and the *Rêve de Bonheur* of Dominique Papety." *Art History,* II (1979), 327–38.

Fitzgerald, Fiona. "The Prints of Lucien Pissarro from 1886 to 1896." M.A. thesis, University of East Anglia, 1981.

Fleming, Marie. *The Anarchist Way to Socialism: Elisée Reclus and Nineteenth-Century Anarchism.* London, 1979.

Forley, Ruth. "Camille Pissarro's *Turpitudes sociales:* Documents of History." M.A. thesis, Adelphi University, 1981.

Galois, Bob. "Ideology and the Idea of Nature: The Case of Peter Kropotkin." *Antipode,* VIII (1976), 1–16.

Ghent, Musée des Beaux-Arts. *Retrospective Théo van Rysselberghe.* Ghent, Belg., 1962.

Goldman, Emma. *The Social Significance of the Modern Drama.* Boston, 1914.

Goustine, Christian de. *Pouget: Les Matins noirs du syndicalisme.* Paris, 1972.

Griffiths, Richard. *The Reactionary Revolution: The Catholic Revival in French Literature, 1870–1914.* London, 1966.

Guérin, Daniel. *L'Anarchisme: De la doctrine à l'action.* Paris, 1965.

Hadjinicolaou, Nicos. "On the Ideology of Avant-Gardism." *Praxis,* VI (1982), 39–70.

Halperin, Joan Ungersma. *Félix Fénéon: Aesthete and Anarchist in Fin-de-Siècle Paris.* New Haven, 1988.

Hansen, Eric C. *Disaffection and Decadence: A Crisis in French Intellectual Thought, 1848–1898.* Washington, D.C., 1982.

Hemmings, F. W. J. *Culture and Society in France, 1848–1895: Dissidents and Philistines.* New York, 1971.

Herbert, Eugenia W. *The Artist and Social Reform: France and Belgium, 1885–1898.* New Haven, 1961.

Herbert, Robert L. "Les Artistes et l'Anarchisme." *Le Mouvement social,* XXXVI (July–September, 1961), 2–19.

———. "City vs. Country: The Rural Image in French Painting from Millet to Gauguin." *Artforum,* VIII (February, 1970), 44–55.

———. "Industry in the Changing Landscape from Daubigny to Monet." In *French Cities in the Nineteenth Century,* edited by John M. Merriman, 139–64. London, 1982.

———. *Neo-Impressionism.* New York, 1968.

———. "*Parade de cirque* de Seurat et l'Esthétique scientifique de Charles Henry." *Revue de l'art,* L (1980), 9–23.

———. "Seurat and Emile Verhaeren: Unpublished Letters." *Gazette des Beaux-Arts,* 6th ser., LIV (1959), 315–28.

Herbert, Robert L., and Eugenia W. Herbert. "Artists and Anarchism: Unpublished Letters of Pissarro, Signac, and Others." *Burlington Magazine,* CII (1960), 473–82, 517–22.

Hobsbawm, Eric J. *The Age of Capital, 1848–1875.* New York, 1975.

———. *The Age of Empire, 1875–1914.* New York, 1987.

———. "Socialism and the Avant-Garde in the Period of the Second International." *Le Mouvement social,* CXI (April–June, 1980), 189–99.

Homer, William Innes. *Seurat and the Science of Painting.* Cambridge, Mass., 1964.

Horner, G. M. "Kropotkin and the City: The Socialist Ideal in Urbanism." *Antipode,* X–XI (1979), 33–45.

House, John. "Meaning in Seurat's Figure Paintings." *Art History,* III (1980), 345–55.

Humbert, Jeanne. "Le Poète Paul-Napoléon Roinard, 1856–1930." *La Rue,* XXI (1976), 97–99.

———. *Sebastien Faure: L'Homme, l'Apôtre, une Epoque.* Paris, 1949.

Hunisak, John M. "Rodin, Dalou, and the Monument to Labor." In *Art the Ape of Nature: Studies in Honor of H. W. Janson,* edited by Moshe Barasch and Lucy Freeman Sandler, 689–705. Englewood Cliffs, N.J., 1981.

Hutton, John. "A Blow of the Pick: Science, Anarchism, and the Neo-Impressionist Movement." Ph.D. dissertation, Northwestern University, 1987.

———. "Camille Pissarro's *Turpitudes sociales* and Late Nineteenth-Century French Anarchist Anti-Feminism." *History Workshop Journal,* XXIV (Autumn, 1987), 32–61.

———. "'Les Prolos Vagabondent': Neo-Impressionism and the Anarchist Image of the *Trimardeur.*" *Art Bulletin,* LXXII (1990), 296–309.

L'Immagine del socialismo nell'arte, nelle bandiere, nei simboli: Mostra per il 90° della fondazione del PSI. Venice, 1982.

Isaacson, Joel. *The Crisis of Impressionism, 1878–1882.* Ann Arbor, Mich., 1980.

Jay, Robert Allen. "Art and Nationalism in France, 1870–1914." Ph.D. dissertation, University of Minnesota, 1979.

Jensen, Richard Bach. "The International Anti-Anarchist Conference of 1898 and the Origins of Interpol." *Journal of Contemporary History,* XVI (1981), 323–47.

Joll, James. *The Anarchists.* 2nd ed. Cambridge, Mass., 1979.

Jourdain, Francis. "Paul Signac, peintre et logicien." *La Pensée,* No. 63 (September–October, 1955), 18–23.

Kilroy-Silk, Robert. *Socialism Since Marx.* London, 1972.

Kornfeld, Eberhard, and Peter A. Wick, comps. *Catalogue raisonnée de l'oeuvre gravé et lithiographié de Paul Signac.* Bern, 1974.

Lambert, Jean, and Joelle Saiac. "Les Almanachs socialistes et anarchistes, 1891–1914." 2 vols. Dissertation, University of Paris, 1973.

Larsen, Neil. *Modernism and Hegemony: A Materialist Critique of Aesthetic Agencies.* Minneapolis, 1990.

Lee, Ellen Wardwell. *The Aura of Neo-Impressionism: The W. J. Holliday Collection.* Indianapolis, 1983.

Lefranc, Georges. *Le Mouvement socialiste sous la troisième république, 1875–1940.* Paris, 1963.

————. *Le Mouvement syndical sous la troisième république.* Paris, 1967.

Lehmann, Andrew George. *The Symbolist Aesthetic in France, 1885–1895.* Oxford, 1950.

Le Nuëne, Patrick. "Les Soldats de l'Industrie de François Bonhommé: Idéologie d'un project." *Histoire et Critique des Arts,* IV–V (May, 1978), 35–61.

Lespinasse, François. *Charles Angrand, 1854–1926.* Rouen, 1982.

Levin, Miriam R. *Republican Art and Ideology in Late Nineteenth-Century France.* Ann Arbor, Mich., 1986.

Lindemann, Albert S. *A History of European Socialism.* New Haven, 1983.

Lipton, Eunice. *Looking into Degas: Uneasy Images of Women and Modern Life.* Berkeley and Los Angeles, 1986.

Lossier, Jean G. *Le Rôle social de l'art selon Proudhon.* Paris, 1937.

McGraw, Roger. *France, 1815–1914: The Bourgeois Century.* London, 1983.

Magne, Jacqueline. "Forain et l'Affaire Dreyfus." *Nouvelles de l'estampe,* No. 8 (March–April, 1973), 9–13.

Maitron, Jean. "Jean Grave, 1854–1939." *Revue d'histoire économique et sociale,* XXVII (1950), 105–17.

————. *Le Mouvement anarchiste en France.* 2 vols. Paris, 1975.

————. *Pierre Kropotkine et "le Manifeste des Seize."* Paris, 1951.

Marlais, Michael. *Conservative Echoes in Fin-de-Siècle Parisian Art Criticism.* University Park, Pa., 1992.

Mauner, George. *The Nabis, Their History, and Their Art, 1888–1896.* New York, 1978.

Mayeur, Jean Marie, and Madeleine Rébérioux. *The Third Republic from Its Origins to the Great War, 1871–1914.* Translated by J. R. Foster. New York, 1984.

Meadmore, W. S. *Lucien Pissarro: Un Coeur Simple.* London, 1962.

Medlyn, Sally S. "The Development of Georges Seurat's Art with Special Reference to the Influence of Contemporary Anarchist Philosophy." M.A. thesis, University of Manchester, 1976.

Melot, Michel. "Camille Pissarro in 1880: An Anarchistic Artist in Bourgeois

Society." Translated by Alan Wallach and Carol Duncan. *Marxist Perspectives,* II (Winter, 1979–80), 22–54.

Miller, Martin A. *Kropotkin.* Chicago, 1976.

Moférier, Jacques. "Symbolisme et Anarchie." *Revue d'histoire littéraire de la France,* LXV (1965), 223–28.

Moses, Claire Goldberg. *French Feminism in the Nineteenth Century.* Albany, N.Y., 1984.

Moss, Bernard H. *The Origins of the French Labor Movement, 1830–1914.* Berkeley and Los Angeles, 1976.

————. "The Political Origins of Revolutionary Syndicalism." In *Proceedings of the Second Meeting of the Western Society for French History,* 281–87. Austin, Tex., 1975.

Nettlau, Max. *Elisée Reclus: Anarchist und Gelehrter, 1830–1905.* Berlin, 1928.

The New Painting: Impressionism, 1874–1886. San Francisco, 1986.

Newton, Joy. "Zola and Pissarro, with Four Unpublished Letters." *Laurels,* LI (1980), 89–99.

Nicolson, Benedict. "The Anarchism of Camille Pissarro." *The Arts,* II (1947), 43–51.

Niess, Robert J. "Zola's *Paris* and the Novels of the *Rougon-Macquart* Series." *Nineteenth-Century French Studies,* IV (1975–76), 89–104.

Nochlin, Linda. *The Politics of Vision: Essays on Nineteenth-Century Art and Society.* New York, 1989.

————. "Seurat's *Grande Jatte:* An Anti-Utopian Allegory." *Museum Studies,* XIV (1989), 133–53.

————. *Women, Art, and Power, and Other Essays.* New York, 1988.

Noland, Aaron. *The Founding of the French Socialist Party, 1893–1905.* Cambridge, Mass., 1956.

Noszlopy, George T. "The Embourgeoisement of Avant-Garde Art." *Diogenes,* LXVII (1969), 83–109.

Orton, Fred, and Griselda Pollock. "Les Données bretonnantes: La Prairie de représentation." *Art History,* III (1980), 314–44.

Patsouras, Louis. *Jean Grave and French Anarchism.* Dubuque, Iowa, 1978.

Perrot, Michelle. *Les Ouvriers en grève, France, 1871–1890.* 2 vols. Paris, 1974.

Pessin, Alain. *La Rêverie anarchiste.* Paris, 1982.

Pick, Daniel. "The Faces of Anarchy: Lombroso and the Politics of Criminal Science in Post-Unification Italy." *History Workshop Journal,* XXI (1986), 60–86.

Pierrot, Jean. *The Decadent Imagination, 1880–1900.* Translated by Derek Coltman. Chicago, 1981.

Poggioli, Renato. *The Theory of the Avant-Garde.* Translated by Gerald Fitzgerald. Cambridge, Mass., 1968.

Pogu, Guy. *Théo van Rysselberghe: Sa Vie.* Paris, 1963.

Pollock, Griselda. "Artists' Mythologies and Media Genius, Madness, and Art History." *Screen,* XXI (1980), 57–96.

————. "Stark Encounters: Modern Life and Urban Work in van Gogh's Drawings of the Hague, 1881–1883." *Art History,* VI (1983), 330–58.

————. *Vision and Difference: Femininity, Feminism, and the Histories of Art.* London, 1988.

Quinsac, Annie Paule. *La Peinture divisionniste italienne: Origines et Premiers Développements, 1880–1895.* Paris, 1972.

Raynaud, Ernest. *En marge de la mêlée symboliste.* 3rd ed. Paris, 1936.

Rearick, Charles. "Festivals in Modern France: The Experience of the Third Republic." *Journal of Contemporary History,* XII (1977), 435–60.

————. *Pleasures of the Belle Epoque: Entertainment and Festivity in Turn-of-the-Century France.* New Haven, 1985.

Rébérioux, Madeleine. "Culture et Militantisme." *Le Mouvement social,* XCI (April–June, 1975), 3–12.

————. "Zola et la Critique littéraire socialiste et anarchiste, 1894–1902." *Europe,* XLVI (April–May, 1968), 7–16.

Reszler, André. *L'Esthétique anarchiste.* Paris, 1973.

Rewald, John. *Georges Seurat.* New York, 1946.

————. *Seurat and His Friends.* New York, 1953.

Richardson, John Adkins. *Modern Art and Scientific Thought.* Urbana, Ill., 1971.

Rookmaker, H. R. *Synthetist Art Theories: Genesis and Nature of the Ideas on Art of Gauguin and His Circle.* Amsterdam, 1959.

Rose, Millicent. "The Letters of Camille Pissarro." *Modern Quarterly,* n.s., III (Autumn, 1948), 25–34.

Rosensaft, Jean Bloch. "Le Néo-Impressionnisme de Camille Pissarro." *L'Oeil,* No. 223 (February, 1974), 52–57, 75.

Roslak, Robyn S. "Neo-Impressionism, Organicism, and the Construction of a Utopian Geography: The Role of the Landscape in Anarcho-Communism and Neo-Impressionism." *Utopian Studies,* n.s., I (1990), 96–113.

————. "The Politics of Aesthetic Harmony: Neo-Impressionism, Science, and Anarchism." *Art Bulletin,* LXXIII (1991), 381–90.

————. "Scientific Aesthetics and the Aestheticized Earth: The Parallel Vision of the Neo-Impressionist Landscape and Anarcho-Communist Social Theory." Ph.D. dissertation, University of California at Los Angeles, 1987.

Rossel, André. *La Belle Epoque, 1898–1914.* Paris, 1982.

Rubin, James Henry. *Realism and Social Vision in Courbet and Proudhon.* Princeton, 1980.

Ruckhaberle, Dieter, ed. *Théophile-Alexandre Steinlen, 1859–1923.* 2nd ed. Berlin, 1978.

Russell, John. *Seurat.* London, 1965.

Salmon, André. *La Terreur noir: Chronique du mouvement libertaire.* Paris, 1959.

Schapiro, Meyer. *Modern Art—Nineteenth and Twentieth Centuries: Selected Papers,* New York, 1979.

Seigel, Jerrold. *Bohemian Paris: Culture, Politics, and the Boundaries of Bourgeois Life, 1830–1930.* New York, 1986.

Serret, G., and D. Fabbiani, comps. *Armand Guillaumin, 1841–1927: Catalogue raisonnée de l'oeuvre peint.* Paris, 1971.

Shikes, Ralph E. *The Indignant Eye: The Artist as Social Critic in Prints and Drawings from the Fifteenth Century to Picasso.* Boston, 1969.

Shikes, Ralph E., and Paula Harper. *Pissarro: His Life and Work.* New York, 1980.

Shikes, Ralph E., and Steven Heller. "The Art of Satire: Painters as Caricaturists and Cartoonists from Delacroix to Picasso." *Print Review,* No. 19 (1984), 8–125.

Signac, Paul. "Message aux artistes." *Commune,* II (1934), 1035–38.

———. "Signac." In *Ceux qui ont choisi: Contre le fascisme en Allemagne, contre l'impérialisme en France,* 23. Paris, n.d. [1933?].

———. "Le Sujet en peinture." *L'Encyclopédie française.* Paris, 1935.

Silverman, Debora L. *Art Nouveau in Fin-de-Siècle France: Politics, Psychology, and Style.* Berkeley and Los Angeles, 1989.

Song, Misook. *Art Theories of Charles Blanc, 1813–1882.* Ann Arbor, Mich., 1984.

Sonn, Richard David. *Anarchism and Cultural Politics in Fin-de-Siècle France.* Lincoln, Nebr., 1989.

Spitzer, Alan B. "Anarchy and Culture: Fernand Pelloutier and the Dilemma of Revolutionary Syndicalism." *International Review of Social History,* VIII (1963), 379–88.

Springer, Annemarie. "Terrorism and Anarchy: Late Nineteenth-Century Images of a Political Phenomenon in France." *Art Journal,* XXXVIII (1979), 261–66.

Stafford, Barbara Maria. "'Les Deux Edifices'—The New Areopagus and a Spiritual Trophy: Humbert de Superville's Vision of Utopia." *Art Quarterly,* XXXV (1972), 50–73.

Stromberg, Roland, ed. *Realism, Naturalism, and Symbolism: Modes of Thought and Expression in Europe, 1848–1914.* New York, 1968.

Sutter, Jean, ed. *The Neo-Impressionists.* Translated by Chantal Deliss. Greenwich, Conn., 1970.

Swart, Konraad W. *The Sense of Decadence in Nineteenth-Century France.* The Hague, 1964.

Tabarant, Adolphe. *Camille Pissaro.* Paris, 1924.

———. *Maximilien Luce.* Paris, 1928.

Tagg, John. "The Idea of the Avant-Garde." *Artery,* XII (Summer, 1977), 4–10.

Tailhade, Laurent. *Masques et Visages.* Paris, 1925.

Thibert, Marguérite. *Le Rôle social de l'art d'après les Saint-Simoniens.* Paris, 1926.

Thomson, Richard. "Camille Pissarro, *Turpitudes sociales,* and the Universal Exhibition of 1889," *Arts Magazine,* LVI (April, 1982), 82–88.

———. "'Les Quat' Pattes': The Image of the Dog in Late Nineteenth-Century French Art." *Art History,* V (1982), 323–37.

———. *Seurat.* Oxford, 1985.

Thorold, Anne. "The Pissarro Collection in the Ashmolean Museum, Oxford." *Burlington Magazine,* CXX (1978), 642–45.

———, comp. *Artists, Writers, Politics: Camille Pissarro and His Friends.* Oxford, 1980.

———, comp. *A Catalogue of the Oil Paintings of Lucien Pissarro.* London, 1983.

Tuchman, Barbara. *The Proud Tower: A Portrait of the World Before the War, 1890–1914.* New York, 1967.

Walker, John A. "Art and Anarchism." *Art and Artists,* XIII (May, 1978), 16–19.

———. "Post-Impressionism." *Marxism Today,* XXIV (March, 1980), 19–21.

Ward, Mary Martha. "Camille Pissarro in the 1880s." Ph.D. dissertation, Johns Hopkins University, 1983.

Weber, Eugen. *France, Fin de Siècle.* Cambridge, Mass., 1986.

———. *Peasants into Frenchmen: The Modernization of Rural France, 1870–1914.* Stanford, Calif., 1976.

Weisberg, Gabriel. "François Bonhommé and Early Realist Images of Industrialization." *Arts Magazine,* LIV (April, 1980), 132–35.

———. "Jules Breton, Jules Bastien-Lepage, and Camille Pissarro in the Context of Nineteenth-Century Peasant Painting in the Salon." *Arts Magazine,* LVI (February, 1982), 115–19.

Wilson, Nelly. *Bernard-Lazare: Antisemitism and the Problem of Jewish Identity in Late Nineteenth-Century France.* London, 1978.

Wolff, Janet. "The Invisible *Flâneuse:* Women and the Literature of Modernity." *Theory, Culture, and Society,* II, No. 3 (1985), 37–46.

Woodcock, George, and Ivan Avakumovic, eds. *The Anarchist Prince: A Biographical Study of Peter Kropotkin.* New York, 1950.

Zeldin, Theodore. *France, 1848–1945.* 5 vols. Oxford, 1979–81.

Zemel, Carol. "The 'Spook in the Machine': Van Gogh's Pictures of Weavers in Brabant." *Art Bulletin,* LXVII (1985), 123–37.

Zupnick, I. L. "The Social Conflict of the Impressionists." *College Art Journal,* XIX (1959–60), 146–53.

Index